STRUGGLE AND SURVIVAL
IN COLONIAL AMERICA

Struggle

and Survival

in Colonial

America

Edited by

David G. Sweet

and Gary B. Nash

University of California Press

Berkeley • Los Angeles • London

University of California Press
Berkeley and Los Angeles, California

University of California Press, Ltd.
London, England

© 1981 by
The Regents of the University of California

Printed in the United States of America

1 2 3 4 5 6 7 8 9

Library of Congress Cataloging in Publication Data

Main entry under title:

Struggle and survival in colonial America.

    Includes bibliographies.
    1. America—History—To 1810 2. America—
History—To 1810—Biography. 3. America—Biography.
I. Sweet, David G. II. Nash, Gary B.
E18.82.S77   920'.0091812   80-14413
ISBN 0-520-04110-0

✳ CONTENTS

General Introduction

GARY B. NASH AND DAVID G. SWEET

*T*his collection of essay-biographies had its inception in a chance meeting during which the editors, a historian of the United States and a historian of Latin America, discovered that each had long been fascinated by the lives of little-known but remarkable individual human beings from the inarticulate lower strata of colonial society. The experiences of such people, surfacing from time to time in the documents with which we work, had captured our imagination in ways different from the ordinary interest in historical information. These fleeting acquaintances had left us feeling enlightened and inspired, because their lives provided vivid insights into the real workings of societies difficult to bring into focus. They had also left us with some frustration: while such stories were clearly illuminating, they were difficult to communicate to serious students of history except as anecdotes in classroom lectures.

As we discussed the stratagems by which these men and women seemed to have coped with their circumstances, it became clear to us that there was indeed a great deal to be learned about the colonial period of American history through a closer examination of the experiences of such extraordinary "ordinary" people. Believing that others must also have stumbled on such characters in the course of their research on more traditional subjects, we broadcast an appeal for contributions to a book of capsule biographies of unknown early Americans and their struggles to survive. The initial results were promising. Then for more than two years we coaxed and counseled, corresponding with a great number of people in many places and at the same time experimenting with writing serious historical essays about "unimportant people"—essays that would be both scholarly and entertaining, both substantial and interesting to a general readership. In the course of doing this we learned that some of the best stories of individual experience are too fragmentary for exposition in essay form, and that more needs to be done with combining the experiences of many people to sketch composite pictures of ordinary colonial life. But that will be a different project.

This book assembles some of the fruits of our search. It is a collaborative effort by twenty people, for the most part unknown to one another, to break through the crust of a scholarship that has focused on political and institutional history to the nourishing substance of the real history that lies below. In the stories assembled here we provide glimpses of the hard-to-trace process of social transformation that has been taking place since earliest times, with the full participation of all people. "To study the laws of history," wrote Leo Tolstoy in *War and Peace*, "we must completely change the subject of our observation, must leave aside kings, ministers and generals, and study the common infinitesimally small elements by which the masses are moved."[1] This book, though not pretending to discover any laws of history, is a response to Tolstoy's challenge to take a closer look at the central concerns of most human beings and at the details surrounding real human experience. It is also a response to the lesson of social science and our present-day lives and times that "life is with people" rather than with abstractions.

Our first plan was to group the stories by racial categories, perhaps even with separate volumes for Indians, blacks, whites, and racially mixed persons. Race, after all, was a highly salient factor in colonial America. Colonial society was organized to a considerable extent around racial distinctions. While the impact of race varied with the modes of

production, the national origins and religion of the colonizers, the geographical conditions, and other factors, all early
American societies were essentially quadripartite in the
functional roles they assigned to Native Americans, Europeans, Africans, and those who fell in between. The colonial
relationship inherently involved the extraction of wealth by
overseas subjects for the enrichment of metropolitan rulers
and investors and a colonial aristocracy. As this process developed in America, the forced manual labor of Indians and
Africans became indispensable to an economic development
that "respectable" Europeans supervised with the assistance
of "half-breeds" and declassé whites.

Within this basic framework of New World colonization,
life was undoubtedly worst for Native Americans. This was
true not only because they were dispossessed of their land,
enslaved, and even exterminated by the invaders, but also
because they were the victims of a massive and relentless
biological warfare, in which sooner or later all Indian populations were decimated by Old World diseases to which they
had no genetic immunity. This holocaust left societies and
individuals in desperate straits, hard pressed merely to survive, and in many cases willing to exchange surrender for
sustenance. It was a circumstance of immeasurable assistance to the European takeover.

Among the immigrants to this hemisphere, the most severe hardships were visited upon Africans. Brought in chains
in staggering numbers in the largest forced migration in history, they were thrust into a system of forced labor that
became increasingly efficient in its exploitation of human
beings and resilient in the face of such reformist attacks as
were occasionally directed against it. Hence there is a powerful logic behind the focus on race relations in studying colonial America, a focus that obliges us almost automatically
to think in terms of red, white, and black when we survey the
lives of ordinary people.

Yet color cannot by itself satisfactorily demarcate the experiences of the common people of America in any period.
Though Europeans and their light-skinned descendants were
better off most of the time than Native Americans or Africans and their swarthy descendants, every inhabitant of both
continents has until comparatively recent times faced the

real possibility of an early death by disease or violence. Most people, even stalwart freeholders and artisans, have been obliged to work hard all their lives for a precarious subsistence, while seeing wealth accumulated by the few. In colonial times, moreover, nearly everyone was subject to an authority that might in the name of religious orthodoxy, national allegiance, racial purity, gender prerogative, or class privilege impose harsh physical and psychological punishment, imprisonment, ostracization, or exile on any but the most privileged members of society. It is hardly an exaggeration to say that for three centuries after the first European landfall most of the colonizers and colonized were locked into a system that functioned mainly for the enrichment of kings, merchants, and gentleman adventurers in Europe, as well as a small minority of large landholders, merchants, and officials in the New World.

Rather than thinking exclusively in racial categories, therefore, we have found it more satisfactory to consider these stories in the light of three kinds of structural inequality—those determined by race, class, and sex. This view of asymmetrical power relations lies behind the insight of Albert Memmi, the Tunisian essayist on colonialism, who probed the resemblance of oppressed people to each other the world over:

> Their own peculiar features and individual history aside, colonized peoples, Jews, women, the poor show a kind of family likeness: all bear a burden which leaves the same bruises on their soul, and similarly distorts their behavior. A like suffering often produces similar gestures, similar expressions of pain, the same inner paroxysms, the same agony or the same revolt.[2]

The real subject of this book is, however, not the history of oppression in early America but the striving of colonial people—and their extraordinary ability—to live life more fully and creatively than their external circumstances would seem to have allowed. The essays reveal this striving at work even in the most discouraging of contexts, such as those of Juan de Morga and Gertrudis de Escobar, slaves in seventeenth-century Mexico. They make it clear that people alone and in collectivities, at every level of society and from every racial and ethnic group, customarily found ways of coping with the many hazards that surrounded them and the social system that contained them. For the most part, they survived their hardships rather than being overcome by them; some even managed to thrive in the face of everything. It is this theme of struggle and survival, cutting across the lines of race, sex, and class, which organizes this series of brief life stories into a significant whole. An understanding of the modes of coping with colonial life can offer valuable insights into human ingenuity and resilience, as well as into the institutional mechanisms of the harsh and disorderly societies set up on foreign soil by the Spaniards, Portuguese, French, English, and their subject peoples between the sixteenth and eighteenth centuries. Hence we may come to understand better the societies that have descended from them—harsh and disorderly enough still—within which people still struggle for survival today.

We are concerned, then, with women and men engaged in personal campaigns to survive and even to succeed in a social landscape filled with obstacles. What we have assembled is not a random sample but a miscellany of lives that may not be representative of the great variety of ways in which life was lived in the New World colonies but that is nevertheless suggestive of a good many of them. These are not Horatio Alger stories about individuals triumphing against adversity, although a few exceptional characters managed at least to reach advanced ages and a few others succeeded modestly in business. Neither are they Howard Fast stories about people triumphing against oppression, although a few of the subjects did inflict a wound or two on those who were grinding them down, usually in the process of losing against heavy odds. The former kind of story would violate historical truth by representing the colonies as wide-open lands of opportunity for the audacious, which they were only exceptionally. The latter kind would violate historical truth by suggesting that ordinary folk had the wisdom to fathom the intricate workings of the colonial system and the collective strength to stand up to it and prevail, which they had only occasionally.

Successful upward striving and heroic resistance are both part of the historical record of the people of colonial America, to be sure, and both may be seen here at odd moments. The essays mainly dwell, however, on the far less dramatic, more mundane level of mere survival. By so doing, they provide better characterizations, we believe, of the difficult reality of everyday life in the colonial world. Theirs is an America of tumultuous change, bewildering complexity, persistent brutality, odd beliefs and priorities, the unceasing process and paradox of real human experience. These life stories tell us that nothing was very fixed in colonial life; that institutions, though often starkly oppressive, were usually permeable; that informal power relationships were as important as prescribed ones; that the labyrinth of solitude through which resisters and accommodators were dispersed was an enormous one without maps.

In attempting to understand why the subjects of our stories were more likely to try to adapt and survive than to challenge directly the power of their rulers, it has been helpful to keep in mind the concept of cultural hegemony, as developed by the Italian Marxist Antonio Gramsci and employed since by social historians of the oppressed, such as E. P. Thompson and Eugene Genovese. Gramsci's compelling thesis was that ruling classes are able to obtain and maintain the consent of those subject to them because their rule gains legitimacy even in the eyes of the most dispossessed members of society. By acting paternalistically and insisting that all ranks and both sexes are organically connected through specific responsibilities and rights, the members of the elite foster the notion that they customarily use their authority responsibly and for the good of the whole. Ultimately, according to Gramsci, this idea becomes a far more powerful instrument in the hands of those at the top of the social hierarchy than guns or clubs could ever be, for while class or racial or sexual conflict is not eliminated, it is largely muted by the workers' acceptance of those who mold and perpetuate the social system. Cultural hegemony, writes Genovese, is "the seemingly spontaneous loyalty that a ruling class evokes from the masses through its cultural position and its ability to promote its world view as the general will."[3]

In our context, Gramsci's cultural hegemony is perhaps most evident in the stories taken from colonial Mexico or New Spain, where the male ruling-class world view was effectively disseminated through the power of the Catholic Church, which served as a branch of the state and penetrated at least superficially into every home in every stratum of society. Authoritarian measures were regularly employed to maintain the colonial order in New Spain, as everywhere, but naked force was usually not required. This was in part true because the Church, which enjoyed the respect and support of the common people and sometimes acted to defend them against the worst excesses of the European laymen, preached docility. Similarly, the racist and sexist ideology of the ruling class was easier to perpetuate because many people of mixed race, full-blooded Indians and Africans, and white women internalized the notions of the superiority of European culture and the naturalness of male domination that were manifest in the work of the Church. These dominated people even came to share the white man's disdain for the members of other ethnic groups. "Not the least of the misfortunes caused by oppression," writes Memmi, "is that the oppressed come to hate each other."[4] This assimilation of ruling class and colonialist values and ideology, so brilliantly exposed by Gramsci (and by Memmi and Frantz Fanon for our own times), can be seen in several of our stories to have served the masters of New Spain and the other American colonies very effectively.

We must not be misled by the impressive examples of hegemonic mechanisms that did exist in the colonies, however, into accepting the notion that the establishment of such mechanisms guaranteed hegemony. Many of the essays assembled here, including several from New Spain, show how difficult it always was in the days before mass communication for the arbiters of cultural norms and the possessors of economic and political power to gain the complicity of ordinary people in a social system designed principally to exploit them. The closer we look at the behavior of people not in power, the clearer it becomes that most people subscribed to an upper-class male system of values only some of the time and for some purposes. They could not be relied on to sustain these values, and they were unlikely to allow them to get in the way of their elemental struggles to survive and create a satisfactory life for themselves.

What needs to be recognized is that in colonial America a long history of insubordination and undeferential behavior ran parallel to a long history of imperfect hegemonic control by the elite. There is no doubting that the social and psychological leverage held by men of wealth and power was enormous or that the "popular mentalities of subordination," as Thompson has called them,[5] always hindered the development of any sort of class consciousness and collective struggle against structural inequalities and exploitation. But we must also take note of the persistent attempts to evade, resist, and even overthrow hegemonic control among laboring men and women in every part of the hemisphere. Such attempts were present from the beginning but grew stronger in the eighteenth century, as the power of the Church and the aristocracy became weaker vis-à-vis the state, the bourgeoisie, and the common people. It is precisely the pervasiveness and the multifaceted creativity of individual resistance, adaptation, and survival that are brought into focus by the essays in this book.

Social historians have lately devoted much effort to recapturing the experience of the "inarticulate" in an effort to correct the historical myopia produced by too exclusive a focus on the rich and powerful. This long overdue historical revisionism is not merely a quest for an aesthetic balance or for "simple justice." The examination of the circumstances of life for the great mass of common people and for women in every period and the study of their ways of thinking and acting are essential if we are ever to test the hallowed historical generalizations made from the study of the select masculine few, on which our understanding of life in society and the process of politics is primarily based. Some saw the need for this kind of reexamination long ago. In 1856 the famous American traveler and planner Frederick Law Olmsted remarked that:

> Men of literary taste . . . are always apt to overlook the working classes, and to confine the records they make of their own times, in great degree, to the habits and fortunes of their own associates or to those of people of superior rank to themselves of whose sayings and doings their vanity, as well as their curiosity, leads them to most carefully inform themselves. The dumb masses have often been so lost in this shadow of egotism, that, in later days, it has been impossible to discern the very real influence their character and condition has had on the fortune and fate of the nation.[6]

It is only a century later that the historical profession, itself derived from the upper stratum until recently, has taken Olmsted's challenge to heart.

To do so, historians have had to overcome two biases. The first pertains to sources that were long thought to be unavailable or too intractable for the study of the "lower orders" or for the study of women. The essays in this book are a part of the rapidly expanding body of proof that this is not the case. The second bias is ideological. In probing the lives of the anonymous masses historians have had to overcome one of the master assumptions of premodern times, namely, that uneducated laboring people as well as women were moved by passion (the baser impulses in human nature) rather than by reason (which guided rich and educated males). Common people and women, it used to be said by colonial Englishmen, Spaniards, and Portuguese, could not calculate their own interests rationally and were therefore hardly worth studying or listening to in any context. The "rabble," the "unthinking multitude," the "mob," the "common herd," the "distaff side," and the "frailer sex" are only a few of the terms with which the colonial elite discredited ordinary people and contrived to preserve its belief that educated and materially successful men were alone entitled to make decisions for society. Power in the hands of the majority could lead only to anarchy and chaos. Either the people would miscalculate their own interests or they would be manipulated by morally bankrupt persons wishing to use them for their own ends. Imbibing such beliefs and tied primarily to male ruling-class documents, historians have also tended either to ignore the "ignorant lout," the "sheeplike masses," and the "passive female" or to pay them only passing attention as unimportant supernumeraries in the great historical tableaux.

In recent years a number of historians have exposed the myth of an unthinking and unconscious mass of people for the self-serving instrument of ruling-class power that it is. E. J. Hobsbawm, George Rudé, E. P. Thompson, and others have demonstrated that the frequent crowd actions and popular demonstrations of the preindustrial era represented purposeful and discriminating participations in the process of history rather than blind lashings-out as suggested by the myth.[7] Carried from the collective to the individual level, this reconceptualization of lower-class behavior demands that when we examine the experiences of such ordinary struggling people as those who are introduced in this book, we take their actions seriously, as reflections of their ideology and self-interest. This is not to say that irrationality, superstition, and spontaneous emotion play no role in the lives of ordinary people. They do, as of course they have always done in the lives of the rich and powerful. But passion and reason may now be seen to have functioned alongside one another in the decisions of women and men of all classes in any period, and neither serves to characterize one class, race, or sex more than another.

In recapturing the lives of the historically inarticulate we must avoid another pitfall, which is the construction of a pantheon of people's heroes. There were, of course, heroes from the lower ranks. They are worthy of attention, and a few of them even appear in this book. But most people, then as now, were made of less illustrious clay. For the most part, then, this book brings together the stories of men and women who were not exceptionally wise, heroic, or virtuous. Some exhibited these characteristics on occasion, and a few lived out their lives fired by an unquenchable thirst for social justice or an unremitting determination to forge a new and better world. But more commonly the figures portrayed here were self-centered, opportunistic, and sometimes even cowardly—like most people throughout the annals of history and today. Their understanding of their world was often circumscribed, their morals were flexible, their personal relations were far from exemplary, and their successes in life were evanescent. We need not be surprised at this, for it has always been so.

Each of these stories suggests, however, something that has too often been overlooked by historians and social scientists, even critics of the ruling class, namely, that real life has always been lived, even among the obscure members of the "faceless mass," by individual human beings possessing resourcefulness, knowledge, wisdom, and a sense of humor. In colonial America, as elsewhere, people were in the habit of dealing creatively with the social circumstances that surrounded them rather than passively accepting their lot. These stories are about people who were the subjects rather than the objects of their particular local and national histories. Like most others who have inhabited this planet, regardless of race, sex, social status, or formal education, they learned from experience and, little by little, developed the ability to conduct themselves effectively. This does not mean that they usually accomplished their objectives. A slave escaped and was soon recaptured; an artisan secured a measure of independence and then fell back into the trough of dependency; an Indian leader manipulated white traders into certain concessions and then was drawn into a disastrous war. But struggle in itself invested their lives with dignity, for it gave them the sense of worth that comes from a refusal to lie down before those with power. As with Sisyphus pushing the stone up a hill that had no top, it was the daily struggle that gave life meaning. As long as struggle went on, whatever the odds and whatever the outcome, the dominant could never completely dominate.

These multifarious struggles for survival and betterment are important not only as individual examples of human behavior under stress. Collectively, these personal dramas influenced, changed, and sometimes even dictated the course of colonial development. The ordinary people in the pages that follow, and many millions of others like them, were the true motivators of social change in colonial society because they were the producers, consumers, tax payers, tax collectors, law abiders, law deriders, factors, transactors, complainers, maintainers, printers of books, cobblers of shoes, drivers of mules, cultivators of fields, and schemers of schemes. They were also the disseminators of ideas across networks of communication that we have only barely begun to understand. These were the people who overwhelmingly composed the societies from which we are sprung and of which we still know so little. When laws were made or wars declared or ideas enunciated or merchandise put up for sale, it was the active and largely undocumented response of the mass of people that made these abstractions reality. And when the idea of human betterment spread in the world— which was at the bottom of the declarations of independence, the abolitions of slavery, the experiments with democratic government, the establishment of human rights, and the proliferation of literacy and public health that made America the much improved place it is today—that liberating idea made its mark everywhere, not because of a miraculous explosion of French or English mind power among the elite but because of the unspectacular daily interaction of the millions of people in many regions who came to hear of it. Of course there were enunciators and propagandizers of the new truths—we catch glimpses of a few of these intellectuals and utopian reformers in these essays—but ideas were transformed into concrete change because they were heard, believed, and acted upon by thousands of historically anonymous but vitally involved persons, such as those introduced in this volume.

Life is always a struggle, and survival is always a primary goal. Every individual in the long history of colonial America, whether adult or child, male or female, rich or poor, pale-skinned or dark, slave or free, was therefore part of the social process on which these essays focus. But this observation by itself is of little use in trying to understand how ordinary people carved out their individual places in societies based on the structural inequalities of class, race, and sex. Of somewhat more use is a typology, however crude, of the modes of coping with the realities of colonial life. The task in creating such a typology is not to set forth categories into which every individual must be fitted or to prove that the various people subsumed in each division are alike, but only to create a conceptual tool for the analysis of experience. In reading and rereading these stories, we have found that they seem to arrange themselves into four broad categories of coping: collective struggle, individual defiance, individual accommodation, and competition. Each of these categories contains wide variations in behavior; the lines between categories are blurred; and it is clear that many individuals moved from one mode to another at different stages of their lives or even made use of several modes simultaneously. Nevertheless, each of our categories represents an approach to the struggle for survival that is sufficiently different from the others to suggest its own set of possibilities for an understanding of colonial society and the behavior of people within it. In the introductory remarks for each section we sketch some of the dimensions of the category in question as we have come to understand it. But whether or not this exercise in the taxonomy of human experience proves a useful one, we are confident that readers will rejoice as we have done in the company of these twenty-three new acquaintances from the past.

Notes

1. Tolstoy, *War and Peace*, quoted in James A. Henretta, *The Evolution of American Society, 1700–1815* (Lexington, Mass., 1973), p. 1.

2. Albert Memmi, *Dominated Man* (Boston, Mass., 1968), p. 16.

3. Eugene Genovese, "Marxian Interpretations of the Slave South," in Barton J. Bernstein, ed., *Towards a New Past: Dissenting Essays in American History* (New York, 1967), p. 123. For Gramsci's formulation, see John M. Cammett, *Antonio Gramsci and the Origins of Italian Communism* (Stanford, Calif., 1967), pp. 204–206. Genovese's use of cultural hegemony is questioned by Jesse Lemisch, "Listening to the 'Inarticulate': William Widger's Dream and the Loyalties of American Revolutionary Seamen in British Prisons," *Journal of Social History* 3 (1969): 2–3; and "New Left Elitism," *Radical America* 1 (1967): 43–53.

4. *Dominated Man*, p. 11.

5. E. P. Thompson, "Patrician Society, Plebeian Culture," *Journal of Social History* 7 (1974): 357.

6. *A Journey to the Seaboard Slave States, With Remarks on Their Economy* (New York, 1856; reprint 1968), pp. 214–215.

7. See especially Thompson, *The Making of the English Working Class* (New York, 1963); George Rudé, *The Crowd in History, 1730–1848* (New York, 1963); E. J. Hobsbawm, *Primitive Rebels: Studies in Archaic Forms of Social Movement in the Nineteenth and Twentieth Centuries* (New York, 1959).

✷ PART ONE

Survival Through Collective Struggle

Introduction

*F*or the European colonizers of the Americas, the community was a peculiarly fragile organism. Many brought with them a firm commitment to town living as the *sine qua non* of civilized life. Others came with the hope of reestablishing a sense of community that they thought was waning in Western Europe. Armed conflict with the Native Americans provided a strong incentive for clustering together, as did the sometimes menacing strangeness of the American environment. But before long the centrifugal forces in New World society acted as a powerful corrosive on the communal values and modes of behavior of the European settlers, both on the frontiers and within the confines of the colonial towns and cities. Even the New England Puritans, for whom the reknitting of the community lay at the center of their quest for a godly, regenerated society, were plagued by these disintegrative forces. The psychological "sea change" that occurred on the long Atlantic voyage, the extensive availability of land, the need to explore and lay claim to the land for the purposes of mining or farming, the compressed class structure of immigrant society, and the daily experience of competition in an atmosphere of relative law-lessness—all of these nourished individualistic tendencies and helped attenuate the communalistic ethos of both Pro-testant and Catholic colonists.

The communal basis of society remained rather more intact in the Native American cultures and to a lesser degree even among the African slaves as they were assembled to form new communities around the mines, towns, and planta-tions of the New World. At the heart of the community in most Indian societies were the common ownership of land and the notion of a common membership in a sacred natural order. The European concepts of private property and the individual exploitation of nature for profit were powerful disincentives to collective modes of behavior; but the Indian view of things provided a durable basis for communal soli-darity, as the story of Red Shoes of the Choctaw will show, as long as communities survived and greed did not get the best of people. When Indian lands were invaded, or Indian labor and surplus production extorted, or Indian religious practices suppressed, the Europeans presented a challenge to entire communities, and they were very often met by the resistance of an entire community. Communalism among African slaves was concentrated more in the area of religious expres-sion than in open resistance. There were few opportunities for group action within the closely supervised social order of plantation, mine, and household.

Generally speaking, collective struggle was the strategy for survival of those whose value systems prescribed a group rather than an individual pursuit of goals and those whose alternative to unified action was extinction. This was espe-cially true in North America and Amazonia, where the Indian societies that survived early bouts with epidemics and slave raiders were seldom fully conquered and where the conquered were seldom fully incorporated into Euro-Ameri-can society. These "savage" peoples either resisted furiously, as did Opechancanough's Powhatans in the Chesapeake Bay region, or they withdrew collectively from contact. It was only when they lost the basis in territory and numbers for their collective resistance that they lost their collective identity and ceased to exist as peoples.

Elsewhere in Middle and South America, as the story of the Peruvian Vasicuio will reveal, most Indians were corralled into the systems of forced labor and tax collection established by the sixteenth-century Spanish colonial state. Among these peoples tribal identity was to a great extent vitiated, although new communal forms evolved under European influence. In these contexts the Native American languages and domestic culture were maintained, though substantially transformed, and the communal basis for resistance remained viable down into modern times.

Most of the stories in Part I, therefore, concern Native American leaders who led their people in communal struggles for the preservation of their ancient homelands, political autonomy, and the maintenance of cultural integrity. For Indians, whether they lived on the margin of the European system of production or constituted the bulk of its work force, this contest was conducted in the face of devastating epidemics, technological disadvantages, the exacerbation of traditional hostilities between neighboring tribes, and the systematic extraction of Indian land, labor, and surplus production by the Europeans. In spite of these odds, Indian communal resistance was remarkably successful in many cases and for long periods, a fact that is frequently overlooked because historians focus on the ultimate loss of land and political independence by the large majority of Native American people. During several centuries of interaction on the hemisphere's many frontiers, both Indians and whites recognized that the outcome of the struggle was much in doubt.

Collective resistance was particularly effective in areas where more than one European power contended for dominance. It is too often overlooked that in many parts of the hemisphere, as in Red Shoes' Mississippi, António de Gouveia's Brazil, or Jacob Young's Maryland, two or even three European powers struggled for ascendancy at one period or another. In these situations the Indians were far from being mere objects, to be moved about like pawns on a continental chessboard before finally being swept away altogether. This view is part of the myth of the overwhelming cultural and military force of the colonizers and of the Indians' acquiescence when confronted with this power. The strength of the Europeans and the weakness of the native societies have both been greatly exaggerated in the histories of all American countries, where history is written by the descendants and in the languages of the conquerors.

Africans brought a communal system of values to the New World; but in being thrown together in artificial multiethnic communities they were faced with enormous handicaps for collective action. The apparatus of the American slave systems was also designed precisely to prevent communal resistance of any kind. In view of these difficulties it is remarkable that slave rebellions, and the establishment by escaped slaves of maroon settlements, were fairly common in the areas of America where slave populations were not surrounded by a large population of armed whites. When the opportunity for rebellion arose even in English America, as it did for Thomas Peters and his associates during the American Revolution, the response was great indeed.

In general, we may conclude that collective forms of struggle presented themselves where communal value systems persisted or where, as in the late colonial Buenos Aires of Francisco Baquero, groups of alienated or aggrieved individuals forged a collective identity in the face of those who oppressed them. Dispossessed white colonists only occasionally strove collectively to reshape the system that bound them about. Slaves were more prone to do so, where the ratio of blacks to whites was high and where places of refuge from the power of the state were available. But communal resistance was most frequent among those Indians who remained on the perimeter or outside the orbit of European control, or who retained within it a strong sense of communal identity.

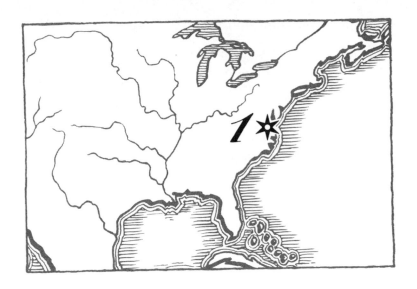

Opechancanough:
Indian Resistance Leader

J. FREDERICK FAUSZ

*I*n May 1607, as the loblolly pines swayed in the spring breeze and the sturgeon were beginning their spawning runs up the broad tidal rivers, a determined band of 105 Englishmen established an invasion beachhead among the fertile meadows and marshy lowlands of Indian Virginia. Only four decades later, with their once-meager numbers now swelled to some fifteen thousand persons, the invaders had made themselves the masters of tidewater Virginia.

The possessors of this rich land—the people the English defeated, displaced, and nearly annihilated in creating the first successful colony in British America—were Algonquian Indians, known collectively as the Powhatans. Because they lost and because historians of the United States have been the political descendants of the victorious English invaders, there have been few attempts to comprehend the personalities or motivations of the Virginia Indians. The legends and tales that abound about the romantic Pocahontas and her father, the "Emperor" Powhatan, have remained popular primarily because they symbolize the so-called superiority and strength of the English conquerors. Pocahontas was a "good Indian" because she renounced her culture and became a converted Englishwoman, while Powhatan confirmed the myths of Indian weakness by capitulating to the whites within a few years after 1607.

While it is true that Pocahontas and Powhatan dealt with the English presence as they saw fit, there was a more characteristic manner of responding to invaders in the context of Powhatan cultural traditions. This was the way represented by Opechancanough (O-puh-cán-can-ō), kinsman of Pocahontas and Powhatan and the much-vilified architect of the bloody Indian uprisings of 1622 and 1644.

Who was this man who has been referred to as the cruel leader of the "perfidious and inhumane" Powhatans, the "unflinching enemy . . . of the Saxon race," and a chieftain "of large Stature, noble Presence, and extraordinary Parts" who "was perfectly skill'd in the Art of Governing"?[1] Although few details are known about his early life or background, Opechancanough, or Mangopeesomon as he was later called by his people, was trained from boyhood to be a leader of the Powhatans in war and in peace.

When the English arrived in Virginia, they reported that Opechancanough was linked by blood and alliance to Powhatan, the supreme chieftain (*Mamanatowick*), who had constructed a proud and strong tidewater Indian empire in the last quarter of the sixteenth century. By 1607 Powhatan ruled the largest, most politically complex and culturally unified chiefdom in Virginia. Called Tsenacommacah (Sen-ah-cómma-cah)—meaning "densely inhabited land"—this Indian chiefdom had a total population of some twelve thousand persons. Forged by conquest, based on efficient administration and common defense, and maintained by force of arms, tribute, religious beliefs, and the authoritarian personality of a determined ruler, Tsenacommacah was a sovereign and extensive political domain. Powhatan was regarded as the great lord of an integrated kinship society administered by carefully selected local chiefs, or governors, of much power and wealth. These tribal leaders were called *werowances* ("he who is rich"), and among them there was none stronger than Opechancanough.

From a cluster of villages located near the present West Point, Virginia, where tributaries form the York River, Opechancanough ruled over the important Pamunkey tribe. The largest single tribe in Powhatan's domain, the Pamunkeys around 1607 had a population of some twelve hundred, including over three hundred warriors. Their territory, called "Opechancheno" after their leader, abounded in fresh water, deer-filled forests, large villages, and acres of planted corn, tobacco, beans, and squash. The Pamunkeys' homeland was also rich in copper and in pearls from freshwater mussels, and Opechancanough's influence derived at least partially from his monopoly of the latter commodity.

The most important source of Opechancanough's power, and a significant factor in explaining many of his later actions, was undoubtedly his role as chief of the most fearsome band of Powhatan warriors. The English often spoke of how disciplined and fierce the Pamunkeys were and reported that Opechancanough was able to mobilize a thousand bowmen in two days' time. His warriors joined battle armed with skilfully made longbows, four-foot arrows, and wooden clubs; their faces and shoulders were smeared with scarlet pigment, and they were adorned with mussel shells, beads, copper medallions, feathers, bird talons, and fox fur.

Despite his considerable power and influence, in 1607 Opechancanough was still subordinate to Powhatan. Although second to his kinsman, Opitchapam, in the line of succession to the title of *Mamanatowick*, he was forced to do the great chief's bidding, just as was any other tribesman less endowed with talent and status. Powhatan had no rivals in tidewater Virginia. As long as he lived, all the *werowances*, including Opechancanough, owed him deference and paid him tribute from the tribes under their control.

In May 1607, only two weeks after the English landed at Jamestown, the *Mamanatowick* mobilized his *werowances* and decided to test the white men by force of arms. It was Opechancanough's duty to keep the more important English leaders distracted some miles upriver from the settlement while other *werowances* attacked James Fort. This assault by several hundred warriors failed to dislodge the English garrison, however, and within days Powhatan altered his strategy. He now decided to offer hospitality to the invaders, and again Opechancanough followed his lead by sending presents of food and overtures of peace to Jamestown.

Similarly, when in December 1607 the *Mamanatowick* desired his first audience with an Englishman, Opechancanough was dispatched to capture Captain John Smith, the most conspicuous leader at Jamestown, and to conduct him safely to Werowocomoco, Powhatan's capital. This Opechancanough did, although some of his own Pamunkey tribesmen called for the death of the white captain.

Opechancanough's inferior position was further emphasized in the February-March 1608 negotiations for a joint Anglo-Powhatan expedition against the Monacan Indians to the west. It was decided that Powhatan and Captain Christopher Newport, "being great Werowances," would not personally lead their forces into battle but would leave the military details to lesser war chiefs—John Smith and Opechancanough.[2]

Although there is no evidence that Opechancanough was ever disloyal to Powhatan in these years, he was an ambitious man who doubtless resented his subordinate status under the *Mamanatowick*. His position became increasingly undesirable after 1608, since while trying to preserve the tenuous peace advocated by Powhatan, he was forced to endure insufferable aggressions by the English. After September 1608 John Smith initiated a purposeful campaign of intimidation, using both threats and force to put Powhatan's people on the defensive. On one occasion Smith captured and imprisoned two Indian warriors, and Opechancanough was obliged to humble himself and negotiate for their release. He sent his own shooting glove and wrist guard to Smith as a token of goodwill and entreated the captain to free the hostages "for his sake."[3] The prisoners were eventually released, but the fact that Opechancanough had been forced to beg meant that the cost in pride had been high.

It was only a matter of time before the brash Smith took still further advantage of his reputed ability to intimidate Indian leaders. In January 1609 he brazenly led a contingent of

1. Captain John Smith harrasses Opechancanough, as Powhatan bowmen charge Englishmen with firearms in background. Virginia, early seventeenth century.

armed Englishmen into Opechancanough's Pamunkey enclave in search of food. When the warriors refused to supply corn to the English, an enraged Smith grabbed Opechancanough by the hair and held a loaded pistol to his chest. He threatened the frightened *werowance* in front of the Pamunkeys and forced the tribesmen "to cast downe their armes, little dreaming anie durst in that manner have used their king." Smith demanded pledges of good behavior and a regular corn tribute from Opechancanough's people and vowed to load his ship with their "dead carkasses" if they ever again crossed him. In addition, soon after this incident Smith physically assaulted a son of Opechancanough and "spurned [him] like a dogge."[4]

Such harsh and shockingly disrespectful treatment of a Pamunkey leader was unprecedented, and Opechancanough's credibility as a war chief and status as a "royal" *werowance* were jeopardized by such incidents. Perhaps as a result of this, sometime between 1608 and 1612 Opechancanough was humiliated by a fellow *werowance* named Pipsco. Pipsco brazenly stole away one of Opechancanough's favorite wives and flaunted his relationship with the woman for years afterward. In the light of such events, how was the Pamunkey chieftain to cope with his own declining status as well as with the larger threat that the increasingly aggressive English invaders posed to all of Indian Virginia?

Matters soon got worse for the Powhatans in general, although Opechancanough's particular position gradually improved after 1609. John Smith's policy of intimidation with limited bloodshed was succeeded in 1609 by a chaotic period during which short-sighted Englishmen senselessly robbed and murdered Indians. Violent retaliation by the Powhatans quickly escalated into full-scale warfare between 1609 and 1614. Although many Englishmen were killed at first, their overall position was eventually strengthened by increased financial and moral support from London, by large supplies of arms, and by the arrival in Virginia of several dozen fighting men under experienced military commanders.

This First Anglo-Powhatan War proved disastrous for the Powhatans. In a series of sharp and brutal engagements, armored English musketeers attacked tribe after tribe until they gained control of the James River from Chesapeake Bay to the fall line. Powhatan, the aging chief, was unable to halt the English advance, but Opechancanough and his Pamunkeys fared better. In November 1609 they decimated an English force that had come to steal corn, and the result was that the leaders of the colony cautiously waited until 1613 before they felt confident enough to invade the Pamunkeys' territory again. Because of their strength in arms and the placement of their villages at some distance from the area of most active fighting along the James River, the Pamunkeys were spared the worst ravages of the war. Relative to Powhatan's declining power and the losses sustained by other area tribes, the Pamunkeys under Opechancanough became ever stronger.

Powhatan, the once-awesome ruler of tidewater Virginia, spent the war years largely in seclusion. The repeated English onslaughts had taken their toll on the energy and abilities of the *Mamanatowick*, already in his late sixties. By this time Powhatan "delighted in security, and pleasure, and . . . peace," and desired to be "quietly settled amongst his owne." He had tired of conflict. "I am old," he told the English, "and ere long must die. . . . I knowe it is better to eat good meat, lie well, and sleep with my women and children, laugh and be merrie . . . then [to] bee forced to flie . . . and be hunted."[5] Powhatan's favorite daughter, Pocahontas, was captured by the English in 1613. In the next year she renounced her heritage, accepted the Anglican faith, and prepared to marry an English planter, John Rolfe. But Powhatan stubbornly refused to capitulate to the English until the Pamunkeys under Opechancanough were attacked by a large force of armed musketeers. Now a broken man, Powhatan meekly accepted a humiliating peace treaty in the spring of 1614. He who might have crushed the English in 1607 found himself, only seven years later, pathetically entreating his enemies for a shaving knife, bone combs, fishhooks, and a dog and cat.

While Powhatan contented himself with making ceremonial tours throughout his domain after 1614, Opechancanough boldly stepped into the power vacuum created by the war. In the year of the peace, Indian informants told colony leaders that whatever Opechancanough "agreed upon and did, the great King [Powhatan] would confirme." The English noted that Opechancanough was the Powhatans' "chief Captaine, and one that can as soone (if not sooner) as Powhatan commande the men." And in 1615 it was reported that Opechancanough "hath already the commaund of all the people." Finally in the summer of 1617, Powhatan, grief-stricken upon learning of Pocahontas's death in England, allegedly "left the Government of his Kingdom to Opachan-ko [Opechancanough] and his other brother [Opitchapam]" and sought refuge among the Patawomeke tribe along the Potomac River.[6]

Powhatan's abdication in 1617 revealed a power struggle among the tidewater Indian *werowances*. At the center of this contest was Opechancanough, who deftly used the English to increase his authority over the area tribes. In 1616 he convinced the proud and quick-tempered governor of the colony, George Yeardley, that the independent Chickahominy tribe had been killing English livestock. This carefully planted information resulted in an English attack during which some forty Chickahominies were treacherously murdered. It was no coincidence that Opechancanough was nearby to witness the slaughter and that he quickly stepped forward to comfort the bloodied and frightened Chickahominies. That tribe then declared Opechancanough their king, gave him their allegiance, and agreed to pay him tribute. As John Smith later explained these events, Opechancanough had succeeded in his plan "for the subjecting of those people, that neither hee nor Powhatan could ever [before] bring to their obedience."[7]

Such maneuvers clearly demonstrated Opechancanough's ambition, and upon Powhatan's death in April 1618 the wily Pamunkey *werowance* became the effective overlord of the tidewater tribes. Opechancanough was finally the "great Kinge," and as "a great Captaine" who "did always fight," he was called upon to use his talents and status in an active, dangerous struggle against the English. But his lust for political control was not only a personal one; it was also an unselfish and desperate attempt to prevent the total collapse of a weakened and threatened Tsenacommacah. Between 1618 and 1622, Opechancanough's priorities were clearly focused on strengthening and revitalizing his people.

The challenges he faced were immense. In the years immediately following the First Anglo-Powhatan War, the English had dispossessed the Indians of much of their best land. This was especially true after 1618, when a boom in tobacco prices sharpened English land appetites, and famine and disease wracked the once-strong Powhatans. Poor harvests made the Indians dependent on their hated enemies for food, while epidemics devastated the Powhatans and even the deer in their forests between 1617 and 1619. Although disease attacked all the tidewater tribes, Opechancanough's Pamunkeys may have suffered proportionately less than other Powhatans because their territory lay at some distance from the English settlements.

In the wake of these tragedies the Powhatans were pitiable but not pitied. Their English enemies regarded the debilitated, depopulated, and seemingly unthreatening Indians more as defeated and downtrodden pawns than as proud and fierce warriors. Complacent in the peace of 1614 and temporarily less dependent on the Indians for food, the English considered the Powhatans merely impotent and troublesome obstacles to the exploitation of Virginia's lands and resources. It was in these exceedingly adverse circumstances that Opechancanough began his methodical consolidation of the remnants of Powhatan's once-united chiefdom, along with the recruitment of tribes like the Chickahominies who had never been a part of Tsenacommacah. It was ironic that although Opechancanough had often displayed his potential for leadership, it was only the harsh presence of the English that brought him to the fore.

Opechancanough's plan depended on manipulating two intertwined social pressures: the desire of the Indians to procure the colonists' muskets and the attempts of the English to convert and "civilize" the Powhatans. The Virginia Company of London, the joint-stock corporation in charge of colony affairs, was sincerely interested in Christianizing and educating Indian youths, and colonial officials approached Opechancanough many times in an effort to borrow or even buy Powhatan children for this purpose. But the chief refused to allow any Indians to live among the English unless they were permitted the use of muskets. Ever since 1607 the Powhatans had been attempting to obtain firearms from the English. Recognizing that this single technological advantage was the key to English domination, Opechancanough was determined somehow to alter the colonists' monopoly of muskets. Faced with his refusal to provide children for Christianization and under unceasing pressure from missionary idealists among the company's investors in London, the Virginia leaders finally allowed some Powhatans to be trained in the use of firearms.

Thus, while the colonists were preoccupied with growing tobacco and were complacent about the Indians' reputed powerlessness, Opechancanough's men were becoming competent marksmen. By 1618 Englishmen were occasionally being killed by Indians using muskets, and it was reported that the Powhatans would be "boulde . . . to assault" white settlements whenever they concluded that English firearms were "sicke and not to be used" against them.[8]

By 1622 Opechancanough's leadership had made the tidewater tribes stronger than at any other time since 1607. The English judged the chief's own stronghold so defensible that three hundred musketeers—more men than had been drawn together in a single force during the First Anglo-Powhatan War—would be required to launch an attack against the Pamunkeys. This was a far cry from the English assessment of a decade before that the Indians were incapable of inflicting harm.

Opechancanough had succeeded in engineering this military renaissance and the psychological revitalization of his people in large part through the efforts of Nemattanew (Nemát-ten-ū), a mysterious prophet, war captain, and advisor, who was himself one of the first Powhatans to become an able marksman with English muskets. Called "Jack of the Feathers" by the colonists, Nemattanew always went about attired in elaborate and unique feather garments, "as thowghe he meant to flye." He was respected by the Powhatans, and by Opechancanough especially, as a charismatic and talented policymaker, while the English called him a "very cunning fellow" who "took great Pride in preserving and increasing . . . [the Indians'] Superstition concerning him, affecting every thing that was odd and prodigious to work upon their Admiration." Significantly, Nemattanew told his people that he was immortal, that he was therefore invulnerable to English bullets, and that he possessed "an Ointment" and special powers "that could secure them" from bullets as well.[9]

By the spring of 1621, as Nemattanew's revitalizing influence grew among the Powhatans, Opechancanough made plans to annihilate the hated English. His first step was to conclude a firm peace with the colony so that the whites would confidently put aside their muskets for plows and allow the Powhatans to move freely among their plantations. Then, further to lure the English into complacency, Opechancanough decided to tell his adversaries what they wanted to hear concerning the religious and cultural conversion of his people.

He was able to accomplish his goals because in 1620–21 the Virginia Company had sent two naive and optimistic reformers to the colony to implement its program for the "civilization" of the Indians. These men were Sir Francis Wyatt, Jamestown's new governor, and George Thorpe, an idealistic proselytizer. They tried to win over Opechancanough's people with lavish gifts, English clothes, and kind words. Wyatt and especially Thorpe set out to undermine Powhatan religion and traditions and to alienate Indian youths from their elders by promoting English customs and Christianity among them. This energetic new campaign seemed especially dangerous to Opechancanough; but he acted coolly and resourcefully in the face of it.

Late in 1621 Opechancanough met with the zealous Thorpe, who had been trying to convert him for months, and to the astonishment of everyone renounced the major teachings of Powhatan religion. He promised to allow English families to live among the Pamunkeys and gave his permission for the colonists to take any lands not actually occupied by the Powhatans! These startling announcements would have amounted to heresy had they been made sincerely, but Opechancanough was purposefully deceptive in initiating the final chapter in his consolidation of power. By lulling Thorpe, Wyatt, and the other Englishmen into complacency, Opechancanough was forging a strategy more subtle in its execution, more ethnocentric in its foundation, and more revolutionary in its potential impact than Thorpe's.

Thanks to the efforts of Opechancanough and Nemattanew, the Powhatans were by this time more strongly committed to their own culture than ever. Opechancanough saw clearly that there could be no Anglo-Powhatan relations based on peace. Every tragedy that could have befallen the Indians had occurred, and the English had brought destruction to the tribes as readily in times of peace as in times of war. A prolonged peace could only result in more seizures of Indian corn and territory and in further attempts to destroy his people's culture. What did the Powhatans have to gain by keeping the peace? What could they lose by breaking it?

From Opechancanough's personal standpoint, everything the English had done before 1621 had served to increase his power and leverage in Powhatan politics; anything they might do from that time forward was likely to weaken his position. The chief's bold strategy with Thorpe nevertheless revealed confidence in the Indians' future rather than despair.

Opechancanough had no intention of leading the Powhatans into physical or cultural suicide; his statements and actions reflected strength and pride, not weakness or desperation.

Opechancanough's plans were suddenly put in jeopardy when in early March 1622 some Englishmen "accidentally" murdered the "immortal" Nemattanew under suspicious circumstances. But Powhatan resiliency and Opechancanough's resolve were confirmed only two weeks later when, as spring breezes once again replaced winter's chill among the pines, an impressive Indian alliance suddenly attacked the English settlements along the entire length of the James River. In this famous uprising of March 22, 1622, Opechancanough's warriors infiltrated white homesteads without arousing suspicion and managed to kill some 330 people before the colony mobilized its forces. Shocked and frightened by this bold and bloody stroke, the English grudgingly recognized Opechancanough's skill as the "Great generall of the Salvages."[10]

The 1622 uprising touched off a ten-year war, and for a brief time Powhatan warriors outdid their enemies, using muskets made in England. Distraught whites reported that the Indians became "verie bold, and can use peeces [muskets] . . . as well or better than an Englishman." With the Powhatans well armed with captured weapons, the colonists feared that they would "brave our countrymen at their verie doors."[11]

This Second Anglo-Powhatan War reached its peak in autumn 1624, when an intertribal force of eight hundred warriors, dominated by Pamunkeys, fought English musketeers in a fierce, two-day battle in open field. In this unusual engagement waged in Pamunkey territory, Opechancanough's warriors fought to defend their homeland and to preserve their excellent reputation among other area tribes. Although the Pamunkeys were eventually forced to retreat, never before had the Indians demonstrated such tenacity under fire. Even Governor Wyatt had to admit that this battle "shewed what the Indyans could doe."[12]

Recognizing Openchancanough's importance to the Indians' courage and persistence, Jamestown officials placed a bounty on his head. The English came close to killing him in 1623 by means of an elaborate plot to ambush and poison several parleying chiefs. Opechancanough was almost certainly present at the meeting, where many Indian leaders died, but somehow he managed to escape the English trap.

The war continued, but by 1625 both sides had come to the realization that the annihilation of their enemies was impossible. For almost three years Governor Wyatt and his commanders had "used their uttermost and Christian endeavours in prosequtinge revenge against the bloody Salvadges" without making Opechancanough or his people submit. The Pamunkey *werowance* had proved a better "generall" than Powhatan, and in 1625 the fatigued English soldiers decided to suspend their twice-yearly campaigns against him. Choosing to plant tobacco rather than to pursue the utter destruction of the Powhatans, the colonists had, in Governor Wyatt's words, "worne owt the Skarrs of the Massacre."[13]

Although the Second Anglo-Powhatan War did not end officially until 1632, the early years of the conflict were the most significant in demonstrating that the Indians' pride had not been extinguished by a decade and a half of disruptive and frequently brutal contact with the Englishmen. By war's end it might be said that Opechancanough had won a qualified victory. If he had not succeeded in annihilating the colonists, he had at least ended the threat of enforced culture change. His people had willingly risked death rather than adopt the Christian religion and English manners. Although many Powhatans did die, their traditions were for the time being preserved.

After peace was agreed to in 1632, there followed a decade of tenuous coexistence between the Powhatans and the English. The Indians had been weakened by the war, and they welcomed an opportunity to tend their fields in peace. In the long run, however, the period after 1632 proved more damaging to the Powhatans than the war years. The Virginia colony developed so rapidly that the Indians' territorial and cultural foundations were quickly and irrevocably eroded. After a dozen years, with nowhere to go and with a smaller and smaller amount of land on which to preserve their traditions and to raise their children, the Powhatans once again chose the desperate option of war.

In the spring of 1644, as the sturgeon and the meadows again experienced nature's season of renewal, the tireless Opechancanough mobilized a new generation of warriors for an even more desperate rebellion. As in 1622, the Powhatans struck at the English plantations without warning and killed some five hundred of the land-hungry colonists. But this uprising proved futile, for by this time the odds against success were overwhelming. In 1646, after almost two years of brutal warfare, the by now infirm but indefatigable Pamunkey chief, who had seen some eighty winters, was captured and murdered by the English.

Opechancanough's death ended a talented and tempestuous career of leadership that spanned four eventful decades. He had known and warred with an entire generation of Englishmen, long since dead. The Virginia governor who captured him in 1646 had been a mere babe in the cradle when Jamestown was founded.

The last of the "true" Powhatans, Opechancanough had symbolized the precontact glory of Tsenacommacah, while adapting to the postcontact exigencies of cultural survival. He had demonstrated resiliency and political resolve in his magnificent effort to save the Powhatan way of life, and he had in fact succeeded in the difficult task of rebuilding and enlarging Powhatan's domain after the first peace with the English in 1614. The Pamunkeys' resort to arms in two bloody wars between 1622 and 1646 reveal that Opechancanough had managed to reinstill pride and purpose in his people.

Opechancanough coped as best he knew how with the strange and aggressive forces of European colonization. Although his indomitable courage and unyielding fight against foreign domination failed to prevent the eventual subjugation of the Powhatans, Opechancanough's refusal to submit was a reassertion of the proud warrior traditions of his culture. He led his people in a struggle for survival while trying to preserve their self-respect. When the Powhatans had to choose between cultural survival and individual sacrifice, they proudly chose death over enslavement. Victory or defeat mattered less to them than the act of resistance.

In this the "Great generall" set a strong personal example. Even as a captive in 1646, the exhausted Opechancanough displayed pride and dignity until the end. Just before he was treacherously shot in the back by an English guard, the aged Pamunkey *werowance*—"so decrepit that he was not able to walk alone," with "Eye-lids . . . so heavy that he could not see"—was protesting the fact that he had been placed on public exhibition like a caged animal.[14] For such a man and such a culture in such an era, the ability to cope was the ability to fight bravely against overwhelming odds and to die with dignity and purpose.

Notes

1. Robert Beverley, *The History and Present State of Virginia* (1705), ed. Louis B. Wright (Chapel Hill, N.C., 1947), p. 61; Edward Waterhouse, *A Declaration of the State of the Colony . . . and a Relation of the Barbarous Massacre* (London, 1622), p. 18; Henry R. Schoolcraft, *Archives of Aboriginal Knowledge* (Philadelphia, 1860), p. 98.

Opechancanough's origins have been the subject of scholarly speculation and folk legend over the centuries. Beverley, the late seventeenth-century Virginia historian, claimed that he was "a Prince of a Foreign Nation, and came to them [the Powhatans] a great Way from the South-West: And by their Accounts, we suppose him to have come from the *Spanish Indians*, some-where near *Mexico*, or the Mines of St. *Barbe*" (Beverley, *History*, p. 61); see also Thomas Jefferson Wertenbaker, *Virginia Under the Stuarts* (Princeton, 1914), p. 80, and Christian F. Feest, "Powhatan: A Study in Political Organization," *Wiener Völkerkundliche Mitteilungen* 13 (1966): 76–77.

Current theories claim that Opechancanough was none other than Don Luis de Velasco, a Virginia Indian who had been captured by Spaniards and converted to Catholicism in the 1560s and who was responsible for wiping out a Spanish Jesuit mission on the York River in February 1571. Opechancanough's birth date (and therefore his age in 1607) are still much-debated keys to confirming or denying such speculations. See the forthcoming works by Carl Bridenbaugh (Oxford University Press) and William R. Swagerty (Ph.D. dissertation, University of California, Santa Barbara).

2. Capt. John Smith, *A True Relation of . . . Virginia* (London, 1608), p. D3^r-v.

3. *Ibid.*, p. E3^v.

4. [William Symonds, comp.], *The Proceedings of the English Colonie in Virginia since their first beginning . . . till this present 1612* (Oxford, 1612), pp. 69, 74.

5. *Ibid.*, pp. 60–61.

6. Ralph Hamor, *A True Discourse of the Present Estate of Virginia . . . till . . . 1614* (London, 1615), pp. 10, 53; Capt. Samuel Argall to Virginia Company of London, March 10, 1617/18, and to

Council for Virginia, June 9, 1617, in Susan Myra Kingsbury, ed., *Records of the Virginia Company of London*, 4 vols. (Washington, D.C., 1906–35), vol. 3, pp. 73–74, 92.

7. Capt. John Smith, *The Generall Historie of Virginia, New-England, and the Summer Isles* (London, 1624), p. 120.

8. *Ibid.*, p. 125; H. R. McIlwaine, ed., *Journals of the House of Burgesses of Virginia, 1619–1658/59* (Richmond, 1915), pp. 33–34.

9. George Percy, "A Trewe Relacyon . . . of Virginia from . . . 1609 untill . . . 1612," in *Tyler's Quarterly Historical and Genealogical Magazine* 3 (1922): 280; Beverley, *History*, pp. 52–53; Smith, *Generall Historie of Virginia*, pp. 144, 151; J. Frederick Fausz and Jon Kukla, "A Letter of Advice to the Governor of Virginia, 1624," *William and Mary Quarterly* 34 (1977): 117.

10. [Anon.], "Good Newes from Virginia" (broadside ballad, ca. 1622–23), in *William and Mary Quarterly* 5 (1948): 354.

11. Richard Frethorne to his parents, April 3, 1623, in Kingsbury, *Records*, vol. 4, p. 61; Report on conditions in Virginia, May 1623, *ibid.*, p. 147.

12. Sir Francis Wyatt to the Earl of Southampton and the Virginia Company, December 2, 1624, *ibid.*, pp. 507–508.

13. *Ibid.*; Governor Wyatt to commissioners investigating Virginia, January 4, 1625/26, *ibid.*, pp. 568–569.

14. Beverley, *History*, p. 62.

Sources

This essay is derived from longer, more detailed works: my dissertation, "The Powhatan Uprising of 1622: A Historical Study of Ethnocentrism and Cultural Conflict" (College of William and Mary, 1977), and a book manuscript, "Quest and Conquest in the Creation of Virginia: An Ethnohistorical Study of Anglo-Powhatan Relations, 1560–1630" (Jamestown MS Prize Finalist). The richest primary sources for ethnohistorical details about early Virginia include: Edward Arber and A. G. Bradley, eds., *Travels and Works of Captain John Smith*, 2 vols. (Edinburgh, 1910); William Strachey, *The Historie of Travell Into Virginia Britania (1612)*, ed. Louis B. Wright and Virginia Freund (Glasgow, 1953); Philip L. Barbour, ed., *The Jamestown Voyages Under the First Charter, 1606–1609*, 2 vols. (Cambridge, 1969); Ralph Hamor, *A True Discourse of the Present Estate of Virginia . . . till . . . 1614* (London, 1615); Susan Myra Kingsbury, ed., *Records of the Virginia Company of London*, 4 vols. (Washington, D.C., 1906–1935); and Samuel Purchas, *Hakluytus Posthumus, or Purchas His Pilgrimes* (1625), modern ed., 20 vols. (Glasgow, 1905–1907). A readable and accurate account of the early contact era is found in Philip L. Barbour, *The Three Worlds of Captain John Smith* (Boston, Mass., 1964).

Suggestions for Further Reading

The best short introduction to Anglo-Indian relations in Virginia is Nancy Oestreich Lurie, "Indian Cultural Adjustment to European Civilization," in James Morton Smith, ed., *Seventeenth-Century America: Essays in Colonial History* (Chapel Hill, 1959), pp. 33–60, a classic overview of the seventeenth century. A readable study of Anglo-Powhatan cultural conflict, as revealed through the careers of antagonistic contemporaries, is J. Frederick Fausz, "George Thorpe, Nemattanew, and the Powhatan Uprising of 1622," *Virginia Cavalcade* (Winter 1979), 111–117. Edmund S. Morgan, *American Slavery, American Freedom: The Ordeal of Colonial Virginia* (New York, 1975), chaps. 1–6, is a well-written interpretation of the early Jamestown years; however, Morgan's comments on Powhatan culture are often misleading and must be read with caution. More accurate in its ethnohistorical details is Christian F. Feest, "Virginia Algonquians," in William C. Sturtevant, ed., *Handbook of North American Indians*, 20 vols. (Washington, D.C., 1978), vol. 15: *Northeast*, ed. Bruce G. Trigger, pp. 253–270. For the ambitious reader who desires an understanding of how current scholars approach Native American history and colonial ethnohistory, I strongly recommend the splendid, provocative work of Francis Jennings, *The Invasion of America: Indians, Colonialism, and the Cant of Conquest* (Chapel Hill, 1975), and the historiographical summary by James Axtell, "The Ethnohistory of Early America: A Review Essay," *William and Mary Quarterly* 35 (1978): 110–144.

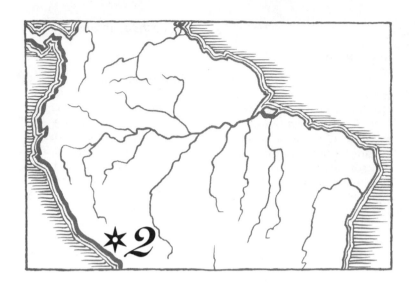

Diego Vasicuio:
Native Priest

ANN M. WIGHTMAN

*V*arucio? Vasicaio? Vasicuio? The scribe who recorded
the testimonies given in the heresy investigations
held in 1671 at San Francisco de los Chichas, near Arequipa in
southern Peru, was apparently not quite sure. But such
careless treatment at the hands of a colonial bureaucrat
would not have bothered Diego at all. He was a quiet, cautious man; and he had managed to survive to an advanced age
by avoiding direct contact with the Spanish imperial system
whenever possible, confronting it only when necessary. This
time, however, the strategy had failed and Diego Vasicuio
was in trouble.[1]

Diego had not taken it personally when his neighbor,
Catalina Paicaua, denounced him to their parish priest as the
leader of a group of Indians who persisted in the worship of
the old god Sorimana. He, too, knew the trick of diverting the

clergy's anger and attention by identifying—or inventing—
"bigger and better sinners." In the course of refuting Catalina
Paicaua's charges, Diego Vasicuio would himself direct
Father Bernardino de Prado, the parish priest, toward investigating a rival cult and its clandestine ceremonies rather
than his own.

Catalina Paicaua had been in a tight spot herself. Either the
spell she had cast to help Teresa Alpana captivate her boy-
friend had not worked and Teresa had complained, or it *had*
taken hold and it was the reluctant lover who had denounced
Catalina for witchcraft. Brought before the parish priest,
Catalina had confessed immediately to the charges made
against her. Yes, she had cast a few harmless spells at the
request of village women. Yes, she knew that witchcraft was
wrong and that she had violated the teachings of the Holy
Church. But did the priest know that a group of his pa-
rishoners in the town of Salamanca regularly committed
even greater sins by praying to an idol called Sorimana? If not,
would he not rather hear her testify about heresy and idol
worshipers than about mere witchcraft? Father de Prado was
more than willing to accept the bargain.

From the beginning of the colonial period, the Spanish
attempt to convert the Indians of Peru into sincere, observant
Catholics had been thwarted by the tenacious survival of
indigenous religious beliefs and practices that the priests
loosely termed "idolatry." The Church had hoped to defeat
this resistance by means of the pervasive influence of the
missionary and secular clergy—enforcing obligatory attendance at mass and catechism classes, introducing a new set of
images to inspire the faithful, and imposing the Christian
calendar and holy days. This program was a central feature of
the imperial framework that the Spaniards constructed to
control the indigenous population. With its help, the colonial
system had indeed succeeded in transforming the social and
economic structure of Indian society (although the extent of
this transformation is the subject of continuing debate).
Despite this effort, however, preconquest religious beliefs
and ceremonies had survived at the community or *ayllu*
level, with relatively little modification and on a very wide
scale. Diego Vasicuio and hundreds like him were the key
elements in this perpetuation of traditional religious

CAPITVLOPRIMERODEVECITA-DOR
CHRISTOBA·DEALBOR
nos uecitador general de las madre yglecia buena justicia —

Juis   cristobal

2. Ecclesiastical *visitador* chides Indian woman accused of witchcraft. Peru, early seventeenth century.

thought. They were influential members of Indian communities, and they worked through individual, informal contacts with their neighbors to hand down gods and gospels from one generation of believers to another.

Diego's parents and grandparents had entrusted him with the stone image of the god Sorimana, and they had taught him to recite the proper prayers and perform the specific ceremonies of his cult. He in turn had repeated their instructions to various Indian women, one of whom was initiating her own twelve-year-old granddaughter into the Sorimana cult at the time Diego was summoned to testify. Father de Prado's investigation of witchcraft had indeed led him to a flourishing, determined, and self-perpetuating group of idol worshipers.

Sorimana's followers were not surprised to be discovered in such an indirect way. Parish priests relied heavily on luck, informers, and hearsay in their "crusade against idolatry." The Holy Office of the Inquisition was not authorized to move against Native American suspects, so the hierarchy had commissioned a series of visiting inspectors who were given blanket authority to detect and punish idolaters in the Indian communities. The *visitas* or inspection tours carried out by these guardians of orthodoxy were sporadic and of varying success. The rivalries between Indian communities that surfaced during the wide-ranging investigations tended to distort the evidence, and as in the present case, to produce denunciations designed to shield the traditional deity of one cult by betraying the gods of others. The Spaniards used the term *guaca* for both the god's physical image and his dwelling place, and Indian "heretics" were able to exploit the resulting semantic confusion when faced with demands for *guacas* by leading the infuriated priests to randomly chosen caves or hillsides rather than revealing the true holy places or surrendering their sacred idols. Diego Vasicuio had protected Sorimana during one such *visita* by simply hiding the idol for the duration of the inspector's stay. But in May 1671 his luck ran out, and he found himself before a parish priest who was determined to eradicate the cult of Sorimana once and for all.

Diego Vasicuio was over ninety years old when he appeared before Father de Prado to answer the charges of heresy. This in itself was remarkable, in view of the fact that in the course of Diego's lifetime and that of his father a population of perhaps ten or fifteen million Native Americans had declined to approximately six hundred thousand as the result of epidemics, malnutrition, starvation, and forced labor under the *mita* system in mines, haciendas, and textile workshops. Even more remarkable was the fact that he had managed to live such a long life without permanently leaving his home community. Tens of thousands of Native Americans had sought to escape the rigors of the colonial labor and taxation systems by migrating, trading the security of a home community for freedom from its *mita* and tribute rolls. Some had fled to remote regions beyond Spanish control; others had found anonymity in the growing urban and mining centers, remaining in them as "voluntary workers" when they finished their terms of forced labor. In the rural sector, harassed and debt-ridden Indians had exchanged communal ties and personal independence for relative security as *yanaconas* under the "protection" of individual Spanish or Indian landholders who were willing to bargain with the tribute collectors or defy the *mita* authorities in order to ensure for themselves an adequate workforce. Those migrants who chose to stay within Indian society became *forasteros*, who settled in other villages to secure the land and labor assistance that would have been theirs by hereditary right in their own communities. The *forasteros* gained access to land by outright purchase, rental, or sharecropping, and they developed relationships with the original residents of their new communities by marrying into existing kinship groups, submitting to the local authorities, and sometimes even evolving their own *ayllu* of *forasteros*, in order to have access to communal labor.

Like many others, Diego Vasicuio had temporarily left his hometown on several occasions—to serve his turn in the *mita* or to find a cash-paying job so that he could meet his tribute obligations. When he was lucky, the Indians from his village had been required to serve their terms of *mita* labor on nearby haciendas; when he was not, they had been forced to work in the dangerous silver mines of Castrovirreyna or in an unhealthy *obraje* or textile workshop.

In theory, only one seventh of all tribute payers—healthy Indian males between the ages of eighteen and fifty—were expected to serve in the *mita* at any one time. After two months they were allowed to return to their home communities for a year of rest. In practice, Diego had to serve with greater frequency due to the combined pressures of heavy death tolls, high migration rates, exemptions from service for the village's political and religious leaders, and the infrequency of government inspections, which would have noted the area's shrinking labor pool and reduced its labor obligations accordingly. In theory, employers who had *mita* workers assigned to their service were bound by government regulations protecting the Indians' physical safety and health, limiting their work hours, and ensuring that they would be paid regularly and at the official rates. In practice, the widespread abuse of these regulations made Indians so fearful of the *mita* that families sometimes mutilated their male infants so that as adults they might be exempt from forced labor service.

Mita service was unfair as well as brutal. Indians who worked as *yanaconas* or "voluntary labor" in the mines and workshops were paid higher wages and often received better treatment. In mining centers, the "volunteers" were usually assigned the less dangerous jobs at the stamp mills and smelting patios, while *mita* Indians worked deep underground in the hazardous tunnels and shafts.

Having served his several terms as a *mita* laborer, Diego must have realized the distinct advantages of migrating permanently from Salamanca. But he had always returned to the village where his family lived and his ancestors were remembered. In addition to kinship bonds and inherited rights to land and labor (and the assistance of a communal workforce when needed), strong spiritual ties held him there, and in particular to a small cave in the hillside of Cantuea. For most of his adult life, Diego Vasicuio had been the chief priest and custodian of the god Sorimana, and an enthusiastic promoter of his cult. It was the close relationship between the god, the sacred stone *guaca* that served as his physical representation, and the place where he exercised his special powers which more than anything else bound Diego Vasicuio to Salamanca.

There he could count on the help of local leaders such as the *curaca*, Don Pablo Uranguaiqua, one of Vasicuio's earliest and most consistent supporters. Whether as a genuine manifestation of his beliefs or as an attempt to increase his power and popularity among the villagers, Don Pablo had always defended the sorceress Catalina Paicaua and had encouraged Diego Vasicuio in his efforts to rekindle the people's flagging interest in the traditional religion by increasing their ritual sacrifices to Sorimana.

By the middle of the seventeenth century, more than a hundred years after the Spanish conquest, the Sorimana cult was flourishing once again in Salamanca. An elderly member named Angelina Vancuipa had replaced the idol's clothing, lost over the years; after she had adorned the *guaca* with beautiful white cloth, Sorimana's status soared. An increasing number of Indians, including Pedro Ninacori, a sacristan of the Catholic church who was later denounced and imprisoned during an ecclesiastical *visita*, had begun participating in the ceremonies that Diego Vasicuio conducted near the Cantuea cave.

These ceremonies were performed at regular intervals throughout the year, on dates chosen by consulting the traditional calendar. The most important celebrations occurred in June, at summer solstice. Angelina Vancuipa's casual comment that the best time for asking Sorimana for gifts of food was "right after Corpus Christi" was especially infuriating to Father de Prado. The celebration of the Corpus in late May or early June was one of the most solemn and prestigious Catholic rites; for the Sorimana cult to use that festival as a prelude to its own traditional holy days or perhaps even to combine the two in some manner was intolerable.

Father de Prado found the ceremonies themselves even more offensive. Never mind that the rites followed the format basic to religions everywhere: praise the god first and then implore him. As succeeding witnesses added detail to the sketchy description provided by Catalina Paicaua, the horrified priest learned how Diego Vasicuio led the Sorimana cult in rituals encompassing every aspect of the venerated union of god, physical representation, and holy ground. At the mouth of the sacred cave, Diego would gently bathe the stone *guaca* in *chicha* (the native corn beer) and then offer the traditional sacrifices of more *chicha*, coca leaves, corn, and fodder. As the grains burned, Diego Vasicuio first spoke and then prayed to Sorimana. His conversations with the god were private. Diego acted as the interpreter of remarks that no one else ever heard, which soon served to emphasize his own special relationship with Sorimana and to add an essential touch of mystery to the ceremony. His prayers, however, were always public and always the same—traditional orations recast to express the harsh reality of life for Andean villagers under the colonial system: "You are the one who gives, the Creator of the Earth. Look at me. I am poor. Give me strength, give me food. Have pity on me. Give me corn. I have nothing. Help me." The central plea of the Indians as they worshiped any god was a simple one: give us food.

The fact that the people of Salamanca prayed to Sorimana specifically for corn, together with their offerings of *chicha* and ground corn, may be of some significance. If the heresy investigators were as careless with the god's name as they had been with Diego's, it may be that they wrote "Sorimana" instead of "Saramama," or "Corn Mother" in Quechua.[2] Unfortunately for our understanding of this story, it was Father de Prado's concern to destroy the idol rather than to identify it correctly.

If the Spaniards were often careless with Indian nomenclature, they were more precise in characterizing the rituals performed. Father de Prado described the Sorimana rites as "idolatrous" and "heretical," but he did not confuse them with witchcraft. Vasicuio had left his ceremonies free of the more sensational popular enchantments incorporated by some other cults. However, Pedro Vaucitama, the priest of the rival gods Vampuvilca and Acocho in Salamanca, was in the habit of mixing magic and prayer indiscriminately. On one occasion, in an incident similar to that which had caused so much trouble for Catalina Paicaua, Vaucituma had promised to reunite a woman and her husband by mingling strands of his hair with hers and imploring Acocho to make the spell effective. Although Diego Vasicuio was well acquainted with local sorcerers such as Catalina Paicaua, he had maintained the purity of the Sorimana rites by refusing to include any such spells. At one point the Sorimana and Vampuvilca rites were similar: both chief priests were said to have "tossed the heavens" in the name of their gods, causing the stars to spin and to streak across the skies. Such were the manifestations of the supernatural powers of gods when each Indian priest believed his deity to be the Creator of Earth with complete control over the physical universe. This innocent drawing of a parallel between "Sorimana, Creator of Earth" and the Christian God who "created the Heavens and the Earth" outraged Father de Prado, and he was not in the least distracted from his horror at such blasphemy by Diego's description of the witchcraft and magic employed in the Vampuvilca and Acocho ceremonies. The priest demanded the immediate surrender of the *guaca* Sorimana.

Diego Vasicuio reluctantly agreed to comply. Accompanied by two men appointed by the priest, Diego left San

Francisco de los Chichas for Salamanca. Sometime later he returned without the stone and with the rather implausible story that Pedro Ninacori, the jailed idolater and former sacristan of Salamanca, had escaped and hidden the *guaca*. Father de Prado was neither fooled nor amused. He threatened repeatedly to jail Diego Vasicuio and was not placated until Angelina Vancuipa's son, Diego Limachi, appeared before him with an impressive-looking stone wrapped in white cloths, which Diego, Angelina, and Catalina Paicaua all identified as the true image of Sorimana. The jubilant parish priest then ordered his men to continue searching for other *guacas*, and at the end of an afternoon's work he was able to record that although some idols had undoubtedly escaped detection, over twenty of these "false gods" had been confiscated and would be forwarded to the ecclesiastical authorities.

Was the stone surrendered to Father de Prado really Sorimana, the god of Diego Vasicuio's ancestors? Probably not. Diego's reluctance to hand over the stone was undoubtedly a piece of artful dissimulation; to produce Sorimana without a protest would have been to arouse the Spanish priest's suspicions. But it was an easy matter for Angelina Vancuipa to wrap an ordinary rock in cloths similar to those she had woven for Sorimana and then to send her son to surrender the false *guaca* instead of the authentic one. If their ancestors had managed to guard Sorimana through more than a century of persecution, why should the men and women of Salamanca surrender his image now?

What then did the priest do to Diego Vasicuio, Angelina Vancuipa, and the other villagers identified as members of Sorimana's cult? The most common punishment in heresy cases was to denounce the convicted idolaters in public, and then to have them whipped by the parish priests or paraded through town carrying a cross or some other visible sign of their repentance. Indians who broke civil or criminal law or who refused to cooperate with heresy investigators would receive harsher penalties, but the ordinary sinner's punishment would usually be mitigated if he could bring himself to put on a convincing display of regret and religious fervor.

Diego Vasicuio and his friends knew this and behaved accordingly. They fell all over each other in their haste to confess that it was "very, very true" that they were idolaters

and had performed scandalous ceremonies and heretical sacrifices, and they claimed that they were surrendering their
false god and asking the true God's help so that they might
"sin no more." They were swearing to these things by the
Catholic God and under the sign of a cross, after all, and not in
the name of Sorimana. What did it matter if they lied to the
parish priest and identified a rock that Diego Limachi had
picked up and wrapped in an ordinary piece of cloth as the
image of their beloved god?

Sorimana was safe. The cautious Diego Vasicuio and his
friends undoubtedly laid low for a while and then resumed
their secret ceremonies just as before. Having once again
adjusted and maneuvered to endure within the colonial system, Diego Vasicuio survived. His rituals, his religion, and his
god survived. Compared with the success of those individuals who became rich and powerful through collaboration
with the repressive imperial order, Diego Vasicuio's achievements may seem to have been insignificant. But survival
through adaptation was the best that most Native Americans
living under European domination could hope for, and it was
something that all too few of them achieved.

Notes

1. The information on which this story is based was gathered in
the course of dissertation research carried out during 1976 and 1977;
the research was made possible by grants from the Henry L. and
Grace Dougherty Foundation and the Social Science Research Council. My thanks to these organizations, and to Mal Bochner, Richard
M. Morse, Irene Silverblatt, and David G. Sweet for assistance in the
preparation of this chapter.

2. This possible connection was suggested to me by Deborah
Poole, personal communication, 1977.

Sources

Diego Vasicuio's story is told in manuscript B1701 of the Biblioteca Nacional del Peru. Supplementary information was drawn from
additional documentation in that collection and from transcripts of
heresy investigations found in the Archivos Arzobispales in Cusco
and Lima. Several *visitas* filed in the Audiencia de Lima section at
the Archivo General de Indias in Seville contributed to the charac-
terization of Father de Prado and of the campaign against Andean
folk religion, as did Pablo de Arriaga, *La extirpación de la idolatría
en el Perú* (Lima, 1920; English trans. Lexington, Ky.: 1968) and José
María Arguedas' edition of Francisco de Avila, *Dioses y hombres*

de Huarochirí (Lima, 1966). John V. Murra provides information on the religious uses of Andean crops in *Formaciones económicas y políticas del mundo andino* (Lima, 1975), and "Rite and Crop in the Inca State," in Stanley Diamond, ed., *Culture in History: Essays in Honor of Paul Radin* (New York, 1960).

At the Seminario de Ideología y Religión of the Primera Jornada del Museo Nacional de Historia held in Lima during November 1976, I benefited from heated debates concerning the extent to which traditional religious thought and Christianity had combined, conflicted, or competed for support in the Andean indigenous community. In particular, Luis Millones' paper, "Religión y poder en los Andes: los curacas idólatras de la Sierra Central," emphasized the varied ways in which Indian political leaders used both magic and traditional religious beliefs to cement their power.

Suggestions for Further Reading

For those who wish to know more about Diego Vasicuio's Peru, the best general sources in English are Henry F. Dobyns and Paul L. Doughty, *Peru: A Cultural History* (New York, 1976) and the articles by John Rowe and George Kubler in vol. 2 of Julian H. Steward, ed., *A Handbook of South American Indians* (Washington, D.C., 1946). A modern view of the Spanish conquest is found in John Hemming, *The Conquest of the Incas* (New York, 1970); James Lockhart provides an in-depth account of the critical formative years of colonial society in *Spanish Peru, 1532–1560* (Madison, Wis., 1968). The drawings and English-Spanish captions of Felipe Huaman Poma de Ayala's *Nueva crónica y buen gobierno* in the edition prepared by Luis Bustios Galvéz (Lima, 1967) present an entertaining and informative view of Indian society. The decline of Indian population has recently been discussed by Nicolás Sánchez Albornóz in *The Population of Latin America* (Berkeley, Calif., 1974), with extensive bibliography; and Henry F. Dobyns records the series of post conquest plagues that were largely responsible for the change in "An Outline of Andean Epidemic History to 1720," *Bulletin of the History of Medicine* 37 (1963): 493–519. For the nature of local government in the Hapsburg era, see Waldemar Espinoza Soriano, "El alcalde mayor indígena en el Virreinato del Perú," *Anuario de Estudios Americanos* 17 (1960): 183–300, and Guillermo Lohmann Villena, *El corregidor de indios en el Perú bajo los Austrias* (Madrid, 1957). The best source for social change in the Indian community is the groundbreaking work of Karen Spalding: "Indian Rural Society in Colonial Peru: The Example of Huarochiri" (Ph.D. dissertation, University of California, Berkeley, 1967), followed by the articles collected in her *De indio a campesino: cambios en la estructura social del Perú colonial* (Lima, 1974). Spalding's "The Colonial Indian: Past and Future Research Perspectives," *Latin American Research Review* 7, 1 (1972): 47–76, assembles a comprehensive bibliography of published and archival materials.

Red Shoes:
Warrior and Diplomat

RICHARD WHITE

*O*n June 23, 1747, Shulush Homa of Couechitto, or Red Shoes as the English called him, fell ill on the trading path leading to the Choctaw nation. As any sick Choctaw would, he made his bed apart from his tribesmen when the English pack train they were escorting stopped for the night. Only one man, a member of a small allied tribe, remained with him when darkness fell. As Red Shoes slept, that man took out a knife, murdered the Choctaw for the French price on his head, and slipped into the night. In the next two years the blood of hundreds more Choctaws would flow in those woods and the ashes of burned and sacked towns would blow through them—the result of the civil war Red Shoes' death helped spark. Red Shoes did not die as a nativist martyr or as a traitor. Both he and his nation were more complex than that. Astute, pragmatic, ambitious, sometimes ruthless, he had acted not as an Indian or even simply as a Choctaw, but rather as the representative of a complex series of groups—his family, his *iksa* (clan), his town, and the common warriors who followed him.

The Choctaws were a nation of more than twenty thousand people at the beginning of the eighteenth century, but theirs was not a centralized state. It consisted of approximately fifty towns, ranging from mere villages to settlements of over a thousand people and organized at various times into three or more districts in what is now east central Mississippi. The nation, in fact, was a league of independent principalities in which the weaker towns were often attached as dependencies to the stronger. Red Shoes lived in Couechitto, the capital of the nation and home of its great chief. He was born there early in the eighteenth century, into what must have seemed a world of chaos and bewildering change. The French had settled the coast from Mobile to New Orleans, and the English the coast of the Carolinas. European disease and European-inspired slave raids ravaged the Choctaws, and European cloth, guns, and tools became necessities tying them into an international trade network that permanently altered their economy. Red Shoes began and ended his career in this changing world; here his loyalties and ambitions were molded and anchored. He did not act defensively in the face of change, nor was he the pawn of Europeans. Instead he moved to seize the opportunities that European contact seemed to offer.

During Shulush Homa's childhood and youth, friendship with the French was a necessity for the Choctaws. Large slaving expeditions of Creeks and Chickasaws, supplied and instigated by English traders, had marched thousands of Choctaws into bondage, killed thousands more, and left the survivors amidst burned fields and ravaged towns. Only French arms and aid had saved the nation. Once armed, however, the Choctaws had quickly recovered and become the bulwark of French Louisiana against the English and their Indian allies. Choctaw civil chiefs received medals from the French, as a token of their status, which entitled them to annual presents of valuable trade goods. In return for their aid to the Choctaws, the French expected gratitude and submissiveness. They got neither: the chiefs regarded the French gifts as a fitting demonstration of their importance to the colonists. Who was tributary to whom long remained an open question.

The chiefs did not grow rich off these presents. They redistributed them to their kinsmen and other followers in the towns. In Choctaw society power was a function of generosity, not wealth, and the chiefs' power increased with every blanket, knife, or bead they presented. They gave away virtually everything but the five or six guns the French allowed each town, letting favored warriors use them in exchange for any deerskins they obtained in the hunt. The chiefs gave the deerskins to the French as gifts, and the French gave them more gifts in return. These too the chiefs redistributed. There always remained, however, more Choctaws than there were goods, and the common warriors—those without *iksa* or family connections with the chiefs—lacked enough blankets, knives, and other manufactured goods. Eventually these warriors began their own trade with the French, but they found French goods scarce and expensive.

Red Shoes, as a common warrior, was on the periphery of these gift exchanges, but in time of war he found other ways to obtain trade goods. When the Choctaws fought as their allies, the French offered scalp bounties and markets for slaves. And in the early 1720s the Choctaws, at French instigation, waged a bitter war with the Chickasaws. Red Shoes fought in these wars, welcoming the trade goods they brought him but coveting his distinction as a warrior far more. In those days, he later recalled, "no one talked of anything but Red Shoes."[1] When the war parties returned, the men gathered, as they had for generations, either before the house of a prominent civil chief or in the square of the town. Here they bestowed new names on those young men who had killed an enemy or otherwise distinguished themselves in battle and gave them the rank of warrior. Sometime after 1720 Red Shoes, whose name at birth we do not know, stood in Couechitto and took a new name, Soulouche Oumastabe, earned by slaying Chickasaws. And as the war continued and more Chickasaws died at his hand, he rose to be the Red Shoes, or war captain, of Couechitto. Shulush Homa, or Red Shoes,

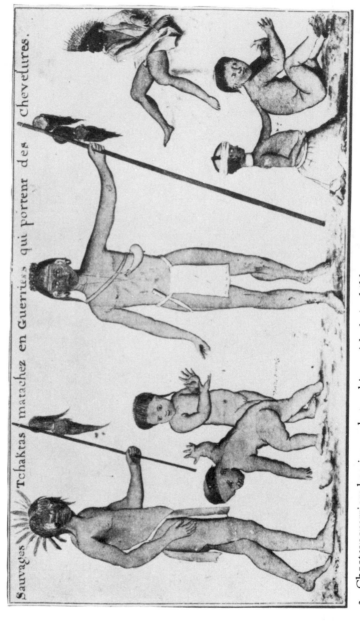

Sauvages Tchaktas matachez en Guerriers qui portent des chevelures.

3. Choctaw warriors bearing scalp trophies, with their children. Louisiana, 1730s.

became his title and his name; it was the highest rank a man of common birth could normally attain in the Choctaw nation.

In the 1720s Red Shoes' town of Couechitto straggled along the hillsides that encircled a small fertile prairie. On the flat lands below the cabins the women planted fields of corn, beans, and squash, which fed the town. Four hundred warriors hunted out of Couechitto and its dependencies then, but little game remained around the village. Red Shoes and the others made their major deer hunts from winter camps to the north and east. When his wives led the small Choctaw ponies loaded with the skins of the deer he had killed back to Couechitto, they brought with them the only commodities he could trade for cloth, pots, axes, guns, and other needed goods. In peacetime Red Shoes, unlike Mingo Tchito, the great chief of Couechitto recognized by the French as head of the nation, received no direct presents from the French. Like other warriors he hunted, traded, and depended on the chiefs for his goods.

Red Shoes' rise to power paralleled the long painful decline of Mingo Tchito and the Choctaw power structure, which Red Shoes helped dismantle. The head chief of Couechitto, as shrewd as Red Shoes and as aware of the rewards to be gained from playing the Europeans off against each other, lacked the boldness of his war captain. Where Red Shoes gambled all, Mingo Tchito hedged his bets. The differences between the two men came to a head in the series of crises that plagued Couechitto in 1729 and the years immediately following.

Corruption, mismanagement, and supply failures crippled the Indian trade of French Louisiana. The warehouses were empty, and the warriors who visited Mobile received only breechclouts, shirts, and scissors for their deerskins. The dissatisfied hunters therefore drifted off to the Chickasaw and Creek villages to trade with the English, whose trade goods were better, cheaper, and more abundant. Mingo Tchito, recognizing his limits, tolerated this "illicit" trade that he could not stop. He was hardly so tolerant, however, of the subsequent French failure to provide the usual presents for the chiefs. His indulgence of trade with the English now turned to active encouragement. Red Shoes became his eager collaborator, enabling Mingo Tchito to appear loyal to the

French while the English contacts widened. As Red Shoes and other warriors traded with the English, Mingo Tchito continued his visits to Mobile to exchange the customary presents with the French commander there. Such exchanges formed the sinews of French-Choctaw cooperation, and it was normally an occasion of courtesy, generosity, and mutual professions of friendship. The French commander, Diron d'Artaguette, like many French officials, was also a trader, who with the diversion of deerskins to the English was losing heavily. When Mingo Tchito presented him with twenty deerskins, the angry Frenchman threw a single limburg blanket on the table and told the great chief to take it or pick up his skins and get out. D'Artaguette had made a personal crisis into a political crisis.

When Mingo Tchito returned home, he dispatched Red Shoes to the English traders with a formal invitation to enter the nation. The English received Red Shoes cordially at the Chickasaw towns, presented him with a coat, and made invidious comparisons between the prosperity of the Chickasaws and the poverty of the Choctaws. The incentives for breaking with the French seemed obvious.

Meanwhile d'Artaguette still had not exhausted his rage. He informed several visiting Choctaws that Red Shoes and Mingo Tchito were women for turning to the English and that they would henceforth not be admitted to Mobile. The first Choctaw to receive this message wisely kept it to himself, but the second conveyed it to Red Shoes. Red Shoes carried the tale to Mingo Tchito, who promptly and ostentatiously hurled his French medal into a stream near the village. To discard the medal, especially so theatrically, was to break with the French, although the symbolic significance of this act was somewhat diluted by the ease with which the medal might be retrieved from the shallow stream.

Mingo Tchito, however, remained a careful man, and Red Shoes could induce him to move only slowly toward an open alliance with the English. Having made his alienation from the French apparent, the great chief waited to see if the French desired to regain his esteem and affections. He knew that trade contacts with the English would help the distant western towns little, and that resentment against the English remained strong in those towns hit hardest by the slavers of the previous generation. The entire nation would not automatically follow northeastern warriors like Red Shoes, who desired English goods. Despite d'Artaguette's anger, the great chief guessed the French would not choose to alienate him further.

He was right. Governor Perier quickly sent Regis de Roullet from New Orleans as his emissary to repair the damage to French interests, and the great chief sent his son to fish up his French medal. Any hopes Red Shoes may have entertained for an open break with the French vanished. The great chief, denying any complicity in the invitation made to the English traders, accepted and distributed new French presents. To win over the warriors, the French agreed to construct a trading house at Couechitto. Red Shoes, with no choice except to follow the lead of Mingo Tchito, bided his time. In council he pointedly reminded the French that his own status as a war captain had not been acknowledged by new presents. The French quickly remedied this, and Red Shoes showed his satisfaction by replacing du Roullet's lame horse with one of his own.

Red Shoes obviously remained the subordinate of Mingo Tchito. The great chief had orchestrated the crisis masterfully; his acts were always as much symbol as substance, and no step he made was irrevocable. The warriors had been appeased, and his own presents had been increased. The French were relieved at the apparent renewal of his loyalty, while the English anticipated his defection. The solution, however, was only temporary. In the next phase Red Shoes brought a cruder, but more forceful, set of tactics into play.

The desire of the warriors for more goods and lower prices lay behind the crisis at Couechitto in 1729; and that was not peculiar to the Choctaws. Soon after the French embassy left Couechitto, the Natchez on the Mississippi, spurred by similar motives and under far worse provocation from arbitrary and arrogant French officials, fell upon the colonial posts and settlements within their territory. They killed the men and took the women, children, and black slaves of the French as prisoners. This attack, coupled with the Choctaw dissatisfaction, prompted rumors among the French of a vast Indian conspiracy against Louisiana. Conflicting reports circulated with regard to Choctaw intentions, and the governor again rushed agents to cement their allegiance. Once more the great chief watched for his advantage. He spoke of renewed English trade, but he allowed Red Shoes to recruit eight hundred Choctaws to attack the Natchez. This army went forth not out of love for the French, but for the ransom the French promised for their women, children, and slaves and for the chance to loot the Natchez towns. The Choctaws moved rapidly so that they would not have to share either the ransom or the booty with other tribes allied to the French. When an initial attack failed to take the Natchez towns, the Choctaws negotiated a truce. In exchange for the French captives and their slaves, the Choctaws would permit the Natchez to withdraw and seek refuge with the Chickasaws. To the French, who had hoped for the annihilation of the Natchez, this was only the first shock. The Choctaws then deemed French ransom offers insufficient and forced the French to raise the offer before returning the prisoners.

In holding up the French in this way the great chief risked little. Believing themselves threatened by an English-sponsored pan-Indian conspiracy, the French could not afford to alienate the Choctaws. As Mingo Tchito awaited the ransoms, he entertained renewed English offers for gifts and trade. In the fall of 1730, however, after his prisoners had been ransomed, Red Shoes emerged from the shadow of Mingo Tchito and announced his intention to plunder any English caravan that entered the nation. This threat was meant as an invitation for the French to solicit his aid, and when the request came Red Shoes accepted it. In March of 1731, even as an uncle of the great chief was threatening to treat the French like so many dogs if they did not stop their constant solicitation for war on the Chickasaws, Red Shoes departed to recruit warriors at a ball game.

To casual European observers the life of Choctaw men sometimes seemed an endless round of hunting, talk, and ball games. Similar to lacrosse matches, usually with twenty players or more on a side, intervillage ball games drew large crowds of participants and spectators. Outstanding ball players were important figures in the nation. A ball game was ideal for talking with warriors from other towns, and Red Shoes circulated among both players and spectators. Ostensibly he was recruiting for a late-season deer hunting party;

actually he was persuading men to follow him against the Chickasaws. Enticed by the French scalp bounty, thirty men followed him from the ball grounds to hunt the Chickasaws, who themselves were hunting deer. Six Chickasaws died at their hands; and eleven more were brought back as captives destined for death or slavery. Shulush Homa had made the white path red. The Choctaw nation was at war.

Red Shoes' campaign that spring was a significant one, whose repercussions would eventually alter the political and social structure of the Choctaw nation; but it was also a decisive moment for the war chief himself. The decision to act on his own meant not only the end of his subordination to the civil chiefs but his alienation from much of the old political order. He had split with Mingo Tchito but also with the accepted ways of achieving power in the nation. He had disrupted the careful maneuverings of the civil chiefs for English and French favors, and he had challenged their limited but real authority among their people. As the French noted, "the sentiments of an ordinary warrior had prevailed over that of the chiefs;"[2] and at the same time the warrior became too powerful a figure to destroy. The French buttressed his position by making him a medal chief with the title of Chief of the Red Warriors in 1732.

This action was unprecedented; the French had never given a medal to anyone but a civil chief entitled to his office by birth and experience. The other medal chiefs refused to recognize the usurper's new status, so that aside from the gifts it brought, the title signified nothing. The civil chiefs had to deal with him because most of his *iksa* and many warriors followed him, but although at times he coerced or bribed other medal chiefs into alliances, Red Shoes never could really be one of them.

Red Shoes survived in the 1730s because he recognized the widening divisions between chiefs and warriors within the nation more clearly than others. Clan and town ties did not vanish, they still held his loyalties, but the real source of Red Shoes' power was his appeal to the warriors. They composed his following, loyal when he secured them trade or scalp bounties, and fickle when the supply of goods dried up. He needed trade goods to hold his men, and the search for them dominated his political life. The French thought they had acquired a tool in 1731, but by 1734 they realized that it was they who were being used. Governor Bienville characterized Red Shoes as an "illdisposed" and dispensable chief.[3] But he refused to disappear, and as long as the French failed to supply adequate goods to the Choctaw civil chiefs he could find a following. Twice during the 1730s he brought English traders into the nation; and in 1738 he delivered virtually the entire nation into the English camp—until the nerve and the trade goods of the colonial officials of South Carolina failed them simultaneously. Twice between 1731 and 1741 he returned to the French. They never trusted him, but as Bienville recognized, he was capable "of doing us either a great deal of harm or a great deal of good."[4]

Shulush Homa's methods were bold and direct. He took risks no other Choctaw leader dared take; and the weaker his position, the more he attempted. He promised wealth to petty English traders and colonial officials if only they would provide him with sufficient presents and unlimited trade. His betrayals were not the modest maneuverings of the civil chiefs but great mutinies that threatened the colonial and tribal balances of power. In 1735 he urged the Choctaws who were accompanying a defeated French army in retreat from the Chickasaw towns to turn on their allies and finish what the Chickasaws had begun. This so outraged Mingo Tchito, ostensibly the commander of the Choctaws, that he attempted to blow Red Shoes' brains out on the spot. But Shulush Homa survived to accompany a second major French expedition against the Chickasaw towns in 1739! On this occasion he conducted unauthorized peace negotiations with the enemy on behalf not only of the Choctaws, few of whom then followed him, but also of the French. He was a man of great audacity and resilience. Time and again his schemes collapsed and he recovered. In the course of his relentless pursuit of trade goods, he passed beyond the boundaries of Choctaw life in the Creek and Chickasaw towns to visit Charleston, travel in Georgia, and negotiate with European traders and governors. His triumphs were astonishing but always temporary; and a steady supply of trade goods forever eluded him.

Red Shoes sought more than simple power and wealth during these years. The possession of wealth itself meant

4. Sketch from a Chickasaw deerskin map of the 1730s, showing locations of the Chickasaw (L) and their friends and enemies, including the English of Carolina (A), the French at Mobile (I) and the Choctaw (K).

little to a Choctaw leader, who redistributed his goods to achieve and affirm his leadership and status. Guileful and persuasive, exploiting the white man to obtain trade goods and parlaying these into power within the Choctaw nation, Red Shoes still sought legitimacy in terms of the old order he was undermining. Negotiating, persuading, giving generously, he acted like the civil chief he could not be. The titles Chief of the Red Warriors, which he got from the French in 1734, and King of the Choctaws, which the English bestowed in 1738, had a hollow ring.[5] They stood outside the realities of Choctaw society, denoting a power and status that no Choctaw possessed and alien to the complex system of precise balances and concessions that had kept the nation whole. Yet Red Shoes took them, settling for such prestige as they brought, but always envious of the traditional status of the civil chiefs.

Red Shoes remained a Choctaw despite his European connections. Loyalty to his clan and his town had a hold on him that is revealed in the failure of his peace attempt of 1740. In that year he sent seventeen men to the Chickasaws, while the French expedition he was accompanying prepared to attack their towns. The Chickasaws, regarding the delegation as spies, executed the entire party. These killings not only outraged the entire Choctaw nation, but they bound Red Shoes to clan obligations of blood revenge. The French made a separate peace, and the civil chiefs refused to cooperate, but for over two years Red Shoes still waged what amounted to a private war on the Chickasaws. He knew that this wasting internecine warfare only helped the French by weakening two strong and dangerous nations on their borders. Yet Red Shoes was faced with a cultural imperative; and his warriors destroyed the Chickasaw cornfields, attacked their hunting parties, disrupted their trade, and killed their people. The result was that a tribe the French had tried unsuccessfully to break for a decade were ready to abandon their homeland by the early 1740s.

Ironically, this devotion to native custom restored Shulush Homa's influence with the French. Since 1739, when Red Shoes' plan to ally the Choctaws with the English had collapsed, Governor Bienville had not only denied him and his followers their customary gifts but had publicly insulted and humiliated them. But after the war against the Chicka-saw Bienville restored his French medal. The civil chiefs remained as hostile as before, however, and this new French alliance proved temporary and insecure. When the Marquis de Vaudreuil replaced Bienville as governor in 1743, French colonial officials warned him against the "polite and dis-sembling"[6] Red Shoes and told him he was held in check only by the opposition of the Choctaw civil chiefs. Vaudreuil decided that Red Shoes demanded "more vigilance and atten-tion than all the rest of his nation."[7]

The new governor's opportunity to confront Red Shoes came when the two men met in December of that year at the annual congress at Mobile. According to custom, the six great medal chiefs of the nation dined daily with the governor. These meals were not a success, for the governor disapproved of Choctaw table manners in general and Red Shoes' exces-sive drinking in particular. Taking the measure of what ap-peared to be a drunken chief, Vaudreuil decided to break him. In council, referring to Red Shoes' low birth, he scornfully expressed surprise that a man "not of the rank to have that mark of distinction"[8] had ever been made a great medal chief and that, after numerous betrayals of the French, he still possessed his medal. He then lectured Red Shoes on his disloyalty and threatened to deprive him of his presents if he caused the French any more trouble. Seeing that he was in the wrong place for open opposition, Red Shoes humbly swal-lowed this abuse and promised the governor he would have no reason to be displeased with him.

Vaudreuil was gratified but not convinced. With the con-sent of the civil chiefs he took measures to centralize the nation under their control, placing each medal chief in charge of eight to ten towns. He then informed every town leader that further presents were contingent on their obedience to the medal chiefs, while the medal chiefs' goods depended on their cooperation with the French. Red Shoes was excluded from this arrangement, as Vaudreuil placed no villages under his control. To complete the scheme, the governor resur-rected the Great Chief Mingo Tchito, in disgrace since his own complicity in Red Shoes' English conspiracy of 1738–39, and recognized him as head of the nation, directly responsible to the French authorities.

Vaudreuil, pleased at the ease with which he had reorganized the tractable Choctaws and humbled Red Shoes, now sought to humiliate him further. When Red Shoes visited Fort Tombeckbe, the French garrison, supply center, and listening post in Choctaw country, he was repeatedly insulted and scorned. Vaudreuil had, however, badly overreached himself. With abundant presents and trade goods and the continuing cooperation of the civil chiefs, he might indeed have broken Red Shoes. But in 1744 a war between England and France erupted, and the English fleet was at pains to choke off the always unreliable supply of French trade goods. This doomed the attempt to centralize the Choctaws under French control, but other developments at first seemed favorable to the French. The Chickasaws asked the French to intercede with the Choctaws for a lasting peace, promising to evict the English if the French would duplicate their presents and trade. Vaudreuil arranged conferences between the Choctaw civil chiefs and the Chickasaws and wrote home for the supplies he would need to carry out the scheme. When the Creeks murdered two Choctaw hunters, Vaudreuil quickly stepped in to quiet that crisis and arrange talks between the Choctaws and Creeks. The Choctaws seemed willing to accept French dominance and Vaudreuil hoped to direct that goodwill into a general Choctaw-Chickasaw-Creek alliance to protect Louisiana from the English. There was no place in this plan for troublesome, unreliable Red Shoes, who himself was deeply resented and strongly opposed by many Choctaw leaders.

Red Shoes, however, knew the Choctaws better than the governor and understood that Vaudreuil's efforts would come to naught if the French pipeline of trade goods was closed. He moved so deftly following his humiliation by Vaudreuil that the governor would not realize for years how artfully he had been manipulated by a man he had supposedly broken. From the beginning the Choctaws had used the Creek negotiations for a surreptitious commerce with English traders at the Creek towns. In November 1744, two Choctaw headmen in the peace mission contacted Lachlan McGillivray, a Scots trader. They bore English commissions from the 1730s that marked them as followers of Red Shoes, and they described the Choctaws as destitute and longing for English trade. They proposed a Choctaw-Chickasaw peace under the auspices of Red Shoes and an agreement for trade with the English. McGillivray relayed the proposal to Charleston.

To succeed in this plan, Red Shoes had to sabotage the Chickasaw-Choctaw negotiations begun by Vaudreuil, but these were already faltering. When the Chickasaws discovered that the French were incapable of supplying them with trade goods, they had suggested to the also impatient Choctaw civil chiefs that they agree to a peace under English rather than French sponsorship. This proposal, so similar to Red Shoes' proposition at the Creek towns, horrified Vaudreuil. What he could not know was that it equally horrified Red Shoes. A Chickasaw peace with the civil chiefs would channel English presents and trade to his rivals within the nation and thus deprive him of the control of the goods he needed to extend his power. When Vaudreuil, desperate to break up an emerging anti-French Choctaw-Chickasaw alliance, sought in 1744 to disrupt the very negotiations he had begun, he tried to make Red Shoes his tool. Red Shoes dispatched his warriors for his own reasons, and they succeeded in reddening the path with enough Chickasaw blood to end the negotiations with the civil chiefs.

It was Blind King of the Chickasaws who first understood Red Shoes' intentions, and in 1745 dispatched emissaries to ask him, rather than the civil chiefs, for peace. Vaudreuil learned how he had been used at the Mobile Congress of March 1746, when Red Shoes failed to appear and the governor discovered that he was in the Chickasaw country opening peace negotiations. Red Shoes, the Chickasaws, and the English bypassed the civil chiefs and aimed their arguments for peace directly at the Choctaw warriors. They argued that while the French paid off the headmen and the warriors got nothing, the English would bring in the trade goods the hunters so badly needed. The French gave the Choctaws only a few guns, which were controlled by the chiefs and distributed largely for warfare. The English would give them many guns to use in the hunt. With goods scarce, the nation destitute, the mass of warriors tired of endless war, and the medal chiefs seemingly concerned only with ensuring their own presents from the French, these arguments proved effective.

Vaudreuil and the civil chiefs joined forces to stop Red Shoes. The commander of Fort Tombeckbe recruited warriors to attack the Chickasaws; and the great chief, Mingo Tchito, moved against his old war captain. A group of his followers attacked a Chickasaw delegation in the western towns, killing one of their important men. The Chickasaws, who by this time must have considered peace negotiations with the Choctaws more dangerous than war against them, demanded satisfaction from Red Shoes if peace was to be obtained. Now it was Mingo Tchito, acting with uncharacteristic ruthlessness, who was covering the plans of Red Shoes with Chickasaw blood. The French also recognized the seriousness of the threat represented by Red Shoes. The Chickasaws awaited satisfaction from the men they had fought so often; and the English waited in the Creek and Chickasaw towns to see if the trading paths would open. To Choctaw and Chickasaw, French and English, it seemed that the fate of the region hung on Red Shoes' response.

Red Shoes brooded over his answer. The Chickasaws wanted revenge, and he did too. The French had scorned and humiliated him, and now he learned that a Frenchman had raped one of his wives. The Frenchman denied it, claiming it was only seduction, an excuse not well designed to appease an already angry Choctaw husband. When Red Shoes' warriors left Couechitto to satisfy the aggrieved Chickasaw nation it was Frenchmen they sought, not Choctaws of the French faction. No one expected this since the Choctaws had never directly attacked the French before. Three Frenchmen were cut down, and Mingo Tchito reflected the astonishment of the nation when he told the French that Red Shoes must have lost his senses. The war chief's actions were carefully calculated, however. He sent word to the French that the murdered men were of "little account" and that he "made no more of the affair than if he had killed the wood rats that ate their hens."[9] Personal satisfaction only complemented political ends. The French scalps appeased the Chickasaws for their dead, and the English for traders they had lost earlier. Red Shoes had also hoped to swing the Creeks into the new alliance by this action, but here he failed.

The French demanded Red Shoes' head. Shulush Homa surrounded himself with bodyguards and placed spies in every village. Assassins paid by the French made several attempts on his life, at one point wounding an English trader and killing his Chickasaw wife in the war chief's house at Couechitto. Red Shoes replied in kind and had his warriors fire into the house of Mingo Tchito. The great chief was unharmed but shaken, and such warnings, together with the spies network, helped to mute the pro-French opposition to Red Shoes within the Choctaw nation.

Red Shoes knew full well that trade goods, not violence, were the key to political control, and he asked for English trade. The colonial officials and private traders responded eagerly, and Englishmen, from Governor James Glen of South Carolina to James Adair, the Chickasaw trader, claimed credit for Red Shoes' revolt against the French. While they sought government grants and trade monopolies to cement the new alliance, Red Shoes completed the swing to the English. He deflated the French hope that revolt would crumble for lack of ammunition and supplies by keeping parties out to guide English traders into the nation. The civil chiefs, surrounded with English goods and French impotence, either lapsed into silence or followed the warriors of their villages into Red Shoes' camp. Support for his chief rivals dwindled to immediate kinsmen.

Red Shoes hoped that the pack trains of private traders would be the forerunners of much larger supplies of guns and presents from the colonial government of South Carolina. In Charleston, his brother Little King promised Governor Glen that they would seize Fort Tombeckbe and build a Creek-Choctaw alliance and a united pro-English Choctaw nation. Glen proved receptive; and he hatched a scheme to obtain a trade monopoly for a company that he helped create. At its head he placed Charles McNaire, freshly arrived from England and without experience in Indian trade. In time Glen's greed and McNaire's incompetence would deprive the Choctaws of trade goods, alienate the bulk of the nation, and condemn their remaining adherents to destruction. But in the summer of 1747, when McNaire arrived in Choctaw country, he found the nation remarkably unified and pro-British. By his count, of the forty-six Choctaw towns only the four nearest Fort Tombeckbe were pro-French, and even there many warriors leaned toward the English.

In June 1747, as the pack train bearing English presents from Charleston approached the nation, Red Shoes took a party to escort the traders to Couechitto. He never returned. Red Shoes died, as the French noted, at "the time he seemed to have most triumphed in his measures."[10] And although his death and the arrival of a French trade ship emboldened the pro-French party, Little King maintained his brother's faction with English goods until English greed and bungling denied him the trade and presents on which his power depended. Only then did a substantial number of towns return to the French and plunge the Choctaws into a bloody civil war. Glen's monopoly now failed to deliver basic supplies, and Red Shoes' old followers substituted clay bullets for lead, ruining their guns in the process. Eight hundred warriors who had followed Red Shoes died in the ruins of their towns, or after being hunted down in the woods and fields, or in the epidemics that accompanied the war. Their scalps were brought to the French for bounties.

Red Shoes, the usurper, had finally reached too far for the civil chiefs and the French, and in the process seemed to them to have threatened the very survival of the Choctaws. The chiefs were not blindly loyal to the French, but they did believe that the French alliance had strengthened both their position and that of the nation. The English were useful to them in reminding the French of the indispensability of the Choctaws; but they were far away and the French were near. An actual alliance with the English, or even an armed neutrality, was much too dangerous. To the French, Red Shoes was a guileful and treacherous savage—a man who knew no loyalty. Yet the enemies of Shulush Homa should not be allowed to sum up his life so easily. Exactly because he used the Europeans so thoroughly and threatened the chiefs so deeply, we must distrust their assessments of him.

Red Shoes challenged the French and English to recognize the realities of his world as fully as he recognized the realities of theirs. That they often failed to do so ultimately made them the tools of his ambition. But Red Shoes sought more than personal gain. He had a vision that the Choctaw nation might grasp the advantages the Europeans had brought without succumbing to their rule. He refused to take the Europeans on their own terms, and he retained a reasonable independence in his dealings with them. Through a period of extraordinarily violent and rapid change, Red Shoes adapted, survived, and took on the new world with an astonishing resilience and optimism. He was ruthless and treacherous when need be, but to lack such qualities in his time and place was to lose all. Even in dying he transformed his nation. He had both grasped and molded the new realities too well, and the victory of the pro-French Choctaws did not change them. A few years after civil war ended, secret emissaries from the new leaders of the nation moved along the trading paths through the Creek towns, once more seeking the fatal embrace of the Englishmen.

Notes

1. Du Roullet to Maurepas, 1729 (Journal of Regis du Roullet), in Rowland Dunbar and Albert Sanders, eds., *Mississippi Provincial Archives, French Dominion*, 3 vols. (Jackson, Miss., 1927–32), 1:33–34. Hereafter *MPA, FD*.
2. Beaudoin to Salmon, Nov. 23, 1732, *MPA, FD* 1:159.
3. Bienville to Maurepas, Sept. 30, 1734, *MPA, FD* 1:237, 240.
4. Bienville to Maurepas, March 28, 1742, *MPA, FD* 3:765.
5. Du Roullet, "Journal," May 7, 1732, *MPA, FD* 1:188, and J. H. Easterby, ed., *The Journal of the Commons House Nov. 10, 1736–1739*, The Colonial Records of South Carolina (Columbia, S.C., 1951), June 1, 1730: 572.
6. Vaudreuil to Maurepas, July 18, 1743. Letterbook 1 (English translation), Loudoon Americana, Huntington Library, LO 9, vol. 1 (2), hereafter LO Amer.
7. *Ibid.*
8. Vaudreuil to Maurepas, Feb. 12, 1744, LO Amer., LO 9, vol. 1 (2).
9. "Journal of De Beauchamps' Journey to the Choctaws in 1746," in Newton Mereness, ed., *Travels in the American Colonies* (New York, 1916): 262.
10. Extracts from Vaudreuil's Letterbook, March 20, 1747, LO Amer., LO 39.

Sources

The standard ethnological source for the Choctaws is John Swanton's *Source Material for the Social and Ceremonial Life of Choctaw Indians*, Smithsonian Institution, Bureau of American Ethnology *Bulletin* 103 (Washington, D.C., 1931), but Swanton's analysis needs revision. Published documents on the Choctaws and Red Shoes are to be found in Rowland Dunbar and Albert Sanders,

eds., *Mississippi Provincial Archives, French Dominion*, 3 vols.
(Jackson, Miss., 1927–32); "An Early Account of the Choctaw In-
dians," *Memoirs of the American Anthropological Association*
(April–June, 1918), which Swanton dates in the 1750s but which
appears to be a report of Father Beaudoin from the mid-1730s; and
the "Journal of De Beauchamps' Journey to the Choctaws," in
Newton Mereness, ed., *Travels in the American Colonies* (New
York, 1916). Gov. Vaudreuil's correspondence is contained in the
Loudon Americana, Huntington Library, and an additional Vaudreuil letter is printed as *The Present State of Louisiana* (London,
1744). There are two quite contradictory English accounts of the
Choctaw Revolt, of which the most reliable is Edmond Atkins,
"Historical Account of the Revolt of the Choctaw Indians" (xerox
copy in the John Carl Parish Papers, University of California, Santa
Barbara). James Adair, *The History of the American Indian* (London,
1775) is less trustworthy. Of the two doctoral dissertations on this
period, Charles W. Paape, "The Choctaw Revolt, a Chapter in the
Intercolonial Rivalry in the Old Southwest" (Ph.D. dissertation,
University of Illinois, Urbana, 1946) is the best.

Suggestions for Further Reading

There is a huge literature on Indian-white relations during the
colonial period. Relatively little of it, however, looks at Indian
motives and views in anything but the most stereotypical and cur-
sory manner. Notable exceptions are two books by David H.
Corkran, *The Creek Frontier, 1540–1783* (Norman, Okla., 1967) and
The Cherokee Frontier: Conflict and Survival (Norman, Okla.,
1962), and the brief article by Nancy Lurie, "Indian Cultural Adjustment to European Civilization," in James M. Smith, ed., *Seventeenth-Century America: Essays in Colonial History* (Chapel Hill,
N.C., 1959).

Neither the lives of individual Indians nor the internal changes
within Indian societies during the colonial period have been adequately treated by scholars, excepting Anthony F. C. Wallace's two
excellent books on the Northeast: *King of the Delawares: Teed-
yuscung* (Philadelphia, 1949) and *The Death and Rebirth of the
Seneca* (New York, 1969). Frederick O. Gearing analyzes political
change within Indian society during the eighteenth century
in *Priests and Warriors: Social Structures for Cherokee Politics in
the Eighteenth Century*, American Anthropological Association
Memoir 93 (Menasha, Wisc., 1962). A more static account of Indian
societies in the area treated by this essay is Charles Hudson, *The
Southeastern Indians* (Knoxville, Tenn., 1976).

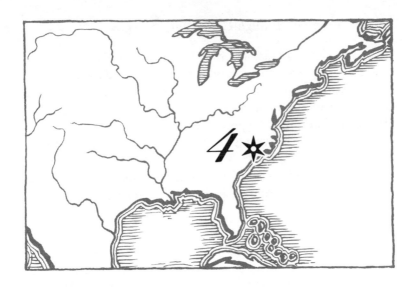

Thomas Peters:
Millwright and Deliverer

GARY B. NASH

*H*istorians customarily portray the American Revolution as an epic struggle for independence fought by several million outnumbered but stalwart white colonists against a mighty England between 1776 and 1783. But the struggle for "life, liberty, and the pursuit of happiness" also involved tens of thousands of black and Native American people residing in the British colonies of North America. If we are to understand the Revolution as a chapter in their experience, we must attach different dates to the process and recast our thoughts about who fought whom and in the name of what liberties. One among the many remarkable freedom fighters whose memory has been lost in the fog of our historical amnesia was Thomas Peters.

In 1760, the year in which George III came to the throne of England and the Anglo-American capture of Montreal put an end to French Canada, Thomas Peters had not yet heard the name by which we will know him or suspected the existence of the thirteen American colonies. Twenty-two years old and a member of the Egba branch of the Yoruba tribe, he was living in what is now Nigeria. He was probably a husband and father; the name by which he was known to his own people is unknown to us. In 1760 Peters was kidnapped by African slave traders and marched to the coast. His experience was probably much like that described by other Africans captured about this time:

> As the slaves come down . . . from the inland country, they are put into a booth or prison, built for that purpose, near the beach . . . and when the Europeans are to receive them, they are brought out into a large plain, where the [ships'] surgeons examine every part of every one of them to the smallest member, men and women being all stark naked. Such as are allowed good and sound are set on one side, and the others by themselves; which slaves are rejected are called Mackrons, being above thirty-five years of age, or defective in their lips, eyes, or teeth, or grown gray; or that have the venereal disease, or any other imperfection.[1]

It was Peters' lot to be sold to the captain of a French slave ship, the *Henri Quatre*. But it mattered little whether the ship was French, English, Dutch, or Portuguese, for all the naval architects of Europe in the eighteenth century were intent on designing ships that could pack in slaves by the hundreds for the passage across the Atlantic. Brutality was systematic, in the form of pitching overboard any slaves who fell sick on the voyage and of punishing offenders with almost sadistic intensity as a way of creating a climate of fear that would stifle any insurrectionist tendencies. Even so, suicide and mutiny were not uncommon during the ocean crossing, which tells us that even the extraordinary force used in capturing, branding, selling, and transporting Africans from one continent to another was not enough to make the captives submit tamely to their fate. So great was this resistance that special techniques of torture had to be devised to cope with the thousands of slaves who were determined to starve themselves to death on the middle passage rather than reach the New World in chains. Brutal whippings and hot coals applied to the lips were frequently used to open the mouth of recalcitrant slaves. When this did not suffice, a special instrument, the *speculum oris,* or mouth opener, was employed to wrench apart the jaws of a resistant African.

Peters saw land again in French Louisiana, where the *Henri Quatre* made harbor. On his way to the New World, the destination of so many aspiring Europeans for three centuries, he had lost not only his Egba name and his family and friends but also his liberty, his dreams of happiness, and very nearly his life. Shortly thereafter, he started his own revolution in America because he had been deprived of what he considered to be his natural rights. He needed neither a written language nor constitutional treatises to convince himself of that, and no amount of harsh treatment would persuade him to accept his lot meekly. This personal rebellion was to span three decades, cover five countries, and entail three more transatlantic voyages. It reveals him as a leader of as great a stature as many a famous "historical" figure of the revolutionary era. Only because the keepers of the past are drawn from the racially dominant group in American society has Peters failed to find his way into history textbooks and centennial celebrations.

Peters never adapted well to slavery. He may have been put to work in the sugarcane fields in Louisiana, where heavy labor drained life away from plantation laborers with almost the same rapidity as in the Caribbean sugar islands. Whatever his work role, he tried to escape three times from the grasp of the fellow human being who presumed to call him chattel property, thus seeming to proclaim, within the context of his own experience, that all men are created equal. Three times, legend has it, he paid the price of unsuccessful black rebels: first he was whipped severely, then he was branded, and finally he was obliged to walk about in heavy ankle shackles. But his French master could not snuff out the yearning for freedom that seemed to beat in his breast, and at length he may have simply given up trying to whip Peters into being a dutiful, unresisting slave.

Some time after 1760 his Louisiana master sold Peters to an Englishman in one of the southern colonies. Probably it was then that the name he would carry for the remainder of his life was assigned to him. By about 1770 he had been sold again, this time to William Campbell, an immigrant Scotsman who had settled in Wilmington, North Carolina, located on the Cape Fear River. The work routine may have been easier here in a region where the economy was centered on the production of timber products and naval stores—pine planking, barrel staves, turpentine, tar, and pitch. Wilmington in the 1770s contained only about 200 houses, but it was the county seat of New Hanover County and, as the principal port of the colony, a bustling center of the regional export trade to the West Indies. In all likelihood, it was in Wilmington that Peters learned his trade as millwright, for many of the slaves (who made up three-fifths of the population) worked as sawyers, tar burners, stevedores, carters, and carpenters.

The details of Peters' life in Wilmington are obscure because nobody recorded the turning points in the lives of slaves. But he appears to have found a wife and to have begun to build a new family in North Carolina at this time. His wife's name was Sally, and to this slave partnership a daughter, Clairy, was born in 1771. Slaveowners did not admit the sanctity of slave marriages, and no court in North Carolina would give legal standing to such a bond. But this did not prohibit the pledges Afro-Americans made to each other or their creation of families. What was not recognized in church or court had all the validity it needed in the personal commitment of the slaves themselves.

In Wilmington, Peters may have gained a measure of autonomy, even though he was in bondage. Slaves in urban areas were not supervised so strictly as on plantations. Working on the docks, hauling pine trees from the forests outside town to the lumber mills, ferrying boats and rafts along the intricate waterways, and marketing various goods in the town, they achieved a degree of mobility—and a taste of freedom—that was not commonly experienced by plantation slaves. In Wilmington, masters even allowed slaves to hire themselves out in the town and to keep their own lodgings. This practice became so common by 1765 that the town authorities felt obliged to pass an ordinance prohibiting groups of slaves from gathering in "Streets, alleys, Vacant Lots" or elsewhere for the purpose of "playing, Riotting, Caballing." The town also imposed a ten o'clock curfew for slaves to prevent what later was called the dangerous practice of giving urban slaves "uncurbed liberty at night, [for] night is their day."[2]

In the 1770s, Peters, then in his late thirties, embarked on a crucial period of his life. Pamphleteers all over the colonies were crying out against British oppression, British tyranny, British plans to "enslave" the Americans. Such rhetoric, though designed for white consumption, often reached the ears of black Americans whose own oppression represented a stark contradiction of the principles that their white masters were enunciating in their protests against the mother country. Peters' own master, William Campbell, had become a leading member of Wilmington's Sons of Liberty in 1770; thus Peters witnessed his own master's personal involvement in a rebellion to secure for himself and his posterity those natural rights which were called inalienable. If inspiration for the struggle for freedom was needed, Peters could have found it in the household of his own slave master.

By the summer of 1775 dread of a slave uprising in the Cape Fear area was widespread. As the war clouds gathered, North Carolinians recoiled at the rumor that the British intended, if war came, "to let loose the Indians on our Frontiers, [and] to raise the Negroes against us."[3] In alarm, the Wilmington Committee of Safety banned imports of new slaves, who might further incite the black rebelliousness that whites recognized was growing. As a further precaution, the Committee dispatched patrols to disarm all blacks in the Wilmington area. In July, tension mounted further, as the British commander of Fort Johnston, at the mouth of the Cape Fear River below Wilmington, gave "Encouragement to Negroes to Elope from their Masters" and offered protection to those who escaped. Martial law was imposed when slaves began fleeing into the woods outside of town and the word spread that the British had promised "every Negro that would murder his Master and family that he should have his Master's plantation."[4] For Thomas Peters the time was near.

In November 1775 Lord Dunmore, the royal governor of Virginia, issued his famous proclamation offering lifelong freedom for any American slave or indentured servant "able and willing to bear arms" who escaped his master and made it to the British lines. White owners and legislators threatened dire consequences to those who were caught stealing away and attempted to squelch bids for freedom by vowing to take bitter revenge on the kinfolk left behind by fleeing slaves.

Among slaves in Wilmington the news must have caused a buzz of excitement, for as in other areas the belief now spread that the emancipation of slaves would be a part of the British war policy. But the time was not yet ripe because hundreds of miles of pine barrens, swamps, and inland waterways separated Wilmington from Norfolk, Virginia, where Lord Dunmore's British forces were concentrated, and slaves knew that white patrols were active throughout the tidewater area from Cape Fear to the Chesapeake Bay.

The opportune moment for Peters arrived four months later, in March 1776. It was then that he struck his blow for freedom. On February 9 Wilmington was evacuated as word arrived that the British sloop *Cruizer* was proceeding up the Cape Fear River to bombard the town. A month later twenty British ships arrived from Boston, including several troop transports under Sir Henry Clinton. For the next two months the British controlled the river, plundered the countryside, and set off a wave of slave desertions. Peters seized the moment, broke the law of North Carolina, redefined himself as a man instead of a piece of William Campbell's property, and made good his escape. Captain George Martin, an officer under Sir Henry Clinton, organized the escaped slaves from the Cape Fear region into the company of Black Pioneers. Seven years later, in New York City at the end of the war, Peters would testify that he had been sworn into the Black Pioneers by Captain George Martin along with other Wilmington slaves, including his friend Murphy Steel, whose fortunes would be intertwined with his own for years to come.

For the rest of the war Peters fought with Martin's company, which became known as the Black Guides and Pioneers. He witnessed the British bombardment of Charleston, South Carolina, in the summer of 1776, and then moved north with the British forces to occupy Philadelphia at the end of the next year. He was wounded twice during subsequent action and at some point during the war was promoted to sergeant, which tells us that he had already demonstrated leadership among his fellow escaped slaves.

Wartime service places him historically among the thousands of American slaves who took advantage of wartime disruption to obtain their freedom in any way they could.

Sometimes they joined the American army, often serving in place of whites who gladly gave black men freedom in order not to risk life and limb for the cause. Sometimes they served with their masters on the battlefield and hoped for the reward of freedom at the war's end. Sometimes they tried to burst the shackles of slavery by fleeing the war altogether and seeking

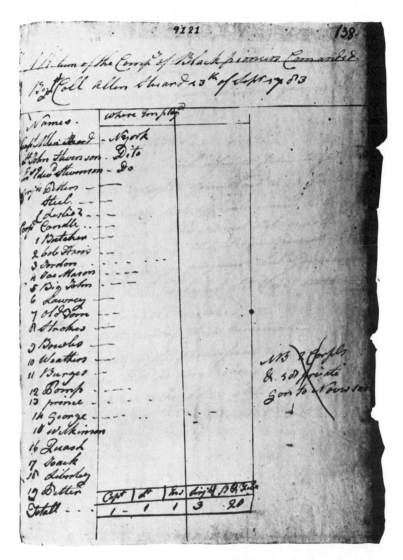

5. Muster sheet for the Black Pioneers, showing Thomas Peters and his friend Murphy Steel as sergeants (fourth and fifth from the top).

refuge among the trans-Allegheny Indian tribes. But most frequently freedom was sought by joining the British whenever their regiments were close enough to reach. Unlike the dependent, childlike Sambos that some historians have described, black Americans took up arms, as far as we can calculate, in as great a proportion to their numbers as did white Americans. Well they might, for while white revolutionaries were fighting to protect liberties long enjoyed, black rebels were fighting to gain liberties long denied. Perhaps only 20 percent of the American slaves gained their freedom and survived the war, and many of them faced years of travail and even reenslavement thereafter. But the Revolution provided them with the opportunity to stage the first large-scale rebellion of American slaves—a rebellion, in fact, that was never duplicated during the remainder of the slave era.

At the end of the war Peters, his wife Sally, twelve-year-old Clairy, and a son born in 1781 were evacuated from New York City by the British along with some three thousand other Afro-Americans who had joined the British during the course of the long war. There could be no staying in the land of the victorious American revolutionaries, for America was still slave country from north to south, and the blacks who had fought with the British were particularly hated and subject to reenslavement. Peters understood that to remain in the United States meant only a return to bondage, for even as the articles of peace were being signed in Paris southern slaveowners were traveling to New York in hopes of identifying their escaped slaves and seizing them before the British could remove them from the city.

But where would England send the American black loyalists? Her other overseas possessions, notably the West Indian sugar islands, were built on slave labor and had no place for a large number of free blacks. England itself wished no influx of ex-slaves, for London and other major cities already felt themselves burdened by growing numbers of impoverished blacks demanding public support. The answer to the problem was Nova Scotia, the easternmost part of the frozen Canadian wilderness that England had acquired at the end of the Seven Years War. Here, amidst the sparsely scattered old French settlers, the remnants of Indian tribes, and the more recent British settlers, the American blacks could be relocated.

Thousands of British soldiers being discharged after the war in America ended were also choosing to take up life in Nova Scotia rather than return to England. To them and the American ex-slaves the British government offered on equal terms land, tools, and rations for three years.

Peters and his family were among the 2,775 blacks evacuated from New York for relocation in Nova Scotia in 1783. But Peters' ship was blown off course by the late fall gales and had to seek refuge in Bermuda for the winter. Not until the following spring did they set forth again, reaching Nova Scotia in May, months after the rest of the black settlers had arrived. Peters found himself leading his family ashore at Annapolis Royal, a small port on the east side of the Bay of Fundy that looked across the water to the coast of Maine. The whims of international trade, war, and politics had destined him to pursue the struggle for survival and his quest for freedom in this unlikely corner of the earth.

In Nova Scotia the dream of life, liberty, and happiness turned into a nightmare. The refugee ex-slaves found that they were segregated in impoverished villages, given scraps of often untillable land, deprived of the rights normally extended to British subjects, forced to work on road construction in return for the promised provisions, and gradually reduced to peonage by a white population whose racism was as congealed as the frozen winter soil of the land. White Nova Scotians were no more willing than the Americans had been to accept free blacks as fellow citizens and equals. As their own hardships grew, they complained more and more that the blacks underbid their labor in the area. Less than a year after Peters and the others had arrived from New York, hundreds of disbanded British soldier-settlers attacked the black villages—burning, looting, and pulling down the houses of free blacks.

Peters and his old compatriot Murphy Steel had become the leaders of one contingent of the New York evacuees who were settled at Digby, a "sad grog drinking place," as one visitor called it, near Annapolis Royal. About five hundred white and a hundred black families, flotsam thrown up on the shores of Nova Scotia in the aftermath of the American Revolution, competed for land at Digby. The provincial governor, John Parr, professed that "as the Negroes are now in this country, the principles of Humanity dictates that to make them useful to themselves as well as Society, is to give them a chance to Live, and not to distress them."⁵ But local white settlers and lower government officials felt otherwise and soon bent the governor to their will. The promised tracts of farm land were never granted, provisions were provided for a short time only, and racial tension soared. Discouraged at his inability to get allocations of workable land and adequate support for his people, Peters traveled across the Bay to St. John, New Brunswick, in search of unallocated tracts. Working as a millwright, he struggled to maintain his family, to find suitable homesteads for black settlers, and to ward off the body snatchers, who were already at work reenslaving blacks whom they could catch unawares, selling them in the United States or the West Indies.

By 1790, after six years of hand-to-mouth existence in that land of dubious freedom and after numerous petitions to government officials, Peters concluded that his people "would have to look beyond the governor and his surveyors to complete their escape from slavery and to achieve the independence they sought."⁶ Deputized by more than two hundred black families in St. John, New Brunswick, and in Digby, Nova Scotia, Peters composed a petition to the Secretary of State in London and agreed to carry it personally across the Atlantic, despite the fearsome risk of reenslavement that accompanied any free black on an oceanic voyage. Sailing from Halifax that summer, Peters reached the English capital with little more in his pocket than the plea for fair treatment in Nova Scotia or resettlement "wherever the Wisdom of Government may think proper to provide for [my people] as Free Subjects of the British Empire."⁷

Peters' petition barely disguised the fact that the black Canadians had already heard of the plan afoot among abolitionists in London to establish a self-governing colony of free blacks on the west coast of Africa. Attempts along these lines had been initiated several years before and were progressing as Peters reached London. In the vast city of almost a million inhabitants Peters quickly located the poor black community, which included a number of ex-slaves from the American colonies whose families were being recruited for a return to the homeland. He searched out his old commanding officer in the Black Guides and Pioneers and obtained letters of introduction from him. It is also possible that he received aid from Ottobah Cugoano, an ex-slave whose celebrated book, *Thoughts and Sentiments on the Evil and Wicked Traffic of Slavery and Commerce of the Human Species*, had made him a leader of the London black community and put him in close contact with the abolitionists Granville Sharp, Thomas Clarkson, and William Wilberforce. Once in touch with these men, Peters began to see the new day dawning for his people in Canada.

Peters had arrived in London at a momentous time. The abolitionists were bringing to a climax four years of lobbying for a bill in Parliament that would abolish the slave trade forever; and the ex-slave was on hand to observe the parliamentary struggle. The campaign was unsuccessful in 1791 because the vested interests opposed to it were still too powerful. But it was followed by the introduction of a bill to charter the Sierra Leone Company for thirty-one years and to grant it trading and settlement rights on the African coast. That bill passed. The recruits for the new colony, it was understood, were to be the ex-slaves from America then living in Nova Scotia. After almost a year in London, working out the details of the colonization plan, Peters took ship for Halifax. He was eager to spread the word that the English government would provide free transport for any Nova Scotian blacks who wished to go to Sierra Leone and that on the African coast they would be granted at least twenty acres per man, ten for each wife, and five for each child. John Clarkson, the younger brother of one of England's best-known abolitionists, traveled with him to coordinate and oversee the resettlement plan.

This extraordinary mission to England, undertaken by an uneducated, fifty-four-year-old ex-slave, who dared to proceed to the seat of British government without any knowledge that he would find friends or supporters there, proved a turning point in black history. Peters returned to Nova Scotia not only with the prospect of resettlement in Africa but also with the promise of the secretary of state that the provincial government would be instructed to provide better land for those black loyalists who chose to remain and an opportunity for the veterans to reenlist in the British army for service in the West Indies. But it was the chance to return to Africa that captured the attention of most black Canadians.

Peters arrived in Halifax in the fall of 1791. Before long he understood that the white leaders were prepared to place in his way every obstacle they could devise. Despised and discriminated against as they were, the black Canadians would have to struggle mightily to escape the new bondage into which they had been forced. Governor Parr adamantly opposed the exodus for fear that if they left in large numbers, the charge that he had failed to provide adequately for their settlement would be proven. The white Nova Scotians were also opposed because they stood to lose their cheap black labor as well as a considerable part of their consumer market. "Generally," writes our best authority on the subject, "the wealthy, and influential, class of white Nova Scotians was interested in retaining the blacks for their own purposes of exploitation."[8]

So Peters, who had struggled for years to burst the shackles of slavery, now strove to break out of the confinements that free blacks suffered in the Maritime Provinces. Meeting with hostility and avowed opposition from Governor Parr in Halifax, he made the journey of several hundred miles to the St. John valley in New Brunswick, where many of the people he represented lived. There too he was harassed by local officials; but as he spread word of the opportunity, the black people at St. John were suffused with enthusiasm and about 220 signed up for the colony. With his family at his side, Peters now recrossed the Bay of Fundy to Annapolis. Here he met with further opposition. At Digby, where he had first tried to settle with his wife and children some eight years before, he was knocked down by a white man for daring to lure away the black laborers of the area who worked for meager wages. Other whites resorted to forging indentures and work contracts that bound blacks to them as they claimed; or they refused to settle back wages and debts in hopes that this would discourage blacks from joining the Sierra Leone bandwagon. "The white people . . . were very unwilling that we should go," wrote one black minister from the Annapolis area, "though they had been very cruel to us, and treated many of us as though we had been slaves."[9]

Try as they might, neither white officials nor white settlers could hold back the tide of black enthusiasm that mounted in the three months after John Clarkson and Thomas Peters returned from London. Working through black preachers, the principal leaders in the Canadian black communities, the two men spread the word. The return to Africa soon took on overtones of the Old Testament delivery of the Israelites from bondage in Egypt. Clarkson described the scene at Birchtown, a black settlement near Annapolis, where on October 26, 1791 some three hundred and fifty blacks trekked through the rain to the church of their blind and lame preacher, Moses Wilkinson, to hear about the Sierra Leone Company's terms. Pressed into the pulpit, the English reformer remembered that "it struck me forcibly that perhaps the future welfare and happiness, nay the very lives of the individuals then before me might depend in a great measure upon the words which I should deliver. . . . At length I rose up, and explained circumstantially the object, progress, and result of the Embassy of Thomas Peters to England."[10] Applause burst forth at frequent points in Clarkson's speech, and in the end the entire congregation vowed its intent to make the exodus out of Canada in search of the promised land. In the three days following the meeting 514 men, women, and children inscribed their names on the rolls of prospective emigrants.

Before the labors of Clarkson and Peters were finished, about twelve hundred black Canadians had chosen to return to Africa. This represented "the overwhelming majority of the ones who had a choice."[11] By contrast, only fourteen signed up for army service in the British West Indies. By the end of 1791 all the prospective Sierra Leonians were making their way to Halifax, the port of debarkation, including four from Peters' town of St. John, who had been prohibited from leaving with Peters and other black families on trumped-up charges of debt. Escaping their captors, they made their way around the Bay of Fundy through dense forest and snow-blanketed terrain, finally reaching Halifax after covering 340 miles in fifteen days.

In Halifax, as black Canadians streamed in from scattered settlements in New Brunswick and Nova Scotia, Peters became John Clarkson's chief aide in preparing for the return to Africa. Together they inspected each of the fifteen ships assigned to the convoy, ordering some decks to be removed, ventilation holes to be fitted, and berths constructed. Many of the 1,196 voyagers were African-born, and Peters, remembering the horrors of his own middle passage thirty-two years before, was determined that the return trip would be of a very different sort. As the ships were being prepared, the Sierra Leone recruits made the best of barracks life in Halifax, staying together in community groups, holding religious services, and talking about how they would soon "kiss their dear Malagueta," a reference to the Malagueta pepper, or "grains of paradise," which grew prolifically in the region to which they were going.[12]

On January 15, 1792, under sunny skies and a fair wind, the fleet weighed anchor and stood out from Halifax harbor. We can only imagine the emotions unloosed by the long-awaited start of the voyage that was to carry so many ex-slaves and their children back to the homeland. Crowded aboard the ships were men, women, and children whose collective experiences in North America described the entire gamut of slave travail. Included was the African-born ex-Black Pioneer Charles Wilkinson with his mother and two small daughters. Wilkinson's wife did not make the trip, for she had died after a miscarriage on the way to Halifax. Also aboard was David George, founder of the first black Baptist church to be formed among slaves in Silver Bluff, South Carolina, in 1773. George had escaped a cruel master and taken refuge among the Creek Indians before the American Revolution. He had reached the British lines during the British occupation of Savannah in 1779, joined the exodus to Nova Scotia at the end of the war, and become a religious leader there. There was Moses Wilkinson, blind and lame since he had escaped his Virginia master in 1776, who had been another preacher of note in Nova Scotia and was now forty-five years old. Eighty-year-old Richard Herbert, a laborer, was also among the throng, but he was not the oldest. That claim fell to a woman whom Clarkson described in his shipboard journal as "an old woman of 104 years of age who had requested me to take her, that she might lay her bones in her native country."[13] And so the shipboard lists went, inscribing the names of young and old, African-born and American-born, military veterans and those too young to have seen wartime service. What they had in common was their desire to find a place in the world where they could be truly free and self-governing. This was to be their year of jubilee.

The voyage was not easy. Boston King, an escaped South Carolina slave who had also become a preacher in Nova Scotia, related that the winter gales were the worst in the memory of the seasoned crew members. Two of the fifteen ship captains and sixty-five black emigrés died en route. The small fleet was scattered by the snow squalls and heavy gales; but all reached the African coast after a voyage of about two months. They had traversed an ocean that for nearly three hundred years had carried Africans, but only as shackled captives aboard ships crossing in the opposite direction, bound for the land of their misery.

Legend tells that Thomas Peters, sick from shipboard fever, led his shipmates ashore in Sierra Leone singing, "The day of jubilee is come; return ye ransomed sinners home."[14] In less than four months he was dead. He was buried in Freetown, where his descendants live today. His final months were ones of struggle also, in spite of the fact that he had reached the African shore. The provisions provided from England until the colony could gain a footing ran short, fever and sickness spread, the distribution of land went slowly, and the white councilors sent out from London to superintend the colony acted capriciously. The black settlers "found themselves subordinate to a white governing class and subjected to the experiments of nonresident controllers."[15] Racial resentment and discontent followed, and Peters, who was elected speaker-general for the black settlers in their dealings with the white governing council, quickly became the focus of the spreading frustration. There was talk about replacing the white councilors appointed by the Sierra Leone Company with a popularly elected black government. This incipient rebellion was avoided, but Peters remained the head of the unofficial opposition to the white government until he died in the spring of 1792.

Peters lived for fifty-four years. During thirty-two of them he struggled incessantly for personal survival and for some larger degree of freedom beyond physical existence. He crossed the Atlantic four times. He lived in French Louisiana, North Carolina, New York, Nova Scotia, New Brunswick, Bermuda, London, and Sierra Leone. He worked as a field hand, millwright, ship hand, casual laborer, and soldier. He struggled against slavemasters, government officials, hostile white neighbors, and, at the end of his life, even some of the abolitionists backing the Sierra Leone colony. He waged a three-decade struggle for the most basic political rights, for social equity and for human dignity. His crusade was individual at first, as the circumstances in which he found himself as a slave in Louisiana and North Carolina dictated. But when the American Revolution broke out, Peters merged his individual efforts with those of thousands of other American slaves who fled their masters to join the British. They made the American Revolution the first large-scale rebellion of slaves in North America. Out of the thousands of individual acts of defiance grew a legend of black strength, black struggle, black vision for the future. Once free of legal slavery, Peters and hundreds like him waged a collective struggle against a different kind of slavery, one that while not written in law still circumscribed the lives of blacks in Canada. Their task was nothing less than the salvation of an oppressed people. Though he never learned to write his name, Thomas Peters articulated his struggle against exploitation through actions that are as clear as the most unambiguous documents left by educated persons.

Notes

1. Quoted in Basil Davidson, *The African Slave Trade* (Boston, Mass., 1961), p. 92.

2. *The Wilmington Town Book, 1743–1778,* Donald R. Lennon and Ida B. Kellam, eds. (Raleigh, N.C., 1973), quoted in Jeffrey J. Crow, *The Black Experience in Revolutionary North Carolina* (Raleigh, N.C., 1977), pp. 27–28.

3. Quoted in *ibid.,* pp. 55–56.

4. Quoted in *ibid.,* p. 57.

5. Quoted in Ellen Gibson Wilson, *The Loyal Blacks* (New York, 1976), p. 109.

6. James W. St. G. Walker, *The Black Loyalists: The Search for a Promised Land in Nova Scotia and Sierra Leone, 1783–1870* (New York, 1976), p. 32.

7. Quoted in *ibid.,* p. 95.

8. *Ibid.,* p. 121.

9. Quoted in Wilson, *Loyal Blacks,* p. 209.

10. Quoted in *ibid.,* p. 205.

11. Walker, *Black Loyalists,* p. 129.

12. Wilson, *Loyal Blacks,* p. 218.

13. Quoted in *ibid.,* p. 230.

14. Walker, *Black Loyalists,* p. 145.

15. *Ibid.,* p. 149.

Sources

Peters' life had to be reconstructed primarily from the records of the British army in America during the Revolution, in the archives of Nova Scotia, and in the correspondence and papers of the English abolitionists with whom he worked. I have relied primarily on material culled from these sources and used in Ellen Gibson Wilson, *The Loyal Blacks* (New York, 1976) and James W. St. G. Walker, *The Black Loyalists* (New York, 1976). There is a short sketch by Christopher H. Fyfe, "Thomas Peters: History and Legend," in *Sierra Leone Studies,* New Series, 1 (1953): 4–13. *King Peters of Sierra Leone* is a novel about Peters written by F. W. Butt-Thompson (London, n.d.). His life as a slave in North Carolina is illuminated by Jeffrey J. Crow's *The Black Experience in Revolutionary North Carolina* (Raleigh, N.C., 1977) and Lawrence Lee, *The Lower Cape Fear in Colonial Days* (Chapel Hill, N.C., 1965).

Suggestions for Further Reading

Students may deepen their understanding of the Afro-Americans' revolution by reading Benjamin Quarles, *The Negro in the American Revolution* (Chapel Hill, N.C., 1961), Ira Berlin, "The Revolution in Black Life," in Alfred F. Young, ed., *The American Revolution: Explorations in the History of American Radicalism* (DeKalb, Ill., 1976), pp. 349–82, and Sidney Kaplan, *The Black Presence in the Era of the American Revolution, 1770–1800* (Greenwich, Conn., 1973). For the postwar experience, Robin Winks, *The Blacks in Canada: A History* (New Haven, Conn., 1971) is valuable, as are Ira Berlin, *Slaves Without Masters: The Free Negro in the Antebellum South* (New York, 1974) and Leon F. Litwack, *North of Slavery: The Negro in the Free States, 1790–1860* (Chicago, 1961).

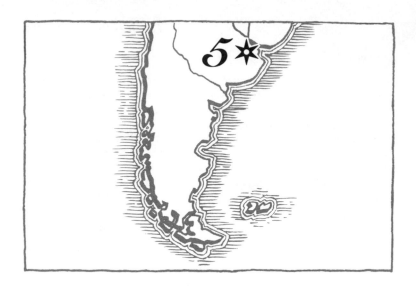

Francisco Baquero:
Shoemaker and Organizer

LYMAN L. JOHNSON

*T*he city of Buenos Aires was a major beneficiary of
Spain's eighteenth-century imperial reform effort. In 1776 the city was selected as the capital of a new
viceroyalty that included the modern nations of Argentina,
Uruguay, Bolivia, and Paraguay. Two years later the city's
economy was further stimulated by a loosening of commercial restrictions that gave its merchants direct access to the
ports of Spain and other Spanish colonies. Taken together,
these reforms produced a rapid increase in the city's population. The military garrisons were augmented, as were the
civil and ecclesiastical bureaucracies. In addition, large numbers of artisans were attracted to the city from the interior,
from Spain, and from other European nations. This large
wave of new arrivals overwhelmed the social order that had
evolved within the context of the city's slow-paced economic

and demographic growth before 1776 and initiated a period of acute competition between the new arrivals and the established residents. Nowhere was this competition more evident than among the contending ethnic and racial factions of the city's artisan community.

Before 1776, there were no efforts by the city's artisans to create legally recognized guilds such as those which had existed in the major urban areas of Spanish America since the sixteenth century. Although the hierarchical nomenclature of master, journeyman, and apprentice was regularly used in Buenos Aires, there were few effective bars that could inhibit an ambitious journeyman, or sometimes even an apprentice, who wanted to open a shop and claim the status of master. In particular, there were no religious or racial prescriptions for access to the skilled trades or mobility within them. As a result, substantial numbers of persons of color, or *castas*, had entered the skilled trades and hundreds had claimed the status of master.

Artisans immigrating to Buenos Aires from Spain and other European nations were horrified by the low status and impoverished conditions experienced by the majority of the city's artisans. To these immigrants, the absence of legally recognized guilds in the city explained the depressed economic circumstances and low social status that were characteristic of the artisan community. One result of this analysis was an effort led by European-born master shoemakers to create a guild. After a brief effort to enlist support from the previously established masters, the European masters called a general meeting to discuss the formation of a self-regulating organization of master shoemakers that would establish and maintain standards of workmanship and commodity prices while protecting the membership economically by restricting competition.

Seventy-one masters met in the house of Juan José Romero in April, 1779. Romero had immigrated to Buenos Aires from his native Cádiz twenty years earlier. His long residence in Buenos Aires made him an effective liaison between the recent immigrants and the creoles and *castas* who numerically dominated the trade. After a brief discussion, the assembled masters agreed to create a guild and accepted Romero's suggestion that an attorney be retained to represent

them. Only forty-two of these masters can be identified by
birthplace and race, but it appears that the meeting included
a representative cross-section of the master shoemakers.
A slight majority of the participants were born in Buenos
Aires, and seven of these were *castas*. The remainder were
Europeans.

One of the nonwhite masters present at this inaugural
meeting was Francisco Baquero, aged thirty-one. Baquero
was a dark-skinned mestizo born in the city. He had entered
the trade as an apprentice at twelve years of age. As was
common, he had left his parents' home and entered the
household of a master shoemaker, where he shared the
meager resources of the master's family. After four difficult,
lonely years, during which he worked from sunrise to sunset
learning the trade and often received harsh corporal punishment for mistakes, Baquero successfully passed the journeyman's test. Although hardworking and frugal, he remained a journeyman, often working on a day-to-day basis,
for nearly a decade until he had acquired his own tools and
enough capital to open a shop. After opening his shop in Calle
Santo Domingo, he married Bonifacia Vera, a woman with
Indian and Negro antecedents, who was six years his junior.
They lived in one small room behind his shop in a building
owned by Don Blas de Castro, a merchant. Although a master
craftsman, Baquero was unable to gain access to the upper-
class clientele who would have assured his material success.
Instead, he was forced to accept repair work and to produce
inexpensive ready-to-wear shoes for a local shopkeeper who,
in turn, marketed them in the neighborhood. Baquero's precarious financial position and his small scale of operation
also prevented him from taking on an apprentice, since he
would have been responsible for feeding, clothing, and
housing the youngster. These circumstances clearly encouraged him to cooperate with the effort to create a guild. A
guild, he had been assured, would stabilize the marketplace
and guarantee the economic well-being of all existing masters.

Although the master shoemakers pooled their funds and
hired a lawyer, Dr. Vicente Cañete, this initial effort had
little success. Cañete petitioned Viceroy José Vértiz for
permission to constitute a guild, outlining in his letter the

benefits that a guild would provide to the larger society. In particular, Cañete argued that, in the absence of a guild, consumers were regularly victimized by inadequately trained masters who produced poor-quality goods. Uninhibited by guild regulations and regular inspections by guild officials, some masters regularly resorted to fraud. Only the creation of a guild, claimed Cañete, could eliminate these practices and benefit legitimate masters by ending the destructive price-cutting competition of their former journeymen and apprentices, who falsely claimed the title of master and opened shops.

The viceroy forwarded Cañete's petition to the cabildo, city council, for consideration. The cabildo then delegated this responsibility to one of its members, who proved to be intemperate and unsympathetic. He claimed that the shoemakers were slow to provide him with copies of guild constitutions from Spain and that, when he persisted, they produced spurious documents. The shoemakers of Buenos Aires, he asserted, lacked the maturity and dependability of Spanish artisans. In his opinion they were a vice-ridden and drunken lot who should not be permitted the exercise of corporate self-government.

This unfriendly critic produced a draft constitution for the guild in July 1780, in which his prejudices were clearly manifest. He suggested three guild officials, two senior masters, and a treasurer. The senior masters were to be selected by the cabildo without consultation with the shoemakers. Only the treasurer was to be elected by artisans, and even he was to be closely supervised by the cabildo's notary. Although the draft constitution provided a market monopoly for recognized masters and also granted these masters the means of controlling their journeymen and apprentices, the heavy-handed attempt to make guild officers the clients of the cabildo so angered the shoemakers that Baquero and others argued for the suspension of the organizational effort.

The issue then remained dormant for eight years before a portion of the 1779 leadership resurrected the project for a guild. Baquero was again one of the supporters of the effort, but by this time Juan José Romero and other Spaniards clearly dominated the group. In their initial communication with Viceroy Marqués de Loreto, Romero and his closest allies reiterated the rationale for a guild previously provided by Cañete. False masters, they argued, were defrauding the public and forcing legitimate masters to abandon their trade. The shoemakers suggested a two-stage process: first, that a formal examination procedure be established to guarantee that only fully trained journeymen became masters; and second, that a fully articulated guild structure controlled by the masters be created. The only restrictive clause in the proposed structure sought the exclusion of "foreigners" from guild offices. Although Baquero and the other nonwhite masters supported these proposals, they were increasingly nervous about their marginal role in the formulation of guild regulations.

The request for permission to create a guild passed quickly through the bureaucracy this time, and in April 1789 the masters met at the home of the wealthy merchant Miguel de Azcuenaga, one of the city's two administrative officers, or alcaldes, to frame a constitution. The draft constitution produced at this meeting immediately led to a bitter and divisive controversy. Juan José Romero protested that the draft violated Spanish law because it failed to exclude foreigners from guild offices. The cabildo attempted to provide a compromise solution by which Spaniards and foreigners would alternate in some of the guild offices. This compromise failed to placate Romero and others who sought the exclusion of foreigners, mostly Italians and Portuguese, from guild offices. At the same time the cabildo triggered a new conflict within the craft by suggesting a system of racial discrimination within the proposed guild.

The 1789 draft had excluded slaves from the rank of master but had permitted free nonwhites full participation in the guild. Baquero and the other free *castas* had easily accepted this exclusion since it benefited them by eliminating competitors from the marketplace. The cabildo refused to go along with the proposal, however, because it financially penalized slaveowners who derived income from hiring the labor of their skilled slaves. Other forms of discrimination, based on race not legal status, however, were more acceptable. The cabildo stated that poor white families hesitated to place their sons as apprentices because they would be forced to mix with nonwhites. Provision should, therefore, be made for the racial separation of apprentices. In addition, they suggested that all nonwhites, except Indians, should be excluded from guild offices and separated physically from whites at meetings, religious observances, and public processions. The enthusiastic acceptance of these discriminatory proposals by many Spanish and foreign masters forced Baquero to begin organizing the black and mestizo masters to resist this attack on their traditional full participation in craft affairs.

Baquero, by this time, had begun to escape his earlier poverty. After years of struggle, he had accumulated sufficient savings to buy a small house for his family. He maintained a shop in the front room, where he and his son and only apprentice, José, worked twelve to fourteen hours per day repairing shoes, making cheap sandals for the poor, and occasionally producing expensive boots and shoes for wealthy customers. Although a mestizo, he had also joined one of the city's segregated militia units reserved for Indians and had quickly become an officer. Because of his status as one of the most established, best-known nonwhite masters and a militia officer, Baquero was looked to for leadership by other nonwhite shoemakers when the prospect of racial discrimination was suggested by the cabildo and endorsed by many white masters.

Baquero's immediate strategy was to identify potential allies among the white masters and forge an effective alliance that would prevent the full implementation of racial discrimination. As a result, Baquero and his supporters evolved a tentative and tenuous short-term alliance with Juan José Romero, the leader of the faction that had sought the exclusion of the Italian and Portuguese masters. Although Romero was an immigrant, his long residence in Buenos Aires had accustomed him to the regular participation of nonwhite masters in craft affairs. This is not to say that Romero recognized Baquero as an equal, but rather that he recognized Baquero's usefulness in his struggle with the foreign masters.

The 1789 draft was modified to incorporate the cabildo's suggestions in an open meeting in January 1791, which attracted most of the city's master shoemakers. The new constitution provided that foreigners married to Spanish citizens or resident in the city for ten years could participate fully in guild affairs. Negroes, mulattoes, and mestizos, however, were completely barred from guild offices. Surprisingly, neither Romero nor Baquero protested the document. Instead, they organized their supporters for the election meeting called for March 14.

One hundred and six masters crowded into the interior patio of the home of the alcalde, Martínez de Hoz, on March 14. The meeting was held after nightfall so that the shoemakers could complete their day's work. The masters were tired, hungry, and terribly uncomfortable in the hot crowded space. Feelings ran high as the bickering factions jostled against each other. Rivals pushed and threatened each other, but a general melee was prevented by some of the older masters who counseled patience. Both the alcalde and a notary, present to record the electoral results, were clearly intimidated by the noisy, combative crowd and were never in control of the meeting. As a result, the supporters of Romero and Baquero were able to subvert the letter and the spirit of the recently accepted constitution. Throughout the proceedings, Baquero and his allies kept up a constant cry, demanding the total exclusion of all foreign masters. Romero's partisans gained control of the balloting and permitted virtually all the nonwhites to vote, despite the constitution's clear prohibition. The result was a total victory for these two groups. Romero was elected guild president and his closest supporters gained the remaining offices.

These events touched off a storm of protest from the recent immigrants, both Spanish and foreign. Citing the disturbances and violations of the guild constitution, they demanded a new election. Although Martínez de Hoz supported the electoral results, the cabildo overturned the election and ordered the shoemakers to frame a new constitution based on the constitution of the guild of shoemakers of Madrid. The process was undermined, however, by the cabildo's selection of Romero to oversee the process.

Under Romero's supervision, the officers elected in the disputed ballot quickly redrafted the guild constitution to incorporate elements of the Madrid document. The major innovation was the creation of a *cofradía*, a Catholic lay brotherhood, to supervise the religious and charitable functions of the corporation. Romero's antiforeign bias was manifested in two discriminatory provisions that eliminated foreign-born masters from guild offices and barred the future admission of foreigners to apprenticeship until the total number of foreign masters was reduced to six. This boldfaced exclusion enraged the cabildo membership, who refused to accept the document. Romero and Baquero subsequently appealed to the chief prosecutor of the royal court and ultimately to Viceroy Nicolás de Arredondo, but the cabildo's decision was sustained. Arredondo sought to end the increasingly bitter struggle by delegating the task of writing a guild constitution to a lawyer who had not previously been involved in the case.

This final document attempted to end the conflict over the participation of foreigners by permitting full membership to all existing masters but barring the future admission of foreigners as apprentices. Following Spanish legal tradition, Indians were permitted full participation in the guild and two guild offices were reserved especially for them. Negroes and other *castas,* however, were relegated to a passive role in guild affairs. They were to be segregated at all public functions and were ineligible to vote for or hold guild offices. This, stated the lawyer, was to avoid "the drunken confusion that would be felt by freeborn whites when mixed with Negroes who were slaves or free. This, truthfully, would be something very strange and indecent."[1] Despite these discriminatory provisions, Francisco Baquero made no effort to prevent the constitution's implementation. Instead, he advised the nonwhite masters to maintain their alliance with Romero and seek to influence the election process within the new guild itself.

The long process begun in 1779 had apparently been brought to a successful conclusion. In June 1792 the guild constitution was published, and the election of guild officers was set for the end of July. However, the deep divisions created by a decade of struggle within the craft had not been resolved, and the three major factions—Romero's antiforeign group, the foreigners and recent immigrants from Spain, and Baquero's nonwhites—used the month and a half hiatus to prepare themselves for the electoral struggle. On the appointed day the master shoemakers met in the home of alcalde Antonio García Lopez to elect the guild officers, and once again the election was tumultuous. The competing groups yelled insults at each other and tried to prevent their enemies from voting. Juan José Romero led the efforts to exclude foreigners. From his position near the front of the room, he challenged the alcalde's interpretation of the guild constitution; and when he failed to win his point, he encouraged Baquero and the other nonwhites at the rear of the room to demand their rights. García Lopez grew increasingly fearful that the meeting would erupt in violence, and finally, after Romero had forced his way to the front of the room yelling threats, he called for a police patrol. Even the presence of the armed police officers failed to quiet Romero, who was finally ejected from the meeting, leaving the leadership of the antiforeign faction to Baquero, who succeeded in manipulating the chaos caused by Romero's arrest to push through the antiforeign slate of candidates. Romero was again elected guild president, and Baquero was elected to one of the two offices reserved for Indians.

This victory was short-lived, however. The foreign masters emerged from the meeting with wide support among native-born white and Spanish masters who feared that, despite the discriminatory nature of the guild constitution, the guild would be dominated by Baquero and his nonwhite supporters. Even some of the creole masters who had previously supported Romero now allied themselves with the European block. The deeply embittered whites immediately requested that the royal court overturn the election results because *castas* had voted and Baquero had been elected to an office reserved for Indians despite the fact that he was a mestizo. When the court decided to order new elections, Baquero protested that the alcalde had permitted the foreigners to use an "adulterated" census that unfairly denied the vote to individuals listed as white or Indian in the "true" census. This he claimed had provoked Romero's protest and the subsequent chaos. Despite Baquero's pleading, however, the court ordered a new election, supervised by the police.

This new election, held in December 1792, resulted in the complete triumph of the foreigners and recent Spanish immigrants. Baquero and the other *castas* were excluded from the meeting, and Romero and his adherents failed to win any guild offices. The future of the guild, however, was immediately clouded by the arrival in Buenos Aires of a royal order demanding the immediate suspension of both the guild and *cofradía* since the shoemakers had failed to gain prior royal approval for their creation. Baquero seized on the weakened legitimacy of the white-dominated guild to organize the Negro and racially mixed masters for an effort to create a separate, segregated guild that would free them once and for all from the control of their white enemies.

Although Baquero was a mestizo who had claimed to be an Indian in order to further his career in the militia and in the guild, he had developed and sustained a strong following among the Negro and mulatto shoemakers, who constituted nearly 90 percent of the nonwhite masters excluded from full participation in the guild. Within days of the arrival of the royal order, Baquero met with forty-eight Negro and other *casta* masters who appointed him as their legal representative and empowered him to seek the creation of a separate guild. In a letter sent to Viceroy Arredondo, Baquero outlined their case. The Negro and *casta* masters had been barred from an active role in the guild, yet were equally responsible for its financial obligations. The whites had demonstrated clearly their antipathy for the *castas* and were now in a position to punish them for their previous opposition through the unfair administration of guild standards. He argued that segregated guilds were sanctioned by Spanish law and had existed for years in Lima, Havana, and Cartagena. In addition, segregated *cofradías* and militia units already existed in Buenos Aires and were run by their members "without scandals or disorders and with a financial regularity that is exemplary."[2] Baquero therefore asked that the *casta* masters be immediately excused from paying dues to the white guild and that the officers of that guild be prohibited from inspecting the shops of the *castas*.

Needless to say, the officers of the guild opposed Baquero's petition. The long effort to create a legally recognized guild in Buenos Aires had been a tremendous financial burden for the master shoemakers, and many debts remained unpaid. As a result, the guild could ill afford to lose fifty dues-paying nonwhite masters. The chief legal officer of the guild, Martín Porra, suggested in his letter to the viceroy that the creation of a separate nonwhite guild would inevitably lead to massive frauds and the erosion of quality in the trade. Baquero and his supporters were, according to Porra, an incipient criminal class that resented the guild's commitment to quality control. The racist assumptions that provided the starting point for this analysis were clearly shared by many whites in colonial Buenos Aires, and the viceroy concurred by refusing to permit the formation of a guild of *castas*. The viceroy also chose to interpret the royal order broadly, so that only the *cofradía* was suspended and the white-dominated guild could continue to function.

Although Baquero appealed this decision, he recognized that the local authorities were committed to the existing guild's white leaders. He therefore sought and received permission from his supporters to pursue their cause at the royal court in Madrid. Having secured the moral and financial support of his colleagues, Baquero wrote Viceroy Arredondo of his intention to appeal to the king "as is the right of all Spanish vassals."[3] Accordingly, he paid a local notary to make a copy of all the documents that related to the long effort to create a guild of shoemakers in Buenos Aires, and he secured passage on a ship destined for Spain.

After arriving in Cádiz in late December 1793, Baquero traveled to Madrid, where he located a notary familiar with the court. He then addressed his appeal to the king and his Council of the Indies on January 17, 1794. After identifying himself as a captain in the colonial militia, he briefly summarized the long effort to create a guild of shoemakers in Buenos Aires. In particular, he emphasized that the *casta* masters were excluded from an active role in guild affairs but were subjected to the same financial obligations as the white members. After dispensing with these necessary preliminaries, Baquero launched into a bitter attack against Viceroy Arredondo, the prosecutor of the royal court, and the members of the cabildo. All these officials, claimed Baquero, were hostile to *castas* and had willingly and knowingly violated Spanish law in an effort to sustain the guild's white leadership. First, they had permitted the shoemakers to hold meetings and frame a guild constitution without the required prior approval from Madrid. Second, the viceroy and prosecutor had again violated the law by enforcing the constitution without receiving royal approval. And finally, even after receiving a royal order to suspend the guild, these royal officials had continued to sanction the continued operation of the guild. The highest officials of the viceroyalty had collaborated in this contravention of the royal will because,

stated Baquero, they shared with the white masters a re-
pugnance for *castas*.

Despite Baquero's reckless willingness to attack the motivations and actions of royal officials, his appeal was sustained by the Council of the Indies in January 1795, and a
royal order was issued permitting the *casta* shoemakers to
hold meetings and formulate a constitution for a segregated
guild. Baquero arrived in Buenos Aires and received the universal acclaim of the *casta* shoemakers. Unwilling to rest on
his laurels, Baquero organized his supporters to produce a
new guild constitution and an accurate census of all nonwhite shoemakers resident in the city. Despite his urgings,
however, this process consumed nearly two years. In part,
this dangerous delay resulted from a growing split within the
ranks of the *casta* shoemakers themselves. Baquero and his
allies had sought a guild because they were personally ambitious and wanted to gain the increased social status and
added income associated with guild offices. Others, however,
had simply wanted to escape the dues, fines, and special
contributions generated by the white guild. These masters
had to be cajoled and pushed each step of the way toward the
creation of the nonwhite guild.

The census of nonwhite shoemakers and the ordinances
for the Guild of Negro and Mulatto Shoemakers were completed and sent to the prosecutor of the royal court on July 6,
1798; he then passed them along to the cabildo. In May of the
following year the cabildo decided to oppose the formation of
both the white and nonwhite guilds on the grounds that
guilds were a restraint of trade and an impingement on individual freedom. The arguments of the new liberal political
economy were clearly in evidence throughout the discussion
that followed. Guilds, according to the cabildo, held back
able young artisans while protecting incompetent masters.
More importantly, however, guilds victimized the consum-
ing public by artificially sustaining high prices and commodity scarcities. Although Baquero quickly appealed this
decision, the royal court and the viceroy upheld the cabildo.

Baquero and his closest allies were bitterly disappointed
but lacked the financial resources to undertake a new appeal
to Madrid. The long litigation with the white masters had
already produced a heavy debt that undermined Baquero's

support among the nonwhite shoemakers and made further monetary exactions impossible. Pedro Nolasco Rivas, a mulatto master who had supported Baquero until the cabildo decision, emerged as his major antagonist over the issue of the guild's debt. By 1799 the *casta* masters owed well over one thousand pesos for legal and notarial fees and the expenditures of Baquero in Spain. In an effort to liquidate this debt without further recourse to the courts, Baquero had assessed each *casta* master sixteen pesos. Seizing on the dissension caused by this levy, Pedro Nolasco Rivas created a powerful faction among the nonwhite masters that demanded Baquero's removal as spokesman. In a letter to the royal prosecutor, he claimed that Baquero had not deserved the trust of his constituents, had gone beyond his mandated authority, and had incurred debts for which the entire corporate membership should not be held responsible. Instead, stated Nolasco Rivas, Baquero should be held personally responsible for the debt. Although this suggestion was probably attractive to the colonial officials who had found Baquero such a durable and resourceful antagonist, the debt remained a corporate problem. In 1806, two mulatto shoemakers who had not participated in the effort to found a separate guild asked the royal court to excuse them from the most recent assessment since "most of the shoemakers held liable for the debt were apprentices when the litigation was begun and had no part in the decisions that led to the debt."[4] No record exists to indicate the final decision of the government on the debt issue, but it does appear ironic that, having opposed the creation of traditional corporations of artisans as an abridgement of individual liberty, the cabildo made successive generations of shoemakers responsible for the debts of their ambitious predecessors.

Baquero escaped responsibility for the entire debt, but he never recovered the 250 pesos he had spent traveling to Spain and arranging for the appeal to the Council of the Indies. Although he eventually recovered from the financial loss, he remained a bitter and resentful man for the rest of his life. He blamed Nolasco Rivas for betraying him and turning the other *casta* shoemakers against him. The allegation that he had embezzled corporate funds and gained other personal benefits from his position had so enraged him that he withdrew entirely from all contacts with other shoemakers, refusing even to join them in public processions and the observances of the feast days of the craft's patron saints. His withdrawal from public life in 1803 obscures our vision of his last years, but we can assume that he died or left Buenos Aires by 1810, since he is not recorded in the city census for that year.

Francisco Baquero's effort to create the Guild of Negro and Mulatto Shoemakers is not to be evaluated in the terms of modern North American views of race and race relations, nor should he be seen as a fighter for the rights of all *castas*. Baquero had been willing to accept the elimination of slave artisans from the rank of master in the guild, even though this discriminatory provision would have financially hurt slave shoemakers as well as their owners. He also failed to oppose publicly the early efforts of the cabildo and some white shoemakers to write discriminatory provisions into the guild constitution. Baquero, like many racially mixed individuals within Spanish colonial society, seems to have had ambiguous feelings about institutionalized racial discrimination. As long as he was accepted as a white and permitted full participation in guild affairs, he accepted the exclusion of others. It was only when it became evident that the faction dominated by recent immigrants would gain control of guild offices and that it was their intention to exclude systematically all nonwhites from an active role in guild affairs did Baquero actively oppose the discriminatory nature of the guild constitution. Baquero, a mestizo, and other racially mixed masters held back from direct opposition to the idea of discrimination until it became evident that the victorious white faction would actually define them as *castas*. Once excluded from the white group, Baquero and his mulatto allies asserted their solidarity with the Negro shoemakers and began efforts to gain a separate guild.

Although the nonwhite masters failed to establish a separate guild, all nonwhite shoemakers benefited ultimately from the dissolution of the white guild. After 1799, the comparative freedom of the previceroyal period reappeared. Nonwhite artisans regained direct access to the marketplace unencumbered by a formal guild structure with its fees, dues, and fines. In addition, no formal mechanism for racial discrimination in the craft survived the debacle of 1799. As a result, nonwhite shoemakers remained a vital and dynamic element within the artisan community until the opening of Buenos Aires to British trade in 1809, and the turmoil of the independence period after 1810, disrupted all the city's artisan industries.

Notes

1. Archivo General de la Nación (hereafter AGN), División Colonia, Sección Gobierno, Interior, Legajo 26, Expediente 4.
2. AGN, División Colonia, Sección Gobierno, Interior, Legajo 54, Expediente 2.
3. AGN, División Colonia, Sección Gobierno, Interior, Legajo 41, Expediente 14.
4. AGN, División Colonia, Sección Gobierno, Justicia, Legajo 51, Expediente 1461.

Sources

Because the struggle to create and sustain a guild of shoemakers in colonial Buenos Aires produced so much litigation, there is an unusually rich legacy of documentation available for the modern researcher. All these records, including administrative reports, the legal opinions of city and imperial officials, the testimony of the participants, and juridical decisions, are found in the División Colonia, Sección Gobierno of the Archivo General de la Nación in Buenos Aires, Argentina. The documents used in my discussion of the first effort to create a guild in 1779 are found in Archivo del Cabildo, 1780–83, and in the published Acuerdos, Archivo General de la Nación, *Acuerdos del Extinguido Cabildo de Buenos Aires*, 47 vols. (Buenos Aires, 1907–34), Series 3, vol. 6, p. 365. Materials generated during the second organizational effort, including lists of master shoemakers and important biographical information on Francisco Baquero, are found in Interior, Legajos 33, 53, and 54. The discussion of Baquero's effort to create a segregated guild, his trip to Spain, and the ultimate failure of the nonwhite guild is based on documents found in Interior, Legajos 41, 54, and 55, Tribunales, Legajo Z4, and Justicia, Legajo 51.

Suggestions for Further Reading

Unfortunately there have been few studies of artisans in colonial Spanish America. The problem is further compounded for students who are unable to read Spanish. The literature in English is limited to James Lockhart, who devotes one chapter of his excellent *Spanish Peru, 1532–1560* (Madison, Wisc., 1968) to artisans, and to my recently published article on another artisan group, "The Silversmiths of Buenos Aires: A Case Study in the Failure of Corporate Social Organization," in *Journal of Latin American Studies* 8, 2 (1976): 181–213. The standard work on the artisans of Mexico is Manuel Carrera Stampa's *Los gremios mexicanos* (Mexico City, 1954). The only other book-length study is Hector Humberto Samayoa Guevara's *Los gremios de artesanos en la ciudad de Guatemala* (Guatemala, 1962).

There are a limited number of articles on artisans in Spanish. Of special interest is Samayoa Guevara's study of an attempt to reform the Guatemalan guilds, "La reorganización gremial guatemalense en la segunda mitad del siglo XVIII," in *Antropologia e historia de Guatemala* 12, 1 (1960): 63–106. A discussion of the importance of guild regulations as a source for social history is found in Richard Konetzke, "Las ordenanzas de gremios como documentos para la historia social de Hispanoamérica durante la época colonial," *Revista Internacional de Sociologia* 5, 18 (1947): 421–449. Finally, there is Emilio Harth-Terré and Alberto Márquez-Abanto's detailed analysis of the role of artisans in colonial Lima, "Las bellas artes en el virreinato del Peru, Perspectiva social y económica del artesano virreinal en Lima," *Revista del Archivo Nacional del Peru* 31 (1963): 353–446.

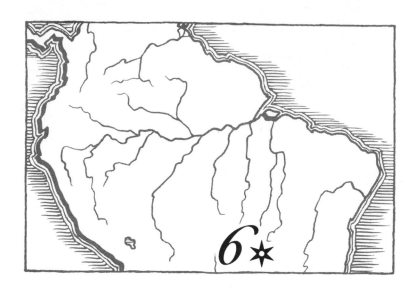

Damiana da Cunha:
Catechist and *Sertanista*

MARY KARASCH

The stony plateau of Goiás was a treacherous environment in which to adapt and survive, and for two centuries few Europeans were tempted to leave the fertile coast of Brazil to try to extract a living there. Short, scraggly trees twisted into surprising shapes. Continuous rain eroded, flooded, and mired people and animals in mud for six months, until the dry season descended with its endless sun and choking dust.

The hills of Goiás hid gold, however, and in time the frontiersmen and adventurers from Portugal and São Paulo penetrated the forbidding terrain with their gangs of African and Indian retainers to try to discover its treasure. Fighting, conquering, enslaving, and destroying the owners of the land, the new men established their mining camps and cattle ranches and set slaves to extracting fortunes for them.

Wherever enough gold was found, the outsiders erected towns. The rest of the country was left to its original inhabitants, and the outraged Indians fought where they could to recover some portion of what they had lost. They stole cattle, waylaid mule trains, and killed isolated settlers where they found them. The outsiders retaliated without much success; but whenever the violence grew severe enough to disrupt the flow of gold to Europe, their ruler would order the roads cleared at all costs, and the shipments of gold increased.[1]

Of all those who fought the invaders of Goiás, the Caiapó[2] succeeded in making themselves most troublesome. They attacked travelers and severely hampered communications on the road that ran from Cuiabá in Mato Grosso through Vila Boa (now Goiás) and on to Rio de Janeiro or São Paulo. They refused to make peace or to settle alongside other nations in the fixed villages which the colonists considered indispensable, or to change their beliefs and ways of life. For fifty years of the eighteenth century they gave the outsiders ample reason to fear and hate them, determined never to forget how their land had been invaded and their people enslaved. But in time, inevitably, some began to change.

The transition period for one group of the Caiapó began in 1778, with the arrival of Governor Luís da Cunha Menezes in Vila Boa, the capital town of the captaincy. Since the discovery of gold, the main function of the governors had been to locate and develop mines and see to the collection of the royal-fifth tax on their production. Menezes found, however, that mining was in a slump and that many former miners had turned for survival to subsistence farming or cattle raising. They no longer displayed the old adventurers' readiness to embark at the first rumor on a fruitless search for gold; and the governor, therefore, met with limited success in his efforts to increase the shipments of gold. His second project was to suppress the obstreperous Caiapó in the south of the captaincy; and this was more favored by fortune. During the five years of his administration, he did more to pacify the hostile Indians than any of his predecessors and thereby earned a commendation from his sovereign.

The governor's strategy for this conquest was to pursue a policy of gentle persuasion, offering presents to the Caiapó to cease their depredations and live in peace with the settlers. In

1780 he organized an expedition of fifty men with three Caiapó interpreters, who were to penetrate the *sertão* or back country of the Claro River and make contact with them. The captain was a soldier named José Luís Pereira, familiar with the Caiapó and their customs through having fought in many wars against them. Pereira's instructions, which a historian says "breathed peace and protection to the Indians," enjoined him to give presents of iron tools and other trade goods to the Caiapó in the name of Her Majesty Queen Maria I. In five months the expedition returned, claiming to have accomplished the pacification of the Caiapó without losing a man. They had even persuaded a group of thirty-six Indians to return with them to meet their great captain.

The Caiapó who entered Vila Boa in 1780 were led by an old man, Romexi, sent in place of their principal chief, Angraí-oxá, to verify the promises made by Pereira. Accompanying him were six warriors, women, and children. Luís da Cunha welcomed the expedition with musket and cannon fire and received the envoys at his headquarters in full dress uniform and in the company of all his staff. With great gravity he assured Romexi and his people of the full protection of Her Majesty's government, so long as the Caiapó would cease their hostilities toward her vassals. The ceremonies concluded with a Te Deum or hymn of thanksgiving in the main church, after which for some days the visitors enjoyed a series of parties given in their honor. With this the conquest of the ferocious Caiapó appeared complete.

Romexi and his group remained for nearly a month in the capital, during which time the old man's sister fell sick, was baptized, died, and was buried in the church with solemn rituals. Several children were baptized as well; and the governor then sent the Caiapó to São José de Mossamedes, an *aldeia* (village) that had been established near Vila Boa in 1755 for pacified individuals of the Xavante, Carajá, and Carijó tribes among others. The purpose of this visit was for the Caiapó to see how the *aldeia* Indians lived, so that they might return and persuade their people to come and settle there for good. Romexi was also given rich presents for the great chief, Angraí-oxá, but the old man, pleased with the reception he had received, was reluctant to depart. It was only after a series of entreaties by the governor that he could be persuaded to leave for home in the company of Pereira and his men. Then on the way Romexi refused to go any further, claiming that he was too old and tired and wanted to end his days among the whites, and sent his six warriors to bring his people from their home village.

Why did the Caiapó allow themselves to be pacified so easily after decades of fierce resistance? Part of the answer may lie in the prolonged drought the region had experienced in 1780, followed by exceptionally heavy rains in 1782. The penetration of cattle ranchers and their herds into the region in recent years had greatly reduced the hunting territory of the Caiapó; and when the governor offered them both food and a favorable location for resettlement, they may have been compelled by necessity to accept. Finally, as happened in many another frontier situation, it seems likely that the Caiapó had grown dependent during their years of intermittent conflict with the settlers on the iron tools and firearms that only the outsiders could provide. At this point it may have seemed preferable to establish peaceful relations in order to obtain a steady supply of these vital goods, rather than relying on the unpredictable outcome of raids. There is evidence that groups of Caiapó had on several occasions made peace for long enough to master the outsiders' military tactics and lay in a supply of firearms—and that once armed they had resumed their attacks on mule trains and outlying ranches.

In May of 1781 the news reached Vila Boa that a larger group of more than two hundred Caiapó, led by their great chief Angraí-oxá, were making their way toward the capital. At the end of that month the governor welcomed the new delegation with all the pomp and ceremony at his disposal. The Indians camped near his "palace"; and a month later the new era of friendly relations between the people of Vila Boa and the Caiapó was confirmed by the baptism of 113 Caiapó children. Luís da Cunha Menezes himself served as godfather to the children of Angraí-oxá and other chiefs. The alliance between the two peoples was thus cemented, in Catholic as well as in Indian eyes, by means of a ritual alliance between their leaders.

It was through this gala ceremony, or one in 1780, that the Indian heroine of Goiás—granddaughter of Angraí-oxá and

later teacher, missionary, mediator, frontierswoman, and expedition leader—entered the historical record. She and a
brother were baptized and given the Christian names of Damiana and Manoel da Cunha in honor of their godfather.
Shortly thereafter some of the Caiapó went to settle at the
new village of Maria Primeira, named for the Portuguese
queen, which the governor had established for the Caiapó on
the Fartura river some fifty miles (twelve leagues) from Vila
Boa. Damiana went to live as a hostage in the governor's
household, to be raised in something like the European fashion while serving as a symbol of the good intentions of the
Caiapó. As the granddaughter of Angraí-oxá and his wife
Xiunequá, the "little princess" must have enjoyed a high
status among her people from the start, and this may have
carried over to some extent among the Portuguese, who although generally contemptuous of Indians were ever conscious of the quality of a person's birth. We know nothing of
Damiana's experiences with the Menezes family, but it is
possible that for a few months she even attended the "domestic" school founded by the governor in Vila Boa, in which
classes were taught in spinning cotton and weaving on wood-
en looms. However well Damiana may have been received by
Luís da Cunha Menezes and his retainers, the governor was
called back to Portugal in 1783. At that time, the need for an
official hostage from the Caiapó having passed, the child may
have been sent to live as a "domestic Indian" in the *aldeia* of
São José de Mossamedes.

It is not clear whether Damiana da Cunha spent all her
young womanhood in São José, or whether as an interpreter
and half-assimilated person with a partial indoctrination in
the Catholic faith she may also have had some role in the
history of her relatives' settlement at Maria Primeira. Angraí-oxá and his followers had been joined there soon after
they arrived by other groups of Caiapó until in all there were
nearly seven hundred people gathered in four hamlets. Of
these people, almost half were baptized early on—a circumstance suggesting that at that time they were a healthy
population with a high birthrate and a large number of children. The decades that followed, however, were not happy
ones for the "domestic" Caiapó; by 1813 the settlement at

Maria Primeira was so reduced by disease and desertion that it could not function. Its few surviving inhabitants were relocated to the also much-diminished São José so that they might be administered more efficiently; and by that time the population of the two villages together had declined to a pitiful 267.

What is clear is that Damiana must have received a remarkable training for a nonwhite woman on the colonial Brazilian frontier. In the 1820s she impressed foreign travelers with her intelligence, her correct speaking knowledge of Portuguese, and above all with her piety. Before that time she had apparently married and been left a widow. Her first husband, to whom she is said to have been wed at about the age of fourteen, is somewhat romantically recalled in local tradition as having been a Portuguese soldier of the regiment of royal dragoons of Goiás. Nothing is known about him. Then in 1819 or soon after she appears to have married a Brazilian civilian and ex-corporal of the militia named Manuel Pereira da Cruz. Given the racial makeup of the captaincy and of São José at that time, it seems likely that Cruz was a poor mulatto peasant. There are no references to children from either marriage.

Damiana da Cunha's life, as a girl and as a married woman, was lived in the context of the late colonial *aldeia*, the secular descendant of the old frontier mission-station of earlier times. It was there that she developed her ideals regarding the conditions of Indian life in her day, and it was there that she distinguished herself as a communal leader. São José had been established in 1755 to house "domestic" Indians from several tribes, and at its height it had included thousands of people. Then its original inhabitants had deserted or died off, and little by little they were replaced by Caiapó during the later years of the eighteenth century. Beginning about 1800, if not as early as 1783, Damiana's life and the life of the *aldeia* were inseparable. In later years she seems to have become the principal Indian leader of the community, presiding over the last two decades of its transition from missionary outpost to peasant village. She was a loyal supporter of the Church and interpreter of its teachings to her neighbors, and the principal mediator between the *aldeia*'s inhabitants and the colonial and Brazilian state. When she died in 1831, the community disintegrated as one by one the other *aldeias* of Goiás had done many years before.

In 1819 São José de Mossamedes was a village situated atop a hill at the foot of the low mountains of the Serra Dourada. Its buildings were placed around a vast rectangular plaza, with a seldom-opened church, "simple and of good taste," in the center. In each of the four corners of the plaza there was a two-storeyed structure, but the majority of the houses were at ground level. Across from the church was the comfortable residence of the military commander with its portico crowned by the royal arms. Considered sumptuous for its locale, it also served as a summer vacation residence for the governors of Goiás. Other buildings were used as community storehouses. The majority of the tiled-roof houses, built at great expense by the government for the Caiapó, were not occupied by them but by the soldiers stationed in São José to keep order and by about fifty poor mulattoes whom the government had permitted to settle in the town in order to supplement its declining population. Some of them had intermarried with the Caiapó women. Damiana lived in one of the Luso-Brazilian houses, but most of the other Caiapó shunned them as cold and uncomfortable, preferring to live in a group of thatched-roof houses of their own construction that were arranged along the western side of the *aldeia* or scattered in their fields at some distance from the village.

The chief administrator of the *aldeia* was a colonel who lived in Vila Boa and who was in charge of all the settlements of domestic Indians in the province. Directly beneath him and stationed in São José was a corporal of the dragoons with the title of *comandante*, assisted by a soldier from the same regiment and fifteen mulatto footsoldiers recruited in the region. In addition there were a carpenter and a blacksmith. The task of these functionaries was to supervise the semivoluntary labor of the less than three hundred Caiapó who remained in the village, in the cultivation of the *aldeia*'s land and the operation of its cottage industry—in principle for the benefit of the Caiapó, the soldiers, and the state. A Catholic priest was also supposed to be present on a full-time basis to see to the "civilization" of the Caiapó; but in 1819 he was living on his sugar estate at some distance from the *aldeia* and appeared only occasionally to say Mass or perform baptisms. The Caiapó were therefore ruled by their own leaders and the military, with little or no interference from the Church.

The consequence of this military system was the exploitation of the Caiapó. The mulatto soldiers served as overseers of the men in the fields, while a mulatto woman directed the labors of the women on twenty-four spinning wheels and a number of rudimentary looms. After the harvest had been gathered into storehouses, the *comandante* would distribute rations among the families of the Caiapó. They in turn were permitted to sell part of their crop to the soldiers, who were poorly paid and obliged to find their own food and clothing where they served. The surplus was shipped to the director in Vila Boa to be exchanged for salt, tobacco, fine cotton cloth, and iron tools, which he in turn sent to the *comandante* to be parcelled out among the Caiapó. Naturally, such a system permitted each official to rake off dividends for himself and his subalterns. The *aldeia* also had a water-powered mill for grinding corn and a machine for de-seeding cotton, both of which were also operated under official auspices.

The Caiapó of São José had two free days, Sunday and Monday, in which to go hunting and fishing or work in their own gardens of yams and sweet potatoes. They had no significant role in the administration of the village, although the auxiliary functions of communal leaders such as Damiana remain to be clarified, or in the disposition of the products of their communal labor. Those who neglected to work or who displeased the administration in other ways could be punished quite severely by the authority of the *comandante*—a man described by a European traveler as "gross, ignorant, and cruel." The usual punishment for men was confinement without food or water for several days at the mercy of the hot sun and biting insects in the feared *tronco*, or stocks; for women and children, it was numerous blows on the palms of the hands with the *palmatória*, a perforated wooden paddle that raised extremely painful welts. Symbolically, both these instruments were in common use for the punishment of slaves in Brazil.

Jab. 6.

Roda de fiar o algodão.   J.J. Codina inv. 81784.

The Caiapó, not surprisingly, were bitterly unhappy with this regime of ostensibly voluntary servitude. The *comandante* was so afraid of them that he would not leave his house without his sabre. His soldiers stood guard during Sunday Mass in a church where a priest had once been killed at the altar by angry Indians. The Caiapó complained about having to get permission to leave the *aldeia,* about the harshness of their supervisors, and about the backbreaking, monotonous labor involved in foreign-style cultivation. At the same time they were often hungry because of the inequities built into

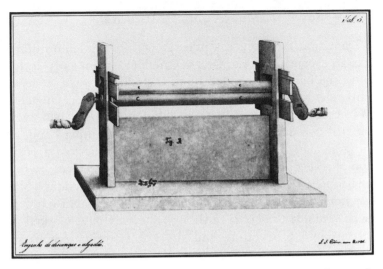

6. Late eighteenth-century Brazilian machines for de-seeding and
   spinning cotton.

the outsiders' system for distributing the products of their
labor. To top off their grievances, the very location of the
aldeia was from their point of view unsuitable. By the 1820s,
after half a century of steadily increasing foreign settlement,
they had no access to good hunting and fishing. People looked
back fondly on their old independent way of life, and even on
the first years of domesticity at Maria Primeira, where the
land had been more fertile, the hunting and fishing more
abundant, and the supervision less intensive.

In these circumstances it was not surprising that when
new groups of Caiapó were brought to São José, the bolder and
more spirited of them were apt to leave at the first opportunity and try to find their way to their cousins in the
backlands. The withdrawal of Indians was so serious a problem that it sabotaged production and the food supply of the
aldeia. The only reliable Indian inhabitants were those like
Damiana herself, who had been raised in the *aldeia* and knew
no other way of life. A traveler noted disapprovingly that
whereas in the old Jesuit missions (well-known to enlightened Europe through the fanciful writings of Voltaire and
others) a single priest had presided peacefully over the productive labors of thousands of Indians, at São José seventeen
armed men were required to supervise the unwilling labors of
less than three hundred!

Damiana da Cunha's situation within this community was an exceptional one. On the one hand, from early childhood she had been trained in the outsiders' ways, at least while she lived in Vila Boa. She had learned their language and become a believer in their religion, and she had even married two outsiders in succession. On the other hand, as the granddaughter of Angraí-oxá she had inherited a position of respect among the Caiapó that was enhanced by her position as a "broker" in relations with the outsiders. She was herself undoubtedly not subject to forced labor requirements outside the home, although she may have worked in cotton cloth production; and she was exempt from harsh physical punishment, at least at the hands of anyone other than her husband. She was certain to have enough to eat even when other Caiapó were going hungry; and as one of the few Indians to have undergone some religious training as a Catholic, she may have been favored by the religious establishment. It is not surprising, then, that as a Christianized Caiapó leader she was concerned rather to hold together the shaky structure of the *aldeia* than to join the recalcitrant Caiapó and endeavor to lead her people out of it.

The *aldeias* of Maria Primeira and São José appear to have enjoyed some tranquility and prosperity during the lifetime of Damiana's grandfather. It was Angraí-oxá who had decided to resettle his people under Portuguese "protection," and his prestige was sufficient to keep them there. But not long after his death, which occurred sometime after Damiana's first marriage, perhaps in the 1790s, the structure of the settlements began to fall apart. Many Caiapó, disgusted with the conditions of their life and unpersuaded by the foreign religion, rebelled or simply deserted with the new weapons they had acquired and learned to use. Many returned to raiding and burning ranches, killing the men and stealing their women and children, making war on the captaincy as their fathers had done half a century before. It was then that Damiana made her first remarkable expedition to the *sertão* and returned with about seventy Caiapó in 1808.

The circumstances of this journey are not yet clear, but what Damiana seems to have done is leave her husband and São José and travel alone to visit the Caiapó in the *sertão* of the Araguaya River, in order to persuade them to return to

São José. According to local legend, her appeal was made on the grounds that only Christianity, even as inadequately taught and more inadequately exemplified by the Portuguese, could raise them above the level of "savages." It seems more likely today that she persuaded her fellow tribespeople by reminding them that in the *aldeia* more than in the unpredictable forest they could count on shelter and a reliable supply of food and trade goods and escape the depredations of land-hungry outsiders. By this time for Damiana certainly, and possibly for a number of other younger Caiapó, the old way of life was no longer either practical or desirable. Its resource base had been eroded by pressure from the prospectors and ranchers, burning and tearing down the trees and rendering the land infertile; and the Indians themselves had mostly succumbed to violence and epidemic disease. Damiana may have seen the *aldeamento,* as bad as it was, as the only means of saving her people from extinction.

In 1819 Governor Fernando Delgado Freire de Castilhos organized a new expedition to pacify the Caiapó. This time, rather than call on a soldier to do the job, he commissioned Damiana da Cunha to form a group of armed men "with the object of making an impression on those people." Christianized Indians were often used for catechizing their fellows on the Brazilian frontier, and Damiana seemed more likely than anyone else to be able to persuade the Caiapó. It may be, since the priest of São José was so much absent from the *aldeia,* that Damiana was in practice the principal spokesperson for the Church in the region as well. In any case, her assignment was to find some of those who had fled from São José and persuade them to return.

Before she left on this three-month expedition, Damiana was visited by the French traveler Saint-Hilaire, who found her a jovial and friendly woman with an "open and intelligent physiognomy," and the most respected person in the *aldeia.* Damiana informed her visitor that she intended not only to bring back the Caiapó who had fled but also a good number of her compatriots who were still "savages." She confessed that in the "savage state," her people had "no idea of God," and that it was for this reason that she had requested permission to go after them. She was not confident of success, even though "the respect they have for me is far too great for them to fail to follow my instructions"; but she appeared to be firm in the belief that resettlement was in the Caiapó's best interests, and they would be happier in the long run in the *aldeia* than in the forest.

The expedition of 1819 kept Damiana in the *sertão* for many months, after which she returned to São José with about seventy of her brothers, who were soon baptized. Some of these people left not long afterward, and the war on the frontier was renewed. In 1821 the authorities dispatched Damiana at the head of a third expedition, which returned with "a great quantity" of her people; in the following year the hostilities resumed again. This time it was not only the Caiapó but a number of groups, including bands of fugitive slaves, who fought against the outsiders, soldiers, and settlers and in particular plagued the road to Cuiabá. In retaliation for their attacks, government forces indiscriminately slaughtered the inhabitants of Caiapó villages. As far as can be determined, Damiana was active during this period as a mediator, attempting to make peace between the Caiapó and the authorities in Goiás so as to save her people from further violence.

An unsympathetic Brazilian who visited Goiás in 1824 and apparently did not meet Damiana but gathered hearsay about her, reported that the "Indian Dona Damiana, daughter of one of their captains and married with a soldier of the infantry of the line of Goiás, governs arbitrarily the Cayapó Indians; and when it is necessary for some task, she goes naked, paints herself and leaves for the interior, and leads the Indians just as she wishes."[3] This cryptic comment tells us little about the nature of Damiana's authority, but it does raise an important question about the degree of her assimilation and that of her people. Visitors to São José half a century after its establishment as a community of "domestic" Christian Indians were generally impressed by the lack of "civilization" in the place. The Caiapó knew little of Christianity (one traveler could find none who could recite the Lord's Prayer), and they were unreconciled to the labor regime or the *aldeia*. Few wore much clothing, and they continued to celebrate their traditional feasts and dances. All of this the visitors blamed on lazy and selfish directors and priests and on the half-assimilated tribal leaders, who were in the habit of treating the Indians as slaves and beasts of burden rather than as human beings and Christian vassals of the Crown. By 1824 the village was in complete decadence after years of high mortality and frequent desertion. Only 128 people remained, descendants of the first catechized Indians who had settled there. The authorities seemed to the Brazilian visitor to be so incompetent as to be unnecessary and dispensable; and the Indian leader was a woman capable of going about naked and painted, who exercised authority according to her own notions rather than in a "civilized" fashion.

This depressing picture may help explain why Damiana undertook her expeditions. The village over which in some sense she presided was obviously dying. Fewer and fewer Caiapó lived as Christianized Indians under her authority, and she needed new people to replace those who had died or run away. The religious motives emphasized by the historians of the Goiás may very well have been secondary to more conventional political ones. But be that as it may, toward the end of her life Damiana da Cunha found herself trying to keep an inherited dream of Christian peace and tranquility alive in the face of the disintegration of everything she knew.

After 1822 the government of a newly independent Brazil ignored the maintenance of some colonial institutions such as the *aldeia*; and by the time Governor Miguel Lino de Moraes took office in 1827 São José was one of the few such villages surviving in the province. When the new governor learned of the chronic weakness of Christianization efforts among the rebellious Indians subject to his authority, he feared that he might be blamed in Rio de Janeiro for this failure and turned to Damiana to make another effort at pacification. This time she tracked her fugitive people for seven months to the Camapuã River and the upper Araguaya; and when she returned she was accompanied by 100 Caiapó including two chiefs, who were baptized by the priest and warmly embraced by the governor during an official welcome ceremony.

Toward the end of 1829 groups of Caiapó appeared near Cuiabá and began to renew their attacks on the settlers. Expeditions then drove the Caiapó from Mato Grosso back to the area of the Araguaya and Claro rivers in Goiás. The smoke of their campfires terrorized the settlers, who begged the governor to intervene; and for the fifth[4] and last time Damiana da Cunha accepted the arduous task of leading men into the battle zone of a frontier war. The governor wrote that she was to attract the Caiapó as "our brothers, sons of Brazil," who would always be treated as "free men." She was not to force them to leave their villages but to invite them to come to speak with him in the capital, where they would be treated well and given gifts of iron tools—on the condition that they respected the people of the province and did not rob or kill. If they persisted in rebellion, he would send men to the forest to castigate them because "crimes are deserving of punishment."

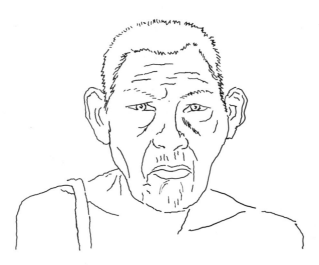

7. Sketch of an elderly Caiapó man from the 1830s.

This time Damiana left São José with her husband, Manuel Pereira da Cruz, and José and Luiza, an Indian couple who had accompanied her on previous expeditions. They traveled for nine months to the upper Araguaya and possibly to the great swampy *pantanal* of Mato Grosso. According to tradition, the trip took them into unhealthy regions where food was scarce, and it was a failure. Damiana fell sick from hunger and a virulent fever, possibly malaria, and only with great difficulty returned to her village. There, after a month during which she was visited by the governor and other officials and cared for by her husband, who was released from his military duties to attend to her, she received the last sacraments and died sometime in February or March 1831.

Damiana da Cunha was buried in the local church as a Brazilian heroine; and with her were buried the last official hopes for catechizing the Indians of Goiás and turning them into "civilized" Christians, self-sufficient agriculturalists able to produce an exploitable surplus under the benevolent direction of military commanders and priests. Her example lived on in the region, however, as did what was by that time the poor Brazilian peasant village of São José de Mossâmedes. As late as the 1930s, a visitor reported that Caiapó catechists were going out to find their "uncivilized" brethren and endeavor to persuade them to give up their customary ways of life and settle among the Christians. By that time they were obliged to travel to remote places indeed, because the Caiapó had long since been killed by settlers or driven out of their old homelands on the Pilões and Claro rivers and Caiapônia. Today's few Caiapó survivors roam the forests of northern Goiás and Pará.

Damiana da Cunha was not one of the heroic Indian resisters; at no time did she take up arms against the outsiders or encourage others to do so. Consistently throughout the period of her political influence she worked to encourage her people to adapt to the settled way of life that provided them with access to the Christian faith, some protection against extermination, and a few of the "amenities" of life on the colonial frontier. While she went to extraordinary efforts to share this way of life with those who lived in the forests, at the same time she resisted total assimilation to the ways of the outsider.

Damiana was an intelligent, able, and forceful woman, a leader used to high status and its prerogatives, who exercised her authority well enough to enjoy the respect and obedience of her people. As the symbol of her authority, she used Caiapó sticks in her ears rather than the trappings of an outsider. Raised in the Caiapó culture of the *aldeias,* she was loyal neither to the culture of the capital nor to the culture of the Caiapó in the backlands. Her commitment was to a Christianized style of Caiapó life that had been worked out over the years by the Caiapó themselves in resistance to authoritarian and corrupt administrators. When that way of life came under attack or was ignored by indifferent officials and priests, she did not sit by passively and watch it collapse but acted on her beliefs and her concern for her people to try to stave off the disintegration all around her. A realist, she had no illusions about the outsiders who worked in the *aldeias* and complained bitterly about their failure to implement their promises to her people. She died sick and exhausted, a "mummy," in the words of a chronicler, much older than the average Indian woman of her day. She had worn herself out in futile efforts to bring peace to the frontier, to preserve the *aldeia* way of life, and to save her people from extinction by the settlers. But neither the unassimilated Caiapó nor the outsiders gave her an opportunity to accomplish her goal of presiding over a group of Christian Caiapó surviving under the protection of a "benign" government. Like people the world over caught between resistance and assimilation to colonial rule and desirous of taking some kind of initiative in the process of their lives, Damiana saw her dreams shredded in the violent collision of cultures and economic ways of life. She and those like her, no longer Indians and not yet Luso-Brazilians, found that there was no place for them in any world other than one of their own making. Damiana tried but failed to make that world a reality in São José de Mossamedes, for in the 1820s as in the 1970s the forces of disease, settler pressure, and government indifference, corruption, and interference were too powerful. The result for those caught between, then as now, was disintegration, death, and disappearance.

Notes

1. "Outsider" here includes not only Luso-Brazilian "white men" but also their racially mixed retainers, African slaves, and Indian allies. In 1804 whites composed only 14 percent of the population of Goiás in a census that excluded the Indians; slaves composed 37 percent of these, and the remainder were free persons of color.

2. The Caiapó (Kaiapó), speakers of a language in the Gê group, were once numerous and roamed widely over a vast region in the modern states of Mato Grosso and Goiás. First encountered by expeditions from São Paulo at the end of the seventeenth century, a portion of them witnessed the enslavement of some 8,000 of their number in 1741 and then fled to the south of Goiás, where they

established themselves in the vicinity of Vila Boa. Today they are virtually extinct in that region, having either died out or migrated to the north of Mato Grosso and Goiás and adjacent Pará; but 200 years ago they were still to be found scattered in a region centering on the Claro and Pilões rivers and the Serra do Caiapó and Caiapônia in Goiás.

3. Raymundo José da Cunha Mattos, "Corographia histórica da Província de Goyaz," *Revista do Instituto Histórico, Geográphico, Brasileiro* (hereafter *RIHGB*) 37 (1874): 305.

4. Most traditions cite only four major expeditions, but she evidently made more than four, since there are references to at least five. Evidently, she made the first expedition on her own, which is not well known, and became famous for the other four, which are better documented because they were made with government support.

Sources

This story has been reconstructed largely from the histories of Goiás and the travel literature of the early nineteenth century. All narratives of Damiana's life are fragmentary, but the best are included in J. Norberto de Souza e Silva, "Biografia. Damiana da Cunha," *RIHGB* 24 (1861): 525–38; Camilo Chaves, *Caiapônia: Romance da terra e do homem do Brasil Central*, 2d ed. (Belo Horizonte, 1943); J. M. P. de Alencastre, "Annaes da Província de Goyaz," *RIHGB* 27 (1864): 5–186 and 229–349, and 28 (1865): 5–167; Zoroastro Artiaga, *História de Goiás*, 2d rev. ed. (Goiânia, 1959); Collemar Natal e Silva, *História de Goyaz*, 2 vols. (Rio de Janeiro, 1935); and Ofelia Socrates do Nascimento Monteiro, *Goiaz Coração do Brasil* (Goiás, 1933). Travel accounts of use for this purpose were Auguste de Saint-Hilaire, *Viagem à Província de Goiás*, trans. Regina Regis Junqueira (Belo Horizonte, 1975); João E. Pohl, *Viagem no Interior do Brasil*, 2 vols. (Rio de Janeiro, 1951); Raymundo José da Cunha Mattos, "Corographia histórica da Província de Goyaz," *RIHGB* 37 (1874): 213–398 and 38 (1874): 5–150; Francis Castelnau, *Expedição às regiões centrais da América do Sul*, trans. Olivério M. de Oliveira Pinto, 2 vols. (São Paulo, 1941); and Hermano Ribeiro da Silva, *Nos Sertões do Araguaia* (São Paulo, 1949). Useful background material was taken from Aires de Casal, *Corografia Brasílica* 1817, vol. 1 (2d ed. Rio de Janeiro, 1945), and José de Souza Azevedo Pizarro e Araujo, *Memórias históricas do Rio de Janeiro, vol. 9* (Rio de Janeiro, 1948), pp. 131–232.

Suggestions for Further Reading

There is unfortunately almost nothing to read in English about the late colonial and early nineteenth-century history of Goiás, other than a few pages in Robert Southey's *History of Brazil* published more than 150 years ago and C. R. Boxer, *The Golden Age of Brazil, 1695–1750* (Berkeley, 1969). Useful Brazilian works include Marivone Matos Chaim, *Os aldeamentos indígenas na Capitania de Goiás* (Goiânia, 1974), an important but incomplete study of the *aldeia* system; Luiz Palacin, *Goiás 1722–1822: Estrutura e Conjuntura numa Capitania de Minas,* 2d ed. (Goiânia, 1976); and Dalísia Elizabeth Martins Doles, *As comunicações fluviais pelo Tocantins e Araguaia no século xix* (Goiânia, 1973), with a good bibliography. For general background, see Ernani da Silva Bruno, *História do Brasil: Geral e Regional.* Vol. 6, *Grande Oeste (Goiás-Mato Grosso)* (São Paulo, 1967). For further reading on the problem of the integration of the Indian populations of Brazil, past and present, see Darcy Ribeiro, *Os índios e a civilização: a integração das populações indígenas no Brasil moderno,* 2d ed. (Petrópolis, 1977); and a recent bibliographical essay by Anthony Seeger and Eduardo Viveiros de Castro, "Resenha bibliográfica: pontos de vista sobre os indios brasileiros," *Boletim Informativo e Bibliográfico de Ciéncias Sociais* 2 (1977): 11–35. On the earlier history of the Caiapó, there are scattered references in John Hemming, *Red Gold: The Conquest of the Brazilian Indians, 1500–1760* (Cambridge, Mass., 1978).

★ PART TWO

*Survival Through
Individual Defiance*

Introduction

*I*n the colonial systems of America, those who possessed power took the normal precautions to discourage any collective defiance of their rule. There was, nevertheless, ample space in the colonial social order for countless individual acts of resistance, rebellion, insubordination, and noncooperation. The frequency of these acts of protest kept the laboring inhabitants of the real world of the colonies from being perceived by their contemporaries, or from functioning, as an army of soulless and predictable drones. At one end of the spectrum of individual defiance were extreme gestures such as the suicidal attack on some oppressive individual or institution. Less hazardous and more frequent were civil and criminal lawbreaking and the various forms of "antisocial" behavior such as banditry, inveterate vagrancy, or a simple refusal to live according to the standards established for persons of one's station. Less overt defiance was manifest in witchcraft, madness, and ecstatic religion—all of which may be viewed as forms of protest against restrictive norms and constituted authority. More modulated still, and presumably most common of all, were the myriad daily acts of noncompliance or noncooperation, sometimes so subtle as to lose themselves in the odd behavior of individuals described simply as eccentric or peevish or dull.

Every society contains large numbers of individuals arranged along this spectrum of individual defiance in ways determined by its particular patterns of culture and modes of oppression. The present collection offers two deviant Catholic priests, an Indian sorcerer, and two indomitable slaves, all from early colonial Latin America. But students of society have barely begun to account for the prevalence of this phenomenon, and they have yet to suggest ways of approaching a comprehensive analysis or a quantification of it. This is true in part because of an absolute lack of information about these matters. But another reason for the failing is a general unwillingness to accept the paradoxical truth that is manifest in the present collection of stories and in the individual experiences of every one of us—that a considerable degree of inequality and exploitation is a feature of every society that has evolved up to now, and that inequality and exploitation are nevertheless painful and destructive contexts for the human spirit. The tacit acceptance of the normalcy of this man-made suffering has led to a singular lack of curiosity among historians and other students of society about the key role that oppression has played in the histories of all peoples and about how individual human beings have contrived to deal with it.

There is no way as yet to make comparative estimates of the frequency of defiance as a mode of coping with life in the American colonies, or to measure changes in the incidence of defiance through time. Individual defiance is by definition idiosyncratic, as the stories that follow will make clear. At present, therefore, we can do little more than recognize its importance in colonial America and speculate that its frequency and mode of expression must have depended on several factors, including the extent to which elites were able to establish cultural hegemony, on their ability to distribute rewards in what was regarded as an equitable way, and on the effectiveness of annealing forces such as religion, family life, and ethnic solidarity. This collection of life stories suggests that the pattern of individual defiance varied greatly from place to place and from one racial group or social stratum to another, and it offers the hope that something may eventually be said about the patterns of defiance, when a few dozen more of the fascinating stories of "ordinary" colonial people have been unearthed and subjected to scrutiny.

Among slaves and forced laborers in the New World, rebellions were infrequent and usually unsuccessful. But individual rebelliousness, like that of Juan de Morga and Gertrudis de Escobar, seems to have been very widespread. The most overt act was running away, or willful withdrawal from the system of exploitation. Studies of slave societies make it clear that this was so common as to be perceived as an endemic problem by every slave-owning class. Another form of individual resistance was psychic withdrawal into an absent dullness, which made the slave or the servant exasperatingly difficult to exploit—a person whose body was available for service but whose vital governing intelligence and initiative had, at least for the master's practical purposes, been shut down. An eighteenth-century planter in Virginia complained: "My people seem to be quite dead-hearted and either cannot or will not work."[1] It was a lament that echoed down the decades wherever slavery took root.

Beyond seeking some form of personal liberation, many slaves defied the system through violent attacks on their masters' persons or property. Most colonies passed special laws against arson and poisoning and steadily increased the severity of punishment for such retributory crimes. As Sidney Mintz observes: "the sharpest evidence of slave resistance is not the historical evidence of armed revolts [but] the codes that legalized branding, flogging, burning, the amputation of limbs, hamstringing, and murder to keep the slaves 'nonviolent.'"[2] Slaveowners lived in great fear of the violence that slaves might perpetrate against them. But the violence in the slave's breast most often did not find expression against the fearsome personnel of the slaveocracy. More often, in desperation it was turned inward in acts of suicide, abortion, or infanticide. Frequently too it was vented on fellow slaves in crimes of passion resulting from ostensibly inconsequential disagreements. These were drastic attempts to slash at the master class, or perhaps at life itself—half-crazed efforts to destroy the rich man's property in human beings, by people driven to the belief that life could no longer be faced or was no longer to be nourished or respected.

Individual acts of defiance seem to have been more frequent among black slaves than among any other group in colonial society. Indians lived for the most part within communities capable of collective resistance, although Martin Ocelotl will be seen operating as a loner at a time when that resistance was low. Europeans had at least the hope of improving their position by collaborating in a system set up for the exploitation of others. But all these groups produced defiant resisters of a life-draining system that offered them too little comfort in the present and too little hope for the future. Understanding that they were being restricted by other men's rules and institutions, they struggled alone in the best ways they could, learning to find and make use of the weak points of the structure in which they lived and labored. This allowed them a measure of retaliation, and it also put effective limits on the ability of others to control them. No sector of colonial society was ever so efficiently managed as to leave people no space in which to engage in some kind of resistance. Men and women learned by resisting that while the authorities could deliver punishing blows against the disobedient, they could also be taught by their subalterns' defiance to temper the daily routine and to concede to their unwilling followers a measure of dignity and autonomy.

Defiance among free persons was most often a matter simply of refusing regular employment, remaining on the margins of society, and choosing to live from hand to mouth. Working-class people of this disposition hired on for short tours of duty as sailors, mule drivers, or day laborers. The more genteel established themselves as retainers of important persons while waiting for an opportunity, as we will see in the story of the reprobate priest António de Gouveia. A great many people everywhere in America also shunned "honest" employment of any kind, taking their living from begging, pickpocketing, gambling, highway robbery, or piracy. Others, like Gouveia and the Peruvian priest Cristóbal Béquer, insisted on flouting the regulations of their employers, remaining in bad odor with the authorities for as long as they lived. All these people, it is important to note, preferred the hazards of falling afoul of a harsh system of justice—which was likely to flog its victims, jail them indefinitely, or condemn them to forced labor—to the daily suffering and indignity, or the boredom, of regular employment.

The stories in Part II suggest to us the possibility that the noncompliers outnumbered the compliers in colonial society—that most individuals, at many points in their lives, engaged in overt or covert acts of resistance to what was after all a socioeconomic system that thwarted the aspirations and affronted the dignity and the sense of equity of large numbers of people. A great deal of noncompliance must have been going on at any given place and time; and even in the most demonstrably oppressive and regimented circumstances of life, such as Gertrudis de Escobar's on the sugar plantation, defiant resistance of some kind or another may be thought of as having been a normal rather than an exceptional phenomenon. Because people were spread across the land more than in Europe, because the agencies of law enforcement and social control were weaker than on the other side of the Atlantic, and because the fluidity of the social situation and the expectations of immigrants encouraged anti-authoritarianism, the New World colonies seem to have become veritable laboratories of individual defiance at the same time they became proving grounds for new systems of human exploitation.

Notes

1. Quoted in Gerald W. Mullin, *Flight and Rebellion: Slave Resistance in Eighteenth-Century Virginia* (New York, 1972), p. 53.
2. Mintz, "Toward an Afro-American History," *Journal of World History* 13 (1971): 321.

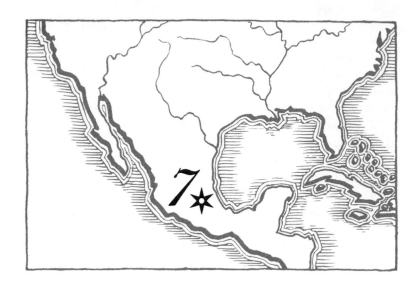

Martín Ocelotl:
Clandestine Cult Leader

J. JORGE KLOR DE ALVA

*P*erhaps as early as 1508, vigilant natives sighted
Spanish ships off the eastern coast of Mexico. All
but unchronicled by the Europeans, these encounters are
suggested by the records from which the wise men of the
Aztecs, with an imagination steeped in their ancient tradition of religious thought, distilled the enigmatic visions and
foreboding omens that alarmed the leaders of the Mexicas
approximately ten years before the conquest of their empire.
Prophecies regarding the fall of Mexico-Tenochtitlan fit well
within the cyclical and eschatological religious views of the
Mexica, which centered on the belief in recurrent destruc-
tions and recreations of historical and religious epochs. It is
understandable, therefore, that Moctezuma, the powerful
lord of the Mexica-Aztec world, was disconcerted by the

many strange signs observed during his reign and saw them as indications of impending doom. In 1518 and 1519, when the arrival of the floating towers and hills of Juan de Grijalva and Hernán Cortés was reported to him, Moctezuma responded to the inauspicious interpretations of these portents by ordering the imprisonment and execution of a number of his priest-diviners and their families.

Among the soothsayers imprisoned during those years, and one of the few to avoid execution, was a youthful religious prodigy named Ocelotl, who had predicted the coming of bearded white men who would wrest control of the land from the great *tlatoani* or emperor. This precocious novice, born in 1496, probably came from a family of important priests or priestesses. His father was a merchant, but as late as 1537 his mother, Eytacli, enjoyed the reputation of being an even more effective sorceress than her son. The family lived in Chinanta (modern Chinantla, Puebla?), where Ocelotl seems to have been born and where his mother continued to live for almost twenty years after the conquest. As a major priest of Chinanta, the young man accompanied nine other native ministers who were sent by the lord of the village to tell Moctezuma about certain ominous signs they had seen sometime around 1519. The resulting imprisonment of a year and twelve days was not to be the last punishment he would incur for divining, or for reporting to unfriendly ears the unfavorable results of his inquiries into the will of the gods.

In 1521 Tenochtitlan fell and Moctezuma was killed, but not before ordering the release of Ocelotl. Caught in the midst of the destruction of the metropolis, the enterprising priest survived the smallpox epidemic unscathed, eluded the massive starvation then ravaging every corner of the city, and escaped the murder and plunder that the Spaniards and their Indian allies visited upon the hapless Mexicas. Like many others, Ocelotl joined the scramble to get out of the burning city and away from the stench of rotting corpses. He made his way to the east bank of the lake surrounding Tenochtitlan, and there in the city of Tetzcoco he set up residence. In addition to the religious training he had acquired in priestly schools before the conquest, Ocelotl had inherited a knack for business from his merchant father; and it was only by combining both of these skills with a remarkable adaptability that the astute priest was able to weather the vicissitudes of foreign conquest and professional displacement. The accomplishment of Ocelotl during the years that followed was to contrive to live in the high style of former times with a minimum of cultural compromise.

As a consequence of the conquest and subsequent Christianization effort in Mexico, the native clergy very quickly lost both office and influence. Many priests were killed or died in the epidemics; and of the individual destinies of those who survived we know practically nothing. The inflexible position of the Roman Church worked to exclude most native rituals and all native priests from an active role in the implantation of the new faith. The fear of confusion or heretical syncretism led the newly arrived friars to ignore the many vague similarities between the observances of the two religions. For Aztecs of the priestly class some features of the new order must have had a familiar feel about them—penitential self-sacrifice, processions, morality plays, and the seminary traditions of religious education—but even here the missionaries were at pains to insist on the differences.

Marginalized by unemployment and the sudden loss of prestige, some indigenous priests continued to celebrate clandestine native services to a greatly reduced following. In the general disarray that followed the dismemberment of the ancient official ecclesiastical structure, these undercover priests were obliged to act independently of each other and according to their own lights and recollections. This isolation and the freedom from the scrutiny of an overseeing orthodox hierarchy inevitably caused the rituals to become grossly simplified, greatly diversified, and subject to a process of continuous change. Impoverished by the eradication of their aristocratic privileges along with the loss of the church lands and the laborers who had contributed to their support, the nomadic Aztec priests were made to charge directly for their services in competition with the mendicant friars. These forlorn survivors were a favorite target of the early Christian missionaries, who were quick to find the imprint of the devil wherever native priests trod. In the course of this

8. Franciscans burning temples in Tlaxcala, as demons flee and Indian neophytes look on "with approval." Sixteenth-century drawing.

persecution the friars labeled the Mexica religious rites as "divination," "sorcery," "witchcraft," and especially "idolatry," limiting the acceptable religious expression of the natives to the bare-bones Catholicism that they preached and that was only half-understood by the recent converts. For baptized natives, a relapse into idolatry was tantamount to heresy; and even before Bishop Juan de Zumárraga initiated his functions as Apostolic Inquisitor in 1536 at least four Indians had fallen victims to the Spanish inquisitorial zeal.

In 1525, one year after the famous Twelve Apostles of the New World arrived to begin the systematic Christianization program, Ocelotl was baptized in Tetzcoco and christened with the Spanish name Martín. However, at the age of twenty-nine, too set in the ancient beliefs to be truly converted and too worldly wise not to be, Martín continued with as many as possible of his old ways under the new name—when necessary, in the semblance of the new faith. Martín went on to make a brilliant career as a native priest, enjoying the favors of many of the lords who made up the remnants of the decimated indigenous aristocracy now serving the Spaniards as local rulers. His influence was felt throughout the region that made up the modern states of Puebla, Tlaxcala, and Mexico, where he made friends among those Spaniards least concerned with matters of religious orthodoxy and had excellent relations with important Indian leaders such as Don Pablo Xochiquentzin, successor to the title of *tlatoani*, whom the Spaniards had appointed governor charged with the administration of the natives in Mexico City. These connections served Ocelotl well, allowing him to amass a small fortune in lands, houses, and jewels by charging handsome fees among his well-to-do penitents, patients, and clients. The conquest had brought about a leveling among the surviving members of the indigenous ecclesiastical hierarchy, and with the destruction of their old division of labor, many underground priests like Ocelotl became skilled in the various arts of folk healing, shamanism, divining, and ministering. Ocelotl exercised all these trades, catering to both rich and poor. His skill at divining, in particular, made him greatly sought out by both natives and Spaniards. All the while, in addition to functioning as a priest, Martín rented land that he used along with his own to produce both indigenous and Spanish fruits and vegetables. Between the two enterprises he became a rich man. In spite of his wealth, Martín was not beyond working in the fields himself and was often seen hard at work alongside his laborers. Don Juan, lord of Guatepeque (Coatepec, Mexico?), was said to have described Ocelotl as a man who, having lived a long time, had come to know many of the lords of Mexico, and everywhere he was obeyed and given anything he demanded, all of which, when received, was redistributed among the people. This reputation for generosity is substantiated by the testimony of many natives who were the recipients of both good advice and useful gifts from this Indian Robin Hood.

Success, unfortunately, brought in its wake the fear, hostility, and envy of many of Martín's contemporaries. Notwithstanding his munificence and caution, the clandestine priest eventually ran afoul of the friars, and he was denounced as a wizard and idolater by some recently converted Indian zealots. In 1530, the *corregidor* in charge of the district of Tetzcoco, Cristóbal de Cisneros, claimed to have heard the townspeople speak disapprovingly of Martín as an evil person who could transform himself into a lion or a tiger. Ocelotl, whose reputation as a great sorcerer was well-known to his neighbors in Tetzcoco, was readily identified as an enemy of the Holy Faith. Wherever the friars preached, his detractors claimed, Ocelotl would follow, declaring that they should move on because he was next. Cisneros also heard Friars Antonio de Ciudad Rodrigo and Juan de la Cruz describe Martín as a troublemaker who was intent on impeding their work, claiming that his constant harangues against the Church were keeping the Indians distant from the Catholic faith. Cisneros was further convinced of the accused heretic's depravity after listening to a former servant of Martín who described the frequent nocturnal visits made by Ocelotl to the lake near Tetzcoco. There the priest would burn *copal*, the native incense, and stand on a raised platform while uttering some occult formulas, after which the "devil" would appear to advise Ocelotl as to what to do and where to go. The *corregidor* put Martín through a highly contrived test requiring him to uncover a piece of gold supposedly stolen but purposely hidden in the blouse of an Indian woman; having failed the experiment he was seized and brought before the president and judges of the Audiencia, the high court and governing body which at that time ruled New Spain.

In sixteenth-century Mexico, when civil prosecution was at hand ecclesiastical harassment could not be far behind. Time after time in Tetzcoco Friar Antonio de Ciudad Rodrigo, who was to cast his shadow over the rest of Martín's life, had threatened and admonished the suspect convert to desist from performing his "idolatrous" native ceremonies, to cease the practice of divination, and to abandon his outrageous claims to being a god! Rumor had it that Martín Ocelotl had taken to calling himself Telpucle (probably a Spanish variant of the Náhuatl *telpochtli*, "young man," which was also used as a name for the supreme Mexica-Nahua deity, Tezcatlipoca) and that in this guise he was greatly revered by the Indians. It was also said that he was immortal, that he foretold the future, that he could turn himself into a cat or tiger at will, that he kept many women, and—what was to be his downfall—that he went about inciting the Indians against the Spanish faith. Martín's tactical response to these charges was to admit the evil of his pre-Christian ways but to deny that he had been guilty of any wrongdoing after his baptism. This ruse was not to prove successful for long.

In 1533 Martín was coerced into a Church marriage by Friar Antonio de Ciudad Rodrigo. The ceremony was an event of great propagandistic value to the Christianization effort. The astute Franciscan convened the neophytes of Tetzcoco and the surrounding area to witness the event, and he then made Martín abjure his ancient faith from the pulpit, renounce his evil lifestyle, abandon his concubines (possibly legitimate wives according to the pre-Hispanic norms under which he had acquired them), and vow to follow the dictates of the Holy Mother Church.

The cunning diviner's vows, made on that occasion to what he considered to be a false deity, left him free in practice to continue exercising his vocation. In the same year, 1533, Martín prophesied that a drought would occur four years thence; and in the course of a business transaction he warned Gonzalo, the lord of Cachula (Quecholac, Puebla?), that he ought to plant much maize, agave, and prickly pear cactus in anticipation of the coming famine. He repeated this caution to many in Guatepeque, where he himself owned and rented extensive farmland. He also predicted the longevity of his friend Gonzalo, to soothe him as he cured him of some malady; and he correctly foretold the death of an elderly Indian named Maquizna. All the while he persevered in the performance of his duties as a clandestine priest of the native religion, celebrating the traditional rituals alone or among the greatly reduced group of diehards who were unwilling to give up the faith of their ancestors.

Late in the spring of 1536, only a growing season or two in advance of the prophesied drought, he sounded a desperate alarm among the natives. This time he distributed *coas*, digging sticks, to facilitate the planting of additional drought-resistant plants and trees. Afraid of what lay ahead, he decided to persuade the Indian leaders of the region to convene at his house near Guatepeque so that he might impress on them the risk that any delay in their preparations would entail. In a secret cellarlike construction below his house he urged his small congregation to plant fruit trees, agave, and cactus. It was not going to rain, he warned, and soon there would be a famine during which, if they failed to cultivate these crops, they would surely perish because the maize was not going to grow. He then distributed some religious paraphernalia, including large colored hollow reeds shaped like swords, blankets of agave fiber, and certain flowers or plants, claiming that they were gifts from Camaxtli (the name given in Tlaxcala and Huexotzinco to the supreme pre-Hispanic god). Finally, in a vein clearly betraying the messianic nature of his calling, Ocelotl added that two apostles with long teeth and nails and other frightful features had come from heaven to inform him that the friars were going to turn into Chichimicli, that is, into the *tzitzimime* that were the pre-Hispanic demons who would descend on the earth at the conclusion of the present epoch and devour everyone! Martín was obviously predicting nothing less than the end of the rule of the Spaniards. In his traditional cosmogony, the consummation of the present historical period meant the possible return of a previous age and, therefore, the need to revert to the ancient faith.

Toward the end of the 1530s the mendicant evangelization was at its height. The Indians seemed to be converting by the millions and the friars, flushed with optimism, were spreading the gospel with relentless vigor. In an attempt to bolster his political and religious influence, which were presumably beginning to wane in the face of the progressive Christianization of the natives, Ocelotl told many of the native leaders and their servants who convened in his cellar that anyone in need of anything was to come to his house. He claimed that this was because everyone in the area had issued from there, and that there, as at an oracle, the truth could always be known. Then in an effort to reassure his guests, ever fearful of the growing punitive powers of the missionaries, he falsely stated that their gathering had taken place with the permission of the friars. As a farewell gesture he dismissed his followers with the prophecy that by the time they each reached their home it would rain, because the clouds were his sisters and he would soon cause them to appear.

In the fall of 1536 Ocelotl was obliged to confront the inevitable. The unfortunate priest's reputation as a wizard and diviner, the rumors that he was immortal and capable of changing his age and nature, and the reports of his continuous preaching against the Catholic faith came to the attention of Bishop Zumárraga, recently installed as head of the Inquisition in Mexico. The bishop saw Ocelotl as a threat to the evengelization effort and decided to act at once; that November he subpoenaed witnesses to inform him regarding the truth or falsehood of the allegations against the scandalous "Martín Ucelo."

Six witnesses from towns in what are now the states of Puebla and Tlaxcala came before the prelate and recounted tales of sorcery, idolatry, and depravity. Martín's gatherings

9. Punishment of a Tlaxcalan *cacique* for practicing "idolatry" in a cave after having undergone baptism. Sixteenth-century drawing.

in his secret cellar, his predictions of drought, death, and health, his magical cures with semi-precious stones placed on the backs and bellies of the sick, his claims that the Spanish medicines killed the patients, and his tirades against the Catholic faith were fully disclosed. The witnesses, speaking under oath, repeatedly contradicted one another in declarations tinged with bias. The most damaging testimony was that presented by two Indians named Diego, residents of Tecalo (Teacalco, Tlaxcala?). Having established that they had been present at a meeting in Martín's house, they explained that he had taken them aside to ask them to carry a message to their cacique, or chief. Martín had asked them to inquire why their lord had dealt so harshly with him, refusing to obey his urgings as if he believed that the law of the Christians was going to remain forever. Ocelotl had advised them to remind the cacique that one was only born to die, that after death there were no pleasures, and that people should therefore amuse themselves while they lived—eating, drinking, and making love, even with the wives of their neighbors—while seizing everything they could from anyone, because that was what life was all about.

This picture of a hedonistic Ocelotl, in rebellion against the austerity of the mendicant friars and their promises of a joyous hereafter, is not corroborated by the other testimony presented in the proceedings. There was, however, a *carpe diem* tradition in some sectors of the Nahua world, which survived into postconquest times. In 1600, Fray Juan Bautista recorded a widespread proverb that suggested one ought to eat and imbibe while one lived, because there would be no returning from hell to enjoy either food or drink.

On November 28, 1536, having reviewed the damaging declarations of seven deponents, Bishop Zumárraga had Martín brought before him. As might have been expected, the spirited and wily Ocelotl denied every allegation presented against him; and wherever the events allowed, he recast the circumstances to give them the most favorable interpretation possible. Convinced that there was no need for further witnesses, the prelate then appointed a defense attorney for Martín and directed the prosecutor, Alonso Pérez, to present a formal accusation. Pérez demanded the most severe penalty allowed for those convicted as diviners, idolaters, and active enemies of the faith, which is to say that he was probably asking that Martín be burned at the stake.

Fray Ciudad Rodrigo, who must surely have been standing in the wings during the accusations, declared on the same day that in view of Martín's past behavior and his great "sagacity, malice, and astuteness," he believed all the charges. Nothing but evil could come from this inveterate enemy of the Church, and God would therefore be best served if he were banished from the land to a place where the natives would neither see him nor hear him. All of this was seconded by another of the Franciscan founders, Fray Pedro de Gante.

There were additional depositions by other witnesses, and Martín was then interrogated by the bishop on the subject of his ill-fated encounter with Moctezuma. The resourceful priest denied having said that Moctezuma had cut him up in pieces and that he had survived by immediately becoming whole once more. Then his denials of the new allegations were heard, and the record of the proceedings was forwarded to Viceroy Don Antonio de Mendoza and the Audiencia of Mexico (including at that time Don Vasco de Quiroga, later bishop of Michoacán). After listening to a reading of the complete trial record, the judges agreed unanimously that Martín Ocelotl should be banished from New Spain and sent to the inquisitors of Seville to be kept in jail for the rest of his life. They reasoned that Martín was impeding the Christianization of the natives and was therefore harmful to the new colonial society. But with a certain air of tolerance, or perhaps with a fear of unpleasant political consequences, they cautioned against sentencing Martín to death. Both sides then rested their cases, the prosecutor demanding the worst punishment possible and the defense attorney begging for leniency on the grounds that Martín was new to the faith and not yet well-versed in it.

On February 10, 1537, Martín was subjected to public humiliation by being ridden on a mule through the streets to the marketplaces of Mexico-Tenochtitlan and Tlatelolco with a crier proclaiming the charges against him in both Náhuatl and Spanish. Following this spectacle, he was taken to the city of Veracruz to embark on the first available ship for Spain. The ship's captain was cautioned that if he did not deliver the prisoner, who was after all wealthy enough to bribe his way to freedom, he would suffer excommunication and a fine of 200 gold pesos. In the meantime Martín's considerable estate was confiscated by the Holy Office.

In the course of auctioning off Martín's substantial holdings in maize, cotton, cloth, jewels, gold, and real estate, the bishop not only learned a good deal about Ocelotl's extensive business dealings and his activities as a moneylender but was surprised to hear that since 1531 Martín had been banned from the towns of Tetzcoco and Tlalmenalco on account of his various transgressions. This allegation may have been a false one used by the natives to keep Martín's true assets hidden from the agents of the Inquisition by denying that Martín had had any recent business relations or still owned any land in those places. It suggests, however, the interesting possibility that Martín may have fallen victim to the machinations of priestly competitors or debtors. The contradictory evidence presented at his trial lends credence to this theory. To manufacture incriminating evidence against a man with Martín's reputation as a sorcerer was virtually to guarantee his conviction and thereby to wipe out any unrecorded debts while at the same time removing his influence in matters of religion. The Inquisition records are filled with instances in which the Holy Office was used to eliminate personal enemies or competitors.

The exact nature of Ocelotl's business activities is unknown, but a brief analysis of the inventory of his estate is illuminating. Included among his real properties were houses and plots of land ranging from one to fourteen acres, located in the present states of Tlaxcala, Morelos, Puebla, and Mexico. Many of these parcels had orchards or commercially usable plantings of agave or prickly pear, or were ready for the cultivation of maize or cotton. Most of the jewels confiscated were semi-precious stones more valuable to the Indians than to the Spaniards. But coins, pieces of silver, and gold beads and ornaments were also seized. The property actually sequestered, which totaled eight lots and almost 400 bushels of maize, various loads of cotton, a dozen blankets, and assorted household goods, was auctioned off for 405½ pesos in gold. In the 1540s a skilled laborer working six days a week would have taken almost twenty-one years to earn this amount, and an unskilled laborer twice that long. Martín's household possessions and ritual paraphernalia in Guatepeque included the following: ten fans and two old plumes, six gourds, nine black cloth trims, two pairs of painted shoes, two tortoise-shell mixers for making cocoa, forty-eight skeins of cotton yarn the size of an orange, two pieces of liquidambar, three bushels of large colored hollow reeds, one embroidered shirt, six bushels of clay gourds, two medium-sized plates with wooden legs, one deer skin, eighteen digging sticks, three bushels of a plant used to make a tawny-colored dye, two censers, one large chisel, seven large jars, twenty-two clay plates, two belts, six bushels of amaranth seed, twelve bushels of beans, some chili peppers, three loads of wood, two rubber balls, one wooden drum, seven frames for making adobe, five mullers for grinding corn with their pestles, two tubes for blowing like those used by the silversmiths, various seats and mats, and four female Indian slaves.

The destitute and tragic Martín Ocelotl seems to have disappeared when his ship was mysteriously lost at sea. His memory, however, remained. In Chinanta, his birthplace, his alleged brother Mixcoatl and a former servant of Martín's named Papalotl continued celebrating the rites and propagating the faith of the ancient past. They did this, however, under the ominous cloud of the ever-vigilant Inquisition, which was to storm into their lives as well before the end of that summer.

Sources

Only two primary sources have yet surfaced that contain information on Martín Ocelotl. Fray Gerónimo de Mendieta notes in Book 2, Chapter 19 of his *Historia eclesiástica indiana* (México, 1971), written in the last decade of the sixteenth century, that Ocelotl was lost at sea near some unspecified port and never heard of again. All other details concerning Ocelotl's life are derived from the record of his trial, which was published by Luis González Obregón in "Procesos de índios idólatras y hechiceros," *Publicaciones del Archivo General de la Nación* 3 (1912): 17–51. The omens concerning the fall of Tenochtitlan are described in detail in the Spanish version of Bernardino de Sahagún, edited by Ángel Ma. Garibay, *Historia general de las cosas de Nueva España* (México, 1975) Book 12, ch. 1. On the punishment of the diviners by Moctezuma, see Hernando Alvarado Tezozómoc, *Crónica mexicana* (México, 1975), Chapter 106. The relationship between the epithet *telpochtli* and Tezcatlipoca is well known. Rémi Siméon points to it in his *Dictionnaire de la langue Náhuatl ou Mexicaine* (Graz, 1963), p. 416. Fray Juan Bautista's proverb is reported in his *Advertencias para los confesores de los naturales* (México, 1600), p. 54.

For additional data on Martín's view of Christianity, along with an analysis of the identification of the *chichimictli* with the *tzitzimime*, see Miguel León-Portilla's "Testimonios nahuas sobre la conquista espiritual," *Estudios de Cultura Náhuatl*, 11 (1974): 26–27. Martín Ocelotl is discussed at length by Jacques Lafaye in *Quetzalcoatl and Guadalupe* (Chicago, Ill., 1976), pp. 20–22. Lafaye's description of Ocelotl's role as "one of the first of those petty native messiahs" is illuminating; so is his explanation of Martín's cosmogony. Robert Barlow includes a reproduction of the native pictographic inventory of Martín's possessions as well as a discussion of his trial before the Inquisition, in "Las joyas de Martín Ocelotl," *Yan* (1954): 56–59. Richard Greenleaf also summarizes the trial record in *Zumárraga and the Mexican Inquisition* (Washington, D.C., 1961), pp. 53–54.

Suggestions for Further Reading

On the status and socioeconomic condition of the natives after the conquest, see Charles Gibson's monumental text, *The Aztecs Under Spanish Rule* (Stanford, Calif., 1964). Jacques Soustelle describes preconquest Mexicas in *The Daily Life of the Aztecs* (Stanford, Calif., 1970). The best book to date on the Christianization of Mexico is still Robert Ricard's *The Spiritual Conquest of Mexico*, trans. Lesley Byrd Simpson (Berkeley, Calif., 1966). Greenleaf's *Zumárraga and the Mexican Inquisition* is useful for its discussion of the Inquisition. For some excellent insights into the native perspective on the Spaniards, Miguel León-Portilla's *The Broken Spears: The Aztec Account of the Conquest of Mexico* (Boston, Mass., 1966) is to be recommended, as is his *Aztec Thought and Culture* (Norman, Okla., 1970) for a well-documented study of Nahua cosmogony and Mexica philosophy in general.

António de Gouveia:
Adventurer and Priest

MANOEL DA SILVEIRA CARDOZO

$\mathscr{A}$ ntónio de Gouveia was an Azorean priest of obscure origins who lived during the incredible years of the sixteenth century, moved about freely in the Atlantic world that the Portuguese had created, and unhinged himself morally and religiously in unhinging times. A deceptively charming man who could endear himself to people in high places, he knew astrology and alchemy, read fortunes, foretold happenings, practiced medicine with the sometime success of the amateur, and believed that he had the key to invisibility. It would be hard to find a better prototype of the worldliness of the clergy of his day—men whose conception of sin was tempered by a primeval innocence—or a better example of the humanism that was at odds with the dark orthodoxy of the court and would not survive the triumphal moralism of the Counter-Reformation.

António de Gouveia spent his youth in the Azores, when the nine islands of the archipelago were already the nerve center of Atlantic shipping. In 1493 Columbus had landed in Santa Maria to tell the incredulous residents that he had reached Cipangu on his voyage beyond the setting sun. He had been the first to touch the Azores on what would thereafter be the regular sailing route from the Gulf of Mexico to the Iberian Peninsula. In 1499 Vasco da Gama's brother Paulo, too ill to proceed to Lisbon on the last leg of the grand expedition to India, was put ashore in Terceira to die. From 1500 on ships sailed from the Azores some twelve hundred miles northwest to Newfoundland and the Grand Banks to fish for cod. And in 1533 Martim Afonso de Sousa returned to Portugal via the Azores after his reconnoitering voyage along the coast of Brazil.

The battlements of St. John, overlooking the ocean at Angra, still stand as mute witnesses to the importance of these strategic islands on the great Atlantic routes. Terceira would soon be the obligatory stopover of Castilian armadas bulging with the produce of Terra Firme and New Spain en route from Havana to the warehouses of Cadiz and Seville. They would be the first landfall in the northern hemisphere for the Portuguese commercial fleets out of Rio de Janeiro, Bahia, and Pernambuco, joined by East-Indiamen and laden with sugar, hides, hardwoods, parrots, monkeys, silks, and porcelains—sometimes as many as 135 cargo ships and men-of-war bound for the home port of Lisbon.

A man of Gouveia's curiosity and wanderlust found himself at the optimum junction of time and place. He was born nine years before Martin Luther nailed his theses to the church door of Wittenberg, and only seven after Hernán Cortés brought the Aztec empire to its knees. He was in his prime when in 1549 Portuguese Jesuits reached Brazil and Japan. He lived during the stirring years of Saint Francis Xavier and Michelangelo, the reigns of the Emperor Charles V, Philip II, and Henry VIII. The age was of unparalleled grandeur for Western civilization, forcing it along channels that it would thenceforth follow, and António de Gouveia, almost unconcerned and certainly unafraid, lived it with the intensity of someone who knew that it would never happen again.

The Lisbon of his generation had already become the "eighth marvel" of the world. Built on the north bank of the most beautiful river in Europe, the city had a population of a hundred thousand "souls" of whom ten thousand were slaves, mostly Guinea blacks. In 1552 the size, wealth, and civilization of Lisbon were beyond compare. The king had moved from the ancient royal residence high above the city on Castle Hill to the new riverside palace overlooking the Yard on the east and a stone's throw from the merchant ships lying at anchor, warehouses, and shipyards that King Manuel the Fortunate had built for his comfort and filled with treasures from the far corners of the globe. The sovereign no longer went about Lisbon on foot or on horseback escorted by a rhinoceros and elephants to clear the way for his entourage, but the streets, reflecting the ever-widening dimensions of the overseas experience, were more alive than ever. There were merchants and sailors, hawkers and craftsmen, money-changers and usurers, slave women hauling water from the public fountains, emptying chamber pots in the river in the daily offering to the goddess Cloacina, carrying cargoes of merchandise and produce. The variety of humanity was endless—men from the Holy House of Mercy on their rounds to pick up the dead for burial, noblemen on horseback or in sedan chairs, friars and clerics on errands of mercy, missionaries assembling for debarkation, pimps and prostitutes flaunting their wares, foreigners from the northern rim of Europe, starry-eyed converts from distant pagan lands, frightened aborigines from Brazil, cautious Indians from Malabar, visitors from China and Japan, Jews, and the occasional Moor—a parade of mankind, intense and kaleidoscopic, unique in Europe.

Every year between 1,500 and 3,000 ships entered the port of Lisbon, the best "on all the coast of the known sea."[1] So many ships unloaded at dockside or anchored in the river facing the Palace Yard that the bay was described in 1608 as a forest of great trees. There were more ships in Lisbon than in all the ports of Italy put together, and it was common to see between 150 and 200 come in with the tide.

What a cornucopia of plenty was disgorged from their holds—the rich products of China, the aromatic herbs of the Spice Islands and Ceylon, the precious stones of India, amber from shores everywhere, the ivory of Angola and ebony of Mozambique, the sugar of Brazil, the textiles of Flanders, the woolens of England, the glass of Venice, the gold tissues of Milan, the silks of Naples and Sicily, the fine boxes of Florence. Everything of value found its way to the Rua Nova dos Mercadores, the Street of the Merchants, a paved thoroughfare twenty-four feet wide and lined with solid walls of buildings five and six stories high—the skyscrapers of the sixteenth century—that extended from the government houses on the east to the vicinity of the Palace Yard on the west. It was the grandest shopping center of Europe, the most bountiful and exotic, and it lives still in illuminated form in King Manuel's famous Book of Hours.

The reputation that Gouveia enjoys as a Renaissance adventurer and rascal goes back very far, but the fuller picture of this remarkable man has been painted by historians of the twentieth century. Chroniclers of colonial Brazil refer to him fleetingly and with disgust. José de Anchieta called him necromantic, Fernão Cardim a magician, Vicente do Salvador the Padre do Ouro or Gold Priest, but expressions of feelings are hardly enough. Had it not been for the publication in 1905 of his dossier from the files of the Lisbon Inquisition, he would have been forgotten. The papers of the Holy Office enable us to bring him back to life; and they reveal a side of the operations of the dread tribunal that has been generally ignored and a slice of life in the heyday of the Age of Expansion that is crying to be told.

Born in 1528 to a family of Old Christians in Terceira, António de Gouveia went to Lisbon at about twenty years of age. There within two years he was made a subdeacon and a deacon and then ordained to the holy priesthood in the chapel of Saint Anne, celebrating his first mass in Gestosa, his father's birthplace near Santa Comba Dão. When and where had he prepared himself for the clerical state? There was no seminary in the Azores, but it is likely that he had been tutored in theology by the local bishop or by qualified priests from the diocese.

In 1557 he said under oath that he had studied Latin and rhetoric at the University of Coimbra, but did not specify the year. It must have been before he sailed for Italy in 1553 to further his education, in theology and medicine in Rome, in theology in Siena. During his Italian sojourn he visited Piedmont and perhaps Savoy and, contrary to canon law, served a stint as a mercenary soldier.

It was apparently on the return voyage from Italy to Portugal that he was shipwrecked near Barcelona. Having lost his belongings in the disaster, he turned to medicine as a means of earning his passage home, though this too was a forbidden profession for priests under the law of the Church. En route from Tarrega to Cervera, he sought out a gentleman who had been suffering from a persistent cough. Gouveia's familiarity with medicinal herbs and his need for money led him to the bedside of the sick man, and the grateful *hidalgo* was as good as new in two months. Gouveia was then asked to cure a woman from the neighborhood but declined. He said that she would soon die (as indeed she did), and nothing would save her. In Valladolid a man told him the secret of a medical sphere that could be used as a purgative. In Extremadura, not far from the Portuguese border, he raised a countess from her sick bed, leaving her with a misshapen name for the record but in good health. In Castile he ran into the apocryphal *Clavicola Salamonis* and the Art of Solomon or treatise on alchemy that circulated as part of the larger work and copied both. For his knowledge of pharmaceutical botany and mineralogy, which contemporaries greatly admired, he relied on Saint Alberto Magnus' medieval encyclopedia of the natural world, *De secretis mulierum et de animalibus, herbis, lapidibus et mineralibus,* passages from which he also transcribed.

Gouveia's first encounter with the Inquisition was in Valladolid during this journey across Spain, but the details of his arrest are not known. Was he accused of superstition, of having made a pact with the Devil, of practicing the proscribed art of medicine? In the absence of Castilian documentation, we must rely on his own later testimony. He confessed that the inquisitors had frowned on a priest who wore clothing plaited with gold under the habit of an heretical mendicant Beguin. (Was he collecting alms by means of this subterfuge?) He had the power, he once boasted, of making people lose their heads. In Castile he had obliged a woman to spend three days in a courtyard, all the while yelling for him. He had once made himself invisible long enough to steal delicacies with impunity from the table of a Castilian gentleman. He had also had a sphere that when placed on the body cured the affected part, but the Inquisition had relieved him of his magical object. These were charges enough to justify his appearance before the inquisitors of Valladolid, but we are without the specifics of his arraignment and interrogation.

When he appealed the sentence (again the particulars are lacking) the inquisitors not only stuck to their guns but also fired new volleys. They had found in his possession a handwritten copy of the Albertus Magnus work and a magic ring with the likenesses of two human faces, one male and one female, and a secret inscription. Ultimately the guardians of orthodoxy and morality must have decided that the case against him was not good enough to justify a harsh sentence, and they released him on bail. By now Gouveia was again out of money and must have felt that the better part of valor was to put himself beyond the reach of the Castilians. He escaped to the safety of Portugal.

Once back home, he applied for membership in the new Society of Jesus, whose glories were those of the empire. In 1549 Saint Francis Xavier had reached Japan, and Manuel da Nóbrega had planted a mission in Brazil. In 1555 the Jesuits were put in charge of the Arts College at Coimbra, and in 1559 Cardinal Prince Henry founded the University of Évora for them. Did the Jesuits realize who this mature applicant was and what he had been up to, or were they taken by his lively mind and fascinating credentials? They knew about his interest in alchemy, for they burned his papers on that fradulent science, but this did not stand in the way of his admission. He was received into the order in December 1555 and took the first three vows in the course of a year. Then in December 1556, without waiting for a required canonical separation, António de Gouveia walked out of the Jesuit residence, presumably the Professed House of São Roque in Lisbon, never to return. Nobody knows why the Jesuit experience did not please him. Months later he declared that by this peremptory act he had automatically been excommunicated, but he had done nothing in the meantime to regularize his situation.

The man who had turned his back on the Jesuits found a room in a lodging house near São Roque and stayed there for a few weeks before moving into the noble household of Dona Isabel de Albuquerque, a sister of Martim Afonso de Sousa, donatary of the Captaincy of São Vicente in southern Brazil and ninth governor of India. We do not know what brought António de Gouveia to the attention of the eminent Dona Isabel. He could hardly have been her chaplain because in this capacity he would have celebrated Mass regularly. However, Father Gouveia said Mass in her oratory only three times in all the months that he lived under her roof. Perhaps he entered the lady's circle as a healer. At any rate he prepared ointments for her and nursed her during her *acidentes*, possibly fits of epilepsy.

Father António might have led his merry and carefree life indefinitely had Bastião Luís, a groom of the queen's chamber, not denounced him to the Inquisition of Lisbon on May 4, 1557. On the basis of this and other testimony, the inquisitors ordered his arrest on charges of superstition, divination, witchcraft, and commerce with the Devil, and placed him behind bars on May 9 to await the judgment of the court—a judgment that was inexplicably postponed for four years.

What had brought him to this pass? There is no suggestion that the Castilian Inquisition had alerted the Lisbon confrères, or that the Jesuits of São Roque had anything to do with his disgrace. Their provincial told the Inquisition during the trial that he was aware of nothing that could involve Gouveia with the Holy Office. A woman from Castile had written to say that he was a person who could not be trusted; and she declared that she did not like his jests and mockery. But these were insufficient grounds to keep a man locked up in jail.

The queen's groom deposed that he had known Gouveia since his return from Spain in 1555. What had disturbed him were the wild stories Gouveia told—that he had learned from Saint Albertus Magnus' famous book how to make himself invisible with the oil of rosemary, a bay leaf, and pebbles; that unseen he had once entered a dwelling in Boa Vista, found two sleeping maidens, blown out the lamp, flung aside the bedclothes, and prepared to enjoy them when an old woman in the room heard the disturbance and put an end to it; that in the presence of witnesses he had once told Mateus de Aguiar, who made pastilles and incense cones for the royal family, that the province of God was spiritual and the province of the Devil corporal and temporal—without adding that God could also give life or death and poverty as well as wealth; that he had done strange things that appeared to be the work of the Devil in Castile; that the magic sphere taken from him by the inquisitors could cure acute constipation simply by being placed on the buttocks; and that in Lisbon he had foretold Dona Isabel's illness by gazing at the stars.

Once while walking with Father Gouveia in Lisbon, Luís reported, they had run into Manuel de Melo, the chief huntsman of the realm. The priest had observed that Melo was a lost man. On another occasion the priest had called on Luís and met his niece. Later the priest told him that if his niece married, her husband would kill her, that she would become a whore if she did not marry, and that in any case she would be violated at home in eighteen months.

Joana Gonçalves, the queen's apothecary and confectioner, testified that she had seen Gouveia four or five times when he was called to the palace to treat a slave woman and had heard it said that he was an alchemist and astrologer. She once asked him to examine her daughter, who suffered from a catarrh that blocked her nasal passages and obliged her to breathe through the mouth. He assured her that the disease was of no consequence, only "a little humor that came from the head."[2] The mother had confided to the priest that she was apprehensive about arranging a marriage for her daughter and had been reassured that the girl would be married before the feast of Saint John the Evangelist.

Dr. Leonardo Nunes, the chief physician of the realm, told the inquisitor that he too knew António de Gouveia and that the priest was familiar not only with herbs that had proved effective in diseases of the eye and phthisis but also with a sphere that served marvelously as a purgative when placed on the hind parts. He had confided to Dr. Nunes that with the philosophers' stone, the fifth essence, and the juice and powder of herbs, he could transmute silver into gold. The chief physician was impressed with a distillation of gold that Gouveia had made and acknowledged that he knew something about medicinal herbs and their use, but for the rest he thought him a "lightweight with little ballast," a magician and buffoon, a man guilty of actions unbecoming to the clerical state. He was also a liar, but the doctor had never heard him say anything contrary to the faith or that could be of concern to the Inquisition.

Gouveia's magic was brought out by others. Dona Isabel's friend, the widow Violante de Sá, understood that the priest could confuse people with the root of cuckow-pintle, had an ointment that when rubbed on the umbilicus made love-making delicious, and could become invisible with pebbles from the gizzards of swallows. Pero Lopes de Sousa, Martim Afonso's son, had asked to be made invisible so that he might enter unseen the bedchamber of his maid, but Gouveia had refused to be a party to it. He had assured Violante that he could make a religious leave his cloister by changing his character and offered for a price to use his powers to make Dona Isabel's nephew abandon the Dominican convent. Astrology, he said, had disclosed her thoughts to him, and he promised that with its help he could get her any husband she wished. By means of moonwort, an herb that shone for two hours after midnight, he could pick locks. Of course he had recourse to the Devil, but what he did he did naturally, without the need of demoniacal intervention. He had predicted the deaths of various famous persons (apparently without success) and bragged that he was in command of supernatural forces that could bend any magistrate to his will. Finally, the widow reported that during the fortnight she had stayed with Dona Isabel, the priest Gouveia had never opened a prayer book.

At his hearing, Gouveia insisted that he went to confession every year and received holy communion but declared that he had not made good confessions lately because of his inability to overcome a certain sin. He admitted dereliction in reading the Canonical Hours and accused himself of having celebrated Mass without reciting them beforehand. When he repeated the prayers of the Church in Latin and in Portuguese for the inquisitor, his Latin was found to have been very good. He admitted to knowing astrology, though only as an autodidact, but insisted that he was ignorant of necromancy and chiromancy or any science that involved the help of the devil. (A few days later he revealed that he had heard the voice of the devil several times, and that the devil had directed his cures, separated the waters of the sea to lead him to a cache of money on the ocean floor, and offered to make him invisible in return for his soul.) He denied that he had a pact with the devil and that he foretold events with devilish powers. His liquifying of gold was not the work of the devil but of man. The recipe was simple: crush gold with honey in a mortar, add ardent spirits and Celidonia water. The concoction cured phlegm and headaches.

A servant of Dona Isabel's household reported that he had said Mass five or six times while he lived there, that he had gone to confession in times of illness only, and that twice priests had gone to the house to administer the sacrament of penance to him. When women of the house wondered why he never fasted during Lent, he replied that the many penitential acts he had practiced in Rome were enough to cover him now. On some Fridays he never went to bed at all but slept fully clothed on an *estrado*, a low platform covered with rugs that was common to the domestic arrangements of the day.

The Inquisition, concerned about Gouveia's interest in soothsaying, alchemy, and the other magical arts, heard Pero Lopes de Sousa depose that he had found Gouveia familiar with astrology and able to draw horoscopes. He had foretold the number of children that Pero Lopes would have, when death would overcome him, his parents, and his aunts; and he had advised Pero Lopes' sister not to go ahead with her wedding plans. A member of Dona Isabel's domestic staff reported that Gouveia had said he would not leave Lisbon until he had transmuted silver into gold, and that he had set up firegrates for that purpose in one of the rooms of the house. The servant also spoke of periodic (apparently epileptic) seizures and had once seen him lying on his bed, eyes closed, mouth foaming, racked with tremors, and held down by force. Another witness testified that indeed he suffered from *acidentes* or fits, but that he recovered quickly. The priest had told him that the way to test a wife's fidelity was to put a diamond ring under her bed pillow and the way to make a man tell what he had done during the day was to apply the ground head of a frog and heart of a dove to his body while he slept.

Coming back to depose once more, the queen's groom of the chamber revealed wild and fanciful things that Gouveia had said: that nobody knew how to govern Portugal; that everything had gone wrong; that all was lost; that António Pinheiro, the chief chronicler of the realm, had not put things in context; that the theologian, philosopher, herbalist, and astrologer António de Gouveia would be called upon to rule the country; that he had power over the king's health, that King Sebastian (then three years of age) would become ill at eleven; and that if he recovered, he would be king of Fez at fourteen.

Although nothing of great moment had been brought to light by these witnesses, António de Gouveia was kept in jail for four years before his case was settled. He was finally found guilty of scandalous acts against the Faith, of practicing medicine without qualifications, of being a victim of his own imagination, of commerce with the Devil, of failure to say the Canonical Hours during a period of three months, of celebrating Holy Mass in the state of mortal sin, and of not abstaining in Lent without need or permission. At the next auto-de-fé he was to present himself with head uncovered, candle in hand, and publicly abjure his heresy. He was suspended from holy orders, perpetually prohibited from practicing medicine, and condemned to the prison of the College of the Doctrine of the Faith, where he would be instructed in the means of salvation.

In 1564, several years after his arrest, the warden of the college reported that the prisoner had escaped during the night. He had gone through a broken railing and climbed over the roof of the veranda to the street. The search began at once and was soon over. Gouveia had a quick change of heart, decided to turn himself in, and threw himself on the mercy of the court. The errant priest explained that he had been led to believe by the warden that he would soon be banished from Portugal, possibly to Seville. For fear of capture by Barbary pirates on the voyage to Andalusia, he had decided to escape and go by land instead. From the college he had gone to see Rui Fernandes, a guard at India House who had supplied him with food during his internment. (The prisoners had to feed themselves.) He had told Fernandes that he had been in prison for seven years, long enough to expiate his sins, and now wanted to be taken to the grand inquisitor himself. Outfitted with other clothes, he had moved in with a fellow Azorean priest while a New Christian friend sought to put his case before the ecclesiastical authorities. The bishop of Miranda agreed to apprise the queen of Gouveia's predicament; the queen told the bishop to let the cardinal know; the cardinal told the bishop to let the inquisitors know; and after a few days Gouveia was arrested once more. Again the inquisitors had no mercy and sentenced him to the galleys for an indefinite period.

The punishment was beyond endurance. After months of forced labor, the repentant Gouveia begged to be freed from "the most pestiferous commerce of men." To remain with it would surely endanger his immortal soul. He had suffered the pains of hell in that outrageous service. He had had to man a battery of guns on a warship sent in hot pursuit of two enemy galleys. A frightful sunburn on the right arm had been so badly treated that he feared it might turn to leprosy. His general health was bad. His new duties left him so weak that he could hardly stand on his feet. At night he slept on a board. The matter was again brought to the attention of the cardinal, who took pity on Gouveia and ordered him released from the galleys, sentenced him to leave the country within thirty days, and prohibited him from returning to Portugal without permission.

Gouveia did not wait for the Cardinal's decision. Seeing himself "in the danger of desperation," he made his escape from the galleys and fled far from the Inquisition's vigilant eye, to Italy, France, and Germany. He found northern Europe burning with heresy. In France his sojourn coincided with the beginnings of the religious wars. It was too much to bear. Returning to the theological security of Lisbon, he again threw himself at the mercy of the Inquisition, begged forgiveness "by the virginity of the Most Blessed Mary" for his notorious faults, and asked for his canonical reinstatement as a priest. In return for these favors, he promised to leave for his native Terceira where "if he should fall, the fire of the good Jesus being unable to consume him, the shame of his fellow-Terceirans and the fear of justice will." Gouveia's contrite words melted the hearts of the inquisitors, anxious as they were to free themselves from the importunities of a priest who was a scandal to the clerical state, and in granting him what he had asked for they admonished him "to reform his conscience and mend his life in every way, practicing all the acts of a good and Catholic Christian, serving as an example of what was expected of him by virtue of the habit that he wore." The sentence was published by the Holy Office on December 5, 1566. After a decade in and out of Inquisition jails, António de Gouveia was free again.

Punishment, alas, was no balm for his deviousness. While waiting for a ship to the Azores, he took off for the Alentejo. At Aljustrel he became involved in a mining project and remained there for months, returning to Lisbon only for secret visits. The inquisitors eventually got wind of what he was up to and had him apprehended. This time he told them disarmingly that he had not gone to Terceira because God had not willed it, and that he did not ask forgiveness because he had done nothing wrong. If he had sinned, the matter was for the confessional, not the Holy Office. In October 1567 the inquisitors found him guilty of disobedience and ordered him deported to Brazil for two years. On the day of the sentencing the bailiff of the Holy Office took António de Gouveia in fetters to the waterfront and turned him over to the master of the ship *São Mateus*. There would now be no escape. With an ocean between them, the inquisitors must have thought that they were rid of the persistent Father Gouveia. Little did they know that the indestructible priest was embarking on the sorriest chapter of his adventurous life and would return to plague them.

If the ship sailed soon after he was put on board, Gouveia must have arrived in Brazil in time for Christmas. He had never been to the tropics before and had only a secondhand idea of what awaited him. But he must have had a good picture of the new land from the family and friends of Dona Isabel de Albuquerque, in whose household he had lived and who was none other than the sister of Martim Afonso de Sousa and Pero Lopes de Sousa the Elder, both among the original lord proprietors or donataries of Brazilian captaincies and both with extensive pioneer experience in Brazil. She was also the aunt of Pero Lopes de Sousa the Younger, Martim Afonso's son, who knew Gouveia, and the first cousin of Tomé de Sousa, the first governor-general of Brazil. It is not likely that he had met Duarte Coelho, the first donatary of Pernambuco, who died in Lisbon in 1554, but it seems probable, granted the restricted size of the establishment in those simpler days, that he was acquainted with old Duarte's two sons, Duarte and Jorge, who were in Lisbon to further their education from 1554 to 1560.

The thirty-nine-year-old priest, worldly beyond his age, who had frequented the grandest courts of Europe and lived in Lisbon on the periphery of the privileged class, arrived in Salvador, the City of the Saviour on the Bay of All Saints, when the only city of Portuguese America was still in swaddling clothes. It had been founded a scant eighteen years before, in 1549, with a hopeful designation as the capital of the crown captaincy of Bahia and State of Brazil but was still little more than a small town. Thirty-five years after its founding, Salvador and its environs would have a population of no more than three thousand Portuguese, eight thousand Christianized Indians, and three or four thousand Guinea slaves. Gouveia landed during the administration of the third governor-general, Mem de Sá (1557–72), the resolute man who had expelled the French from Guanabara Bay and created Rio de Janeiro. Brazil was still no more than a series of such pockets of settlement along the coast, but European colonization had nonetheless begun to take root. There were already eighteen sugar mills in the Captaincy of Bahia in 1570, which produced the luxury commodity avidly consumed in Europe and brought singular prosperity to their owners.

The Jesuit school, called the College of the Children of Jesus, was founded in 1550, only months after the arrival of the first apostles (as the fathers of the new order were called) in 1549, and canonically instituted as the College of Jesus in 1556, but it had not yet attained the excellence that would later characterize it. The Jesuits were exceptional men, and so in another sense were the secular clergy of Brazil: one group practiced virtue, the other license. António de Gouveia was to join the ranks of the wicked. The diocese of Bahia had been erected by Pope Julius III in 1550 in an effort to impose discipline on this uneven clergy. The first bishop, returning to Portugal in 1556, was shipwrecked on the coast of Brazil and ignominiously devoured by cannibals. His successor, Dom Pedro Leitão (1559–75) was in peaceful possession of the see when Father António reached Bahia.

Gouveia probably landed in Salvador without the shackles that he embarked with. Banishment was not, after all, a period of incarceration in another place but intended to be a humane substitute for capital punishment. King John II (1481–95) had believed that the supreme penalty should be imposed only in "ugly" cases. A man "costs so much to raise, and it was a pity to destroy men when uninhabited islands were crying for settlers."[3] Once a deportee reached his assigned destination, he was at liberty to lead a normal life.

Because of his banishment, Gouveia could hardly have expected a warm welcome from the governor-general of Bahia. Mem de Sá was opposed to *degrêdo* as punishment for crimes committed in Europe. "Your Highness should remember," he wrote to the queen regent in 1560, "that you are colonizing this land with deportees, malefactors who mostly deserve the death penalty and whose only calling is to warp evil."[4] The bishop, however, seems to have had no such reservations and certainly none in Gouveia's case. He knew that the deported priest's faculties had been suspended by the Lisbon Inquisition—in the absence of a Tribunal of the Holy Office in Brazil he had the authority of the Lisbon office in his diocese—but they could be restored by letters dimissorial. He asked Lisbon for them, and while awaiting word, authorized Gouveia to preach, celebrate Mass, and administer the sacraments. The vineyard was enormous and priests were few and far between, and it may be that like so many others the bishop was simply taken by Gouveia's attractive personality. To allay suspicion of canonical irregularity, he instructed Gouveia to protect the prelate's reputation by saying publicly that he had dimissorials from the Pope.

An early Jesuit chronicler referred to the Bahia that Gouveia knew as loose, remiss, and melancholy. A short time after his arrival, Gouveia pulled up stakes and left for Olinda, one hundred leagues to the north, but certainly not because the seat of government of Pernambuco was less sinful. The advantages that Pernambuco had over Bahia were geographic, political, social, and economic.

The Olinda that Duarte Coelho, the first donatary, founded in 1535 had grown substantially in fifty years to seven hundred *vizinhos* within the town itself and an additional thirteen hundred in the surrounding countryside, not counting Indians and between four and five thousand slaves.

The captaincy was populous enough to put in battle readiness a militia of three thousand men, including four hundred horsemen.

Chroniclers waxed eloquent over the excellence of Pernambuco. It was almost a Paradise of human life, a province suited for a kingdom, a land of eternal spring free from cruel diseases. Its fertile soil, crossed by rivers that flowed to the sea, produced an abuandance of sugarcane. There were five sugar mills in the captaincy by 1550; by 1584, there were sixty-six (out of a total of 120 for Brazil as a whole). It took forty or more vessels to move the harvest to market each year.

The civility of the captaincy was proverbial. Families gave great banquets on their estates and slept under rich India quilts in beds covered with crimson damask fringed with gold. When the first cane was crushed, the plantation chaplain customarily blessed the operation and the owners celebrated the auspicious occasion by giving a splendid party for their friends. Vanity was the great sin of Pernambuco, even more than in Lisbon. Some men had fortunes of from forty to eighty thousand cruzados and naturally could afford to dress their wives and children in velvets, damasks, and silks.

Pernambuco was also described as the most flourishing, fertile, and opulent land of Brazil. Its climate was deliciously mild, its territory another promised land. The dyewood from its vast forests was famous for its quality, and seven valuable dyes were extracted from it. Its people, polity, nobility, luxury, commerce, buildings, and wealth were unparalleled in all America; its delights were proper to the paradise of the New World.

When Gouveia landed in Pernambuco, the captaincy had not yet fully recovered from the devastation inflicted by the Caeté Indians. During the lifetime of the first donatary, after a terrible initial struggle, the aborigines were kept under control, but when he died in 1544 they rebelled against the Portuguese, led by French soldiers of fortune. Matters came to a head following the shipwreck of the first bishop of Bahia in 1556, when the cannibalistic Caetés ate the hapless prelate. The Crown's revenge was to sentence the Caetés to perpetual slavery in 1557, but the Caetés were more than a match for the settlers. The situation became so desperate that the second governor-general of Brazil was readying himself to succor the beleaguered Pernambucans.

Because of the massive threat to the very existence of the captaincy, old Duarte Coelho's two sons, Duarte Coelho de Albuquerque, the second donatary, and his brother Jorge de Albuquerque Coelho, the third donatary, interrrupted their education in Lisbon at the command of the queen regent to return to Pernambuco (where they had both been born) in 1560 to restore order. Duarte was then twenty-three years of age, Jorge twenty-one. On their arrival in Olinda the new donatary received the government from his mother, took counsel with the leaders of the community, including the Jesuits, and appointed his brother Jorge to destroy the Caetés and bring peace to the captaincy. The moment was indeed grave. By 1560, when the operations against them began in earnest, the Indians had restricted the Portuguese of Olinda to a ribbon of safety two leagues wide. Along the coast the harassment was even more severe.

The relentless war waged by Jorge de Albuquerque Coelho lasted for five years, until 1565, on the eve almost of António de Gouveia's appearance in Olinda. As a result of the hard campaigns, young Jorge had managed to clear an area that extended fifteen leagues inland. The whole coast from the São Francisco to the Iguaraçu Rivers was also safe for the Portuguese. Meanwhile, Duarte the Younger was unexpectedly forced to defend himself from the enemy, this time from threatening European heretics. The military engagement of 1561 against the French Calvinists, forced to abandon Rio de Janeiro by the governor-general in 1560, drove them forever from Recife, the seaport of Olinda that was then no more than a wretched settlement of fishermen and seamen.

As Gouveia was leaving for Pernambuco, the bishop informed his vicar-general there of the conditions under which the priest's faculties had been restored. The vicar-general broke the confidence by relaying the news to Father Rodrigo de Freitas, rector of the New Jesuit College of Olinda, and the rector, probably aware that Gouveia had briefly been a member of the Society of Jesus, wrote to Bahia about him. Gouveia, for his part, lost no time in provoking the Jesuits of

Olinda. In August 1569, Bishop Leitão advised him that he had received complaints about his preaching and had been asked to remove him. The bishop wondered whether or not he had received word from Portugal. He urged him to pressure the authorities in Portugal to pay his salary. This was a matter of honor because he would otherwise be unable to discharge his debts. He also alerted Gouveia to his need for slaves and announced the sending of a domestic to acquire some.

The cordiality of the bishop's letter indicates that Dom Pedro was not fully cognizant of what had in the meantime taken place in Pernambuco. As a matter of fact, because of his squabble with the Jesuits, Gouveia would soon be charged with departures from "our Holy Catholic Faith" and with being a "bad Christian." When Father Amaro Gonçalves arrived to join the staff of the Jesuit College of Olinda in 1568, Gouveia accused him of heresy. It was not difficult to incriminate the Jesuits because they were known as defenders of the Indians against the settlers who were bent on destroying and enslaving them, and Gouveia's powers of persuasion won the principal people of the captaincy to his side and caused the Jesuits enormous embarrassment. This was eventually his undoing. The voice of Luís da Grã, the most influential Jesuit of sixteenth-century Pernambuco, was raised to defend the orthodoxy of his colleagues, and after a while the uproar died down. By that time Grã had been instrumental in getting the bishop to remove Gouveia from the scene and pack him off to Lisbon.

António de Gouveia had in the meantime become popularly known in Bahia and Pernambuco as the Gold Priest, because of his supposed knowledge of mining. His talents attracted the attention of young Duarte Coelho de Albuquerque, and they became friends. In partnership with the donatary, Gouveia headed expeditions to the backlands of Pernambuco to search for gold and silver and capture Indians for the profitable slave markets of Brazil. (By law, only the donatary could enslave Indians.) The Franciscan chronicler Friar Vicente do Salvador speaks of one such expedition, carried out by order of the donatary and made up of thirty white men and two hundred Indians. On arrival at any backland native village, large or small, Gouveia customarily overcame the people by his magical prowess. He would pick the feathers from a cockerel or the leaves from a bough and throw them in the air. Each feather or leaf would bring a black devil out of hell spewing bolts of fire. Filled with understandable terror, the Indians purportedly gave themselves up to the whites without a struggle and were easily tied up and shipped to market.

Duarte's uncle and brother both upbraided the donatary for permitting "so great a tyranny," but even after Gouveia had destroyed the Viatā nation he refused to put a stop to it. Friar Vicente suggests that he may indeed have profited from the nefarious business or been bewitched by the rascally priest.

On raiding parties, according to another source, Gouveia took sacred vessels and paraments of suspected heretical English origin. He was later accused of having celebrated Mass many times in deserted fields among the Indians that he fought, transforming the bread and wine into the body and blood of Our Lord under circumstances of danger and among infidels, in contravention of the sacred canons of the Council of Trent. He would attack Indians even on the day that he celebrated Mass, killing and capturing them, and taking their wives and belongings. Those who survived his brutality were branded on the face and put in chains.

His moral behavior was notoriously reprehensible. When welcomed by the principal people of friendly Indian villages, he would have the temerity to shackle his hosts and whip and beat them. Sometimes he would apply the whip to them himself. Once the Indians were in his power he would baptize them indiscriminately, without asking their permission as the canons required. Other Indians, when illicitly captured, regained their freedom by order of the governor. These hapless people were so superficially Christianized that when they returned to their own kind they abandoned altogether the precepts of the Catholic religion.

There were other examples of his violent disposition. One time in the backlands he took a fancy to a free Indian woman who accompanied Cristóvão Coelho, one of his own men, and forcibly possessed her. Later, when the woman escaped from Coelho's custody, he arrested the man, struck and kicked him, put him in irons, and tortured him with ropes drawn tightly across the brawn of the arms, hoping thereby to learn the whereabouts of the woman. On another occasion he challenged a Portuguese settler to a duel (though priests were prohibited from dueling) but was prevented from carrying out his threat because the man, out of respect for canon law, refused. The following day Gouveia said Mass some seventy or eighty leagues from the nearest Christian settlement without having "reconciled" himself with the adversary. In the course of the doctrinal homily he declared that he was under no obligation to reconcile himself with anybody.

In Pernambuco, as in Portugal, the controversial cleric bragged that he could talk with devils and understood them. He paraded his powers of divination. He scandalized the gentry by saying that it was better for Christians to be eaten by cannibals than buried and consumed by vermin. Granted the moral temptations of a pioneer community, still without firm structures to defend itself against the depravity of people, we may wonder whether or not Gouveia's life in Pernambuco took a turn for the worse because of his conflict with the Jesuits or because of some flaw of character that impelled him to evil. When the bishop of Salvador was apprised by Father Grã and the vicar-general of Pernambuco of Gouveia's outrageous behavior, he ordered the man arrested and returned to Portugal in April 1571.

As the bishop's representative, Father Manuel Fernandes Cortiçado appeared before a surprised judge in Olinda to ask that Father António de Gouveia be apprehended in the name of the Lisbon Inquisition. Gouveia protested vehemently. He insisted on seeing the bishop's order, refused to recognize Cortiçado's authority, and said that those who had accused him of heresy, Judaism, and the desecration of the blessed sacrament in Lisbon were either dead or gone. He was nonetheless arrested, shackled (because the jailhouse was not secure), and taken off to prison. The news of Gouveia's fall from favor spread like wildfire in Pernambuco and aroused the donatary's anger. The day following these events Duarte Coelho de Albuquerque met Father Cortiçado at the door of the principal church of Olinda and told him in a peremptory manner to return to his parish in Itamaracá as soon as the Gouveia business was over. Yet Coelho and the other friends of Gouveia were powerless to do anything more.

Cortiçado informed the Lisbon inquisitors of his actions in May 1571. He had had trouble, he wrote, in carrying out the bishop's order of arrest because the leading people of Pernambuco were on Gouveia's side. He reminded the Holy Office that Brazil "is a new land and does not need men of education." On his side of the Atlantic nobody paid attention to the Inquisition, and it was difficult to get information from people who had no fear of the Holy Office.

On May 4, António de Gouveia was formally handed over to the master of the ship *São João* that would take him to Lisbon, along with a sealed packet of legal documents for the Inquisition. The case of the Gold Priest and the controversies that it aroused were not put to rest so neatly. King Sebastian, not pleased with Duarte Coelho de Albuquerque's role in the Gouveia affair, ordered him back to Lisbon as well. Sailing from Pernambuco in 1572, the governor ended his days far from home, in Morocco—a victim of the ill-fated battle of Alcácer-Quibir of 1578, which was to cost Sebastian his life and the kingdom of Portugal its independence.

Gouveia, meanwhile, languished in a Lisbon jail without word from the judges. The promoter of justice of the Inquisition reviewed the record carefully and found no grounds for a guilty verdict. He approached the cardinal, thinking that his highness might have made up his mind, but the grand inquisitor was not to be involved. He told the promoter to let Gouveia stay where he was, hopeful that the law and justice would take their inevitable course. Gouveia later petitioned the Inquisition for his release on the grounds that he had been detained without cause. He considered himself a good Christian who had achieved notable things for God and king in Brazil. He had of course celebrated Mass five or six times in the backlands of Pernambuco, but within canonical prescriptions. He had always placed his wooden altar in an enclosed area behind a palisade. When the bishop prohibited him from saying Mass under these conditions, he obeyed. He had not gone to confession on his forays because no priest accompanied him; there was nobody to confess to. Besides, he had not been aware of being in a state of mortal sin.

Having made sure that Gouveia had actually been ordained and was not an imposter, the inquisitors interrogated him about his state of life in February 1573 without uncovering any irregularities. The evidence against Father António was not incriminatory enough for a tribunal of faith, but even so the case against him was not dismissed and his detention continued.

António de Gouveia surfaced once more on January 10, 1575, when a fellow prisoner reported that the priest hoped to go to Venice. What an optimist Gouveia must have been, in the face of overwhelming adversity, to entertain the thought of liberation! On December 30, Gouveia did ask the inquisitors to make up their minds about him so that he could prove his innocence, but to no avail. His latest incarceration had already lasted three years and three months.

On this plaintive note, António de Gouveia passes out of history. His most critical biographer, the eminent Serafim Leite, calls him a cleric who "lived an inconsistent and adventurous life. He tried his hand at a number of vocations in superficial ways that were foreign to moral principles." What Leite does not tell us is that Gouveia was not a man broken on the rack or bent to the wheel, forced to conform to customs and values alien to his way of being. He managed very well on his wits, and he spent a life, however punctured by mishap, that tells dramatically how broad the parameters were of thinking and feeling during the period of transition between the looser humanism of the early sixteenth century and the stricter ethic of Tridentine renewal.

Notes

1. João Brandão, *Tratado da majestade, grandeza e abastança da cidade de Lisboa na 2ª metade do século XVI (Estatística de Lisboa de 1552)*, ed. Anselmo Braamcamp Freire e Gomes de Brito (Lisboa, 1923), p. 99.
   2. Unless otherwise indicated, all direct quotations in this essay are taken from Pedro d'Azevedo, "António de Gouveia, alchimista do século XVI," *Archivo Histórico Portuguez* 3 (1905): 179–208, 274–86, on which see "Sources" below.
   3. Garcia de Resende, *Chorónica qve tractra da vida e grandíssimas virtudes, e bandades, magnánimo esforço, excellentes costumes, e manhas, e claros feytos do Christianíssimo Dom João Segundo deste nome . . .* 2d ed. (Lisboa, 1596).
   4. *Annaes da Biblioteca Nacional do Rio de Janeiro* 27 (1906), p. 229.

Sources

The indispensable work on the life of António de Gouveia is Pedro A. d'Azevedo, "António de Gouveia, alchimista do seculo XVI," *Archivo Historico Portuguez* (Lisboa), 3 (1905): 179–208, 274–86. An account of the man's life is followed by the transcription of his dossier from the files of the Inquisition in the Arquivo Nacional da Torre do Tombo of Lisbon. The most critical treatment of the Brazilian phase of Gouveia's career is by Serafim Leite, *História da Companhia de Jesus no Brasil*, vol. 1 (Lisbon-Rio de Janeiro, 1938), pp. 461, 480–84. Leite's is also the best bibliography.

Two chronicles of the sixteenth century provide word pictures of Pernambuco only a few years after Gouveia's residence there: Fernão Cardim, "Informação da missão do p. Christovão de Gouvêa ás partes do Brasil anno de 83, ou narrativa epistolar de uma viagem e missão jesuitica . . . desde o anno de 1583 ao de 1590," in the larger work published under the same author's name, *Tratados da terra e gente do Brasil*, ed. Baptista Caetano, Capistrano de Abreu, and Rodolfo Garcia (Rio de Janeiro, 1925); and Gabriel Soares de Sousa, *Tratado descriptivo do Brasil em 1587*, ed. Francisco Adolfo de Varnhagen, 3d ed. (São Paulo, 1938).

For the warfare against the Indians of Pernambuco, 1560–65, see Bento Teixeira Pinto, "Naufragio Que passou Jorge de Albuquerque Coelho Vindo do Brazil para este Reyno no anno de 1565," in Bernardino Gomes de Brito, *Historia tragico-maritima*, vol. 2 (Lisbon, 1736), pp. 3–59. The latest edition of this work appeared in Lisbon in 1971. The religious chroniclers of colonial Brazil have something to say about Pernambuco but almost nothing about António de Gouveia. Two may be mentioned: Simão de Vasconcelos, *Chronica da Companhia de Jesu do Estado do Brasil*, vol. 1, 3d ed. (Lisbon, 1865), pp. 99 ff.; and António de Santa Maria Jaboatão, *Orbe serafico novo brasilico*, vol. 1 (Lisbon, 1761), pp. 10–11, 87–91.

Suggestions for Further Reading

For the Lisbon that Gouveia knew, the reader is referred to the appropriate sections of Júlio de Castilho's *Lisboa Antiga*. For the years immediately before and after his time, see Júlio Dantas, "A Era Manuelina," in *História da Colonização Portuguesa do Brasil*, vol. 1 (Porto, 1921), pp. 3–25; and Fernando Castelo-Branco, *Lisboa Seiscentista*, 3d ed., (Lisbon, 1969).

Alexandre Herculano, *History of the Origin and Establishment of the Inquisition in Portugal*, trans. John C. Branner (Stanford, Calif., 1926), has become, *faute de mieux*, the standard work. It is marred by nineteenth-century moralism and a secular concept of man.

Manoel de Oliveira Lima's "A Nova Lusitânia," in *História da Colonização Portuguesa do Brasil*, vol. 3 (Porto, 1924), pp. 285–323, should be read in conjunction with his larger work, *Pernambuco seu desenvolvimento historico* (Leipzig, 1895).

Alexander Marchant, *From Barter to Slavery: The Economic Relations of Portuguese and Indians in the Settlement of Brazil, 1500–1580* (Baltimore, Md., 1942) continues to be an important survey for the period covered. The student should also not overlook the classic book by Gilberto Freyre, *The Masters and the Slaves: A Study in the Development of Brazilian Civilization*, trans. Samuel Putnam, 2d ed. (New York, 1956).

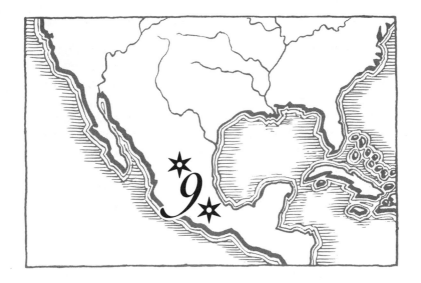

Juan de Morga
and Gertrudis de Escobar:
Rebellious Slaves

SOLANGE ALBERRO

*J*uan de Morga and Gertrudis de Escobar were young
mulatto slaves who lived in central Mexico, the
heartland of the colony of New Spain, during the
middle years of the seventeenth century. They have come out
from a forgotten past to a place where we can half see them,
thanks to a series of documents containing details of their exceptionally harsh experiences with the colonial labor system
that have been preserved in the archives of the Mexican
Inquisition. The documents reveal two indomitable personalities engaged in a struggle to survive, amid the hardships
imposed on individual human beings by two of the key sectors of the colonial economy—silver mines and sugar plantations—in both of which the labor of African slaves and their
American-born black and mulatto descendants, whether

NOTE: Translated by David G. Sweet.

slave or "free," was a crucial factor of production. They also shed an interesting light on the contradictory roles of the Holy Office of the Inquisition and other public institutions within the social order of New Spain.

The principal source for Juan de Morga's story is a heart-rending letter he wrote to the abbot of the convent of Jilotepec, just north of Mexico City, in the year 1650. In a trembling hand and with no notion of basic spelling or punctuation, Morga wrote with the urgency of one suffering from a profound anguish that he was guilty of many heinous sins and in particular that he had made a pact with the Devil. He was a blasphemer; he did not attend Mass; and what was more serious he did not believe in God and had no intention of believing in him unless he were first given absolution for his many sins. Finally, Morga warned that if the authorities were to return him to the cruel master from whom he had escaped in Zacatecas, he was determined to renounce the faith altogether. The desperate but repentant petitioner then pled with the abbot to arrange to have his case heard before the Tribunal of the Inquisition in Mexico City before it was too late, making the priest and any others who might read his letter responsible for the welfare of his soul. It was by means of tactics such as these that Juan de Morga managed to have himself transported to the capital city later that year, and at last won the chance to tell his piteous story to the awesome panel of priests who served as the official arbiters of righteousness in Spanish colonial society.

Juan had been born a slave in the city of Oaxaca in about 1627. He was the son of a European secular priest, Atanasio de Morga, by a locally born African slave woman named Petrona, who was presumably resident in the father's household. No more is known of Morga's early life, except that he seems to have had no brothers or sisters nor any other relatives except for his paternal grandmother and an uncle who was a Dominican friar; that unlike most other slaves of his day he learned to read, write, and work with figures in at least a rudimentary way; and that at the age of twenty-three he was unmarried.

In 1646 the young Juan was serving as the slave and trusted assistant of a kindly public accountant in Mexico City, one Antonio Millán, when he "misbehaved" in some way that has not come down to us. Rather than face punishment, he went boldly around to see one of his master's associates, who was a vendor of officially stamped paper, to borrow the considerable quantity of 375 pesos (approximately the full purchase price of a skilled and healthy young slave at that time) in Millán's name. Then he borrowed a horse with saddle and bridle from another man and set out across the southern mountains for Oaxaca.

Back home once more, Juan passed himself off as a freedman and entered the service of a secular priest. Then some months later his money ran out, and he resolved to try and make his way down to Guatemala. On the road just above Tehuantepec, however, the hapless fugitive was apprehended by a Dominican friar, a friend of Morga's uncle, on behalf of a fellow-priest from the nearby convent of Nexapa who was brother to Morga's owner, the Mexico City accountant, Millán! So close-knit yet far-flung was the network of leading citizens in the vast and sparsely populated territory of seventeenth-century New Spain that it was not impossible simply by transmitting the physical description of a fugitive, whether by word of mouth or through the precarious mails, to arrange for his capture in a village several hundred miles away from the capital. This series of connections also suggests the possibility that Juan de Morga's sale to Mexico City as a boy had been arranged through family channels by his father. But however that may be, the conscientious Friar Millán had Juan placed in chains and then sequestered him in his own monk's cell at Nexapa, awaiting instructions from the capital.

Two or three months later, the accountant sent word that he had decided to pardon his slave and that his brother should release Juan from his chains and escort him back to his home in Oaxaca. This was done without mishap; but just two weeks later Morga was clapped in irons once more—this time for having gone out one night to sleep with a young woman with whom he was acquainted. Shortly thereafter he was shipped back to his owner in the capital, still in chains, for a new disposition. Millán informed him that as a token of affection, and in appreciation of Juan's previous services, he would forego having him flogged for his crimes. Rather he would send him to the house of an acquaintance in Zacatecas, the principal center of silver mining in New Spain at that time, where Morga might find and have himself bought by an employer more to his liking.

Soon afterward the unrepentant Juan set out northward from the capital to make the long walk along the rutted cart trail through Querétaro and the Bajío to the great city of mines. There were several hundred black and mulatto slaves and perhaps as many freedmen in the mining district at that time, employed for the most part in the above-ground processing of silver ore rather than in the actual mining of it— because they sickened and died very easily in the cold and wet of the mines. There were a number of ways in which an enterprising slave might hope to get together the money he needed to buy his freedom or acquire a bit of property in Zacatecas. Juan must have believed that he was on the way to a land of opportunity, because if he had foreseen any part of what awaited him he would most assuredly have run away once more while the running was good.

Not long after reaching Zacatecas, still exhausted and with his feet sore and bleeding from the journey, Juan de Morga underwent the disagreeable chance encounter that sealed his fate. Walking on the street with the agent of Antonio Millán, he ran across a haughty mestizo gentleman by the name of Diego de Arratia, a small-time entrepreneur in the mining industry, who was dressed in dark and unimpressive clothing and who appeared to Juan to be the retainer of some estate owner. Arratia observed that Juan was an unusually handsome slave and offered to buy him. Juan remarked with arrogance that there were plenty of Spaniards in Zacatecas and that he would very much prefer to serve one of them.

In speaking thus, Morga expressed the common adherence by people of color, the *castas* of colonial Mexican society, to the racial prejudices of the society around them. Blacks and mulattoes generally held Indians and mestizos in low regard (though they might also try hard to infiltrate the Indian communities, in which they could count on some measure of acceptance and might aspire to positions of influence, and where from time to time they might even make good an escape from the system of slavery). They also seem to have accepted the colonial standard that elevated white people above all other members of society; and if obliged to serve, they preferred to serve the powerful.

Juan's remark was in any event a stinging insult to Arratia; and although the mestizo retained his composure, from that moment on he became the bitter enemy and cruel tormentor of the unfortunate Morga. He bought him on the spot, saying that he could make use of him as a secretary and clerk; and he took him on his own mule back to his house. But as soon as they got there, he had Juan placed in chains and branded on the face with a rebus drawing of the letter "*s*" and the figure of a nail (*clavo*) to signify to all his permanent status as a slave (*esclavo*). Morga, previously unaccustomed to such harsh treatment, fell into a state of shock because of the pain and was seriously ill and dispirited for many days.

Once restored to health, he pled with Arratia to remove his shackles, swearing that he would serve him faithfully without them; but the new master replied that he intended never to remove them as long as Morga lived, revealing in that way that the hatred he felt toward this handsome slave who had dared to humiliate him was implacable. In desperation, Morga picked up a goad and tried to escape. Defending himself as best he could, he attempted to run to the house of the *corregidor*, the principal royal official of the city, to ask for his merciful intervention. But as Morga's luck would have it, an officer friend of Arratia's arrived just at that moment with a harquebuss and seized the mulatto, just as another slave threw a rock that caught the runaway squarely in the face. Between them, the men were able to tie the struggling Juan to a large stone; whereupon Arratia beat him so mercilessly with a variety of objects that his victim lost the power of speech for several days and was left with deep scars on his body—scars that were still visible months later when he was recounting his story to the inquisitors.

Once again Morga fell gravely ill. But this did not deter Arratia from coming in to beat him again day after day or from having him branded once more—this time with a hideous mark that extended from ear to ear—and obliging him to continue working throughout. It is clear that such treatment was contrived not only to punish Morga for his insult but also to deprive him by means of systematic disfigurement of the physical beauty that had attracted his tormentor to him in the first place. Two weeks later, when the sadistic Arratia had the bandages removed from Juan's face to see if his wounds had healed, he complained that the letters from the first brand were too small and called in a barber-surgeon to enlarge them with his lancet while Morga sat tied to a chair.

Following this torment, Juan remained in chains for five months until he managed to have them removed temporarily through the intercession of sympathetic outsiders. Then one day, in a fit of depression over the continuing cruelty of his master, he succeeded at last in making his escape to the *corregidor's* house. There he begged that Arratia be ordered to sell him to someone else as a matter of common Christian decency; but the *corregidor*, anxious to solve the problem with a minimum of effort, preferred to have Morga thrown in jail for safekeeping. Arratia then managed to get him back by means of a simple ruse. He sent a secular priest friend, Padre Juan de Lescano, who assisted in the management of the labor force in the mines, to pick Morga up at the jail claiming to have bought him from Arratia. Once they got back to Lescano's house, the priest and a servant tied Morga up and locked him in a room. Shortly thereafter the terrible Arratia appeared to put the shackles back on his slave (dealing him a crippling blow on the leg with his hammer as he did so), swearing to Juan all the while that he was bound never to sell him, even if he were offered a thousand pesos.

Arratia then leased Morga out for five months to work in the stamp mill of an *hacienda de minas*, where silver ore was crushed in preparation for the smelting process. It appears that Arratia's business at this point was hiring out his gang of slaves to others rather than administering his own establishment. At the stamp mill Juan was put to work at the hardest tasks. One day, as he was lugging out a load of slag, his master appeared suddenly and attacked him without provocation—flogging him so violently amid curses and threats that he succeeded in ripping great strips of skin from his body. After this, Morga found himself at the limits of desperation, and on several occasions he contemplated committing suicide (as he later admitted), by simply sticking his head under the great pounding iron blocks of the stamp mill, so that it would be smashed to pieces with the ore.

The miserable Juan was still quite capable of anger, however, and it may have been this that kept him afloat. He was particularly incensed at his betrayal by Padre Lescano, who might have been expected to offer comfort to an abused fellow-Christian rather than to collaborate in his persecution. One day, when Lescano was visiting the mill, Morga reproached him for having taken part in Arratia's plot. The priest replied that Arratia had first agreed and then in effect refused to sell Juan to him at the last minute, demanding an excessive sum in payment. It was hard to see what could be done to temper the master's blind hostility to this slave. If Morga would take his advice, he would simply promise Arratia humbly to serve faithfully forever—and hope that by this exemplary demonstration of meekness he might persuade him to relent. But Juan's sufferings had brought him to the very brink of death; he was beyond temporizing and for the time being saw no means of escaping his cruel fate.

At about this time, however, Arratia seems to have experienced some financial setback or another and been obliged to modify his way of doing business. One day he announced that he was going to have to lease an ore-processing hacienda and operate it himself in order to keep from having to sell his slaves. A few days later, as the Christmas season was nearing, he had Morga released from his chains once more. But this was only a temporary respite. It was not long before Arratia had the chains replaced to punish Juan for having gone out at night without permission to borrow a guitar from an Indian friend and go carousing, and he ordered him flogged again into the bargain. Then on the same day he assigned him to man the winch on a water pump, despite the fact that he had not eaten and could barely stand after a sleepless night and a morning of agony. A little later the foreman found a little unpumped water in the shaft and had Juan stripped, strung up, and flogged for the second time that day. Then he sent him down to take charge of another pump, knee-deep in cold water at the bottom of a well. There the slave was barely managing to maintain consciousness when a compassionate mine guard came by, saw his plight, and had him brought up to the surface. Once again Morga contemplated putting an end to his suffering by throwing himself down a mineshaft. At this point even the implacable Arratia noticed how pale, exhausted, and despairing his slave had become after so much work, hunger, and physical punishment—and decided that it was best to have him relieved of duty and removed from his chains.

Morga understood by this time that he had no hope of salvation as long as he remained in Zacatecas. So he determined to escape; and at the first opportunity he stole a horse and fled headlong to Mexico City. There he took refuge in the household of an influential nobleman, whom he begged to buy him from Arratia, or have him bought back by the accountant Millán, or even sent to a sugar plantation, where he was sure that the conditions would be preferable to his life in Zacatecas. When that failed, Morga took his case to the vicar-general of the Mercedarians, who agreed to buy him and send him to the mines of Zacualpan, which were operated by his order. But as Morga was leaving the Mercedarian convent to return to the house of a mulatto friend with whom he was staying, he was apprehended by the men who had been sent after him by Arratia. They handed him over to Florián de Espina, the owner of an *obraje* or woollen textile mill in nearby San Pablo, to be kept hard at work and prevented from escaping while they waited for orders from Zacatecas.

Undaunted, Morga wrote to the mayor of San Pablo in an attempt to persuade the civil authorities to intervene on his behalf. The mayor sent a policeman and scribe to the woollen mill to take his testimony, and then enjoined Espina from handing the slave over to the representatives of Arratia until the case had been resolved. In the meantime some friends of Morga's had arranged his betrothal to a black woman named Micaela, the slave of a local peanut dealer, which also had the legal effect of immobilizing Juan until after the wedding had been celebrated.

Arratia did not desist. His men first succeeded in frightening off Micaela by threatening to buy her and take her to the dreaded Zacatecas along with her new husband. Once she had broken her engagement, they were able to grease palms and pull strings, despite the obvious justice of Morga's case, and have him removed from the woollen mill to their custody. Then they set off with him on the road back to Zacatecas. It was at this point, while being returned to the scene of his torment, that Juan grew so desperate as to renounce God in his heart and turn to the Devil for assistance. One night his captors tied him tightly to a large sack of goods so that he could not run away. Juan called upon Satan and was surprised to find at that moment that the sack could easily be burst open. Once free, he began to fashion a noose of his ropes with which to hang himself—feeling that he could no longer endure the sufferings that awaited him. But then his captors stirred, and, startled, he ran off to hide among the maguey plants that were scattered in the plain. The guards set off in hot pursuit and captured him without difficulty; and while one broke his sword over Juan's head, the others beat him mercilessly. Then they dragged him back to the camp, flogged him, and left him tied up until they could resume their journey in the morning. At another stopping place, Morga tried to commit suicide by asking for a glass of wine to calm a pain in his stomach and then drinking it with a fistful of salt—hoping ingenuously that this mixture would turn out to be poisonous.

When the party got back to Zacatecas, Arratia received Morga with the treatment that by this time was to be expected: he hit him in the mouth with a hammer, breaking off one of his teeth; he put manacles and leg irons on him; he ridiculed him for having tried to present his case to the authorities; and he sent him back to the stamp mill. After a while he removed him from that work, taking this opportunity to inform Juan that it would be useless to attempt any further escapes since he was prepared to spend all his money if necessary to bring his hated slave back from wherever he went—even from under the protection of God himself. Then he sent Juan to work at the Quebradilla mine.

One morning, when Morga was getting off late to work, Arratia tied him behind his horse and dragged him around the encampment over rocks and gullies and spiny plants until he was horribly wounded; and then he sent him to get about his duties as usual. That evening after work, Morga stopped for a minute beside a wall in a state of profound desperation and amid tears called once more upon the Devil to help him escape from this life of torture. An Indian miner stepped up and took pity on him, seeing his gaping sores; and when he had heard the circumstances of Morga's desolation he told him there was an herb that would prevent his master from doing him any more harm—and that he could have it if he would agree in exchange to serve the Devil on a permanent basis. Juan accepted the pact and promised to do what was expected of him, which was that he cease attending Mass and praying to the saints, that he mention not a word of this undertaking to anyone, and that from then onward instead of invoking the assistance of God in his trials he invoke the assistance of Satan. The Indian thereupon gave him an amulet containing some grains of mustard seed.

Sure enough, on the following day to Morga's great surprise, the attitude of Arratia toward him changed as if by a miracle. His master spoke to him gently and treated him kindly; he sent out to have two suits of clothing made for him; and he insisted on taking him with him wherever he went. This situation continued for more than a year without a relapse. But then as the Lent season of 1650 drew near, Morga repented of having made his pact with the Devil. He was overtaken by profound sadness when he realized that he would be unable to accompany his fellow servants to receive the sacraments of confession and communion; and one evening, weeping, he threw his mustard-seed amulet into the fire—swearing to God that he would throw himself on the mercy of the Inquisition if he ever fell back into sin. But all this repentance was to no avail, because when the time came Arratia claimed that there was too much work to be done at the mine and refused to allow his slaves to go and fulfill their obligations to the Church, or Morga to reconcile himself with God.

A couple of months later a squabble broke out between two young women at Arratia's *hacienda de minas* over the apparently still irresistible Morga. Taking advantage of the uproar, and perhaps fearing that the argument might serve as a pretext for further torments, Juan saddled up a horse, stole a harquebuss and a sword from where they were hanging, and galloped off into the flat country at midnight—determined this time to make his way back to the capital and deliver himself to the Inquisition. As dawn broke on the Camino Real, however, he ran across a man who recognized him and hastened to report the runaway's whereabouts to his master. Shouting a prayer to Saint Anthony of Padua, Morga reversed direction and headed north toward Parral in an effort to confound his pursuers. But after two hours of galloping, he saw that another mulatto retainer of Arratia's, armed with a lance, was riding in pursuit and gaining on him. So he got off the road to hide, prayed again to Saint Anthony, and was favored as if by a miracle when his pursuer passed by a short distance away without seeing him. Recovered from his fright, Juan stopped in at a small ranch, whose owners gave him a place to stay for three days. His luck had changed at last. At one point Arratia with four armed men arrived at the ranch to ask whether anyone had seen him. His kindly hosts replied that they had not; and afterward they went so far as to give him a horse on which to make his way to Mexico City.

Morga then rode furiously toward the capital, barely escaping capture in San Miguel. In San Juan del Río he traded his exhausted horse for a mule, and with the new mount he made his way to Jilotepec. There he was arrested and detained by a commissioner of the Santa Hermandad, the voluntary police force famed for its arbitrary methods, which had been established to put down the endemic banditry of the Mexican countryside. He asked to be taken before the Inquisition, but the local representative of the Holy Office refused when he guessed that the plea was no more than a manuever to make good Juan's escape from a harsh master. It was then that Morga managed to obtain pen and paper and address his moving petition to the abbot of Jilotepec—exaggerating some of his sins and inventing others, to oblige the priest to send him on to the tribunal. This letter, as it turned out, was intercepted by the Hermandad and never reached its destination. But Morga in the meantime was advancing his cause by other means. He pretended to experience frightful visions of being pursued by the Devil, which caused such an impression on the incredulous inhabitants of Jilotepec that under pressure from them the authorities determined to hand him over to the Inquisition.

The Holy Office found itself faced with a delicate case. At the outset, in an effort presumably to discourage Juan from lying, the judges warned him that there would be no question of removing him from the power of Arratia, since that was the function of the civil courts. They would, however, order an investigation into his charges with reference to the behavior of Arratia as necessary background to their discussion of his aberrant behavior as a Catholic. All the witnesses who were called upon coincided in describing the vengeful mine operator as a hateful character. A carpenter who knew the situation at Arratia's *hacienda de minas* well observed that the slaves there were so badly treated that they were all desperate and often spoke of murdering their master. He testified further that having found Morga to be someone a cut above the majority of slaves—as a reasonable man able to read, write, and figure—he had himself tried on various occasions to intervene in his favor when he had seen Arratia venting his frenetic hatred on the slave.

In August 1650, Arratia sent an agent to the capital to bring Juan de Morga back once again. But despite its warning to Morga, the Inquisition refused to hand him over; and months later it went so far as to forbid his even being sold to anyone in Arratia's employ. A year later the long-suffering Morga was delivered to one Mateo Días de la Madrid, who presented papers to prove that he had purchased him from Diego de Arratia for the amount of 400 pesos. We have no way of knowing today whether this freed Juan de Morga to end his days in tolerable circumstances (perhaps serving as the slave of an ordinary householder in Mexico City), or whether "la Madrid" too was a party to the machinations of the vengeful Arratia. The considerable publicity that had been given to the case, the mild sentence handed down by the Inquisition (which had satisfied itself with a reprimand in open court for Morga's backsliding and flirtations with Satan), and the decree that he was not to be returned to his master may very well have discouraged Arratia from pursuing the matter at last. However, given the vastness of New Spain, the relative weakness of its institutions, and the great difficulty of enforcing government orders in remote places, it is entirely possible that the calvary of Juan de Morga had not yet come to an end.

✻ ✻ ✻

When Gertrudis de Escobar first came before the court of the Inquisition in 1659, she was a free young mulatta woman of only fourteen years. Her father had been Juan de Garibay, a black slave born and raised in the capital city, but Gertrudis had never known his parents. Her mother had been Beatriz Domínguez, the mulatta daughter of a free black woman of the city named Ana de Escobar. Beatriz had served as a slave in the household of a Captain Antonio "de Chayde" [Echaide], where Gertrudis had been born. It is not clear how her freeborn mother had entered the slave status, nor how Gertrudis, the daughter of slaves, had become free. Both parents appear to have died or to have lost contact with their daughter while she was still a child. In addition she had five brothers and sisters, about whom no information has survived, and was acquainted with two aunts, an uncle and several cousins—all of them free mulattoes. As a small girl she had been put to work in the convents of Mexico City as a servant to well-to-do cloistered nuns; and at the time of her first arrest she was employed by a Mother Juana de la Cruz at the nunnery of the Queen of Heaven.

The circumstances in which Gertrudis' time of trials began were these: one day, to punish the girl for some misbehavior or another, the nun removed her slippers and with no hint of Christian kindness began to beat Gertrudis while at the same time an Indian servant woman hit her with a handful of heavy keys. In these parlous straits, the child denied God several times by repeating some blasphemous language she had learned from a shiftless mulatto of the neighborhood known as Scorpion. Horrified, the nun soon reported this unchristian behavior to the Holy Office (without of course acknowledging her own fault in the matter), and this gave rise to an arrest and routine inquiry, as a result of which Gertrudis was found guilty of blasphemy and condemned to the standard punishment of being paraded through the streets in public humiliation after an auto-da-fé. Her detention in the calaboose of the Inquisition had in the meantime given rise to costs in the amount of nineteen pesos, which she was unable to pay and which were to come back and haunt her later on.

On the evening after her public disgrace, Gertrudis was picked up from the patio of the headquarters of the Holy Office by a priest named Martín de la Estera y Echaide (perhaps a relative of the citizen in whose household Gertrudis had been born). Estera behaved like a man who was afraid he was being watched. He took her first to the house of a silversmith. Then after half an hour or so he took her to his own house, where Gertrudis' aunt Maria Pérez served as housekeeper assisted by her daughter Brianda, aged twenty, and several other children. Gertrudis was conducted stealthily into the house and led to the priest's room, where she found her aunt and cousins already waiting. At the outset of their conversation, Maria and Brianda urged Gertrudis to do whatever the priest suggested.

The priest then announced that he needed Gertrudis to go and serve on the sugar plantation of Zacatepec near Cuernavaca, which belonged to Don Mateo de Lizama. The nature of his connection with Lizama is not clear. Gertrudis refused outright, saying that Lizama and his wife were infamous for the cruel punishments they meted out to their workers; and she informed the group that her own preference was to go to work in the well-known Mexico City *obraje* of Cardoso. Brianda interjected that the textile mill was located in the heart of the capital, and that if Gertrudis were sent there, after the humiliation of the auto-da-fé, everyone would see her on the way to Sunday Mass—which would bring dishonor on the entire family. The plantation, however, was in the country, where no one would know her. Gertrudis replied that she had already been seen by everyone during her penitence, and that it would be no novelty to see her on her way to church! She refused to go to the sugar works but observed bitterly that she was beginning to get the impression that her relatives intended to sell her there whether she wanted to go or not. At this the aunt went into a fury and began to slap her amid threats and obscenities.

Brianda continued the argument, insisting that it was not in Gertrudis' best interests to remain in the city; and soon another cousin, Juliana, a woman of about thirty, arrived to assist her mother and sister in the task of persuasion. Juliana asked her mother crudely, pointing to Gertrudis: "What does this lump have to say about it, anyway?" The reply was that the problem had been solved, and that the child was ready to go to the terrible plantation. The priest had assured Gertrudis in paternal tones that Mateo de Lizama was well-known to him and would treat her well, paying her a real [a day?] in wages in addition to her food, and that he would not force her to work on holidays. At length, seeing that there was so much pressure for her to agree, Gertrudis asked whether it was the decision of the inquisitors that she should go to the plantation—and when the priest assured her that it was, she put aside her resistance to the idea. But she did notice that following their conversation the priest gave her aunt, as the purchase price for the girl, a considerable quantity of money (a "bundle larger than a melon"), and left her ten additional pesos with which to buy the child some clothing.

Gertrudis' Aunt Maria outfitted her with some colored petticoats such as those normally worn by mulatta women in the city, and a new tight-fitted sleeveless jacket or jerkin, and a blouse that had belonged to her cousin Brianda. Two days later, when a muleskinner from Don Mateo's plantation arrived in the city with a load of sugar, he stopped by at Father Estera y Echaide's house on the way back for Gertrudis. The girl was put on a mule and covered with a blue tablecloth so that she would not be recognized; and her cousin Pancho was sent along to see that she got safely out of the city. Once the mule train had passed the suburbs, Pancho returned home with the tablecloth. The mule train wound its way through Churubusco, Coajomulco, and Tachuloaya; and four days later, on the feast day of the Immaculate Conception, it reached the sugar mill of Zacatepec.

No sooner had they arrived than Gertrudis was sent out to help with the backbreaking work of cutting cane in the fields. Each adult worker was expected to cut twenty-five rows of cane in a long working day; the youthful and inexperienced Gertrudis was expected to do just the same. After two weeks she was punished with fifty lashes one evening for having failed to fulfill her quota. Then for a time she was put back to work in the harvest; and later she was sent to feed cane into the rollers of the grinding mill. This was heavy and dangerous night work, beginning at eight o'clock in the evening and finishing in the morning, which required her to handle the enormous amount of cut cane required to fill fifteen huge boiling vats with the sweet juice. Many of those assigned to this work, which was reserved for women, lost hands or arms when they got them caught between the rollers. All of this, we may recall, was being demanded of a girl who was still only fourteen. On one occasion Gertrudis was punished with twenty-five lashes for having stopped to eat a bite of food outside of the scheduled time. Then she was put to work at a man's job, driving the draft animals that walked round and round to provide the motor power of the mill.

When Gertrudis ran away for the first time, she remained hidden in a canebrake for three days and then came back because a free black woman offered to intercede so that she would not be punished. The mill foreman pardoned her as promised; but when don Mateo learned what she had done, he ordered that she receive 300 lashes and threatened to have her flogged even more if she ran away again. This punishment was made especially terrible when Lizama noticed that the slave assigned to whip her was taking it easy and sent for another to administer the last fifty lashes with special intensity. Then she was fitted with leg irons and chains and sent back to the canefields with a quota increased to thirty rows a day instead of twenty-five.

One day Gertrudis was seen cutting cane in her shackles by a Dominican friar from the nearby convent of Tlaquiltenango who had happened to know her when she lived in Mexico City. The friar went to see Lizama to ask that he remove her chains, and the owner acceded. But as soon as he left, don Mateo had Gertrudis flogged again for having sought the intervention of an outsider. Then he replaced the chains and kept her in them for another five months until a cousin of Gertrudis' named Felipe (the son of her Aunt Maria Pérez) came down to the mill to inform Lizama of the death of one of his relatives in the capital. Felipe was able to persuade the master to allow his cousin to move around unencumbered.

One Sunday the wedding of two black slaves was celebrated at the mill. After the religious ceremony, which was attended by all the workers, the midday bell rang to send most of the people back to the fields. Gertrudis went off along with the rest. But suddenly she dropped everything and ran back to join the celebration, in an outburst of rebellion and with the spontaneous desire for a little fun. This was enough to have her put back in chains for another two months—until another visiting friar, a brother-in-law of the plantation owner, was instrumental in having the irons struck from her legs once more.

Three months later, having failed once again to complete her day's quota, Gertrudis was flogged again with great cruelty. This time she decided to take advantage of the fact that she was not in chains to try to escape. At the first opportunity she ran away through the canefields and took refuge at the nearby plantation of Santa Inés, where she thought that no one would know her. But the labor force of the sugar-growing valleys of Cuautla and Cuernavaca was a very unstable one, with free workers moving back and forth between one mill and another until everyone pretty much knew everyone. So one day in the patio at Santa Inés, Gertrudis ran into Diego García, a freedman who had recently worked as harvest foreman for Mateo de Lizama. García was surprised to see her; so Gertrudis explained that she was a free woman and had left Zacatepec because she could not put up with the hardships imposed by Lizama. García then exclaimed, in front of numerous witnesses, that Gertrudis was a liar and that he knew her to be a slave who had been sold by the inquisitors to don Mateo for the sum of 300 pesos.

Gertrudis had been put to work as soon as she arrived at Santa Inés; and as it turned out she had met there among the plantation hands several people who had been among those sentenced by the Holy Office in the same auto-da-fé with her. Among them was the mulatto Scorpion, from whom she had learned the blasphemies that had been the cause of her difficulties in the first place. In the ensuing discussion of his young friend's legal status, Scorpion recalled having known her as a free young woman in the capital and expressed surprise at seeing her made a slave. García said that Scorpion was a liar too and left after placing Gertrudis in a cell to keep her from escaping once more. Don Andrés, the operator of the Santa Inés mill, was attracted by the ruckus and came to find out what was happening. With him was a young barber-surgeon who had also known Gertrudis and her family in Mexico; and while Andrés was having the girl put in chains, he objected that he knew her to be a person of "free condition." The discussion grew livelier, as those who had known Gertrudis as a free person confronted those who had known her as a slave. Scorpion suggested that perhaps she had been sold by the inquisitors themselves, as seems to have happened on occasion when the owners of slaves hauled before the tribunal proved incapable of paying their court costs. Indeed, there is some evidence that the Holy Office sold free persons on occasion for the same purpose.

Gertrudis, for her part, exclaimed that it was impossible that the inquisitors had sold her, because if they had, she would have been informed of the fact when she was sentenced and put up for auction on the block. In these remarks she revealed her considerable intelligence, common sense, and familiarity with the norms of the religious and social life of the colony. None of these things had happened, she said. Rather, she had been taken by night to the house of her Aunt María Pérez. The barber then ventured the opinion that what the inquisitors had not dared to do had been done by her aunt: she had sold her young niece as a slave without regard for her status as a free person. He offered to travel to Mexico City, uncover the facts of the case, and thereby restore Gertrudis to liberty.

Following this discussion, Gertrudis waited at Santa Inés for a month to see what might happen, working at one task and another to pay for her keep. But don Mateo was determined to get her back; and he sent the son of his overseer over to fetch her. Arriving at the mill, the young man arranged to talk privately with don Andrés about the case; but Gertrudis barged in to present herself before the two men and declare in no uncertain terms that she was a free person, that she wanted the Inquisition to be informed of what had happened to her, and that she would wait for their decision at Santa Inés. She preferred working in chains at Santa Inés, she said, to working unencumbered at Zacatepec. Don Andrés, impressed by the young woman's fierce determination, decided not to return her to his neighbor. But don Mateo was not satisfied with this decision, and two days later he sent for her once more.

When Gertrudis, who was working in the canefields at the time, heard that another agent of don Mateo was at the mill asking for her, she burst out shouting and threatening to kill herself if she were sent back to the hated Lizama. It was an explosion of desperation, something not uncommon among slaves in colonial society, which often enough did lead to their committing suicide. Suicide was a means not only of putting an end to a life that was hard to tolerate but also of taking vengeance on the owner by destroying the valuable merchandise in which he had invested money and maintenance, and frustrating his expectation of future productivity and childbearing. It was a Sunday, and later Gertrudis took advantage of the gathering together of people to repeat her claim that she was a free person and that she had not been sold by the inquisitors to anyone. By this point in her travail, it is clear that Gertrudis had come to understand clearly the situation into which she had fallen and the means of her salvation. She had strong suspicions, confirmed by the conversations at Santa Inés, about how she had been enslaved; and from then on her determination to free herself did not falter. Her main objective was somehow to get into contact with a representative of the Inquisition, who she was sure could be persuaded to remove her from the clutches of her owner.

In the meantime it was agreed that Gertrudis should be returned to don Mateo. Before leaving Santa Inés, she was taken by the foreman to the smithy to have her shackles removed; and once she was free the foreman said to her: "Mulatta, I have removed your chains. Don't just stand there! Run! Go wherever you like." He thought that her best plan might be to seek the protection of the elderly Dominican friar who was just then saying Mass at the mill, and who was a familiar of the Holy Office. Gertrudis ran to collar the friar and had just begun to tell him her story when the agent of don Mateo burst in, denying everything she said and assuring the Dominican that the girl had in fact been purchased by his master from the Inquisition. The priest refused to intercede, and Gertrudis was taken away in a state of despair. Seeing that there was no way to avoid going back to Zacatepec, she allowed herself to be put on a mule after exacting a promise that she would not be flogged when she got there.

The promise was kept; but soon afterward don Mateo wrote from the capital that the foremen were to clap her in irons once more—and in this condition she remained for many months. With the complicity of a gang foreman and an old slave woman of the estate, the administrators determined to have Gertrudis married to a blind black slave named Hipólito of about twenty years of age, who was in charge of operating the bellows in the smithy. Gertrudis refused to accept this and also refused a match with a slave named Domingo, who had asked don Mateo to be married to her— knowing that if she married a slave she would become a slave herself and be irremediably lost. But Hipólito, in order to oblige her to accept, persuaded the girl that he had heard that if she did not marry him she would be kept in chains for the rest of her life. This was a terrible alternative, because it was clear that it would be harder to be in chains than married. For this reason she decided at length to go through with the wedding, which was to be celebrated by the Dominican chaplain of the plantation at the earliest opportunity.

The Catholic Church required that slaves and others be left free to choose their own mates; and it was always ready to reprimand slaveowners who arranged marriages between their dependents in the pursuit of their proprietary interests. But the Church had no means of preventing masters from pressuring slaves before the ceremony or from taking reprisals against them afterward if they did not do as they were told. The Dominican was undoubtedly aware of the real circumstances in which this strange decision to marry into slavery had been made, but he was either unable or unwilling to prevent the marriage on that account.. The banns were published, and it was at that time that Gertrudis learned that don Mateo had indeed bought her as a slave and became finally convinced that the betrayal had been perpetrated by her aunt and cousins and the priest Estera y Echaide. This was the harsh reality for many people of color in the colony. With parents often dead, or removed from their children, or never legally married, with grandparents left back in Africa, with other relatives carried off by disease or chained in servitude, not even the protective mechanisms of the family could be relied on. And even when some affective tie remained, there was a danger that it might be sacrificed at any time for some temporary alleviation of the conditions of chronic poverty. Gertrudis had been sold into slavery at fourteen by the only relatives who remained to her.

On the day of this sad travesty of a wedding, and at the request of the friar who was to perform the ceremony, don Mateo agreed magnanimously to remove the shackles from the bride. After the ceremony Gertrudis, who never thought of Hipólito as her husband, worked unencumbered for about four months. Then one day, having received a terrible flogging once again, she decided to attempt another escape. After hiding for two days in the canebrakes, she returned to the mill under the protection of a field guard and somehow managed to avoid being punished. But a few days later, after another flogging, she ran away once more.

This time she made it as far as the village of Tachuloaya on the road to Mexico City, where she made the mistake of dropping in at the church because a religious festival was in progress. There she met the friar, a brother-in-law of don Mateo, who had once interceded to have her removed from her shackles at Zacatepec. Such encounters were not surprising in a country with a very small population, few towns, and widely extended families. The friar was surprised to see her free; but Gertrudis explained to him with a straight face that she was a free woman who was simply out on a holiday. She also reminded him that all her problems had had their origin in the incident with Mother Juana of the Convent of the Queen of Heaven, who happened to be the good friar's sister! The friar therefore offered her his protection if she would agree to return to Zacatepec, and he promised to persuade don Mateo to provide her with some clothing and with better treatment than before. Gertrudis accepted, returned, and remarkably enough was actually pardoned by Lizama with no more than a reproach for having gone about saying that she was a free woman when in reality she was a slave.

Back at work at the sugar mill, Gertrudis was assigned to the boiling room and was getting by tolerably well until one day some cane syrup was spilled on the ground from a broken trough while she was in charge. The administrators had her flogged once again and thus provided the occasion for a new escape. This time she found some men who were willing to have her travel with them through the mountains to Mexico City, where she hoped to find a man whom she had known when she was in the Inquisition jail, and who she hoped might help put her in contact with the inquisitors as her only and final hope. On the way, however, she paid a visit to the sugar estate owned and operated by the Holy Office at Santa Ana de Amanalco near Cuernavaca and pled with its administrator, the secular priest Andrés Gamero de León, that he put her story before the tribunal.

Gamero made her welcome and put her to work for wages; he also listened to her story, and in February 1662, he submitted to Mexico City the long report upon which this reconstruction of Gertrudis' experiences is primarily based. In passing, he pointed out that the young woman appeared to be a devious person of violent character—but that the sugar mill of Zacatepec was indeed famous throughout the region for the excessive cruelty with which slaves were punished there and the many deaths that had resulted. During the ensuing two months, the priest had his hands full with Gertrudis, because as it turned out she was much given to drunkenness, to scandalizing her fellow workers with her coarse language and her licentious way of life, to constantly running away, and to selling or pawning the clothing she was given in order to pay for intoxicating beverages. But he kept her on nevertheless, and at length the long-awaited resolution of the case arrived from the Inquisition in Mexico. It would be necessary to "moderate the girl" by putting her into chains once more and obliging her to work for a time. Then she was to be set free.

What can have happened to Gertrudis de Escobar? It is reasonable to assume that in time she joined the caste of marginal citizens of the colony, the embittered victims of unrelenting social violence, moving back and forth in the wide-open and dangerous underworld of the colony, living by "hard work and miracles." It may be that she returned to the capital to obtain definitive proof of her free status and to trouble her hateful family with her presence. It may even be that don Mateo managed to get her back, determined not to lose his investment and taking advantage of his connections.

✳   ✳   ✳

Both Juan and Gertrudis were able to overcome the unbelievably difficult circumstances of these relatively short periods of their lives, thanks to an extraordinary vitality, strength of character, lively intelligence, and above all a familiarity with the norms of urban and institutional life in the colony. Paradoxical though it may seem today, to the powerless people of color in seventeenth-century Mexican society the principal hope for protection against the unbridled authority of an owner or employer in a mine, hacienda, or plantation was the series of civil or religious institutions, which despite their integration into the system of colonial exploitation existed to impose some sort of regulation on a disorderly society. What contributed more than anything else to destroying the life opportunities for individual people in colonial society was the arbitrary exercise of authority, and what contributed most to protecting them was the system for the regulation of society, unfortunately weak and distant and for the most part ineffective, which was represented by bureaucratic organizations in the capital. The Inquisition itself, never in truth a philanthropic organization, was obliged on occasion to intervene in behalf of the powerless despite itself, for the simple reason that it was bound to hold up certain norms of behavior for the society and to do everything in its power to see that they were respected.

Juan and Gertrudis are excellent examples of the gifted individuals, intelligent and spirited, who were so badly employed by a colonial society whose productive forces were not yet sufficiently developed to absorb the human resources that it had available. People like them played a large role in the armed struggle to destroy the restrictive colonial social order that began a century and a half later under the leadership of Hidalgo and Morelos. Both were indomitable rebels against the oppressive circumstances into which they had been thrown. Gertrudis, far from being a model of "femininity," became a violent, insolent, drunken, and shameless woman—and by this means managed to triumph over her luck. But both of them understood that in order to accomplish their goals they were obliged to channel their rebelliousness into a patient and determined utilization of the established institutions of society, encouraging discussions in which they could argue the merits of their cases, arousing public interest, and even building scandal around themselves. This combination of rebelliousness and adaptation to the social norms was the only available means for survival for the powerless racially mixed and African and Indian majority of the inhabitants of colonial Spanish America.

Sources

Materials for the story of Juan de Morga were found in the Archivo General de la Nación in Mexico City, Ramo Inquisicion, Tomo 454, f. 253ff. Gertrudis de Escobar's story has been reconstructed from documents in the same repository, Tomo 446, f. 161ff.

Suggestions for Further Reading

The circumstances of life for slaves in Central Mexico during the seventeenth century are explored in Gonzalo Aguirre Beltran, *La poblacion negra de Mexico, 1519–1810: estudio etnohistorico* (México, 1946; rev. ed 1972), and Colin Palmer, *Slaves of the White God: Blacks in Mexico, 1570–1650* (Cambridge, Mass., 1976). For the general history of black people in colonial Latin America, see Rolando Mellafe, *Negro Slavery in Latin America* (Berkeley, 1975); Leslie Rout, *The African Experience in Spanish America* (Cambridge, 1976); Roger Bastide, *African Civilizations in the New World* (New York, 1972); Richard Price, *Maroon Societies: Rebel Slave Communities in the Americas* (New York, 1973); and Eugene Genovese, *The World the Slaveholders Made* (New York, 1969), Part 1.

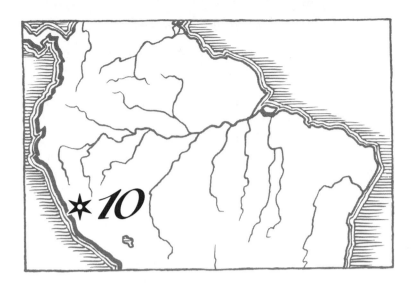

Cristóbal Béquer:
Wayward Prebend

PAUL B. GANSTER

*O*ne day in January 1753 a notary sent by the ecclesiastical authorities of Lima recorded that in the monastery of San Agustín he had seen the body of don Cristóbal Béquer, a prebend of the cathedral chapter, laid out on a "funeral bier, garbed in the vestments of a priest, with lights on the sides, ready to be buried in said convent."[1] Thus ended the tumultuous life and career of a man who neither made his peace with colonial society nor learned to exist comfortably within the boundaries of acceptable conduct. Nevertheless Béquer survived to a relatively ripe old age and lived a life of comfort in which he usually did as he pleased.

Even in death Béquer was a nonconformist. As a member of the cathedral chapter, he would have been entitled to a dignified funeral attended by the chapter and by representatives of the great corporate bodies of the city, and then to interment inside the cathedral. Most chapter members did opt for burial in the principal church of the realm; it was the most prestigious location for eternal repose, and to have oneself buried there was to affirm the corporate solidarity of the ecclesiastical hierarchy in death as well as in life. Some of the chapter prebends from the most important colonial families were interred in family vaults in one or another of the Lima churches, but not Béquer. By choosing to be put away in a monastery, he had the last laugh on people with whom he had been wrangling for years.

Little in Béquer's family background foreshadows his quarrels with the Church or accounts for his irascibility. He was born in Lima in 1693, the son of Captain Guillermo Béquer and doña Juana Barraza, also *limeños*. Doña Juana died before 1700, leaving the Captain to raise Cristóbal and his brother, Pedro. Guillermo, a merchant of moderate means and a member of the Consulado, was also an officer in one of the volunteer merchant companies that had been organized late in the seventeenth century to deal with pirate attacks on the coast of western South America. Such meritorious service to the Crown would be useful in the future if he had occasion to seek royal favor or request an honorific title. Although Guillermo never actually sallied forth against the pirates, his uncle Captain Nicolás Verdugo had been killed in 1686 leading his troops against the hated Protestant freebooters at the port of Pisco, on the south coast of Peru—a fact that reflected favorably on the family name. Cristóbal's grandfather had also served the king for a number of years, as military commander of a force of one hundred men who had conquered Santa Cruz de la Sierra in the Audiencia of Charcas, opening the region to Jesuit missionaries. The paternal line of the Béquer family had been in Lima for five generations and claimed descent from the house of Brabante Béquer founded in Flanders. Their accumulated services to the crown and long residence in the Indies, together with Guillermo's position as a merchant of the Consulado, clearly established the family in the lower ranks of the Peruvian nobility. With a bit more money and some judicious planning, they might have been upwardly mobile; as it was, the Béquers suffered the opposite fate.[2] Their troubles began in

1714 when Cristóbal, his brother Pedro, and their father were all implicated in a murder.[3]

During the late afternoon of September 28 of that year, Pedro Béquer was walking along a street in the heart of Lima when he spotted don Pedro de Torres, the chief police guard for the merchants' shops, leaning over the display counter in a tobacco shop. Pedro quickly pulled out his sword and dagger and rushed into the establishment where he repeatedly stabbed Torres in the back, killing him instantly. Witnesses later indicated that Cristóbal, dressed in the habit of a lay brother, had been riding up and down the street all afternoon on a mule, closely scrutinizing the tobacco shop. When the killing occurred he had ridden off in such great haste, presumably to advise his father of the event, that he had nearly trampled several passing pedestrians. Although the reason for the murder cannot be established in the available documents, one witness suggested that Pedro and Cristóbal had developed a special enmity for Torres after he had apprehended them while breaking into their own father's store.

The authorities were surprisingly slow to respond to the outrage. But some weeks later, when it became clear that arrests were about to be made, the brothers sought refuge in the Bethlehemite monastery in Lima. Hiding in a convent was merely a tactic to delay and frustrate the legal proceedings since the right of church asylum did not apply in crimes of blood such as this. Captain Béquer then unsuccessfully attempted to have the case tried in the military courts out of respect for his rank and affiliation. As one of the prerogatives of wealth, such attempts to sidetrack justice were commonly employed by high-status persons in colonial Peru, often with success for a decade or two. Yet when the machinery of royal justice finally moved into high gear, publishing edicts and sending out the public crier to name Pedro as the murderer and Cristóbal as the accomplice and to order them to appear before the magistrates, it was clear to the brothers that their situation was precarious. Consequently, they left the monastery, fleeing to the nearby mountains, and went into hiding. Not long afterward Pedro died there of unknown causes, but Cristóbal remained, still afraid to return to the capital. Left holding the bag, Guillermo suffered a public disgrace and confiscation of his worldly goods, including two slaves. He then dropped from the scene, appearing no more in the records of the Consulado or in the documents concerning the misadventures of his son. Family fortunes had reached a low point.

How and why Béquer joined the priesthood only a few months after the murder are a mystery, partly because of the vagueness of the autobiographical statements he prepared. For one thing, Cristóbal was not academically inclined (though he presumably studied grammar as a youth in Lima, he never learned Latin). And by 1714, when he was twenty-one and many of his peers had gone on to the *licenciatura* and *maestria*, Béquer had not yet been awarded the *bachillerato*. Although he eventually claimed to have earned the *licenciatura*, he never stated from which institution the degree came—an unusual omission, for candidates for ecclesiastical posts almost invariably indicated their university affiliations. The circumstances surrounding his ordination are equally puzzling. Through cunning he seems to have been able to keep his past obscured and to ingratiate himself with the bishop of nearby Huamanga, obtaining holy orders in that diocese.

One wonders about Béquer's decision to embrace a life in the Church. Whereas colonial families often destined one or more sons for service in the Church as a matter of pious custom, they usually made at least some attempt to ensure that the young men were intellectually and spiritually qualified for such work. True vocations were relatively scarce, however, and by the early eighteenth century, newcomers entered the ranks at least of the secular clergy in much the same way as they would enter any other career. Although a full-time position in the upper hierarchy conferred special prestige and status, it seems likely that most of those who were ordained went on to lead quite ordinary lives as property managers, professors, lawyers, or businessmen, whether or not they were assigned at some point to a parish. At twenty-one Béquer's general attitude and lack of devotion to his studies were not indicative of a clerical vocation; moreover, from an early age he was "perverse and vicious" and about the time of his ordination was described as showing "depraved and vicious inclinations."[4] It may be that he chose the priesthood simply to shield himself from the consequences of his earlier scrape with the law.

Béquer kept on the move for several years, as though to keep one step ahead of his past. By the early 1720s he was in the city of Cuzco, and in 1728 he surfaced in the diocese of Cuzco as assistant to the parish priest of Puno. In that post he demonstrated little of the good sense and tact that were usually required for winning the support of superiors and advancement in the Church hierarchy. A priest who knew him then recalled that he was "gruff, violent, and quick to advance untenable arguments." It is remarkable that though these attitudes and mannerisms stayed with Béquer for the remainder of his life, his career prospered. In 1732 the Bishop of Cuzco appointed him interim priest of the Indian parish of San Sebastian Caminaca in the province of Azángaro, a post for which he was not technically qualified as he knew no Indian language.

Dissatisfied with the status and limited financial prospects of a humble interim priest and longing for the social intercourse of the city, Béquer boldly marched off to Lima after only a short time in Caminaca. There he addressed a petition to the viceroy, claiming that he was a poor cleric without means of support and begging permission to journey to Panama in search of gainful employment. Panama, a crossroads on the only legal trade route between Spain and Peru, was centrally located in the empire, but because of its unhealthy climate it was a place where there was little competition for positions of any sort. Lima, then as now, suffered a surfeit of professional men, including priests. The viceroy was no doubt pleased to have one less cleric scrounging for a living in his capital. The appropriate licenses were dispatched, and in June of 1733 Béquer was off to the Isthmus.

The sly cleric had no intention of remaining in Panama, the sweltering pesthole, but had planned all along to continue his journey to the court in Madrid. There he would join the great throng of aspiring creoles from the Indies who hoped to wangle or bribe their ways into lucrative appointments. The royal court was so beseiged with office seekers that the authorities were reluctant to grant licenses to travel to the Peninsula, particularly to unlettered clerics with less than respectable backgrounds. But in Panama, whence ships left with some frequency for other ports in the Caribbean and Spain, it would not have been difficult for a resourceful man of the cloth to sign on as a ship's chaplain or even as a crewman and thereby make the voyage without being subject to close scrutiny. Béquer seems to have done this—his guile and brazenness probably having served him well in Madrid—for in May of 1736 the king issued a *cédula* naming him to a vacant *media ración* on the cathedral chapter back in Lima. This was a remarkable achievement since by family background, education, and prior service as a cleric he was very poorly qualified for appointment to a high ecclesiastical post and since it is unlikely that Béquer could have obtained letters of recommendation from important people in Lima. (Petitions for such letters would have stirred an interest in his background and brought to light the murder case of 1714). At best then, he would have carried recommendations from the prelates of Cuzco and Huamanga and perhaps Panama. Although successful candidates for high ecclesiastical posts were frequently obliged to employ considerable financial resources in pursuit of their goals, a person with Béquer's cunning may well have pulled the whole thing off without resorting to a generous use of cash. One can only speculate as to how he actually acquired the Lima appointment.

Once assured of his *media ración,* Béquer showed little haste in embarking for Peru. It was not until May of 1738, two years after receiving the king's appointment, that he appeared in Cádiz requesting a license to sail for the Indies with a servant who claimed to be a native of Tucumán, in the Río de La Plata area. Although important people commonly travelled with servants to the New World, Béquer was denied authorization to do so because no witnesses could be produced to attest to the birthplace of his retainer, and the authorities were unwilling to allow the emigration to the Indies of Europeans of such low degree. The wayward cleric was always putting himself in such suspicious situations, skirting the limits of custom and law.

In January 1739, however, Béquer was back in Lima and had been accepted by the cathedral chapter and the archbishop and installed in his new post. The chapter was a key institution in the organization of the secular church, and played a very important part in the religious, social, economic, and political life of Lima and its suffragan area. The official

responsibility of its members was to see the perpetual observance of the canonical hours in the cathedral; in practice,
both as a corporate body and as a collection of individuals,
they served the archbishop as assistants for the administration of the archdiocese, where their talents were utilized in
many different ways. They staffed the ecclesiastical courts,
in particular the Court of Testaments, Bequests and Pious
Works, which controlled one of the major sources of commercial credit in that society of many merchants and no
banks. Chapter prebends supervised the nunneries of Lima;
they also served as professors, as members of the voting
assembly, and as chancellors or even as rectors of the city's
University of San Marcos. The chapter was present as a body
on all major public occasions in colonial Lima: festive celebrations in honor of the birth of an heir to the throne, the
public entrance of a new viceroy, or the funeral of a colonial
notable. Between the death of the archbishop and the install-
ment of his successor, the chapter assumed most of the powers of the prelate. Because members of the chapter were men
of great stature in colonial society, it was the chief ambition
of clerics to be promoted to this august corporation.

As holder of a *media ración,* Cristóbal Béquer was at the
lowest level of the chapter hierarchy; nevertheless his post
was an enviable lifetime benefice that carried with it the
prestige of membership in the principal group of secular
priests in the colony. While the salary brought by his post was
itself adequate for a respectable level of living, as an associate
of the chapter he had the opportunity for garnering additional
income by serving on special commissions within the far-
flung ecclesiastical establishment.

Lima was a city very much dominated by the Church, both
secular and regular. Prior to the earthquake and destruction
of 1746, some sixty thousand inhabitants resided in the more
than two thousand city blocks that were laid out in the grid
pattern typical of Hispanic settlement in the New World.
The life of the city, and indeed that of the entire Viceroyalty
of Peru, centered on the main square that was overlooked by
the imposing cathedral, the seat of the chapter. Although
there were many splendid mansions of the nobility and a
number of impressive edifices housing the civil government,
the urban architecture of the colonial capital was dominated
by religious structures. There were six handsome parish

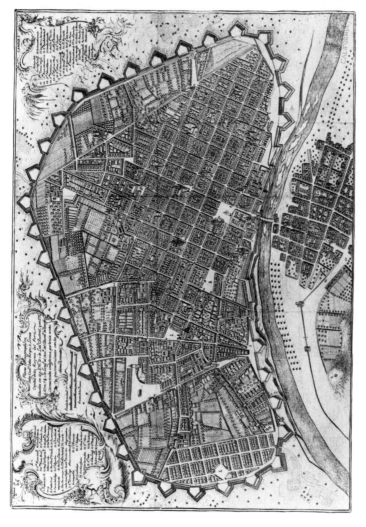

10. Béquer's Lima, with the cathedral on the main square just above the bridge over the River Rímac to San Lázaro.

churches, a dozen monasteries, nineteen nunneries, ten hospitals, the Inquisition, a number of orphanages, and numerous colleges. In total, some seventy buildings were classified as "churches."

Religious buildings and private residences intermingled with commercial establishments in the central section of the city. The shops of artisans were grouped by trade on the same block or street; the Calle de los Roperos was where used clothing was sold, the Calle de los Sombreros was the location of the hatmakers as well as the silk dealers and weavers, and so forth. Scattered throughout the city were pharmacies and *pulperías*, general stores that also dispensed *chicha*, a maize beer consumed by the lower classes. On the busy central streets and in nearby public squares the various levels of Lima's society mingled as they went about their daily business.

The Church set the tone for much of the public life of the city. Public occasions such as the reception of a new viceroy or the celebration of the birth of an heir to the throne always had a large religious content; a mass was held in the cathedral, and the chapter marched through the streets along with representatives of the other corporate entities of the capital. The *auto de fé* or public castigation of penitents by the Inquisition afforded a great public spectacle, and almost daily religious festivals were to be seen as the *cofradías*, or religious brotherhoods, staged processions in honor of their patron saints.

The Church, particularly the secular church, was an intimate part of society. Most upper-class families had several children who found careers in it: some entered the secular church hierarchy; many were ordained and then went on to pursue careers as professors, lawyers, or businessmen; and many, both male and female, entered the regular orders. By the time Béquer returned to Lima to assume his chapter post, more than six thousand persons or a tenth of the total population were members of the regular and secular clergy in the city. Most of the seculars, both chapter members and parish priests, had been born in Peru. Their fathers, uncles, brothers, grandfathers, and cousins formed the core of the men who staffed the other great institutions of the capital—the Audiencia, the town council, the treasury, the military, and the

Consulado. The corporate entities of colonial Lima were linked through families, and it was through family ties as well as through institutional structures that the members of the cathedral chapter influenced the flow of colonial life.

Béquer and his chapter colleagues were expected not only to lead in the affairs of both church and society, but to set examples in moral and ethical matters as well. It must be kept in mind, however, that standards of priestly behavior, carefully delineated in canon and civil law, were tempered considerably by broader societal attitudes in colonial Peru. The various courts and officials charged with enforcing the law generally demonstrated a class bias in acquiescing to behavior at the upper levels of society that would not be tolerated in the other ranks. Wealthy men, and those with family and personal influence or who were associated with one of the powerful corporate bodies (such as the city council, the guild of merchants, the Consulado, or the cathedral chapter), were often able to remain above the law. Illicit love affairs, the fathering of illegitimate offspring, brawling, and gambling were among the upper-class peccadillos that were customarily ignored.

The general emphasis on form rather than substance, legality rather than reality, meant moreover that as long as a "respectable" person maintained at least the appearance of conforming to the norms, he or she most likely would not run afoul of the law. Both Crown and Church, accepting the fact that individual lapses and weaknesses were persistent features of colonial clerical life, often winked at transgressions carried out discreetly. When the misconduct of a prebend began to be a topic of common gossip and could no longer be overlooked, the wayward cleric would be admonished privately by his superior. Prelates were hesitant to institute proceedings in the ecclesiastical courts, as this could often lead to an unseemly power struggle with the chapter. Likewise, the civil authorities were reluctant to intervene, as difficult and interminable jurisdictional disputes might result. When the archbishopric was vacant, the chapter was especially apprehensive of proceeding vigorously against one of its members, lest it bring on a factional conflict that would tax the energies of the elderly clerics, who needed all their powers for the administration of the archdiocese. Now and again, however, a priest caused such a public scandal that the highest church and civil officials were forced to act. During the late 1740s Béquer's unorthodox behavior produced just such a situation.

At first, it appears that his past escapades, his lack of adequate training, and his malevolent disposition were either forgotten or ignored or perhaps just well concealed by the cautious Béquer. For a few years after assuming his post he was on his best behavior, though even then participating absolutely minimally in chapter affairs. He attended few of the twice-weekly meetings and assumed none of the extra responsibilities for the governance of the ecclesiastical establishment with which other prebends customarily became involved; nevertheless as late as 1743 he was esteemed or at least tolerated enough by his colleagues to be awarded a vacant chaplaincy, a normal perquisite providing supplemental income for the chapter members.[5] Béquer's model deportment may perhaps have been due to the forceful presence of Archbishop Escandón, a prelate known for having kept a close watch on his clergy. But Escandón died in 1745, leaving the see vacant for a six-year period that was to witness the deterioration of Béquer's behavior and lead to his eventual downfall.

Shortly after the chapter assumed governance of the archdiocese, Béquer's more undesirable traits began to resurface. Argumentative as ever, one day he became involved in a terrible dispute in the sacristy of the cathedral with don Thomas Berris, one of the choir chaplains. Béquer's passions became so aroused that in a fit of anger he snatched up one of the large church keys that was lying about and smashed the chaplain over the head, producing a copious gush of blood. Berris survived to denounce the incident, prompting the chapter to make a formal inquiry and to admonish Béquer to mend his ways in the future.

Precisely the opposite occurred. Béquer's behavior grew more outrageous by the month, perhaps encouraged by the relatively mild response to his assault on Berris. Such excesses were serious but not infrequent occurrences among the temperamental limeños of the epoch. Colonial Peruvians placed a great deal of importance on outward appearances, ceremonies, and social courtesies, as indicators of rank, power, prestige, and honor. Significant personal and political conflicts were often waged over seating arrangements at public ceremonies or matters of the tone of address or appropriate clothing; the discourteous were sure to make enemies. Béquer's attack on Berris could be taken care of within the ecclesiastical establishment, accustomed to dealing with occasional outbursts between haughty clergymen, because he had not offended anyone with sufficient influence to demand and attain satisfaction.

Béquer, however, also unwisely affronted the powerful. Once at a public ceremony, the Marqués de Cáceres made some courteous remarks to the irascible priest; Béquer somehow took offense and "seriously offended him, with great detriment to his honor." When Marqués complained to those present about the misuse he had suffered, he was told to pay no attention to what was merely the cantankerous nature of the prebend. But Cáceres was among the first to testify in the later proceedings against Béquer, recounting the priest's transgression with great emotion. On that occasion all of those who commented on Béquer, from the viceroy on down to shopkeepers, were to remark at the lack of respect he had customarily shown to others. Béquer's alienation of the influential in society made him vulnerable for all of his misdeeds, but it was his lascivious interest in women that led directly to his downfall.

After the terrible destruction of Lima by the earthquake of October 1746, when the attentions of civil and ecclesiastical officials turned to the crises of maintaining order and rebuilding the city, there was little time left for disciplining an obstreperous cleric. Moreover, with the damage and destruction of most of the buildings of the city, the *limeños* began to frequent the streets, parks, and public squares more often than had been customary, providing numerous witnesses to Béquer's escapades. For his part, the prebend took to stalking the main plaza at night "in lewd solicitation of all the women, whom he tried, in a violent fashion, to persuade to accept his depraved goal," and made himself notorious in the process. A priest who lived in the archbishop's palace that fronted on the plaza reported having observed one evening a group of women "fleeing with no less fear than from a pirate" and crying out "Ay! Here comes Béquer!" A presbyter of the same neighborhood claimed that late one night during Holy Week he had been lounging in the doorway of his quarters when two frightened women who were total strangers burst into his room. When he inquired as to the reason for their precipitous entry, they replied that they were trying to escape from Béquer, who had been pursuing them for blocks, and that the presbyter's room seemed to be the only refuge at hand. They begged him to close the door, which he did, and then refused to leave until he had strolled around the plaza for a while to make sure that it was safe for them to venture forth.

The salacious prebend's most serious problem centered around his passion for doña Fabiana Sotomayor, a widow who kept a carpentry shop in Lima. It is probable that at one time she had been his paramour, but during the period with which we are concerned the widow spurned the attentions of Béquer, who nevertheless chased her with utter abandon. A later complaint on doña Fabiana's behalf stated that "for a long time he has pursued her through all available means for his lewd ends; and since the supplicant did not admit to this pretension, not only because of the sinful nature of it but because of his evil disposition, he has been unceasing in his hostilities towards her." The rejected Béquer eventually made her life so miserable that she found it difficult to attend to the duties of running her shop and earning her living. One day he had followed her chaise through the city streets; when she alighted, he had attacked her, beating her with a whip and leaving her bruised and battered. Béquer had also verbally chastized the widow, going about the town claiming publicly that she was really a mulatta and that her father was a man of obscure origins who had been engaged in hauling dirt and garbage with burros before becoming a petty merchant.

Béquer's wrath extended to doña Fabiana's circle of friends and particularly to don Martín Julián de Gamarra, a lieutenant in the Spanish infantry and fellow shopkeeper, with whom Fabiana spent a good deal of time. Whenever don Cristóbal came across the hated Gamarra, in the streets or in his shop in the Calle de los Judíos, he would accost and insult him. Gamarra later recounted that one day, when he

11. *Limeños* of the early eighteenth century.

was sitting alone in his place of business writing up some accounts, Béquer had rushed in and grabbed him by the throat, screaming that he was "a *sambo* dog as well as other injurious words." Gamarra had been most reluctant to use force against a clergyman, but he did have to defend himself and so grabbed a measuring rod to ward off the attack. Only this action and the gathering crowd of spectators had forced the prebend to leave.

Don Francisco Xavier Oyague, another merchant friend of doña Fabiana, also felt Béquer's wrath. One afternoon the priest had spotted Oyague and the widow Sotomayor together in a chaise near the stone bridge that connected the center of Lima with the refreshing alameda in the fashionable suburb of San Lázaro. The area around the bridge was a favorite gathering place for limeños, where they frequently stopped to chat with friends and observe the smart set of Lima society passing by in their carriages to or from San Lázaro. When Béquer came upon Oyague and doña Fabiana, he flew into a great rage, grabbing a rock and throwing it at the merchant whom he viewed, as a witness stated, as his "rival for the wicked possession of that woman."

As the scandal broadened, these recipients of Béquer's fury found the situation intolerable and began to seek some sort of protection. Doña Fabiana practically had to go into hiding, and her carpentry business suffered accordingly. Oyague and

Gamarra were deeply offended by the public insults of the prebend, but were unable to obtain satisfaction because of his priestly status and his prestige as a member of the cathedral chapter. Initially, all three had been reluctant to complain to the ecclesiastical authorities, assuming that the churchmen would protect their own. Finally, they did register protest with the cathedral chapter that was administering the vacant archbishopric, Gamarra even appearing personally before them to explain the problem. Then when the chapter declined to take any formal action, they sent their accusations directly to the viceroy. The Conde de Superunda, a forceful administrator, forwarded the grievance to the cathedral chapter with a strongly worded letter ordering them to take the necessary steps to correct the intolerable conduct of their colleague. The next day, the intimidated chapter reluctantly decided to proceed against him. Two canons of the chapter were appointed as judges for the case and began forthwith to draw up charges against Béquer.

At this the unruffled Béquer initiated a campaign to frustrate the judicial process as well as to harass his accusers. He demanded that Fabiana and Gamarra post the appropriate bond for the charges; Gamarra demanded that Béquer do the same, and the dispute dragged on. In the meantime Béquer stepped up his attacks on his enemies. One Sunday he chased Fabiana's carriage through the streets; when he caught up to her on the outskirts of the city, he began to beat her. She escaped only when Béquer's companion momentarily restrained him. Francisco Xavier Oyague complained that Béquer had publicly threatened to beat him to death, and was always stalking around the arcade on the main plaza looking for him. Oyague had encountered him there several times, but fortunately important and respected individuals had been present who restricted the priest to threats. These Oyague had tolerated out of respect for his antagonist's clerical status. Nevertheless when he went out in public he had always to be on guard, for he was reminded of the murder of the merchant guard years before:

> The other day, finding myself in the shop of don Pedro Aspur with my back to the street (which is how the deceased [merchant guard] don Pedro de Tores was in the shop of don Alonso Estrada when murdered by the aforementioned), I turned around at the moment that don Cristóbal was about to enter, but when seeing

that I had my sword on my belt, he confined himself to merely threaten me.

Oyague begged the chapter somehow to restrain the prebend, warning that if worse came to worst he would defend himself by whatever means necessary.

Despite the overwhelming evidence and the continuing charges, Béquer successfully delayed the judicial proceedings against him for many months. While the case was still in progress in the Lima ecclesiastical courts, he tried to have it appealed to the court of second instance in Huamanga, where he had been ordained years before and where he no doubt still had friends. Had a decision in Huamanga gone against him, he might have appealed to the court of third instance in Trujillo in northern Peru, a process which would have taken years. But as the attempt to appeal within the ecclesiastical court system failed, he asked that the secular court of the Royal Audiencia take cognizance of the case, arguing that he could not receive a fair hearing in the church courts. The Audiencia rejected Béquer's petition in April 1750, but the resourceful prebend had nevertheless delayed the matter for more than a year.

The case dragged on slowly until September when Dr. Julian López de Maturana arrived from Spain with a royal appointment to the *media ración* that ought by this time to have been vacated by the promotion of Béquer to the next highest post on the chapter, a *ración*. The chapter was thrown into a quandary: it was unthinkable to promote Béquer while he remained under the cloud of suspicion, yet it was unjust and dangerous to deny Maturana his seat on the chapter, for he was a member of the prestigious order of San Juan and a man well connected at court in Spain and linked by blood and friendship to the upper levels of Peruvian society. The prebends fired off a long letter to the king, explaining how in the circumstances it was impossible to promote Béquer and asking for instructions.

Meanwhile the proceedings against the reprobate Béquer began to produce some results. When the judges had taken formal testimony in April 1750 and found the evidence overwhelming against the prebend, orders were issued to confiscate his property and to imprison him in the same Bethlehemite monastery where he and his brother had sought refuge in 1714. Béquer, however, slipped away before the order could be carried out and installed himself in the monastery of San Francisco, claiming ecclesiastical immunity. Avowing that ecclesiastical immunity did not apply in this case since corporal punishment was not involved, the chapter notified Béquer that he was under arrest in the Franciscan monastery. Two months later the two judges for the case went to the monastery, confronted Béquer in the cell where he was residing, and attempted to take his statement. Ever recalcitrant, the prebend refused to cooperate and spent the whole time lambasting his judges. Despite this defiant stance, however, it was clear that justice would soon mete out the appropriate punishment.

Béquer was unable to make himself welcome even among the genial Franciscans. The guardian of San Francisco wrote to the chapter that some shoe buckles belonging to the prisoner had been stolen and that the prebend was accusing one of the friars of the crime. This had thrown the entire monastery into a frenzy, for wild accusations and rumors had begun to circulate, bringing suspicion down on servants and friars alike. The guardian bemoaned the state of his monastery and beseeched the ecclesiastical judges to dispatch Béquer's case quickly. The friar also subtly indicated that the monastery community was not fond of Béquer and that it suffered his presence only out of respect for the traditions of sanctuary in the Church.

Through dispatches from the chapter, the viceroy, and the ecclesiastical court, news of the Béquer affair reached the Council of the Indies in Spain by the middle of 1751. The Council determined that the hierarchy of Lima needed to be prodded to take swift action. The new archbishop, who arrived in Lima in July of 1751, was instructed to investigate the entire problem and take appropriate action; at the same time, an order was issued cancelling Béquer's promotion and directing that the chapter grant the vacant *ración* to López de Maturana in his stead.[6] In this way Béquer's victims were to be avenged. But before the despatches reached Lima, the wayward prebend had died. Although confined in his last months to the Franciscan monastery, he had successfully avoided prosecution, remaining to the end a law unto himself.

Notes

1. Archivo General de Indias (hereafter AGI), Lima 531, 1752, lista de pretendientes a la media racion, vacante por muerte de don Cristobal Béquer.

2. For information on Béquer's family, see his printed autobiographical statement *(relación de méritos y servicios)* in AGI, Charcas 411, no. 39. Béquer's brief *poder para testar* is to be found in Lima, Archivo General de la Nación, Sección Notarios, Valentín de Torres Preciado, 5 May 1752; that of his brother Miguel Carlos Béquer is in Juan Nuñez de Porras, 29 December 1700. For a discussion of the social structure of Lima in the eighteenth century and a detailed treatment of careers of the secular clergy and the role of the chapter in colonial life, see Paul B. Ganster, "A Social History of the Secular Clergy of Lima during the Middle Decades of the Eighteenth Century" (dissertation, University of California, Los Angeles, 1974), ch. 1 and *passim*.

3. The description of the murder case is to be found in AGI, Lima 530, 1749, autos criminales sobre varios excesos que sugue Fabiana de Sotomayor y Dn. Martin Julian Gamarra contra Lic. D. Xptobal Bequer, prebendado.

4. *Ibid.* Unless otherwise indicated, all direct quotations are from this document.

5. Archivo Capitular de Lima, Actas de Cabildo, 5 julio 1743 and *passim*.

6. AGI, Lima 531, consulta, 9 julio 1751.

Suggestions for Further Reading

There are few works in English that deal with the secular church and society in late colonial Peru. For a discussion of the secular church and the societal context, see Ganster, "A Social History." The best introduction to Peruvian social history is James Lockhart, *Spanish Peru, 1532–1560: A Colonial Society* (Madison; Wisc., 1968). Important aspects of the institutional life of Béquer's Lima are treated in the following: John Preston Moore, *The Cabildo in Peru under the Bourbons* (Durham, N.C., 1966); Luis Martin, *The Intellectual Conquest of Peru: The Jesuit College of San Pablo, 1568–1769* (New York, 1968); and Mark A. Burkholder and D. S. Chandler, *From Impotence to Authority: The Spanish Crown and the American Audiencias, 1687–1808* (Columbia and London, 1977). Also see Mark A. Burkholder, "From Creole to Peninsular: The Transformation of the Lima Audiencia," *Hispanic American Historical Review,* 52 (1972) and Leon Campbell, "A Colonial Establishment: Creole Domination of the Audiencia de Lima During the Late Eighteenth Century," *Hispanic American Historical Review,* 52 (1972). Interesting information on the parish priests is to be found in Antonine Tibesar, "The Lima Pastors, 1750–1820: Their Origins and Studies as Taken from Their Autobiographies," *The Americas,* 28 (July

1971). An impressionistic treatment of Béquer's Lima is Jean Descola, *Daily Life in Colonial Peru* (New York, 1968). Contemporary descriptions of Lima are to be found in the following: Robert Ryal Miller, ed., *Chronicle of Colonial Lima: The Diary of Josephe and Francisco Mugaburu, 1640–1697* (Norman, Okla., 1975); *A True and Particular Relation of the Dreadful Earthquake which Happened at Lima, the Capital of Peru . . .* (London, 1806); and [Rene Courte de La Blanchardiere], *A Voyage to Peru* (London, 1753).

★ PART THREE

*Survival Through
Individual Accommodation*

Introduction

*A*n important aspect of the struggle for survival within the colonial social order was the effort merely to get by, or to get ahead slowly but surely by accommodating to the colonial system as it stood. At first glance, accommodationist behavior appears to be the reverse of struggle. It connotes a meek acceptance of the system, an abject judgement that resistance is futile. But this simplistic view of an important human strategy for survival does scant justice to people's creative adaptation to an exploitative but also an apparently indestructible colonial social order. The people who chose this strategy were often strong-willed enough; but they were obliged to recognize that they lacked the physical and organizational resources with which to oppose their masters openly or confront the repressive power of the state. Not even the confessedly meek and cowardly, those willing to stoop to self-degradation in the effort to stay alive and healthy, may safely be dismissed as people who accepted oppression and gave up the struggle. Behavior might be manipulated successfully by the powerful; but thought was relatively free. Accommodation was as often as not a subtle form of defiance, a mask of servility hiding a defiant spirit, as in the "puttin' on ole Massa" of North American slaves.

The meaning of accommodation can be seen with special clarity in the experiences of the women whose stories predominate in Part III. To be female was to be socially inferior, politically powerless, and intellectually inaudible. It was the common view of men in all parts of colonial America that it was God's will for women to live out their lives under the direction of fathers and husbands, beloved and even idealized, but viewed in a very real sense as a kind of property. Despite this handicap, women, like men laboring within the structures of inequality defined by class and race, were far from passive in accepting the roles assigned to them. In countless ways they contrived to bend or break the social restrictions that bound them and give vent to individuality and creativity in determining to some extent the conditions of their lives. Sometimes this was done with the approval of men complacent about a partial relaxing of the definition of "women's place"; and sometimes it was done in defiance of men. Most of this resistance was carried out, however, within the accommodationist mode. Communal leadership and outspoken individual defiance were rare, the examples of Damiana de Cunha and Gertrudis de Escobar notwithstanding.

In much of colonial America, the scarcity of European women combined with the monopoly of wealth and power by European men made provisional arrangements with Indian, African, and especially mulatto or mestizo women the custom. The women who rose to meet this need and opportunity most assuredly played an active rather than a passive role in the social process of the colonies. They sacrificed the psychic comforts of life among people of their own kind for the chance to achieve greater security and a higher standard of living for themselves, an improved status and greater economic opportunity for their children, and some access to people in the seats of power. This strategy for survival has been dismissed as a sellout or as a passive yielding to the superior power (or sexuality) of the European male. But the stories of doña Isabel de Moctezuma and Beatriz de Padilla suggest another view of the hundreds of thousands of women of America who stepped purposefully into this key role. These women emerge here as spirited and intelligent historical actors, motivated by personal ambition, by an instinct for the preservation of self and family, and in some instances by love itself.

There was a positive side to accommodation in colonial society that lay not only in its active character but also in the genuine affirmation of new values that must often have gone along with it. For powerless people in the colonies, accommodation was not merely a tactic for survival, it was also a long-term strategy. As such, it necessarily involved not only concessions to the power of European men but also a willingness to learn from them, to incorporate aspects of the conquerors' outlook into one's own. This involved, far from abandoning one's will in the face of the mechanisms of hegemony, actively taking the lead in a dynamic process of social and cultural transformation. It was precisely this positive tradition of accommodation, this embracing of some European traits and values while rejecting others inwardly and passing on a new amalgam to one's children, that was at the heart of the central process of sociocultural transformation in the history of America. *Mestizaje,* the blending of races and cultures into a new people and a new culture unlike its ancestors and yet very much a piece with all of them, has long been seen as the wellspring of Latin American society. In North America the same process occurred, with the important difference that the overwhelming immigration of European men and women made it possible for colonial society to dispense with its few "half-breed" children, thrusting them back to their mothers' peoples. The blending that made North America was therefore primarily a commingling of different strains of European blood and culture, while alongside it a process more comparable to Latin America's was taking place among black people and Native Americans. The unique cultural and demographic situation of America at the end of the colonial era was the chief product of a long and fruitful process of accommodation.

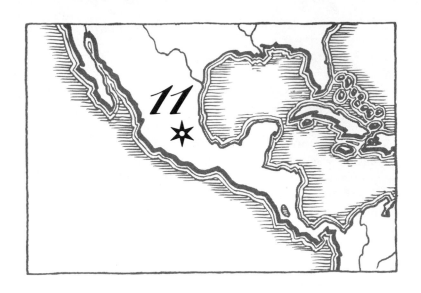

Isabel Moctezuma:
Pioneer of *Mestizaje*

DONALD CHIPMAN

n 1502 the Aztecs of Central Mexico observed the
death of the Emperor Ahuitzotl with a solemn
state funeral of four days' duration. Ahuitzotl had been the
last of three successive brothers to rule the empire, a fact
that complicated the selection of a new sovereign. After some
maneuvering, the late emperor's nephew Xocoyotzin prevailed over several of his brothers and cousins, and in 1503 at
the age of perhaps thirty-five he assumed power as Moctezuma II. At the new ruler's side was his legitimate wife,
Teotlalco, who had been distinguished from a host of concubines by virtue of a formal marriage ceremony.

The marriage of young Aztec noblepersons was contracted
between the families of the two parties and celebrated with a
nuptial dance followed by a feast. When the young couple
retired to the wedding bed, the parents symbolically tied the
skirt of the bride to a blanket covering the groom. For three

days the newlyweds remained in a closed bedroom, attended
only by a female servant who periodically brought them food
and took care of their needs. Without this ceremony a couple
was not properly united; and without it no children could
claim legitimacy or inheritance. If one may believe chroniclers of the Spanish conquest, by 1519 Moctezuma II had
fathered 150 children, of whom fifty or more were sons; at
one point the emperor is believed to have had fifty women in
various stages of pregnancy. Whatever the actual numbers, it
is clear that only a few of his offspring were legitimate heirs
by Aztec standards. In 1509 or 1510 the first-born child of
Moctezuma and Teotlalco was a female named Tecuichpotzin, meaning perhaps "little royal maiden." When Moctezuma consulted his daughter's horoscope in the Aztec book
of fate, he found to his amazement that she would have many
husbands. How this could be possible within the confines of
Aztec custom was beyond his comprehension. After the birth
of Tecuichpotzin, Teotlalco also bore the Aztec emperor an
undetermined number of legitimate sons.

By 1520 the Aztec emperor and his family had unwillingly
fallen captive in his capital of Tenochtitlan to a small force of
Spaniards and Indian allies led by the conqueror Fernando
Cortés. Following an ill-advised and fearful slaughter of Aztec nobility by the impetuous Pedro de Alvarado, the populace of Tenochtitlan rose in massive rebellion. Moctezuma,
in collaboration with the Spaniards, attempted unsuccessfully to quell the uprising. Shortly thereafter the emperor
died under circumstances that have never been resolved.
Before his death, Moctezuma had asked Cortés to assume
custody and care of his one legitimate and several illegitimate
daughters. They included Tecuichpotzin, later known to the
Spaniards as doña Isabel, and her three half-sisters, known as
doñas Ana, María, and Mariana. The conqueror also had in
his power several sons of Moctezuma II.

The rebellion in Tenochtitlan, far from being quieted by
the entreaties of Moctezuma, intensified in late June 1520,
ultimately forcing Cortés to retreat from the Aztec capital via
the Tacuba causeway on the night of June 30. This *noche
triste,* as it is known in Spanish sources, was also the final
night for some four hundred Spanish soldiers. Lost on the
causeway were doña Ana and perhaps a legitimate son of
Moctezuma. According to Cortés, two other legitimate sons

were captured by the Aztecs, of whom one was crazy and the other a paralytic. What is certain is that doñas Isabel, María, and Mariana were reunited with their people, for all were captured from the fleeing and panicky Spaniards by the temporarily victorious Aztecs.

For Tecuichpotzin this was the beginning of a matrimonial odyssey that was to deliver her to five husbands—two Indians and three Spaniards—as well as to an extramarital liaison with Cortés. The Aztec princess was first wed to her uncle, Cuitláhuac, brother of Moctezuma II, who had been elevated to emperor by the rebellion of 1520. Within sixty days Cuitláhuac had fallen victim to smallpox, a disease carried into Mexico by the Spaniards that would contribute substantially to their conquest. Because Tecuichpotzin was no more than eleven years of age at this time, it is generally assumed that her first marriage was unconsummated. Soon after Cuitláhuac's death, however, she was claimed as the bride of her cousin Cuauhtémoc, the last Aztec emperor. According to testimony given years later by her fifth husband, Juan Cano, it appears that Tecuichpotzin was married to Cuauhtémoc in the ceremony of tied blanket and skirt. Cano also maintained that Cuauhtémoc had ruthlessly consolidated his power by imprisoning and later killing Asupacací, the last legitimate son of Moctezuma II and the brother of his bride.

For approximately one year Tecuichpotzin remained with Cuauhtémoc, enduring the vengeful siege and destruction of Tenochtitlan perpetrated by Cortés and his captains. When the Aztec capital fell on August 13, 1521, Cuauhtémoc made a desperate attempt to escape across the water of Lake Texcoco in a large canoe accompanied by his young wife. Pursued and overtaken by the fastest Spanish brigantine, Cuauhtémoc is alleged to have said, "I am your prisoner and I ask no favor other than that you treat my queen, my wife, and her ladies-in-waiting with the respect they deserve due to their sex and condition."[1] Taking doña Isabel's hand, Cuauhtémoc then stepped aboard the brigantine. With the emperor taken prisoner, the Aztecs in boats on the lake made no further attempt to escape, choosing to share the fate of their leader.

For Tecuichpotzin, soon christened Isabel, life continued for three decades, during which she figured as the most prominent Indian woman in colonial Mexico and as a pioneer of *mestizaje.* Cuauhtémoc's days, unfortunately, were numbered. He was separated from his wife, subjected to horrible torture in the Spaniards' quest for treasure they believed was buried in the rubble of Tenochtitlan, and then forced to accompany Cortés on the arduous Honduran expedition from 1524 to 1526. En route to Honduras, Cuauhtémoc was tried, convicted, and hanged by Cortés for allegedly plotting an insurrection. Cuauhtémoc has been remembered as a martyr of Mexico and a symbol of its Indian heritage. Doña Isabel's career was less dramatic, but her procedure for coping with the Spanish conquerors undoubtedly had greater impact on the forging of the Mexican nation.

It was not until the late spring of 1526, when Cortés returned to Mexico, that doña Isabel learned of her husband's tragic fate; she was then sixteen or seventeen years old. Marriage to another Aztec nobleman was out of the question, since the Spaniards had eliminated most of those who had been of the appropriate rank and would in any event have been unwilling to allow the establishment of a new family with pretensions to the Aztec throne. Another consideration was that Moctezuma's daughter was a symbol of great legal and sociological importance to the Hispanization and Christianization of Mexico. This was not lost on the shrewd conqueror.

On June 26, 1526, Cortés granted to doña Isabel and her descendants the revenues and income from the important town of Tacuba, as well as from the several smaller villages that were subject to Tacuba. It was a rich inheritance by the standards of the newly established colonial society, although paltry in comparison with the patrimony that might have been due doña Isabel from her father. Altogether this grant of *encomienda,* pending approval by the crown, included twelve *estancias* and the pueblo of Tacuba for a grand total of 1,240 houses and several thousand Indian vassals. Significantly, Tacuba was a "perpetual" grant, similar to the Marquesado del Valle bestowed on Cortés in the late 1520s. Exempted from the restrictive laws that curtailed *encomienda* in the sixteenth century, Tacuba accompanied Isabel through each of her Christian marriages and provided her family with a handsome yearly income. The advantages of a perpetual grant are borne out by the fact that Tacuba, which had ranked ninth in size of tributary units in the immediate post-conquest era, was the largest *encomienda* in the Valley of Mexico by 1566. Each of the eight larger *encomiendas* originally awarded to Spaniards had escheated to the crown by the 1560s.

In awarding the *encomienda* of Tacuba to doña Isabel, Cortés was at pains to establish that Moctezuma II had served as a willing and valuable collaborator in furthering the work and realms of the king of Spain. Making no mention of the times that Moctezuma had tried to ambush his army on its march to Tenochtitlan, he stressed only that the emperor had placed himself under obedience to the king and that he had lost his life in a vain attempt to restore the fidelity of his misguided subjects. The "señor de Tenochtitlan" had been a "defender of Spaniards," and "a sympathizer of the Catholic Faith," and as such must be viewed as having been the legitimate ruler of his lands. In making doña Isabel the *encomendera* of Tacuba, Cortés claimed to be be discharging his conscience as well as the king's for having appropriated lands that by right belonged to Moctezuma. It was an argument worthy of a Renaissance diplomat. The crown quickly approved of Isabel's grant and of others bestowed by Cortés on the surviving children of Moctezuma. By awarding these *encomiendas,* the crown hoped to forestall the possibility that the emperor's heirs would later lay claim to much greater inheritances—as in fact they attempted to do. The crown also established by this means the important legal principle that Spanish law took precedence over any natural rights of Indian inheritance.

Cortés had at least one other object in mind when he made this grant of *encomienda* to doña Isabel. It would provide her with a suitable dowry for the marriage he was about to arrange, which he foresaw would be of great significance to the evangelization of Mexico. On June 27, 1526, just one day after his grant of *encomienda* to Isabel Moctezuma, Cortés appointed an old friend and associate to the post of visitor general of Indians. The appointee, Alonso de Grado, was specifically charged with the responsibility of investigating any mistreatment of the Indians and of instituting legal proceedings to punish the guilty. Grado, an Extremaduran like many of the conquistadors, had come to the New World at an early age. He had been an *encomendero* on the island of Española in 1514 and a charter member of the Cortés expedition to Mexico in 1519. Then, having accompanied the army of the conqueror on its march inland until its first pitched battle with the fierce Tlaxcalans, he had been frightened by the smallness of the Spanish force when compared with the seemingly endless horde of hostiles and had agitated for a retreat to Veracruz where they might be reinforced with troops sent by the governor of Cuba. But Cortés had repudiated the governor's sponsorship and destroyed his own fleet at Veracruz, thereby committing himself to victory. Grado was sent back to the coast for the duration of the conquest and established there a record for exploiting the Indians, demanding payments from them in foodstuffs, jewels, and pretty Indian women. He was also guilty of disloyalty to Cortés by meeting secretly with adherents of the governor of Cuba. After the occupation of Tenochtitlan in late 1519, Cortés ordered Grado arrested and brought to the capital in chains. He then dismissed the charges against him, and from that point on Grado remained on solid terms with the conqueror. Cortés, when awarding doña Isabel as a bride in 1526, extolled Grado's lineage and character. Bernal Díaz, of more honest pen, portrayed don Alonso as a sharpster, clever with words both spoken and written.

As the wife of a prominent conquistador, doña Isabel would become a model of Hispanicized Indian womanhood whom Cortés expected others to emulate. The mixture of races in New Spain was to be founded in principle on the legitimate grounds of holy matrimony, providing a solid matrix for a new society. Perhaps even more important, it was to be expected that the daughter of the Aztec emperor, whose namesake had been the most Catholic queen of Spain, once thoroughly converted to the Faith would also by her example hasten the evangelization of the country. Years later there was little doubt in the mind of doña Isabel's fifth husband, Juan Cano, that his wife had indeed served this lofty purpose:

> Although born in our Spain [Mexico], there is no person who is better educated or indoctrinated in the Faith. ... And it is no small benefit or advantage to the tranquility and contentment of the natives of this land, because she is the gentlewoman of all things and a friend of Christians, and because of respect and her example quiet and repose are implanted in the souls of the Mexicans.[2]

12. Doña Isabel de Moctezuma with her first Spanish husband, Alonso de Grado. Painting from a sixteenth-century codex.

Doña Isabel remained married to Alonso de Grado for less than two years. By 1528 don Alonso was dead of unknown causes, whereupon the solicitous Cortés moved the young and childless nineteen-year-old widow under his own roof to join the ranks of his Indian mistresses. She was, according to several eyewitnesses, a comely young lady (Bernal Díaz found her "a very pretty woman for being an Indian"). In a short time the Aztec princess was pregnant with the conqueror's child; and although Cortés himself had no intention of taking her as his wife, he did begin arrangements for her second Christian marriage.

This time the choice fell on one Pedro Gallego de Andrade. Don Pedro had arrived in Mexico shortly after the conquest was completed in 1521. An Extremaduran from the province of Badajoz, he had served in the conquests of Pánuco, Michoacán, and Colima. In compensation for these efforts he had received an *encomienda* town with the sonorous name of Izquiyuquitlapilco and a high-born but pregnant bride. Some four or five months after Gallego's marriage to doña Isabel, a daughter sired by Cortés was born in his household. She was christened doña Leonor Cortés Moctezuma and was the first of seven children to be born to the Aztec princess. Soon afterward the infant was placed in the home of Licentiate Juan Altamirano, a cousin of Cortés by marriage and subsequently chief administrator of the conqueror's vast estates in New Spain. There doña Leonor lived as a ward until the occasion of her marriage.

In 1530 doña Isabel bore Pedro Gallego a son named Juan (Gallego) de Andrade Moctezuma. The celebration in Tacuba of don Juan's birth was a gala event marked by fiestas and banquets with honored guests in attendance. The sacrament of baptism for the infant was administered by none other than His Excellency Juan de Zumárraga, first bishop of New Spain. For Pedro Gallego it was a proud moment. His aristocratic Indian wife had given him a son; the revenues of Tacuba and his own *encomienda* made him a wealthy man; he was on good terms with the governors in Mexico City; he moved in the highest social circles; and the bishop himself had sprinkled holy water on his first born. But the moment was short-lived. Within two months Gallego was dead—like Grado of undetermined causes—and at twenty-one doña Isabel had been widowed for a fourth time. None of her husbands had survived for more than a few years; her first, Cuitláhuac, for only sixty days. With such a record she might well have assumed that potential suitors would not tempt fate by rushing her to the altar. But such was not the case. In the spring of 1532 the wealthy doña Isabel was married for a fifth time to Juan Cano de Saavedra. This marriage, as it turned out, would prosper for nearly two decades.

About Juan Cano we know quite a lot, more because of his marriage to Isabel Moctezuma than for his own accomplishments. He too was an Extremaduran, the son of a commander of the royal fortifications in Cáceres. The Cano family had been distinguished for its service to the Catholic monarchs during the final phases of the Spanish reconquest. The grandfathers of Juan Cano had fought in Granada; an uncle had been a member of the retinue of the ill-fated Prince Juan, the only son of Ferdinand and Isabella. Cano was born near the turn of the sixteenth century, journeyed to the New World at eighteen, and was a member of the Pánfilo de Narváez expedition to Mexico in 1520. After the defeat of Narváez by Cortés, Cano became an adherent of the conqueror, participated in several conquests, and received a rather poor *encomienda* in compensation for his services.

When Juan Cano married doña Isabel, his fortunes changed for the better. He shared the lucrative revenues from Tacuba, and with this as a base he threw himself into a series of legal appeals designed to increase his wife's inheritance as a descendant of Moctezuma II. For Isabel, life with her fifth husband provided the first years of tranquility since early adolescence. She bore five children within ten years of marriage: Gonzalo, Pedro, Juan, Isabel, and Catalina. A sixth child in her household was Juan de Andrade Moctezuma, the product of her marriage to Juan Gallego. Her days were spent acquiring personal effects and instructing her daughters in the Catholic faith; she attended to her favorite charities; and she perhaps served as an example to the natives of Tacuba of a devout Catholic and Hispanicized woman who had bridged the worlds of Spaniard and Indian. When the governors of Mexico were brought to trial in the 1530s for their conduct in office, doña Isabel was the only Indian woman to be subpoenaed as a witness against them. She testified that the officials had extorted a bed from her home and had made illegal demands for special tribute from the Indians of Tacuba.

In 1542, shortly after the birth of his fifth child, Juan Cano traveled to Spain for a sojourn of two years' duration. He visited relatives in Cáceres, transacted business matters, and spent several months in Madrid in his continuing attempt to establish the "natural" rights of doña Isabel to her patrimony. Then on his way back to Mexico in 1544 Cano stopped off briefly in Santo Domingo, where he recounted to the official chronicler of the Indies, Gonzalo Fernández de Oviedo, his wife's claim as the only surviving legitimate heir of Moctezuma II, the fate of her brother at the hands of Cuauhtémoc, and the symbolic importance of her Hispanization and conversion to other Indians of Mexico.

In 1550 doña Isabel drew up her last will and testament. Among the executors of her estate was Juan Altamirano, the guardian of Leonor Cortés Moctezuma. In her will doña Isabel stated that she had possessed neither furniture nor jewels at the time she wed Juan Cano, a somewhat surprising declaration in view of her previous marriages to Grado and Gallego. But she maintained that only after her marriage to Cano had they acquired personal effects of considerable value, such as tapestries, carpets, cushions, embossed leather, pillows, and bedding. She specifically requested that these items be given to her daughters, doñas Isabel and Catalina. The single most important clause in the will was the disposition of Tacuba and its lucrative rents.

After doña Isabel's death in 1550, Tacuba would become a center of litigation that occupied courts in Mexico and Spain for years to come; it would set children against the surviving parent and brothers and sisters against each other, embittering relations beyond repair. It was the intent of doña Isabel that the bulk of Tacuba become the inheritance of her eldest son, Juan de Andrade, and that a much smaller portion go to Gonzalo Cano, her eldest son by Juan Cano. In the event that these two died without heirs (which did not happen), their inheritance was to pass to her third son, Pedro Cano, and his heirs. The remainder of doña Isabel's estate, less one-fifth for burial expenses, was to be divided equally among her six legitimate children. She did not mention her illegitimate daughter by Cortés, nor did she provide for her husband, who had property in Spain. As a gesture of compassion for "Indians natives of this land," the slaves held by doña Isabel and Juan Cano were to be freed of services and obligations and permitted to live as *personas libres*. The great lady's body was to rest in the church and monastery of San Agustín in Mexico City, which had for some time been a favorite charity. Not long after doña Isabel's death, the executors of the estate provided token recognition of Leonor Cortés Moctezuma as an heir and set aside a small legacy for her.

It is apparent from doña Isabel's will that she still held hope that the Spanish crown would restore her patrimony as heir to Moctezuma II's vast lands and that this expanded inheritance might also be divided equally among her six legitimate children. Perhaps it was this possibility that persuaded Juan Cano to leave Mexico and return to Seville, where he resided until his death some twenty years later. In Spain he remained active in the courts, contesting the disposition of Tacuba in his wife's will and maintaining a steady barrage of petitions to the crown asserting doña Isabel's natural rights as the heir of the Emperor Moctezuma II.

✳　✳　✳

What became of Isabel Moctezuma's seven children? A brief summary of their lives is a suitable epilogue to her story. Doña Leonor remained under the custody of Juan Altamirano until the early 1550s, when she was wed to the wealthy Juan de Tolosa, a man more than twenty years her senior and discoverer of the silver mines of Zacatecas. Leonor bore Tolosa a son who took religious vows and became the vicar of Zacatecas, a daughter who married Juan de Oñate, future colonizer and governor of New Mexico, and a second daughter who married into the Zaldívar family, prominent in the history of the mining frontier and New Mexico.

By 1551 Juan de Andrade Moctezuma had married María de Castañeda, the daughter of a conquistador. As the principal heir to Tacuba, he had become alienated from his stepfather and half-brothers, who had instituted a lawsuit designed to divest him of his inheritance. After almost twenty years of bitter litigation, the Cano family won a decision in the case that stripped Andrade of all but a sixth of Tacuba's revenues, with the remainder going in equal parts to each of Juan Cano's and doña Isabel's five children. While his estate was tied up in lawsuits, Juan de Andrade and his family resettled in Seville. There he tried his hand at business, a distasteful but necessary alternative to living off rents. However, his commercial venture was a failure, and he spent two years in prison for unpaid debts. Andrade died in Seville in 1576 or 1577, leaving five children as heirs. His descendants eventually became titled nobility as the Counts of Miravalle.

Gonzalo and Pedro Cano de Moctezuma, the first two sons of Juan Cano and doña Isabel, married and spent their lives in Mexico, where they and their children formed with some distinction a part of the colonial nobility. Their descendants include the families of Audelo Cano Moctezuma and Raza Cano Moctezuma, a few of whom were admitted to the Order of Santiago. The youngest son, Juan, was rather more successful. It appears that he accompanied his father to Spain in the early 1550s and married a woman of Cáceres, the seat of his father's property. There he built the Moctezuma Palace, which still stands, and set up an entailed estate, which passed on his death in 1579 to his own eldest son, don Juan. From this branch of the family also came titled nobility, the Count of Enjarada, the Dukes of Abrantes and Linares, and the families of Toledo Moctezuma, Carvajal, and Vivero, several of whom were also admitted to military orders.

Isabel and Catalina, the daughters of Juan Cano and doña Isabel, became novices of the convent of La Concepción in Mexico City shortly after the death of their mother. La Concepción was the oldest nunnery in the capital and housed the daughters of several prominent conquistadors. Its novices were normally the legitimate children of Spaniards more than thirteen years of age, blessed with good health, an ability to read, write, and handle figures, and a 4,000-peso dowry. Doñas Isabel and Catalina were mestizas, but of sufficient "quality" and means that the rules of La Concepción might be relaxed to accommodate them. Once admitted to the order, they took their vows of poverty so seriously as to renounce the share of the revenues of Tacuba that was adjudicated to them in the 1560s, and to arrange to have it bestowed in perpetuity on their father and surviving brothers.

In 1590, after half a century of litigation, a landmark decision regarding the heirs of Isabel Moctezuma was reached in the court of Philip II. In exchange for a permanent renunciation of their natural rights as heirs of Moctezuma II, a general settlement was made with the several grandchildren and great grandchildren of the emperor that granted them revenues from vacant *encomiendas* in Mexico for themselves and their heirs in perpetuity.

The 1590 settlement formalized the legal obligations of the Spanish crown to the many heirs of the Aztec princess Tecuichpotzin. It also vindicated doña Isabel's decision, made more than half a century before, to link her destiny with that of the Spanish conquerors who had destroyed her nation and to contribute to the establishment of a new society on Mexican soil.

Notes

1. Francisco Javier Clavigero, *Historia antigua de México*, 2 vols. (México, 1917), vol. 2, p. 201. I wish to acknowledge continuing support from the Faculty Research Committee of North Texas State University and a grant-in-aid (1976) from the American Philosophical Society for my research on the descendants of Moctezuma II.

2. Gonzalo Fernández de Oviedo, *Historia general y natural de las Indias*, 5 vols. (Madrid, 1959), vol. 4, p. 260.

Sources

The principal secondary sources for this essay are Burr C. Brundage, *A Rain of Darts: The Mexica Aztecs* (Austin, 1972); Cottie Burland, *Montezuma: Lord of the Aztecs* (New York, 1973); Charles Gibson, *The Aztecs under Spanish Rule, 1519–1810* (Stanford, 1964); and two articles by Amada López de Meneses appearing in the *Revista de Indias* (1949 and 1952). Anyone wishing to study Mexican nobility is advised to consult G. Fernández de Recas's *Cacicazgos y nobiliario indígena de la Nueva España* (México, 1961) and his *Mayorazgos de la Nueva España* (México, 1965); R. García Granados's *Diccionario biográfico de historia antigua de Méjico*, 3 vols. (México, 1952–53); and Doris Ladd's *The Mexican Nobility at Independence, 1780–1826* (Austin, 1976). For Mexican genealogical studies, R. Ortega y Pérez Gallardo's *Historia genealógica de las familias más antiguas de México*, 3 vols. (México, 1908–10) is basic. Archival sources for the study of Isabel Moctezuma and her descendants are housed primarily in the Archivo General de Indias (Seville), Sections Patronato, Justicia, and Audiencia de México; and in the Archivo General de la Nación (Mexico City), Sections Vínculos and Tierras.

Suggestions for Further Reading

For specialized studies of Mexican colonial society, readers are referred to appropriate sections of the *Handbook of Latin American Studies*. Peggy Liss's *Mexico Under Spain, 1521–1556: Society and the Origins of Nationality* (Chicago, 1975) emphasizes the transfer of societal institutions from Spain to Mexico in the first half of the sixteenth century, while Robert Padden's *The Hummingbird and the Hawk* (Columbus, Ohio, 1967) addresses the social and religious adjustments of Indians in the early colonial period. Insightful commentary on colonial life may be found in Richard Greenleaf's *Juan de Zumárraga and the Mexican Inquisition, 1536–1543* (Washington, D.C., 1961) and in his *The Mexican Inquisition of the Sixteenth Century* (Albuquerque, N.M., 1969). For the encomienda system, see Leslie Byrd Simpson, *The Encomienda in New Spain* (Berkeley, Calif., 1950). Excellent studies of Mexican society in the seventeenth century are Irving Leonard's classic *Baroque Times in Old*

Mexico (Ann Arbor, Mich., 1966) and Jonathan Israel's recent work *Race, Class, and Politics in Colonial Mexico: 1610–1670* (London, 1975). Two fine monographs, which are principally economic studies but nevertheless contain important social history, are Peter Bakewell's *Silver Mining and Society in Colonial Mexico: Zacatecas, 1546–1700* (New York, 1971) and David Brading's *Miners and Merchants in Bourbon Mexico, 1763–1810* (New York, 1971). François Chevalier's *Land and Society in Colonial Mexico* (Berkeley, Calif., 1970, earlier editions in French and Spanish) and William Taylor's *Landlord and Peasant in Colonial Oaxaca* (Stanford, Calif., 1972) treat both the *latifundio* and rural society. For the affairs of prominent families, see the items listed above by G. Fernández de Recas and Doris Ladd. Special attention is again directed to Charles Gibson's indispensable *The Aztecs Under Spanish Rule*.

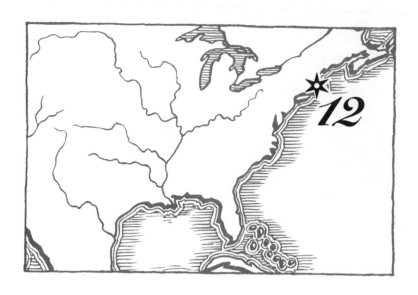

Squanto:
Last of the Patuxets

NEAL SALISBURY

As every American schoolchild knows, a lone Indian named Squanto rescued the Pilgrims from the wilderness by teaching them how to plant corn and introducing them to friendly natives. In so doing, the textbooks imply, he symbolically brought about the union of the European colonizers and the American land. Though contemporary events and critical historical inquiry are now undermining this myth, Squanto's story retains some significance. For when placed in its historic and cultural context, it reveals the range of truly human, if prosaic, qualities called forth among Native Americans during the early colonization of New England.

As befits a mythic hero, the time and circumstances of Squanto's birth are unknown. His birth date can only be inferred from what the sources say and do not say. The first-hand descriptions of him, written between 1618 and his death in 1622, do not suggest that he was strikingly young or old at that time. All we can safely conclude is that he was probably in his twenties or thirties at the time he was forcibly taken to Europe in 1614.

Though Squanto's early years are obscured by a lack of direct evidence, we know something of the cultural milieu that prepared him for his unexpected and remarkable career. Squanto and his fellow Patuxet spoke an Algonquian dialect that they shared with the other natives around Plymouth Bay and west as far as the near shore of Narragansett Bay. Moreover, its differences from other dialects in what is now southern New England were minimal, so that the Patuxet could communicate with the natives throughout this region. Like other coastal villages below the mouth of the Saco River, Patuxet was positioned to allow its inhabitants to grow crops, exploit marine resources, and have easy access to wild plants and animals. In accordance with the strict sexual division of labor maintained by virtually all eastern North American Indians, Squanto's major activities would have been to hunt game and to engage in certain kinds of fishing. He would also have fashioned a wide variety of tools and other material items and participated in the intensely ritualized world of trade, diplomacy, religious ceremonies, recreation, warfare, and political decision making that constituted a man's public life.

The training of young men in precontact southern New England was designed to prepare them for that world. Of the Pokanoket, closely related to the Patuxet, the Plymouth leader Edward Winslow wrote, "a man is not accounted a man till he do some notable act or show forth such courage and resolution as becometh his place."[1] A New Netherland official noted that young Pokanoket men were left alone in the forest for an entire winter. On returning to his people in the spring, a candidate was expected to imbibe and vomit bitter [poisonous] herbs for several days. At the conclusion of his ordeal, he was brought before the entire band, "and if he has been able to stand it all well, and if he is fat and sleek, a wife is given to him."[2]

As a result of such training, young Algonquians learned not only how to survive but also how to develop the capacities to withstand the severest physical and psychological trials. The result was the Indian personality type that Euroamericans came to characterize as stoic, the supreme manifestation of which was the absolute expressionlessness of prisoners under torture. Though the specific content of such training did little to prepare Squanto for his later experiences in Malaga, London, or Newfoundland, it imparted a sense of psychological independence and prepared him for adapting to the most demanding environments and situations.

Patuxet men such as Squanto also exercised their independence in making political judgments and decisions. As elsewhere in southern New England, the band, consisting of one or more villages, was the primary political unit. Its leader, the sachem, was drawn from one of a select group of lineages elevated in prestige above the rest. The sachems distributed garden plots to families and exercised certain judicial prerogatives. They also represented the band on diplomatic and ceremonial occasions. But a sachem's power was derived directly from the band members. To secure economic and political support he or she needed leadership ability as well as a family name. Band members could oblige a faltering sachem to share the office with a relative or step down altogether. Moreover, major political decisions were reached through a consensus in meetings attended by all adult males. Squanto came from a world, then, where politics was a constant and integral component of a man's life.

Squanto was even better prepared for his unusual career if, as seems probable, he was a *pniese* in his band. In preparation for this position, young men were chosen in childhood and underwent unusually rigorous diets and training. The purpose of this preparation was not simply to fortify them and develop their courage but to enable them to call upon and visualize Hobbamock, a deity capable of inflicting great harm and even death on those he did not favor. Hobbamock appeared in many forms to "the chiefest and most judicious amongst them," in Winslow's words, "though all of them strive to attain to that hellish height of honor."[3] It is clear that those who succeeded in the vision quest had developed the mental self-discipline demanded of all Indians to an extraordinary degree. By calling on Hobbamock, the *pnieses* protected themselves and those near them in battle and frightened their opponents. They constituted an elite group within the band, serving as counselors and bodyguards to the sachems. They were universally respected not only for their access to Hobbamock and for their courage and judgment but for their moral uprightness. Because of his psychological fortitude, his particularly astute grasp of Indian politics and protocol, and his continued sense of duty to his band after its demise, it is quite likely that Squanto was a *pniese*.

The few recorded observations of Patuxet during Squanto's early years show that it was a very different place from the "wilderness" the Plymouth colonists later found there. Both Samuel de Champlain, in 1605 and 1606, and John Smith, in 1614, noted that most of the coast between Massachusetts and Plymouth bays was under cultivation. The colonists were told, probably by Squanto himself, that in Plymouth Bay "in former time hath lived about 2,000 Indians."[4] The population of the surrounding area—that is, of the Indians

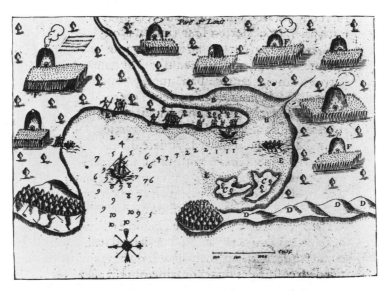

13. Champlain's map of "Port St. Louis" or Patuxet (Plymouth Harbor) in 1605. Note the numerous wigwams, garden plots, and people.

with whom the Patuxet maintained the closest relations— was probably between twenty and twenty-five thousand in 1615. Most of these natives were concentrated in village communities ranging in size from five hundred to fifteen hundred individuals. Squanto was thus accustomed to a more densely settled environment than we might expect and was probably as comfortable in the European cities he later visited as in the tiny colonies.

Though no one could have known it at the time, Squanto was born at a turning point in the history of his people and his region. For a century Europeans had been trading and skirmishing with, and sometimes kidnapping, Indians along the coast. At the time of Squanto's birth, however, these activities had not been extended south of Canada on a regular basis. Infrequent visits from European explorers and traders and the natives' own well-established exchange routes brought some iron tools and glass beads to Patuxet. But these were too scattered to induce any economic or cultural changes of a substantive nature. Unlike the fur-trading Indians to the north, the Patuxet and their neighbors had not become dependent on European trade items for their survival.

The turn of the century marked an intensification of French and British interest in New England's resources. The differing economic goals of the colonizers from the two countries gave rise to differing attitudes and policies toward the natives. The French were concerned primarily with furs. Following Champlain's explorations of the New England coast in 1605 and 1606, French traders using his descriptions and maps began to visit the Indians annually and to cultivate an extensive trade as far south as Cape Cod. Their goals encouraged the maintenance of friendly relations with stable Indian bands and even the development of broad regional ties among the natives.

For the English, however, furs were at best a useful by-product of more pressing interests. Beginning with Bartholomew Gosnold's expedition in 1602, they showed a preference for resources such as fish and sassafras that did not require the cooperation of the natives. Moreover, they thought in long-range terms of making Indian land available to Englishmen for farming, a goal that virtually guaranteed

eventual conflict with the natives. Indian allies were cultivated, but only for purposes of assisting the English in establishing themselves, and the methods used were generally
more coercive than those of the French. Nearly every English
expedition from Gosnold's to that of the Mayflower generated hostility with the Indians. By 1610 taking captured
Indians to England had become routine. Would-be colonizers
such as Sir Ferdinando Gorges hoped to impress their captives with the superiority of English culture, to learn as much
as they could about the lay of the land, and to acquire medi-
ators with the local Indians. They also displayed their captives prominently in order to attract financial and public
support for their projected colonies.

John Smith, the former Virginia leader, witnessed the results of the competition between the two colonial strategies
when he explored the coast from the Penobscot River to Cape
Cod in 1614. Smith found that he had arrived at the end of an
active trading season. Aside from one Englishman's cozy
monopoly at the mouth of the Pemaquid River, all the ships
were French. Though the better-endowed region north of the
Pemaquid had yielded twenty-five thousand skins that year,
Smith judged the south capable of producing six to seven
thousand annually. He himself had retrieved thirteen hundred pelts, mostly beaver, in the wake of the French departure. He also found that all the Indians in the region he visited
were friendly with one another through three loose regional
alliances. Ostensibly formed to resist incursions from the
Micmac in eastern Canada, the friendship chain had an
economic function as well, for Smith noted that some primarily horticultural Indians in southern New England traded
corn to Abenaki hunting groups farther north whose concen-
tration on the fur trade was apparently leading to food
shortages. In return the horticulturalists obtained some of
the Abenaki's supply of European trade goods. Though only
minimally developed by 1614, this trade was already foster-
ing a specialized division of labor among France's clients in
New England.

The extent of Patuxet's participation in the corn trade is
unknown. But Squanto and his people were producing substantial fur surpluses by the time of Smith's visit in 1614 and
had gained at least some acquaintance with the Europeans.

From the visits of Champlain, Smith, and the traders, Squanto had learned something of European approaches to trade, diplomacy, and military conflict and had witnessed some of their technological accomplishments. But the regularized trade was less than a decade old. And the ease with which groups of Patuxet men were manipulated by Smith and his officer, Thomas Hunt, in 1614 suggests that they had not developed the wariness toward Europeans, particularly the English, of the more experienced Indians to the north.

Squanto's life reached a sudden and dramatic turning point with Hunt's visit. Smith had returned to England, leaving Hunt in charge of his fishing crew to complete the catch and carry it to Malaga, Spain. Before departing, Hunt stopped at Patuxet. Using his association with Smith, who had left on friendly terms, he lured about twenty natives, including Squanto, aboard. Quickly rounding Cape Cod, he drew off seven more from Nauset and then turned east for Malaga. Hunt's action indelibly marked the English as an enemy of all the Indians in the Patuxet-Cape Cod region. In the words of Sir Ferdinando Gorges, Hunt's action resulted in "a warre now new begunne betweene the inhabitants of those parts and us," and John Smith condemned Hunt for moving the Indians' "hate against our Nation, as well as to cause my proceedings to be more difficult."[5]

Native outrage at Hunt's action was reinforced by the near-simultaneous return of an earlier Indian captive, Epenow, a sachem of Capawack (Martha's Vineyard). Epenow had been seized three years earlier and taken to Gorges in England. On constant public display, he learned English well and impressed Gorges and others as "a goodly man of brave aspect, stout and sober in his demeanour."[6] Thus his tales of gold on Capawack were eagerly seized upon, and in 1614 Gorges commissioned a voyage under Nicholas Hobson, accompanied by Epenow as a guide. Epenow had apparently planned his escape all along, but the news of Hunt's deed hardened his desire for revenge. As the ship drew near his island, Epenow escaped under a cover of arrows from the shore. A fierce battle ensued with heavy casualties on both sides. Among the injured was Hobson himself, who returned to England empty-handed. Epenow thereafter constituted one source for the anti-English sentiment that would persist in the region to the founding of Plymouth colony six years later.

Meanwhile Squanto and his fellow captives reached Malaga, where Hunt tried to sell them as slaves. A few had already been sold when, according to Gorges, "the Friers of those parts took the rest from them and kept them to be instructed in the Christian faith."[7] What happened to Squanto in the next three years is not clear. Particularly intriguing are questions about the extent and influence of his Catholic instruction and the means by which, in William Bradford's words, "he got away for England."[8] We know only that by 1617 he was residing in the London home of John Slany, treasurer of the Newfoundland Company, where he learned or at least improved his English and his understanding of colonial goals. In the following year he went to Newfoundland itself, presumably at Slany's instigation. Here he met for the second time Thomas Dermer, an officer with Smith in 1614 who now worked for Gorges. Dermer was so impressed with Squanto's tales of Patuxet that he took him back to England to meet Gorges. Though the strategy of employing captive Indians as guides had backfired several times, Gorges was ready to try again. He saw in Squanto the key to countering the recent successes of the French and reestablishing England's reputation among the Indians. For his part Squanto knew, as had earlier captives, how to tell Gorges what he wanted to hear in order to be returned home. In March 1619 he and Dermer were bound for New England.

Moving in the circles he did, Squanto undoubtedly knew something of the epidemic that had ravaged New England, including Patuxet, during his absence. A Gorges expedition under Richard Vines had witnessed what Vines called simply "the plague" at Sagadahoc in 1616 and reported on its effects. Most notable was the immunity of the English; while most of the Indians were dying, Vines and his party "lay in the Cabbins with those people, [and] not one of them ever felt their heads to ake."[9] This immunity and the 75 to 90 percent depopulation among the Indians make it clear that a virgin soil epidemic of European origin had been planted in New England's isolated disease environment. Though the specific instigator cannot be identified because of the frequency with which Europeans were visiting New England, it is noteworthy that the stricken zone, as reported by Dermer in 1619, was the coast from the Penobscot to Cape Cod—precisely the area encompassing the loose coalition of Indian groups engaged in trade with the French and each other. At its southern extremity the epidemic spread west to the Patuxet's allies, the Pokanoket, at the head of Narragansett Bay, but not to their Narragansett rivals on the western side. Such an outline suggests that the epidemic spread via established exchange routes that were shaped to a great extent in response to the fur trade and the accompanying developments.

Squanto found his own village completely vacated. Most of its inhabitants had died, but some had fled inland to other villages. He surely noticed, as did others, the undergrowth that had overtaken the formerly cultivated fields and the vast numbers of unburied dead whose "bones and skulls," in one Englishman's words, "made such a spectacle. . . . it seemed to me a new found Golgotha."[10] The depopulation was so great that the Narragansett were able to force the weakened Pokanoket to abandon their position at the head of Narragansett Bay and to retain only the eastern shore.

The Narragansetts' avoidance of the epidemic gave them a greater advantage than that derived from numbers alone. In the view of their stricken neighbors, the Narragansetts' good health reflected their faithful sacrifices to the deity, Cautantowwit. The ritual worlds and belief systems of the stricken Indians, however, had been badly shaken by the epidemic. The usual practice of gathering with the *pow-wow* (shaman) in a sick person's wigwam could only have served to spread the disease more rapidly. With even the *pow-wows* succumbing, the Indians could only conclude that their deities had aligned against them. And being unable to observe the proper burial rituals, the survivors had to fear the retribution of the dead. The Indians' perception that they had lost touch with the sources of power and that others controlled the access to them would be a critical factor in facilitating Squanto's later political success.

As Dermer's expedition traveled overland from Patuxet in the summer of 1619, Squanto's presence and diplomatic skill enabled the English to break through the antagonisms toward them and to make friendly contacts at Nemasket (near Middleboro) and Pokanoket (near Bristol, Rhode Island). For once an Indian captive had performed as Gorges hoped. But as Dermer returned to his ship and prepared to sail around Cape Cod, Squanto took his leave to search for surviving Patuxets. On his own, Dermer was unable to persuade the Indians at Monomoy (now Pleasant Harbor) of his good intentions. He was captured and barely succeeded in escaping. After a seemingly cordial meeting on Martha's Vineyard with Epenow, the former Gorges captive, Dermer was attacked off Long Island and again managed to escape. Returning to New England in the summer of 1620, he was captured by his newly made friends at Pokanoket and Nemasket and released only after Squanto interceded on his behalf. Dermer, with Squanto, then proceeded to Martha's Vineyard, where they were attacked by Epenow and his followers. Most of the crew was killed this time, while the luckless captain escaped with fourteen wounds and died in Virginia. Squanto was again made a captive, this time of the Indians.

In a letter written after his release at Nemasket, Dermer attributed his reception there to his hosts' renewed desire for revenge. He noted that another English crew had just visited the area, invited some Indians on board their ship, and then shot them down without provocation. The incident could only have revived the Indians' suspicions of the English that had prevailed before Squanto's return. These suspicions were now focused on Squanto himself, as Dermer's accomplice, and led to his being turned over to the Pokanoket with whom he remained until he was ransomed by the Plymouth colonists in March 1621.

The Patuxet-Pokanoket-Cape Cod region was vastly different in the autumn of 1620 from a decade earlier when French traders had begun to frequent it regularly. Fewer than 10 percent of its twenty thousand or more former inhabitants were still living, and they were now consolidated into a few bands. The region was vulnerable as never before to exploitation by outsiders. The once-powerful Pokanoket and their sachem, Massasoit, had been subjected to a humiliating tributary relationship with the Narragansett, who were emerging as the most powerful aggregation in New England because of their size and their control of Indian-European trade links east of Long Island. Moreover, the decimated Indians could no longer count on the fur trade as a means of compensating for other weaknesses. Always limited in both the quality and quantity of its fur resources, the region's loss of most of its hunters now made it an unprofitable stop for traders.

Though a captive, Squanto was able to capitalize on the Pokanokets' despair. "He told Massasoit what wonders he had seen in England," according to a future settler, "and that if he could make English his friends then Enemies that were too strong for him would be constrained to bow to him."[11] He did not have to wait long to be proved right. In December 1620, less than six months after Dermer's departure, word reached Pokanoket that a shipload of English colonists had established a permanent settlement at Patuxet.

Like the other Puritans who later settled New England, the group at Plymouth (for so they renamed Patuxet) was motivated by a combination of religious and economic motives that shaped their attitudes toward the natives. Their experience with persecution in England and exile to the Netherlands had sharpened their desire to practice their exclusionary, intolerant separatism without external interference. Moreover, though seeking distance from English ecclesiastical authorities, the settlers were attempting to reinforce their English identities. They had abandoned their Dutch haven for fear that their children would be assimilated there. Finally, though ostensibly migrating to fish and trade for furs, the colonists sought land to improve themselves materially and, they supposed, spiritually. Though Plymouth lacked the sense of divine mission of the later nonseparatist Puritan colonies, its goals of religious and ethnic exclusivity and an abundance of land had obvious implications for its relations with the natives.

These implications were apparent in Plymouth's early policies and attitudes toward the Indians. In a major promotional pamphlet published in 1622, Robert Cushman restated what had already become a familiar justification for dispossession of native lands:

> Their land is spacious and void, and there are few and do but run over the grass, as do also the foxes and wild beasts. They are not industrious, neither have art, science, skill, or faculty to use either the land or the commodities of it, but all spoils or rots, and

is marred for want of manuring, gathering, ordering, etc. As the ancient patriarchs therefore removed from straiter places into more roomy . . . . so is it lawful now to take a land which none useth, and make use of it.[12]

Cushman's statement was consistent with the emerging European doctrine of *vacuum domicilium*, by which "civil" states were entitled to the uncultivated lands of those in a "natural" state. Though Plymouth's own "civility" was formalized by the hastily contrived *Mayflower* Compact, its financial backers had anticipated its need for more than an abstract principle to press its claim—among its own people as well as among any natives they might encounter. Accordingly, they had hired Miles Standish, a soldier of fortune fresh from the Dutch wars, to organize the colony militarily. It was Standish who would shape Plymouth's Indian policy during its first generation.

Standish began to execute this policy even before the *Mayflower* arrived at Patuxet. Landing first at Cape Cod, the settlers aroused native hostilities by ransacking Indian graves, houses, and grain stores. At Patuxet they also stirred suspicions during the first four months of their stay. But their own situation grew desperate during their first New England winter. They lost half their numbers to starvation and disease, and as inexperienced farmers they were ill-prepared for the approaching planting season. In this condition they could no longer expect to alleviate their shortages through pilferage with impunity. The impasse was broken one day in March 1621 by the appearance of Samoset, a sachem of the Pemaquid River band, which had been trading with the English for more than a decade. Samoset learned the needs and intentions of the colony and returned a few days later with Squanto.

The Pokanoket had been watching the Plymouth group throughout the winter. With Samoset and the newly useful Squanto offering advice and experience, they concluded that the time was ripe to befriend the settlers instead of maintaining a hostile distance. Such an alliance would enable them to break from the hold of the Narragansetts, whose haughty demeanor stung even more than that of the English. Nevertheless, the decision was not to be taken lightly. Bradford wrote that the Indians did first "curse and execrate them with their conjurations" before approaching the settlers.[13]

But this description betrays his fear of witchcraft as it was understood by Europeans, rather than his comprehension of Indian rituals. More likely the Pokanoket were ritually purging themselves of their hostilities toward the English. Samoset and Squanto arranged the meeting between the Pokanoket and Plymouth colony that resulted in their historic treaty. In it each side agreed to aid the other in the event of attack by a third party, to disarm during their meetings with each other, and to return any tools stolen from the other side. But in addition to these reciprocal agreements, several others were weighted against the natives. Massasoit, the Pokanoket sachem, was to see that his tributaries observed the terms; the Indians were to turn over for punishment any of their people suspected of assaulting any English (but no English had to fear being tried by Indians); and, the treaty concluded, "King James would esteem of him [Massasoit] as his friend and ally."[14] The meaning of the last honor was made explicit by the colony's annalist, Nathaniel Morton, who wrote that by the treaty Massasoit "acknowledged himself content to become the subject of our sovereign lord the King aforesaid, his heirs and successors, and gave unto them all the lands adjacent to them and theirs forever."[15] Morton made clear that among themselves the English did not regard the treaty as one of alliance and friendship between equals but as one of submission by one party to the domination of the other, according to the assumptions of *vacuum domicilium*.

For the Pokanoket, however, the meaning of a political relationship was conveyed in the ritual exchange of speeches and gifts, not in written clauses or unwritten understandings based on concepts such as sovereignty that were alien to one party. From their standpoint, the English were preferable to the Narragansett because they demanded less tribute and homage while offering more gifts and autonomy and better protection.

The treaty also brought a change in status for Squanto. In return for his services, the Pokanoket now freed him to become guide, interpreter, and diplomat for the colony. Thus he finally returned to his home at Patuxet, a move that had, as we shall see, more than sentimental significance. Among his first services was the securing of corn seed and instruction in its planting, including the use of fish fertilizer, which he learned from his own people or from the Newfoundland colonists.

Squanto also enabled Plymouth to strengthen its political position in the surrounding area. He helped secure peace with some bands on Cape Cod and guided an expedition to Massachusetts Bay. His kidnapping by anti-English Indians at Nemasket and subsequent rescue by a heavily armed Plymouth force speaks compellingly of his importance to the colony. Moreover, this incident led to a new treaty, engineered in part by Squanto, with all the Indian groups of Massachusetts Bay to the tip of Cape Cod, including even Epenow and his band. By establishing a tributary system with the surrounding Indian bands, the colony was filling the political vacuum left by the epidemic and creating a dependable network of corn suppliers and buffers against overland attack. But it also incurred the resentment of the Narragansett by depriving them of tributaries just when Dutch traders were expanding their activities in the bay. The Narragansett challenged Plymouth's action in January 1622 by sending a snakeskin filled with arrows. On Squanto's advice Plymouth's leaders returned the skin filled with powder and shot. The Narragansett sachem, Canonicus, refused to accept this counterchallenge, in effect acknowledging the colony's presence and political importance.

However effective in appearance, Plymouth's system of Indian diplomacy was fraught with tensions that nearly destroyed it. A Pokanoket *pniese*, Hobbamock (named for his patron deity), became a second adviser to Plymouth in the summer of 1621. Whether the English thought that Hobbamock would merely assist Squanto or would serve to check him is unclear. In any event, Squanto was no longer the only link between the colony and the Indians; indeed, as a Pokanoket, Hobbamock had certain advantages over him. As one whose very life depended on the colony's need for him, Squanto had to act decisively to check this threat to his position. His most potent weapon was the mutual distrust and fear lingering between English and Indians; his most pressing need was for a power base so that he could extricate himself from his position of colonial dependency. Accordingly, he began maneuvering on his own.

Squanto had been acting independently for several months before being discovered by the English in March 1622. As reconstructed by Edward Winslow:

> his course was to persuade [the Indians] he could lead us to peace or war at his pleasure, and would oft threaten the Indians, sending them word in a private manner we were intended shortly to kill them, that thereby he might get gifts to himself, to work their peace; . . . so that whereas divers were wont to rely on Massasoit for protection, and resort to his abode, now they began to leave him and seek after Tisquantum [Squanto].[16]

In short, he sought to establish himself as an independent native political leader. At the same time he endeavored to weaken the Pokanoket's influence on Plymouth by provoking armed conflict between the two allies. He circulated a rumor that Massasoit was conspiring with the Narragansett and Massachusett to wipe out the colony. The English quickly verified the continued loyalty of the Pokanoket but, though angry at Squanto, were afraid to dispense with him. Instead they protected him from Massasoit's revenge, which brought tensions into the Pokanoket-Plymouth relationship that were only finally assuaged when Squanto died later in the year.

In seeking to establish his independence of Plymouth, Squanto was struggling for more than his survival. As Winslow put it, he sought "honor, which he loved as his life and preferred before his peace."[17] What did honor mean to Squanto? For one thing, of course, it meant revenge against the Pokanoket, not only for threatening his position at Plymouth but for his earlier captivity. But it meant more than that. Squanto appears to have made substantial inroads among Indians loyal to Massasoit in a short period of time. Winslow indicated, unknowingly and in passing, the probable key to this success. The news of Massasoit's alleged treachery against Plymouth was brought, he said, by "an Indian of Tisquantum's family."[18] Contrary to the Plymouth sources (all of which were concerned with establishing the colony's unblemished title to the land around Plymouth Bay), there were certainly a few dozen Patuxet survivors of the epidemic at Pokanoket, Nemasket, and elsewhere. Though Squanto undoubtedly sought the loyalty and tribute of others, it was to these relatives and friends that he would primarily have appealed. The honor he sought was a reconstituted Patuxet band under his own leadership, located near its traditional home.

Squanto's hopes were shattered when his plot collapsed. With Massasoit seeking his life, he had, in Bradford's words, "to stick close to the English, and never durst go from them till he dies."[19] This isolation from other Indians and dependence on the colonists helps explain the latter's willingness to protect him. In July, Squanto again engineered an important breakthrough for Plymouth by accompanying an expedition to Monomoy, where suspicion of all Europeans persisted. The Indians here had attacked Champlain's party in 1606 and Dermer's in 1619. Standish's men had taken some of their corn during their stop at Cape Cod in November 1620. Now, as Winslow phrased it, "by Tisquantum's means better persuaded, they left their jealousy, and traded with them."[20] The colony's take was eight hogsheads of corn and beans. But as the expedition prepared to depart, Squanto "fell sick of an Indian fever, bleeding much at the nose (which the Indians take for a symptom of death) and within a few days died there."[21]

By the time of Squanto's death, Plymouth colony had gained the foothold it had sought for two and a half years. The expedition to Monomoy marked the establishment of firm relations with the last local band to withhold loyalty. Moreover, the trade in corn was no longer an economic necessity, remaining important primarily as a means of affirming tributary relationships. These accomplishments would have been infinitely more difficult, if not impossible, without Squanto's aid. But it is questionable whether his contributions after the summer of 1622 would have been as critical. Thereafter, the colony's principal dealings were with the hostile Massachusett and Narragansett Indians beyond Patuxet's immediate environs. Moreover, the world in which Squanto had flourished was vanishing. A rationalized wampum trade had begun to transform Indian-European relations in southern New England. And the end of the decade would bring a mighty upsurge in English colonization that would surround and dwarf Plymouth. Within the restrictions imposed by his dependence on Plymouth's protection, Squanto would have adapted to these changes. But his knowledge and skills would no longer have been unique nor his services indispensable.

It is difficult to imagine what direction the life of this politically and historically isolated man, who valued "honor" above all else, might have taken in the coming decades. It is in this light that we should read his well-known deathbed conversion wherein he requested Bradford "to pray for him that he might go to the Englishmen's God in Heaven; and bequeathed sundry of his things to sundry of his English friends as remembrances of his love."[22] He was acknowledging that after eight years of acting with honor in alien settings, he had been cornered. Dying so ignominiously, the last Patuxet would have found it ironic that later generations of Americans celebrated him as a hero.

Notes

1. Edward Winslow, "Good Newes from New England," in Alexander Young, ed., *Chronicles of the Pilgrim Fathers* (Boston, Mass., 1841), p. 363.

2. Isaack de Rasieres to Samuel Bloomaert, c. 1628, in Sydney V. James, Jr., ed., *Three Visitors to Early Plymouth* (Plymouth, Mass., 1963), p. 79.

3. Winslow, "Good Newes," p. 357.

4. Emmanuel Altham to Sir Edward Altham, September ? 1623, in James, *Three Visitors,* p. 29.

5. James Phinney Baxter, ed., *Sir Ferdinando Gorges and His Province of Maine* (Boston, 1890), vol. 2, p. 211; Edward Arber, ed., *Travels and Works of Captain John Smith,* 2d ed. (Edinburgh, 1910), vol. 1, p. 219.

6. Baxter, *Gorges,* vol. 2, pp. 20–21.

7. *Ibid.,* vol. 1, p. 210.

8. William Bradford, *Of Plymouth Plantation,* ed. Samuel Eliot Morison (New York, 1967), p. 81.

9. Baxter, *Gorges,* vol. 2, p. 19.

10. Thomas Morton, *New English Canaan,* ed. Charles Francis Adams, Jr. (Boston, 1883), pp. 132–133.

11. Phineas Pratt, "A Declaration of the Affairs of the English People that First Inhabited New England," Massachusetts Historical Society, *Collections,* 4th series, 4 (1858): 485.

12. Dwight B. Heath, ed., *A Journal of the Pilgrims at Plymouth,* orig. title: *Mourt's Relation* (New York, 1963), pp. 91–92.

13. Bradford, *Plymouth Plantation,* p. 84.

14. Heath, ed., *Journal*, p. 57.

15. Nathaniel Morton, *New Englands Memoriall*, ed. Howard J. Hall (New York, 1937), p. 24.

16. Winslow, "Good Newes," p. 289.

17. *Ibid.*, pp. 289–290.

18. *Ibid.*, p. 287.

19. Bradford, *Plymouth Plantation*, p. 99.

20. Winslow, "Good Newes," p. 301.

21. Bradford, *Plymouth Plantation*, p. 114.

22. *Ibid.*

Sources

The pervasiveness of myth and the paucity of hard evidence have discouraged serious biographies of Squanto. Leonard A. Adolf, "Squanto's Role in Pilgrim Diplomacy," *Ethnohistory* 11 (1964): 247–61, assembles the best known facts of Squanto's life but with little context or interpretation. More imaginative are Frank Shuffleton, "Indian Devils and Pilgrim Fathers: Squanto, Hobomock, and the English Conception of Indian Religion," *New England Quarterly* 49 (1976): 108–116; and Ronald Sanders, *Lost Tribes and Promised Lands: The Origins of American Racism* (Boston and Toronto, 1978). All these authors would have benefited from the ethnohistorical background provided by T. J. Brasser's "Early Indian-European Contacts," in Bruce G. Trigger, ed., *Northeast*, vol. 15 of *Handbook of North American Indians*, gen. ed. William C. Sturtevant (Washington, D.C., 1978), pp. 78–88. On native culture, I have relied heavily on the handful of careful European observers who recorded it in the seventeenth century. Among secondary analyses based on these sources, I have drawn especially on M. K. Bennett, "The Food Economy of the Southern New England Indians, 1605–75," *Journal of Political Economy* 63 (1955), 369–97, on subsistence; and William S. Simmons, "Southern New England Shamanism: An Ethnographic Reconstruction," in *Papers of the Seventh Algonquian Conference, 1975*, ed. William Cowan (Ottawa, 1976), pp. 217–57, on religion. Douglas R. McManis, *European Impressions of the New England Coast, 1497–1620* (Chicago, 1972), provides useful background on the pre-Plymouth visitors. On the epidemic, see Sherburne F. Cook, "The Significance of Disease in the Extinction of the New England Indians," *Human Biology* 45 (1973): 485–508; Alfred W. Crosby, "'God . . . Would Destroy Them, and Give Their Country to Another People . . .'," *American Heritage* 29 (Oct.–Nov. 1978): 38–43. The last year and a half of Squanto's life is recorded in the several histories cited in the notes, especially those by Winslow, Bradford, and Thomas Morton. Squanto's best known contribution has been examined most thoroughly in Lynn Ceci, "Fish Fertilizer: A Native North American Practice?," *Science* 188 (4 April 1975): 26–30.

Suggestions for Further Reading

The standard reference on all aspects of southern New England Indian history and culture is Bruce G. Trigger, ed., *Northeast*, vol. 15 of *Handbook of North American Indians*, gen. ed. William C. Sturtevant (Washington, D.C., 1978). Francis Jennings provides a fine, provocative introduction to Indian-European relations in seventeenth-century New England in *The Invasion of America: Indians, Colonialism, and the Cant of Conquest* (Chapel Hill, N.C., 1976). The earliest stages of those relations, including the background for this chapter, will be detailed in Neal Salisbury, *Manitou and Providence: Indians, Europeans, and the Making of New England, 1500–1643* (forthcoming, New York, 1981). For theoretical, methodological, and historiographical perspectives on ethnohistory and the history of Indian-white relations, see James Axtell, "The Ethnohistory of Early America: A Review Essay," *William and Mary Quarterly* 35 (1978), 110–144.

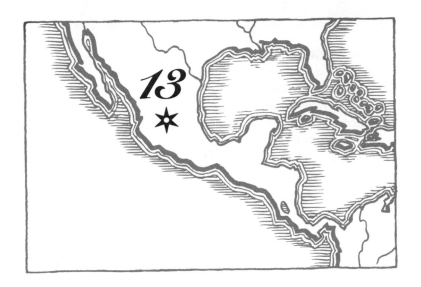

Beatriz de Padilla:
Mistress and Mother

SOLANGE ALBERRO

*I*n 1650 there was a great scandal in the sleepy town of Lagos, near Guadalajara in western New Spain. The shameless mulatta Beatriz de Padilla was accused by the royal agent don Juan Sánchez de Vidaurre, an influential gentleman of the country, sixty-four years of age and the owner of several farms and ranches in the vicinity, and by a secular priest and some others, of having caused dreadful and mysterious things to happen to two of her lovers. According to the charges she had poisoned the first of them, a priest who had been serving as commissioner of the Holy Office of the Inquisition in Lagos, and then, several weeks later, she had driven the lord mayor of Juchipila crazy through the exercise of magic. Informed of this development and alarmed at the

---

NOTE: Translated by David G. Sweet.

possibility that one of its representatives might have been done away with in this cold-blooded fashion with impunity, the Tribunal of the Inquisition in Mexico City summoned the alleged murderess to the capital. In the meantime, it instructed its new commissioner in Lagos to undertake a complete investigation of the case.

On the prisoner's dock in Mexico City, Beatriz informed the inquisitors in spirited language that she was not a mulatta but a lighter-skinned *morisca,* the daughter of a white man and a mulatta. She said that she was about thirty years old, unmarried and without any "respectable" means of supporting herself. She had been born in Lagos, the daughter of a don Lorenzo de Padilla (a descendant of one of the best families of Guadalajara, she was proud to attest, and brother to the late Gaspar de Padilla, who had served for a time as a secular priest in Lagos). Her mother was an unmarried mulatta serving woman named Cecilia de Alvarado, who had been born a slave in the Mexico City household of the viceroy don Luis de Velasco. Cecilia had been an only child whose mother died in childbirth, and as a young woman had been taken to Lagos to serve as housekeeper to the parish priest there, don Francisco Pérez Rubín. She was still employed by this priest more than thirty years later, when the scandal broke around her daughter.

Cecilia had borne two other children, younger than Beatriz, by different fathers. They were Francisca Ramirez, who had been legally recognized and declared a free person by her father, a white man of the neighborhood, and Francisco de Alvarado. Francisca was the wife of the administrator of a cattle ranch in Zacatecas, but she lived with their several children in Lagos. Francisco, the unrecognized son of a Basque immigrant long since dead, had been blinded some two years before Beatriz' trial. He was unmarried and also lived in Lagos. Beatriz had begun her life as a slave, inheriting her mother's status, but both she and Cecilia had at length been granted their freedom thanks to the benevolence of their employer and presumably their own satisfactory service in the priest's household. At the time of her arrest and removal to Mexico City, Beatriz had been a housekeeper and mistress in the service of don Diego de las Mariñas, the lord mayor of

Juchipila, for the loss of whose senses she was being held responsible.

Like her mother, Beatriz was a woman who had led an active and somewhat irregular private life. Never married, she had brought two sons and two daughters into the world. The eldest was Agustín Ortiz, then fourteen, the son of the priest Diego Ortiz Saavedra, with whom Beatriz had interacted happily for eight years and whom she was now accused of having poisoned. Seven-year-old María, who was being raised by Beatriz' mother, was the daughter of one Hernando López de Lara, and her children Micaela, five, and Diego, four, were the fruits of her union with Diego de las Mariñas. Asked to provide a little more detail about the history of her life and loves, Beatriz replied that when she was only thirteen or fourteen years old she had whipped an Indian woman without cause and had been taken to Guadalajara for two months—apparently in an effort to get her away from Lagos until the furor died down. There she had stayed in the houses of doña Maria Ortiz, a sister of the priest Diego Ortiz, who was already her secret lover, and of another elegant lady. This visit would seem to have had a great influence in establishing the ideal of a standard of living to which the ex-servant girl hoped to become accustomed.

After returning to Lagos, she had first gone to live with Diego de las Mariñas in the village of Nochistlán. But her friendship with the priest Diego Ortiz was already of long standing, having begun when Beatriz was an adolescent and still lived with her mother in the household of Father Pérez Rubín. It would appear that Ortiz was the man whom she really loved throughout. Two years before his death the commissioner had reversed his earlier policy and determined to make his relationship with her a public one. At that point he had taken her away from Mariñas to live with him at his hacienda of Moya, some two leagues distant from Lagos. It is a powerful testimony to the strength of the affection that Beatriz had managed to inspire in Mariñas in the meantime that after Ortiz' death he was willing to take her back with him.

The witnesses hostile to Beatriz, whose testimonies were taken during the inquiry, were unanimous in declaring that the mulatta had made life miserable for the lovelorn commissioner of the Holy Office during all the time that she had remained in his house. In their view, she had literally reduced the man to idiocy before finishing him off by placing poisonous powders in his bath.[1] Before entering into relations with her, they recalled, he had been in excellent health, with an indomitable character and an evil disposition. Afterward he had lost his hair and grown very sickly, and he had lost control of his faculties to such an extent that he was often to be seen walking and talking to himself and laughing out loud for no reason at all. Beatriz replied that none of this was true, and that if the truth be known it was she who had suffered a greater loss than anyone else with the death of don Diego— because the priest loved her very deeply and had made her the lady of a household where she never lacked for anything. After his passing she had been beset with poverty and persecuted by her enemies. The priest's love for her had grown even more profound after their son Agustín had been born, she recalled. From then on he had often remarked that when he died, the hacienda of Moya would be hers to administer to support their son and another girl whom Ortiz had adopted. This last determination was, as it turned out, to be the chief cause of Beatriz' difficulty with the authorities.

Beatriz confessed that she had been less than exemplary in her conduct while exercising authority in the household of Diego Ortiz. She remembered having been an unduly harsh taskmistress to the slaves and domestic servants, despite the fact that she had served as a slave housemaid herself as a young girl. In particular, she admitted to having been especially cruel toward a lying and gossipy slave named Catalina la Garay—beating her frequently or spattering her with hot grease—and moreover that she had had this woman branded. But she denied that Diego Ortiz had suffered any transformations of character or behavior in her company. He had always had the custom of talking to himself, though she had never seen him laugh without reason. He had indeed lost some hair, but only on the face, where two spots had appeared like birthmarks that were free of whiskers. But something none of the witnesses had mentioned was that he had suffered from an illness that caused him to complain frequently of severe headaches and flatulence and colic, and Beatriz believed that it was this that had carried him off.

Certain witnesses testified that the silver chamberpot in which Beatriz prepared the water for Diego Ortiz' bath had turned black on account of the menstrual blood she was in the habit of putting into it in an effort to poison her lover—and that when someone had pointed this out to the faithless mistress, she had replied that the skin of a prickly pear had fallen into the water and given it its red color. Beatriz responded sharply and astutely to this charge that, in the first place, blood would not cause silver to turn black, and, in the second place, she was not so foolish a person as to tell the whopper about the prickly pear skin, since everyone knew that the red color of the prickly pear was not the same as the color of blood. But most of the process was not so easy. The young woman was obliged to defend herself vigorously against the calumnies of her accusers, and in the course of doing so she took pleasure in providing many interesting details concerning life in the village of Lagos.

The folks back home, she pointed out, were green with envy at the fact that the lovers of Beatriz had all been important men who were crazy about her, such as the commissioner of the Holy Office and the lord mayor of Juchipila. Often people had asked her by means of what charms or love potions she was able to attract such admirers, and Beatriz recalled that she would reply with a laugh that the only charms or potions she employed were those she carried between her legs! But public opinion had a hard time accepting the fact that a mere *morisca,* and an ex-slave at that, could come to enjoy the devotion of such important men by any such natural means as simple seduction, or youth and beauty, or sincerity in affection combined with a lively intelligence and a sparkling wit. The only convincing explanation for many was that she must be having recourse to magical procedures that were mysterious and dangerous, not to mention illegal.

As the trial proceeded, however, it became clear that something further lay behind the scandal, namely, a complicated situation within the family of the late commissioner, Ortiz. He had lived for years under constant pressure from his mother, doña Luisa Ortiz, his sister's husband, the drunken but "respectable" royal agent Juan Sánchez Vidaurre, and their daughter María. These envious relatives had woven a veritable conspiracy against Beatriz when they realized that the priest was genuinely enamored of her and that he proposed to leave his entire estate to her and to their illegitimate son. It was they, together with their slaves and retainers, who had plotted to dispose of one whom they perceived as a contemptible upstart in any way they could.

Beatriz maintained that when Ortiz had died, the family had been in such a hurry to bury him that there had been a rumor in Lagos that they had buried him alive. She recalled that on that day the relatives of the deceased had descended on the house like a flock of buzzards, picking through his property and making off with the most insignificant objects. Doña Luisa had gone so far as to make off with a bird cage belonging to Beatriz, which she had gotten from some boys who had gone out looking for birds to snare in the countryside. Not satisfied with this, the greedy sister had later invented the preposterous charge that Beatriz only kept birds on hand so as to be able to use them in the preparation of her love charms.

Ortiz, said Beatriz, had for his part felt a great distrust toward his family—knowing full well that they despised her and would do their best to frustrate his desires in the disposition of his estate. At one point, in an effort to win them over, she had begged Diego to name Luisa and her husband, Juan Sánchez Vidaurre, as godparents of their son. Ortiz had resisted the idea strongly, though in the end he had agreed to her request. But all of this had been to no avail. It was the *compadre* Sánchez Vidaurre and his wife who had first circulated the rumor that Beatriz was a sorceress and then put it about that she was a murderess as well. They simply could not accept the genuine love that Beatriz insisted had existed between the late priest and herself, and much less the certain loss of a prosperous hacienda. Once launched by the envious relatives of Ortiz, the conspiracy had quickly broadened to serve as a channel for the rancor of all the leading citizens of Lagos—people who saw in the relationship between the commissioner and the *morisca* the beginning of a dangerous process of social dissolution. Having a colored mistress of low social standing was no scandal in colonial society; on the contrary it was a common practice, even among priests. But to demonstrate an exclusive affection for one's concubine in public, to put her in charge of one's household, and above all to make her the heir to one's estate were altogether unheard of. And this was especially hard to swallow when the woman in question was as outspoken as Beatriz and as indiscreet as she in boasting about her amorous and social successes.

The clamor against Beatriz had eventually been joined by no less a personage than the *licenciate* Andrés López, don Diego Ortiz' replacement as commissioner of the Holy Office in Lagos. López was called upon to receive formally the depositions of the witnesses who testified against Beatriz. Before she left for the capital he committed the error of warning her not to speak out against the hostilities that had been directed against her in Lagos if she wanted to avoid being muzzled as she stood before the tribunal. Andrés López' hatred for Beatriz derived from the facts that at some point she had been the lover of his brother Hernando López de Lara, the father of Beatriz' second child María, and that the sister of these two men, Catalina de Lara, had been abandoned by her fiancé don Diego de las Mariñas some years before, when he had "lost his head" and decided instead to take the humble Beatriz as his mistress! This intricate web of licit and illicit relations between civil and ecclesiastical functionaries and their female relatives, which seems to have been typical of the society of colonial Mexico, had left a bitter residue in the broken marriages, the frustrated ambitions, and the envies of many people. Beatriz was being made the scapegoat for all of them.

Catalina la Garay, the slave woman who had been so cruelly treated by Beatriz when she lived at the hacienda of Moya, had moved on later to become the servant of Ortiz' sister doña Luisa. As a resentful ex-servant, she was able to contribute many valuable pieces of information to the preparation of the case against Beatriz, recounting with prejudice the details of the day-to-day life of the couple. All this notwithstanding, the Tribunal of the Inquisition was persuaded by the intelligent and sincere defense of Beatriz de Padilla (if not by her beauty, or by the recollection that she had been the beloved companion of a brother). To be doubly certain, the judges had Catalina la Garay brought to testify in Mexico City. Catalina confessed, apparently after a session in the torture chamber, that she had made up all her accusations. Then, so that her fate might serve as a lesson to all the evil-tongued gossips of Lagos, she was taken home and punished with 200 lashes administered in the streets of the village. Beatriz, for her part, was acquitted and allowed to return to her home town without any sort of punishment or reprimand.

At the time of Beatriz' release from the jail of the Inquisition she had returned to her the following items of personal property, which had been sequestered by the Holy Office at the time of her arrest. The list gives some indication of the conditions of material comfort in which the mistress of a leading citizen of the provinces might expect to live:

two sheets of Rouen linen
a pillow with its casing
a white bedspread and blanket
a mattress stuffed with cane leaves
two white shirtwaists
five embroidered blouses
two chambray petticoats
a Spanish woolen skirt
a blue petticoat adorned with Spanish flannel
a used green woolen skirt
one blue embroidered handkerchief
an embroidered linen bonnet
a red cloak
a piece of coarse frieze cloth
an old hat
two pairs of new slippers

We may assume that the disgust felt by the respectable society of Lagos toward the beauteous Beatriz was in no way diminished by the sight of her triumphant return—especially in view of the fact that during the trial she had exposed to public criticism all the petty dealings and machinations of her detractors. It seems likely, however, that she returned to the household of the not at all crazy lord mayor of Juchipila with her position as beloved and respected concubine enhanced rather than diminished—and that there was little that anyone could do to harm her from that time forward.

The mulatta mistress as a social type has always attracted the attention of the students of colonial society, and it may be that her importance has been exaggerated. There is still a mysterious aura about women of this sort, a lingering suspicion that perhaps they did make use of love potions or other magic that turned their white owner-keepers into their sexual slaves. But without discarding the possibility that there may sometimes have been some basis to these charges, it is worth pointing out that in a colonial society the woman of low caste and swarthy skin, operating in a more marginal position than the white woman, was also less subject to a series of severely restrictive social regulations. A woman such as Beatriz had in her favor, in addition to the attractions of her physical person and the color of her skin, a relative freedom of movement, a freedom to walk, talk, and dress pretty much as she saw fit, and an opportunity to give full reign to spontaneity and naturalness in her interpersonal relations. These freedoms were not available to the "respectable" white woman, whether Spanish or Creole, who was obliged to concern herself always with what others might say and to do her best to adhere to the norms of society not only in every social interaction but also, since domestic servants were nearly always present, in the most intimate details of her private life.

The women of color in New Spain, whether of African or Indian extraction, performed—however unconsciously—a fundamental role in the historical development of Mexican society. The vital impulse that led them to join their flesh with the white men's and give birth to the white men's children was the biological response of a social group that found itself despised by the existing social order. What legitimate hopes for helping to mold the future might a black person or an Indian in mid-seventeenth-century Mexican society reasonably entertain? Few, if any. But the same people might save some elements of their culture—a rhythm, a musical instrument, an esthetic ideal, a culinary principle, perhaps a formula of courtesy—if they embraced the partial survival represented by the process of genetic and cultural *mestizaje.*

The blacks and Indians who lost hope killed themselves, or they allowed their line to come to a halt by means of abortion, amenorrhea, and sterility—the physiological manifestations of a rejection of life. But the Indian, black, and racially mixed women who had their babies, who struggled so that their fathers would recognize them, free them if they were slaves, provide for them, perhaps provide them with some education—these women were making possible the survival of their own kind over the long period. They were refusing to die. These women, for the most part despised by their contemporaries (and so little understood today), also were those who helped make life a little less harsh than it would otherwise have been for the European immigrants themselves. They forged the details of the domestic culture that gives a unique flavor to the home life of Mexican families even today. And above all they guaranteed the survival of many races in the new humanity that populates most of the Americas in our own time.

Notes

1. "Bath" here translates *lavatorio,* which may also have meant "enema." The context does not make clear which is intended.

Sources

The materials for Beatriz de Padilla's story are to be found in the Archivo General de la Nación in Mexico City, Ramo Inquisición, Tomo 561, ff. 219 *et seq.*

Suggestions for Further Reading

Reading on the main subjects introduced by this story is unavailable so far in any language. For an introduction to some key aspects of the society in which Beatriz de Padilla lived, see Jonathan I. Israel, *Race, Class and Politics in Colonial Mexico, 1610–1670* (New York, 1975); Irving Leonard, *Baroque Times in Old Mexico: Seventeenth-Century Persons, Places and Practices* (Ann Arbor, Mich., 1959); and J. Eric S. Thompson, ed., *Thomas Gage's Travels in the New World* (Norman, Okla., 1958). For an approach to the complex and little-understood workings of the seventeenth-century Mexican Inquisition, see José Toribio Medina, *Historia del Tribunal del Santo Oficio de la Inquisición en México* (México, 1952), and Julio Jiménez Rueda, *Herejías y supersticiones en la Nueva España (los heterodoxos en México)* (México, 1946). The larger issue of race mixture and race relations in colonial Spanish America is discussed most usefully in Magnus Mörner, *Race Mixture in the History of Latin America* (Boston, 1967) and Richard Konetzke, "El mestizaje y su importancia en el desarrollo de la poblacion durante la época colonial," *Revista de Indias* 7 (1946).

Catarina de Monte Sinay:
Nun and Entrepreneur

SUSAN A. SOEIRO

*O*ne August morning in 1758, Catarina de Monte Sinay,
enfeebled by old age and illness, called for the convent's scribe to dictate her last will and testament. It was the
usual summer's day—damp, cloudy, and punctuated by sudden showers. The odor of mildew hung heavily about the
nun's cell and bedclothes. For a few hours each day a rectangular window at the corner of the room allowed a narrow
beam of light to cross the floor. The glimmering rays shed by
two oil lamps dimly outlined her cot, a writing table, two
chairs, a chest, and a few treasured images of saints in the
sparsely furnished cell.

These belongings revealed little of Catarina's activities
during a long life in the convent. As she lay approaching her
final hours, she reflected on the immensity of her wealth.
How had she come by it? No doubt it had been God's will. She
was reminded of the need to petition the archbishop in order

to dispose of her property as she intended. The matter was urgent; life was fading. She asked her slave to summon the confessor in haste. There was much to repent in so short a time. Scenes of her cloistered life appeared before her mind's eye, and she was drawn into the past ever more quickly.

On a clear bright day in 1696, the young novice, Catarina de Telles Barretto, stood at the portals of the Destêrro Convent of Bahia in Brazil, about to become Madre Catarina de Monte Sinay. Catarina had looked forward to this day of celebration. The nunnery had only recently been founded and professions there were still feted with all the pomp and pageantry of a marriage ceremony. The procession began, and it was splendidly colorful. First came the images of the saints, held high for all to see; behind them came the church dignitaries—archbishop, canons, deacons, and vicars—in the full regalia of their office. Marching friars chanted hymns to the Lord. The town's notables—the leading merchants and planters, the aldermen of the municipal council, and even many of the well-bred ladies borne in sedan chairs on the shoulders of slaves—thronged the narrow streets to attend the spectacle. Bells chimed and drums beat in exuberant celebration, and from time to time ships in the harbor sounded their cannonry. Following the festivities, removed from their midst, Catarina vowed to God, the Virgin, Saint Francis, and Saint Clare that she would forever honor her sacred promise to live in poverty, chastity, and obedience.

To Catarina the occasion signified her spiritual wedding; on entering the cloister, she symbolically dedicated her life to being a "bride of Christ." While she prayed that the blessed bond with her Lord would endow her with the virtues she would need for religious perfection, she rejoiced inwardly that the hard-fought battle to become a nun had been won. In a moment she was alone in the awesome presence of the archbishop, D. João Francisco de Oliveira, who solemnly questioned her to determine if her decision to profess had been voluntary and sincere. She had no doubts at all. Catarina and her three sisters had been raised to become nuns, and to be admitted to the exclusive Destêrro Convent was a stroke of good fortune. The convent was the only one in Brazil. Before its creation it had been necessary for the well-bred young women of the colony in whom the religious vocation was discovered to brave the long and dangerous voyage across the Atlantic to profess in a convent in Portugal or in the Azores. How many other girls had petitioned the archbishop for a coveted place in the Destêrro? The competition had been intense. But as the daughter of João de Couros Carneiro, scribe of the municipal council, she had been selected over other applicants. Since the council had been the original patron of the nunnery, the daughters of councilmen were preferred.

Life in the nunnery held few mysteries for Catarina. For six years she had lived there as a pupil and secular ward of the nuns, and her older sister had taken the veil there just three years before. After Catarina's father had pledged a dowry of 600,000 *réis* and offered a contribution to the sacristy, she was permitted to enter the novitiate. When she had spent a year studying religious discipline with the *Mestre da Ordem*, the community voted to allow Catarina to make her vows. She was delighted to exchange the white veil of a novice for the prestigious black one of a nun.

Catarina was proud and grateful that the king had at last rewarded the people of Bahia with a nunnery. Over the last century and a half the city had gradually matured into the administrative, commercial, and ecclesiastical center that befitted its position as a colonial capital. Ringed by walls for its defense, Bahia was divided into an upper and a lower segment. The portion that rested atop the plateau was the formal core of the colony. Here, clustered about a large square, sat the royal treasury, the high court, the offices of the municipal council, and the governor's palace. Off slightly to one side was the Brotherhood of the Misericórdia, known for its charitable services; to the other was the cathedral and the bishop's palace. Formidable mansions lined the streets leading away from the city's main square. Nature had endowed the site with special beauty. From the convent Catarina could see the striking panorama of glistening rooftops perched above the crystalline blue waters of the Bay of All Saints and the white sandy beaches that ringed it. In her mind's eye she could see the activity in the market district below: the prattle of the vendors, the melodic cries of itinerant peddlers hawking their contraband wares, the strange calls of turbanned African women dressed in long and fulsome colored skirts, and the distant beating of drums and twanging of a *berimbau,* which marked the rhythm of a foot-fighting dance of African origin, the *capoeira.* Down the steep hillside, the lower city was a bustling port. Cargoes of European goods were unloaded alongside gangs of half-starved Africans, herded together to be auctioned off as slaves. Sugar, tobacco, and leather stood crated and wrapped, piled at the quay for shipment. Around the docks and in the cafés and shops there were groups of men huddled about anxiously discussing the size and timing of the sugar harvest.

Now, at the dawning of the eighteenth century, these were troubled times for Bahians. Prosperity in the past had come mainly from the sale of sugar to the European market, and other goods such as cattle hides, tallow, or tobacco had been of secondary importance. Until the latter third of the seventeenth century, by virtue of her superior natural harbor, rich tropical soils, and a growing region interspersed by connecting waterways, Bahia had maintained her position as the world's leading sugar producer. The sugar planters, many of whom were close friends and associates of Catarina's father, dominated the town's most respected social and political positions as councilmen, magistrates, and royal officials. All were aware that the past success of sugar had depended not only on an unlimited supply of arable land but also on a tractable, cheap, and dependable source of labor—African slaves. While sugar was in its heyday, slaves had come to fill all of Bahia's labor needs from the canefields to the innermost recesses of the cloister.

Bahia had thus become the linchpin in a tricontinental trade between Europe and Africa. Fabrics, furniture, tools, manufactures, and foodstuffs were imported into Bahia from Lisbon. In return, the fleets to Portugal carried sugar as well as whale oil, dyewood, and hides, for cattle raising had also become a prominent seventeenth-century activity. The ships leaving Bahia for African ports carried goods that could readily be exchanged for slaves—beads, trinkets, rum, brandy, and great quantities of tobacco, specially prepared to please the palates of African princes by sweetening with molasses.

Catarina's childhood coincided with the beginnings of Bahia's depression. In the 1670s, when competition from the British, French, and Dutch islands in the Caribbean drove the price of sugar down, Bahia entered a period of painful decline. Droughts, floods, and epidemics ravaged the land in the wake of financial disaster. Many fortunes, so quickly made, were as easily lost. The once splendid palatial residences of the upper city showed signs of decay and disrepair. Weeds overran walls whose sparkling white was now stained with the relentless growth of green and brown tropical mosses. Many planters had already abandoned their city homes and retreated to the remains of their now idle estates.

Catarina, however, did not need to preoccupy herself with such weighty concerns. These worldly problems were the domain of the menfolk. As a young woman from a good family, her life would fit the expected pattern: she would either marry or enter the convent, and the latter alternative had been chosen for her. In either case she was not expected to do much more than learn to sew and embroider, prepare tasty delicacies, read her prayers and hymns, and manage a few household slaves. Business affairs were properly left to men.

But life in Bahia was not all business. The Church gave life its other meanings. The Destêrro Convent mounted a plateau on the heights of the upper city, roughly midway between the Convent of Carmo to the north and the house of Benedictines at the city's southern rim. Between them and a skyline dotted by church spires lay the main square, the Terreiro de Jesus. Here the Jesuits had founded their school, where each day they taught more than sixty young men their lessons in Latin, philosophy, mathematics, and theology. The Jesuits had earned their central position by being the first missionaries to arrive when the land was still wild and peopled by the cannibal Indians. Only later in the seventeenth century had the Carmelites, Benedictines, and Capuchins founded their houses. Alongside the Jesuit seminary stood the cathedral, the seat of the archdiocese. For a long time Bahia had been only a bishopric, but now its august prelate had jurisdiction over the parishes of the captaincies of Bahia, Rio de Janeiro, and Pernambuco as well and served them as the ultimate authority on moral, ethical, and religious questions. As he stood before her, Catarina was reminded that this man exercised the final word on the economic as well as the spiritual affairs of her nunnery.

Catarina rarely reflected on the presence of the Church in Bahia because it was so well integrated with the natural order of things. Saints days and holy days marked the passage of the seasons, while St. Francis Xavier perennially watched over Bahia as its patron saint. Catarina considered herself a devout person and always tried to follow the Lord's teachings. But religion was far more than devotion to a set of precepts or even an unfailing faith in God's omniscience. Her faith imbued her life with meaning that was both intensely personal and broadly universal. Her awareness of her own small place in a grander cosmic design gave Catarina a sense of humility; she was one person in the vast flock of the Lord. Yet her communication with God was direct and immediate, since every procession, every ceremony, and every pageant reminded her of his presence. But what especially drew her to her faith was the drama and the spectacle that commanded her participation—the procession, the colors, the rhythm of movement and sound. This was the pulse of religious life. The ceremony, ritual, and display were intensely evocative. At the core of Catarina's faith was the profoundly inspired state she experienced, both from the celebratory mood of the procession and through the droning liturgy of the Mass. Reliving the passion or the birth of Christ, Catarina knew first despair and then elation. Finally, she would be released from the pain of grief by the joy of attaining forgiveness. Thoroughly enthralled by the ritual, Catarina could feel her soul purified and cleansed of its guilt.

Finding and following the right path to salvation was not, however, an easy matter. Catarina was fortunate to have within the cloister a model of saintly behavior. Madre Victória da Encarnação was one of those rare persons whose faith required her to suffer in imitation of Christ. She was already a living legend, popularly canonized, though she had entered the convent only a few years before. Victória's background was similar to Catarina's. Their fathers had been born in Portugal and had emigrated to Brazil—Victória's as an army officer in the campaign against the Dutch some fifty years before and Catarina's as an immigrant in search of his fortune. Both men, anxious for the well-being of their souls in a society overrun by greed and depravity, had raised their daughters to be nuns.

Since Madre Victória had lived to become such an exemplary religious, the story of her reluctant entry into the convent in the first place seemed all the more remarkable to

Catarina. Although her father was renowned as a God-fearing man and master of a pious household, Victória had at first refused to obey him and take the veil. Never was a young woman more obstinate. But then, it was rumored, the Lord had visited her in her dreams, first with gentle and sweet urgings that she become his bride. Victória had resisted still, and it was only after she had had a vision of her terrifying descent to hell, trapped in the stinking and fetid hold of a ship, that she was convinced that life in the Destêrro was the road to her salvation.

Once in the convent, Victória lived the austere and blameless life of a saint. Catarina found her example awesome and inspiring, although she regretted that she could never attain the same humility. Victória could not bear to hear herself praised, not even with a complimentary word about the purity of her faith. On the contrary, she gloried in self-denigration. It was whispered about the convent that one day she had been discovered eating from the same plate as a dog. Victória found solace in the vilest insults, as in the time when a slave came to the kitchen for her mistress's portion when Victória was serving. Dissatisfied with what she received, the slave heaved the plate at Victória and struck her square in the face. Victória, nonplussed, simply asked, "Have things come to this?"[1] Not a reprimand, not even a complaint against an outrage committed by a slave! Victória perceived herself as a victim, but a blessed one, chosen to suffer. She had been designated to atone not only for her own sins of the flesh, but also for those of the entire community and the society at large. For a moment Catarina faced the painful thought that the nunnery might indeed be in need of someone to do penance on its behalf. She was young then, a woman of sheltered life herself, and not yet privy to the conversations of the older nuns, but even she had heard rumors of scandals. Nuns had been reprimanded for holding illicit conversations at the window-grilles and for sending messages to persons outside the convent. Friars and other churchmen had entered the cloister on the flimsiest of excuses! More than once the nuns had refused to reveal these violations to the archbishop himself in order to conceal their wrongdoings.

Catarina reassured herself that surely the presence of a model of saintliness in their midst would redeem at least some of the community's sins. Victória's deeds were whispered among the nuns, sometimes in reverent amazement, sometimes almost in disbelief, although she herself never sought her sisters' attention. She tried to conceal the brutal punishments she inflicted on her weak body and abstained from joining them at meals, eating only bread and water. Rarely did she spend more than three hours sleeping, occupied as she was during most of the day and night in prayer, self-mortification, and good works. Under her coarse habit she always wore a hair shirt. Catarina had often seen blood spattered on the walls of the choir, where Victória did her nocturnal penance with barbed wires or with whips made of the strings of violins and raw leather that she had twisted herself. On Fridays she performed the seven stations of the cross, bearing a cross so intolerably heavy that two other nuns could not carry it. At every station, she disciplined herself anew—sometimes so cruelly that she was obliged to cover her bruised and swollen face for the rest of the week in order to prevent others from taking pity on her.

Madre Victória was known too for her miracles and her charitable deeds. Once several slaves caught the terrible smallpox. Usually sick slaves were removed from the cloister and abandoned to their fate. But Victória had insisted on tending to them in her own small cell. This she did until they had all miraculously recovered, while at the same time preventing anyone else from falling ill with the disease. Even after her death Madre Victória retained her heavenly endowed powers of healing. Catarina recalled that a religious had long been ill with a tumor in her throat, which refused to respond to any of the normal remedies like bleeding, leeches, cuppings, or herbal brews. As a last resort, the nun put some earth from Victória's grave into a cup and drank it. Immediately after, the swelling in her throat subsided, and the cup itself retained a sweet fragrance.

There was much in the past to give Catarina pause. Although sugar growing had given rise to a plantation-based society and had lent some semblance of respectability to the land, eighteenth-century Brazil was still a haven for fortune seekers and entrepreneurs of all types. The discovery of gold in the 1690s in the interior had attracted rootless adventurers from Portugal and the rest of Brazil and brought disorder and lawlessness in its wake. Bahia was not unaffected. The city was jocosely known as the Bay of All Saints and All Sinners. Madre Victória had been a saint among sinners. Catarina prayed fervently that her presence would spare the community and the city from eternal damnation. Catarina knew that she and her family, one of the most distinguished and prosperous in the city, were among the guilty souls for whom Madre Victória had suffered her painful vigils. Her father had been the scribe of the municipal council, and this office had passed to her brother João in 1716. For all the strength of family ties, Catarina was forced to admit, if only to herself, that João did not always honor their family name. He had been mainly interested, like many another leading citizen of the colony, in making money. In 1724 he had petitioned the crown on the grounds that he was being unjustly deprived of income from his office as scribe of the municipal council by the creation of several villas in the nearby *Recôncavo* of Bahia, each with its own scribe. Since the revenues of these new offices had been taken from him, João believed that each of the new scribes ought to pay him 20,000 *réis* annually. The crown in its wisdom had seen fit to deny this request.

From that time forward her brother's fortunes progressively worsened until he succumbed to a thoroughly unChristian life of debauchery and dissolution. He had been married for some years to the daughter of a respected merchant, and although the couple had one child, they had never been compatible. Catarina, whose naiveté was nurtured by her cloistered life, was reluctant to accept the full panoply of her brother's sins. Still she felt infinite sympathy for his abused wife. João had openly installed his concubine, the wife of a convict who had been exiled to Angola, in his home. To add to the horror of the situation, he often beat his wife ferociously and then closeted her in a tiny room where she received only a single ration of *farinha* (the same diet as a slave) each day. Fortunately, the authorities had eventually gotten word of the poor woman's circumstances, and she and her daughter had been removed to the protective custody of the retirement house of the Misericórdia. Catarina reflected gratefully that her conventual life had spared her from any such abuse.

These events, painful to recall, had come and gone with the passing of time. Years elapsed quickly in the convent, where the routine was repeated daily except for the occasional interruption of a *festa*. Catarina had always found the regular rhythm of convent life satisfying. She had taken comfort in the elaborate daily ritual. The day was divided by the canonical hours, with seven times set aside for prayer and devotion. The community awoke early to the sound of the chimes of matins. Mornings were spent in work or study, a time when many of the sisters sewed or embroidered. Interrupting the morning hours was a short Mass; later, a more elaborate High Mass was celebrated, and then, vespers ceremonially ended the day. Catarina always attended meals in the refectory, although many in the community chose to be served privately by their servants.

On holidays the routine was broken by special festivities. Once a year at the time of the archbishop's visit, there was a splendid banquet with many courses elaborately prepared and delicately spiced with saffron and imported herbs. The repast culminated in a glorious array of sweets and dumplings baked by the nuns. On rare occasions the Destêrro opened its church doors to the town's notables. Catarina recalled one Christmas when the celebration grew especially lively. The nuns had presented a Christmas pageant, followed by a musical recital. Some of the nuns became somewhat overexuberant in their dancing and posturing, Catarina recollected. Perhaps their behavior could be considered undignified—even raucous—and their musical talent wanting; but critics who took this for a lack of religious vocation were mistaken. In these times there were few religious who were not given to an occasional transgression.

Catarina was reminded of her own shortcomings as a nun; she had often failed to live up to her creed, but all the same she was deeply committed to and content with convent life. It provided her with the companionship of her sisters and other friends, spared her from the possibility of serving an unpleasant husband, allowed her time for solitude and contemplation, and gave her life a purpose and a sense of mission. She prayed that her soul would earn its place in heaven.

✳   ✳   ✳

Now, as death approached, Catarina had drawn up her will and was taking stock of her life, as the Lord would surely do in his heavenly ledger. Fortunately she had maintained a simple and unaffected style of life, considering the wealth she had amassed. She had few personal belongings beyond some essential pieces of furniture, some china, and some cuts of cloth. By comparison, her extravagant sister nun, Leonor da Madre de Deus, the daughter of a sugar mill owner, had died leaving her cell stocked with extraordinary possessions. Included among them were cookie sheets and trays imported from India and candy molds from Macao, fine pieces of porcelain and silver, and two exquisite desks, one of rosewood and another inlaid with tortoise shell, at which she had read her impressive collection of Latin works and written the notes of her diary. Catarina had indulged no such vanity. She had neither acquired fine and stylish habits decked with ribbons or embroidered sleeves, nor worn rouge, nor dyed her hair like some of the Clarissas. Catarina's sins had been of another order. She knew that she had been lacking in humility and had in fact taken great satisfaction in her own intelligence and her skill at business and financial dealings.

Catarina reflected that perhaps she had acquired her financial acumen from her father, who had always been alert to the chance for a profitable undertaking. Once he and several other officials had been the subject of an official inquiry for having collected excessive fees from their offices. She too had known an inclination and talent for making money, and in a period of over half a century she had built up a working capital of 4,402,000 *réis*[2]—a considerable sum equal approximately to half of the wealthy convent's total annual income. (And far from the state of poverty she had vowed to accept.) How had Catarina been drawn into these pursuits? She could hardly recall. To whom had she extended her first loan? Was it to the mill owner José Pires de Carvalho or to Paulo de Argolo, who had requested the loan of a few *milréis* as a personal favor? Surely, the Lord would not find these transactions with friends of her family usurious?

Her fortune had accumulated gradually over the years, as the product of various enterprises. First, she earned a handsome income from money she placed on loan. Catarina admitted that she had frequently let her sentiments rather than her business sense guide her in these dealings and that she often had trouble collecting her debts. But then, so did the nunnery, which was a more formidable lender. Catarina counted among her debtors residents of regions as far afield as Ilheus, Rio de Janeiro, and Minas Gerais. Three hundred thousand *réis* were owed to her in Minas Gerais as the result of the sale of one of her recalcitrant slaves to José Jacome Raposo. She believed it to have been a just decision to sell that young African woman; she had become impossible to handle, and the hard work of the mining regions might teach her a lesson in discipline. Not long before, Catarina had written to Rio de Janeiro to inquire about the reason for Antonio Vieira de Miranda's default on his payments. It turned out that Miranda had died, but his widow responded that she intended to repay his debt. Others in default pleaded extreme financial distress. One apologized profusely that "prison and illness [were the] reasons for the great delay—these were not excuses but [brutal] reality, as [he] was still in prison with all of his slaves and possessions foreclosed."³ Even José de Semedo, the free black who rented one of her houses, and José Rodrigues de Carvalho, the *pardo* (mulatto) mason, still owed her money.

Much of the money she had lent came from her rentals of houses. She owned five substantial residential buildings of whitewashed limestone, which earned at least 160,000 *réis* a year. Like her sister nuns, in accordance with conventual regulations she received an allowance derived from the rental of houses. The property itself was to become part of the convent's patrimony at her death; however, during her lifetime she was entitled to use the income for her personal needs. Many of the religious had houses from which they might derive a small allowance, but few collected more than 100,000 *réis*. Sometimes Catarina paid rents on behalf of others, either out of familial obligation or as an official guarantor. For instance, she dutifully paid the rent of her godmother, the widow of Francisco Barbosa, to the convent of Carmo.

But what had kept Catarina most occupied through the years was her business of preparing and selling sweets. For this purpose she maintained twelve slaves—six males and six females. Gonçalo and Catarina, married, had been with her all her life and were by now quite old. She had purchased several others when they arrived from Africa; two of the younger ones had been born in Bahia. After her death the convent could either keep them for its use or sell them. Although church law forbade the nuns to use private servants and limited those of the community to fifteen, the convent now housed more than four hundred slaves. Over the years most nuns had been granted papal dispensations to possess personal slaves on the grounds of age or infirmity. A few had as many as five or six private attendants. At the death of the nun, unless she had directed otherwise, the slaves automatically passed to the community. Catarina assuaged her conscience with the thought that her slaves were not employed solely for her personal convenience. She could conceive of few illnesses which required the ministerings of five attendants. Catarina occupied her slaves in the preparation and sale of sweets. Some of them worked in the house in the convent's orchard which served as the factory. There the cooking equipment—some twenty-three cookie sheets, a large copper basin, two kettles, other pans and some ovenware—was stored.

Catarina and a few other nuns like her who prepared and sold pastries were known to produce irresistible delights. All manner of customers flocked to the nunnery's doors to sample their specialties. That reckless magistrate, Gregório de Matos, distinguished for his acid tongue and unkind words, had even written a poem about the popularity of the little cakes:

> Friars of pure and flawed existence
> Eat snacks with great persistence
> And remain in such contentment
> As the Popes of all the convent.
>
> If to fatten up the friars
> The nuns were brought to this city
> Better yet had they come to
> Support the infantry.[4]

The tarts and caramels were so tempting that they acquired suggestive nicknames—"little kisses, weaned sucklings, raise-the-old-man, maiden's tongue, married couples, love's caresses, nun's belly, nun's sighs. . . ."[5] Surely, such lascivious epithets had been conceived by those who wanted to mock the nuns and impugn their honor.

Old and dying, Catarina looked back on the sixty years she had spent in the cloister and she wanted very much to end them well, with some assurance of salvation. She reviewed the significant contributions she had made to the Destêrro. Like Madre Victória (if she dared to compare herself), she had especially favored the chapel of the Senhor dos Passos; but unlike her predecessor Catarina had been able to spend enormous sums, more than 2,027,000 *réis*, to provide it with lavish accoutrements. She took great satisfaction in the belief that the elaborately gilded frontispiece of the altar and the chapel's shrines made the chapel an exceptionally worthy place in which to worship her Saviour. Catarina had donated the annual income from one of her houses to provide wax for the chapel's candles. She had lavishly adorned the chapel with silver pieces, among them candlesticks and a fruit bowl, and provided a cabinet in which to store them. Finally, she had donated a slave worth 290,000 *réis*, who had been miraculously spared in a serious illness, to attend to keeping the chapel clean and its ornaments polished.

Catarina's generous gifts to the convent's church had helped to fashion a dazzling temple of azure, white, and gold. The fine tooling and elaborate contrivance of Bahia's baroque craftsmen had created astonishingly detailed sacraria and an elegant altar. Carved images, framed by swirling columns, pointed skyward to a muraled ceiling. Tiles lined an impressive entranceway. Catarina could take pride in the fact that her contributions were both functional and decorative. She had provided chairs for the choir, a spectacularly large hand-wrought silver crucifix, and a silver lamp adorned with gilded flowers and an iron chain. She had placed the sum of 400,000 *réis* on loan to provide an income to buy oil for the lamp. A symphony of color, texture, and ornament in the current style, the Destêrro's church could well be compared with the most elaborate in the city.

The thought of her will called her back to the present. Now that the convent had been provided for, Catarina concerned herself with a settlement for her sisters. She wished to see that her sisters, both nuns, lived out the remainder of their days in comfort. Since the convent was the immediate heir to her possessions, she was required to petition the archbishop for a license to provide her sisters with a legacy. She hoped to give each sister the use of a slave and the income from a house. When her sisters died, the property would automatically pass back to the convent. Catarina also sought to have a gift of 200,000 *réis* granted to an aged and faithful slave. In addition, she asked that 600,000 *réis* be set aside to have Masses intoned for her soul.

Catarina was prepared to face death and even grateful for its imminence. She had had a rich and full existence as a nun, and now she longed to approach her God. In the last year suffering had greatly sapped her strength. Yet she still desperately wished to know the outcome of her petition to the archbishop. Would he, in her dying hour, grant her request? Other nuns before her had petitioned for such special dispensations. But in Catarina's case it was not simply a matter of granting a deathbed wish or of disposing of property. The archbishop's concurrence was necessary to free her conscience of a burdensome weight. All her business affairs—her sale of sweets, her money on loan, her rental of houses, her gifts to the Destêrro and to others—had been carried out without the permission of the archbishop and in direct violation of church law. Without some dispensation, she wondered, were good works enough? Catarina was beset with this anxiety when she died in August 1758. She had spent sixty years of her life cloistered as a religious. She knew that her death would be lamented by the sisters and that her body would be carefully laid out for a wake in the chapel of which she was so fond. But what was the destiny of her soul? Could a nun who had been a businesswoman and a moneylender expect to be rewarded with salvation?

Notes

1. Frei Antonio de Santa Maria Jaboatão, *Novo orbe seraphico brasilico,* 3 vols. (Rio de Janeiro, 1858–61), vol. 3, p. 694.

2. During the seventeenth and eighteenth centuries, the Brazilian currency fluctuated widely in value. The basic unit of currency was the *real* (pl. *réis*); 1,000 *réis* comprised the *milréis*. According to H. E. S. Fisher, *The Portugal Trade: A Study of Anglo-Portuguese Commerce, 1700–1770* (London, 1971), the *milréis* minted in Portugal was worth 5 shillings and 5¾ pence in 1750. Inventories of the belongings of other nuns offer some notion of the buying power of the *real* and the extent of Catarina's assets. In 1731 a healthy female slave sold for 70,000 *réis*, a rosewood wardrobe for 30,000 *réis*, and a

religious figurine for 1,920 *réis*. A married couple who counted among Catarina's slaves, described as "old and useless," were sold for 20,000 *réis*. The rentals from each of her houses ranged from 15,000 to 55,000 *réis* per year.

3. *Arquivo do Convento de Santa Clara do Destêrro (ASCD)*, Caixa 1, Pasta 28, Correspondence, 27/8/1747.

4. Gregório de Matos e Guerra, *Obras completas*, 6 vols. (São Paulo, 1945), vol. 2, pp. 289–91. Translation by author.

5. Gilberto Freyre, *The Masters and the Slaves* (New York, 1966), pp. 259–60.

Sources

The principal documentation on which this biography is based is the manuscript collection housed in the Archive of the Convent of Santa Clara do Destêrro in Bahia, one of the few remaining collections of monastic records in Brazil. Catarina's will, an inventory of her belongings, and her personal correspondence provided a rich and varied commentary on the unusual economic activities of the nun (Caixa 1, Pastas 29, 44; Caixa 2, Pastas 48, 60(II), 63(II), 64, 65(I). Biographical details were culled from the records of the convent, such as the *Book of Entrants and Professions*. Catarina's well-known, even notorious, family was often in the town limelight and was mentioned in the correspondence between the colonial governor and the crown (Arquivo Público da Bahia, *Ordens régias*, vol. 23, doc. 109; vol. 25, doc. 36; Arquivo Histórico Ultramarino, Lisbon, Bahia, Papéis avulsos, Caixa 333). The descriptions of Bahia come from travelers' accounts like that of William Dampier, *A Voyage to New Holland* (1729, reprinted London, 1939); Le Gentil de la Barbinais, *Nouveau voyage autour du monde*, 3 vols. (Paris, 1728–29); Thomas Lindley, *Narrative of a Voyage to Brazil* (London, 1805); from the provisions and letters of Bahia's municipal council, published as *Documentos Históricos do Arquivo Municipal. Atas da Camara, 1625–1700*, 6 vols. (Salvador, [1949–55]); and *Cartas do Senado, 1638–1692*, 5 vols. (Salvador, [1951–53]); from contemporaries like Luis dos Santos Vilhena, *A Bahia no século XVIII*, 3 vols. (Salvador, 1969); and from my own vivid recollections. I have relied on the eighteenth-century Church chronicler Frei Antonio de Santa Maria Jaboatão for the hagiography of Madre Victória and for many insights into baroque Catholicism. In voicing Catarina's impressions of religion and the Church, I have closely echoed his sentiments. For written regulations concerning convents I consulted the compilation by the archbishop, D. Sebastião Monteiro da Vide, *Constituicões primeiras do Arcebispado da Bahia* (Lisbon, 1765), and the Destêrro's conventual rule conceded by the Pope in 1726. Discussion of these regulations more from the point of view of their breach than their observance was found in royal and episcopal correspondence housed in the Arquivo Histórico Ultramarino.

Suggestions for Further Reading

A recent Brazilian movie, *Dona Flor and Her Two Husbands,* filmed in Bahia, captured well the spirit of the baroque past when it turned its lenses on a plump cherub perched atop an altarpiece, leering lecherously at the church's female parishioners. In many ways the lascivious cupid calls to mind the ironic contrasts so typical of the baroque. I have tried to convey some of these contradictory impulses in my biography of Madre Catarina. We see that while the Church dominated society and concern with salvation was paramount in the minds of men and women, venality and corruption ran rampant through all levels of public and private life. While Church doctrine proclaimed the brotherhood of man, Church institutions exploited the labor of a multitude of slaves. Although usury was condemned, the monastic orders were among the leading moneylenders of the colony. However circumscribed the role of women, females nonetheless engaged in entrepreneurial pursuits.

The English reader can find an excellent introduction to the society of colonial Bahia in two works: A. J. R. Russell-Wood, *Fidalgos and Philanthropists* (Berkeley, Calif., 1968), and Stuart Schwartz, *Sovereignty and Society in Colonial Brazil* (Berkeley, Calif., 1973). While these books are primarily concerned with the development of particular institutions (the former with the lay brotherhood of the Misericórdia and the latter with the magistracy), they also vividly portray the social context. Thales de Azevedo, *Povoamento da Cidade do Salvador* (Bahia, 1969) offers a more general social history, albeit in Portuguese. Carl Degler's *Neither Black Nor White* (New York, 1971) provides many seminal insights into the multiracial nature of Bahian society.

The women of the Portuguese colony have recently been discovered by historians. For a view of women both in and outside of the convent, see my article, "The Social and Economic Role of the Convent: Women and Nuns in Colonial Bahia, 1677–1800," *Hispanic American Historical Review* 54 (May 1974): 209–32. I have provided an overview of the feminine orders in their Bahian social, economic, and demographic context in Asunción Lavrin, ed., *Latin American Women: A Historical Perspective* (Westport, Conn., 1978). A more general study is A. J. R. Russell-Wood's "Female and Family in Colonial Brazil" in the same volume.

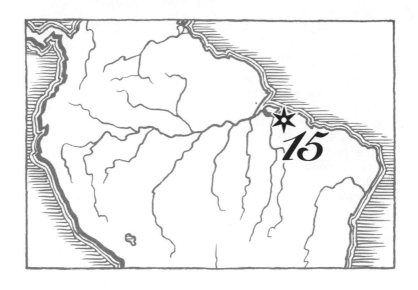

Francisca:
Indian Slave

DAVID G. SWEET

𝓘n 1739 Francisca, an Indian slave woman of the city of Belém do Pará near the mouth of the Amazon River, was persuaded by her young lover, Angélico de Barros Gonçalves, to petition the Portuguese colonial authorities for her freedom. The case was based on the grounds that she had been illegally enslaved in the back country many years before. With the help of the Public Defender of the Indians in Belém, she assembled a number of reliable witnesses to prove this contention at a hearing before the chief justice of the colony. The justice found in her favor; but the case was then appealed by Francisca's owner to the Council of Missions, charged with supervising the administration of the "domestic Indians" of Pará. In the end the litigation was unsuccessful, and Francisca was obliged to remain a slave. This was, as far as can be established today, an exceptional case at law.

Most Indian slaves, in Amazonia and elsewhere in colonial America, lived lives that were so severely constricted by hunger, ignorance, disease and harsh discipline that they had no opportunity for such exercises. They died within a few months or years of their captivity; and for most of them there was little question of striving for an improvement in social status.

Francisca's homeland was more than a thousand miles to the west and up the Amazon from Belém do Pará in the valley of the great Rio Negro, which curves down from what is now the Brazil-Colombia-Venezuela border region to empty into the Amazon at the modern city of Manaus. The Negro was called a "starvation river" by colonial traders and explorers, flowing as it did from rain forest soils so badly leached that the river bore very little of the silt that might raise and enrich the land along its banks during the annual flood. It was never able to support a dense population of fisherfolk and horti-culturists such as once lived along the silt-bearing rivers that flow into the Amazon from the Andes. The people of its basin lived in small, widely scattered groups, or in larger commun-ities which subsisted by trading far and wide, sometimes even bringing in a portion of their food from distant places. It was Francisca's fate to be born in this somber country in a time of hardships and, rather than growing to womanhood in the peaceful company of her own people, to be torn away and made a pawn in strange men's games.

During the seventeenth and early eighteenth centuries, a large, powerful tribe of traders and warriors known as the Manao ranged freely over much of northwestern Amazonia from a base along the middle reaches of the Negro. When first seen by Europeans in about 1640, and again in about 1690, the Manao appeared to be a fierce and warlike people feared by their neighbors. They went entirely naked and kept their heads plucked free of hair—"in order, they say, that they may have nothing to be laid hold of in battle." Their foreheads as far back as the ears were smeared with a black pitch to strike terror in the hearts of their enemies. These were the people among whom Francisca was to spend her childhood. Each flood season they would make their way in swift dugout canoes down through the labyrinth of channels connecting the swollen Negro to the also flooded but immensely fertile and populous valley of the Solimões River, the main stream of the Amazon, to trade. The goods they brought were small platelets of gold for fashioning into ornaments, manioc graters, finely woven hammocks of plant fiber, war clubs, leather shields, and quantities of *onoto* or *urucú*, a red dye for cloth and for faces. Some of these were the products of their own artisanry; others they obtained from trading partners living to the north and west of their home country. The Solimões tribes would provide the Manao traders with certain highly prized shell necklaces, and presumably with cargoes of manioc, smoked fish, pottery, basketry, treecotton cloth, and curare for poisoning the tips of their arrows.[1]

Late in the seventeenth century, this traditional pattern of intertribal trade underwent a process of rapid change. By that time the Portuguese had been established for several decades in a series of small settlements around the mouth of the Amazon in Pará, and the Dutch in even smaller settlements around the mouth of the Essequibo River on the Caribbean coast just north of the lower Negro basin. Both groups of European colonists were endeavoring to extract their fortunes from the tropical forest hinterland. They exchanged trade goods for forest products such as wild cacao, vanilla, sarsaparilla, and certain sweet-smelling barks that could be substituted for East Indian cinnamon and clove, and they corraled Indian men and women as slaves to serve as domestic and plantation workers and as crewmen for the canoes that provided the only available means of transportation into the far interior.

The Dutch were organized as a commercial company, concerned exclusively with profit and anxious to keep both personnel and defense commitments at a minimum. They could deliver large quantities of quality trade goods regularly and at low cost to their factors on the Essequibo. As a result they were able for the most part to stay put and have both Indian slaves and forest products delivered to their trading posts by Indian middlemen, principally the Carib of the lower Orinoco Valley. Other trading peoples in contact with the Dutch roamed inland to the Manao country and acquainted the Manao with such revolutionary technological innovations as the steel axe, knife, and cutlass; the fishhook; the needle; the metal arrowhead or harpoon point; firearms; distilled beverages; and magnificently colored and textured glass beads and pieces of cotton or woollen cloth. Like Native American people everywhere, the Manao quickly incorporated these apparently useful and value-neutral artifacts into their way of life. By so doing they became utterly dependent on their trade with the foreigners, who alone could supply them. This had a far-reaching impact on the commercial activities and ultimately on the social organization and the very destiny of the Manao as a people. Soon they began to barter for slaves rather than for artifacts with their traditional trading partners to the west. When slaves were scarce, they raided other tribes' villages with the purpose of capturing men, women, and children to sell up the Branco to the friends of the Dutch. Among those caught up in this incipient process of social disintegration in the Negro region was the girl Francisca.

During this same era the Portuguese, less organized and less unanimous in purpose than the Dutch, had settled and erected a new exploitative social order on American soil, rather than simply extracting goods from it. They were obliged to obtain most of their trade goods at high prices from the Dutch and other northern European suppliers rather than from manufacturers in their own country, and so they operated at a serious competitive disadvantage. More numerous than the Dutch, the Portuguese settlers quickly required more slaves. By the same token, they could not help but infect more of their Indian neighbors sooner with the same devastating Old World epidemic diseases that had wrought havoc among the native peoples everywhere else in America. The result was that the Portuguese soon had no Indian collaborators who might hope to ensure their own survival by carrying on the Europeans' upriver trade for them. The men of Pará were therefore obliged either to pack up and go home or to try and lay claim to the vast Amazon Valley and its treasures by dint of brute force and sheer audacity. Undaunted, they set out cheerfully on the path of conquest.

By the 1690s, these two frontiers of European expansion had moved close to one another in Francisca's homeland, the lower Rio Negro Valley. There the Indians who traded up the Rio Branco with the Essequibo Dutchmen vied with the

Portuguese and *mestiço* transfrontiersmen who traded with the merchants of Belém do Pará. Around the mouth of the Branco were the Carajaí people, who seem to have traded Dutch goods for slaves with the Manao who lived up the Negro from them to the west. Just downriver from the Carajaí were the Tarumã people, also long-distance traders, who exchanged Dutch goods for slaves (or simply raided for slaves) along the main stream of the Amazon. In the last quarter of the seventeenth century the Manao made war on the Carajaí, either enslaved and sold them or drove them to migrate, and extended their own territory down to the Isle of Timoní, just above the mouth of the Branco. At about the same time the Portuguese transfrontiersmen made war on the Tarumãs, carrying many of them off to Pará, driving others into permanent retreat far up the Branco, and providing a dubious refuge for the survivors in a Jesuit mission village, later run by Carmelites, which was set up to house them on the lower Negro. Not long afterward the Portuguese erected a small fort at the mouth of the Negro (ancestor to the modern city of Manaus), to protect the mission and keep watch on the movements of their new neighbors, the Manao. This westward thrust by the men of Pará was accomplished just a few years before Francisca was born; and as we shall see it was a major factor in determining the course of her life.

Missionaries and soldiers had ostensibly been sent to the Negro to help make the region Portuguese and Christian, to break the trade link with the hated Dutch, and to redirect the entire regional trade in forest products and people toward Belém. Given the vast distances and the limited resources of the authorities in Pará, however, neither group could be either supervised or subsidized on a regular basis. Both were thrown back on their own devices. For a living they competed with the Manao as traders up the Branco to the Dutch, while at the same time they tried to channel the Manao trade in slaves brought from the populous upper reaches of the Negro through their own hands to Pará. They were happy to exchange forest products for Dutch goods; but they were bound that no Rio Negro slaves should make their way to the Essequibo. This would in the long run bring them to war against the Manao; but it was several years before that confrontation came to pass.

Before the fort on the Negro had even been built, an adventurous Portuguese sergeant pushed beyond the mission frontier to establish himself as resident trader in a Manao village across from the mouth of the Branco. The sergeant made friends with the chief there and took his daughter to wife in an effort to cement the commercial alliance. The Manao had already had some violent encounters with the men from Pará and were deeply suspicious of them. They had also been visited by some of the outlanders' tonsured medicine men; and they had had occasion to make it clear to them that as the spiritually powerful rulers of the Negro country they saw no reason to take an interest in the white men's religion. But they were a people who lived by trade; and though the chiefs preferred dealing indirectly with the Dutchmen up the Branco, they could not resist the opportunity that the sergeant and others like him represented. Soon they were exchanging small numbers of slaves, whom they could easily obtain by raiding their weaker neighbors to the west, for occasional shipments of the precious white men's goods from Pará. The sergeant was only the first of a series of "squaw men"[2] through whom this desultory trade was conducted during the first quarter of the eighteenth century.

What the Manao did not understand, to their great misfortune, was that the Portuguese demand for slaves, unlike that of their Indian trading partners, was insatiable. The white men would always require more slaves than the Manao could ever hope to deliver without destroying the entire regional network of intertribal relations. In the end, the men of Pará would lose patience and make war on the Manao, enslaving a great many of them in the process, in order to gain direct access to the populous upper Negro Valley. By 1730 the power of the Manao would be broken forever, and the Manao survivors reduced to working as guides and canoemen for the Portuguese slavers. A century later the tribe would be extinct. But none of this could be foreseen when Francisca was a young woman and the Manao were lords of the Rio Negro.

Francisca's girlhood was spent in the frontier village of the Manao chief Amu, on the Isle of Timoní in the Negro. The name by which she was known there has not come down to us. Her mother appears to have been a woman captured from another tribe and attached to the chief's household either as a servant (if that category of person existed for the Manao) or as one of a number of wives. Whichever was the case, Francisca was Chief Amu's property to dispose of as he pleased. She may have been born among the Manao, as she herself claimed years later, or born elsewhere and brought to the village as a little girl. It seems likely that the date of her birth was between about 1700 and 1705, since she was an adolescent (*mossetona*) when she was taken to Pará in 1718.

In Amu's village Francisca must have lived in a cool circular house loosely constructed of saplings lashed with vines, and with a conical roof woven of palm leaves. She slept in a hammock slung close by those of the many other members of an extended family. Although possibly consigned to some sort of a subordinate status within the village, she undoubtedly enjoyed an easy daily interaction with both children and adults and was probably never flogged by an adult in anger. She bathed once or twice a day in the river. Around her neck she wore an amulet with a bit of wood or a bird's claw, which was designed to protect her against the fearsome demons of the forest and the river and the small *motacu* people with their turned-up feet. By the time she was a young woman, she had learned to tend the corn and manioc plants in the chief's garden; and she could prepare fish, game, and the large manioc pancakes (*beijú*) that Manao men preferred to the manioc meal eaten by most other Amazonian peoples. At the time of her first menstruation, she was wrapped in a hammock, painted, and had her skin incised with the distinctive marks of womanhood. Every year she attended the festival of the first full moon in March, for which the village prepared by storing manioc and smoked fish for months in advance; and during this festival, once she had been initiated, she joined the women in undergoing flogging, with arms crossed over her breasts, to demonstrate her ability to endure pain.

While Francisca was growing up on the Rio Negro, the households and plantations of Portuguese Pará were in chronic need of servants. The several hundred Indians brought there as slaves each year for a century had for the most part failed to reproduce themselves. They tended to die quickly of disease or hunger, and of general discouragement with the forced laborer's life. Each time there was a serious

14. Warrior and hunter of the upper Rio Negro, late eighteenth century.

epidemic, the colonial economy experienced a real crisis from the shortage of working people. Laborers, boatmen, and domestic servants could sometimes be obtained on loan from the Jesuit and Franciscan mission villages near the capital; but they were scarce there as well, and for the same reasons. The result was that rounding up Indians in the backlands had come to be one of the fundamental concerns, year in and year out, of the settlers of Pará.

Each year a few scores of great sailing canoes with forcibly conscripted Indian crewmen would set out for the upper valley to gather the "precious drugs of the backlands," which constituted the colony's only exports. These collecting expeditions made a practice of bringing back as many Indians as they could buy or kidnap. When the upriver tribes committed some act of violence against white men, government slaving troops would be sent out against them as punishment. Finally, beginning in the 1680s, an official system of labor recruitment was devised under which an occasional slave-buying expedition was outfitted and sent up the river by the royal treasury itself. Each expedition was accompanied by a Jesuit chaplain, who was in principle to see to it that no slaves were acquired except through barter with friendly chiefs for the legitimately enslaved prisoners whom they had taken in their customary intertribal wars. This system was of course very readily abused; but once it was established the law required that every slave brought down the river be accompanied by a certificate of legitimate enslavement drawn up and signed by a Jesuit. Any slave found without such a certificate was in theory a free person.

Such people were in fact seldom discovered; and when they did turn up they were never allowed to return home to enjoy their freedom. The labor shortage in Pará was always too critical for that. The few who were intercepted on their way to the slave markets were either released as "free wage laborers" to the custody of an employer in Pará, or they were placed under the jurisdiction of one of the mission villages near the capital—and then made available on a rotating basis as wage laborers to the settlers. The circumstances of life for "free" and slave laborers in the colony were so similar as to be indistinguishable. In practice, the law regulating the slave trade was little observed; and slaves continued to be brought down to Belém under all three traditional systems of recruitment each year and held as captives whether "certified" or not, until long after the trade was officially abolished in 1755.

In September 1717, the season when the cacao-collecting crews sailed forth, a canoe captain by the name of Anacleto Ferreira received a quantity of trade goods from Dona Anna de Fonte, the widow (or at that time perhaps still the wife) of settler Nicolau da Costa of Belém. Ferreira was about to leave for the *sertão* with a canoe belonging to Captain Manoel de Goes of Pará. He signed a receipt for four bundles of white glass beads, two bundles of blue, a dozen pounds of tobacco, a dozen pounds of sugar, two dozen pieces of china, two dozen all-purpose hunting knives, and six matchlocks for muskets.

This was a standard transaction that allowed the stay-at-home settlers and those too poor to outfit their own canoes to take part in financing the forest trade and to have a share in its proceeds. In this case the widow also assisted the expedition by intervening with her uncle, José Velho de Azevedo, the captain-major and acting governor of Pará, to obtain for Ferreira the necessary license for a cacao-collecting trip to the *sertão*. Dona Anna had reason to expect that when Ferreira returned he would bring her a valuable portion of cacao or other "precious drugs," or even better an illegal shipment of slaves to the value of her investment and with a tidy margin of profit.

Some months later a curious transaction took place at the village of Chief Amu on the Isle of Timoní in the Negro. As a gesture of his peaceful intentions toward the slave traders of Pará, the chief gave his daughter (later christened Rosaura) in "marriage" to Anacleto da Costa Rayol, a visiting canoe captain from Belém who had traveled to Manao country in the company of Anacleto Ferreira. According to the several witnesses to this event who were assembled more than twenty years later in Pará, Amu then gave the young woman whom we know as Francisca to the same slave trader as "companion" or personal servant to Rosaura. Ferreira's and Rayol's were illegal private slaving expeditions. They had no Jesuit chaplain with them to interview Francisca, determine the circumstances of her captivity, and draw up the required certificate of legitimate enslavement. If they had brought such a collaborator, he might well have found that she was a free person who might be transported and put to work but could not legally be held as a slave. As it was, Francisca was taken down the river without papers. In the eyes of the transfrontiersmen of Pará she was as surely a slave as any other Indian they might acquire in the *sertão*. It may be assumed that in the eyes of Chief Amu and in her own eyes as well, at that point in her life, she was the property of Anacleto de Costa Rayol or of any other person to whom he might give her, from the day of their transaction and for as long as she might live.

Not long afterward the great canoe commanded by Anacleto Rayol was loaded with a gang of male and female slaves and launched on the river for Pará. In addition to the captain there were probably a dozen crewmen aboard, themselves slaves or involuntary recruits from the mission *aldeias*. These men were kept in docile obedience by a combination of genial treatment with the constant threat and frequent example of brutal physical punishment for the smallest infraction. Their families were held hostage in Pará, and each man knew well that to escape was to throw oneself into a lonely struggle for survival in the unfamiliar forests of the inhospitable Negro, a thousand miles from home. The crewmen received meager rations of manioc meal and salt fish, which they gobbled down hastily with gulps of water from the river during brief interludes in the long days of bending sweating backs to their paddles in the sun. At night they slept on the hard benches of their canoes, and only occasionally were they given the opportunity to fish, hunt, and gather the forest fruits and grubs with which they might restore their exhausted bodies. These men talked little, but they did sing in unison as they worked, a monotonous song that blended with the monotonous rhythm of their work and seemed to lend strength to their aching arms and backs. Francisca sat still in the canoe as it glided down the broad river day after day. She was afraid and had no idea what awaited her, and she must have wished that she understood the crewmen's tongue so that she might ask them what lay ahead.

The slaves being transported were tied to the canoe to prevent their escaping. The strong young men among them had their arms tied behind them around a length of tree-trunk, which exhausted them and lacerated their flesh and thereby discouraged them from even trying to work themselves free. The slaves were fed even less than the crewmen, and after many days of hunger and exposure to the elements several of them were ill and on the verge of dying. Canoe captains in the official trade complained that they often lost a third or a half of a shipment of slaves during the several weeks' journey from the Negro to Pará. The private traders did no better. The dead and the severely ill among both slaves and crew were simply abandoned on the beaches or thrown into the river—food for the alligators and the omnipresent buzzard *urubú*. These horrors of transportation to Pará were comparable to those of the Atlantic "middle passage" of Africans to America, but the slaves of Amazonia were considerably less able to resist them. Francisca was fortunate to survive the journey.

Along the way Anacleto da Costa Rayol seems to have sold Francisca to Anacleto Ferreira for some of Dona Anna de Fonte's trade goods. Farther down they met up with a slaver from São Luiz do Maranhão named Estevão Cardoso, who was returning home by way of Belém with a load of captives from the Negro. Ferreira's canoe was by this time short of crewmen, so he traded Francisca to Cardoso for an Indian man capable of paddling. This was done with the understanding that on his way Cardoso would deliver the girl to Ferreira's employer, Manoel de Goes, in Belém, so that Goes might hand her over to Dona Anna de Fonte in partial payment for the trade goods with which she had supplied him. This was duly done, and within a few weeks' time Francisca had begun the painful process of her "seasoning" as a servant girl of Belém do Pará.

Francisca served in Anna de Fonte's house for twenty years before she brought her petition for freedom before the authorities. What she did there we can only surmise. Undoubtedly her daily routine included assisting in the laborious preparation of food from the manioc plant, and from the variety of

15. Indian women at domestic work in a village on the lower Amazon, late eighteenth century.

fresh fruits, meats, and fish that was available on good days to be fetched from the open-air market by the city's canoe landing along the river. She must have spent a good deal of time laundering clothing to keep her mistress and her mistress' family presentable in the tropical heat. She probably became deeply involved in the religious life of the capital, with its gaudy annual round of festivals and processions and its obligatory frequent attendance at Mass. Little by little she forgot her Manao language and became proficient in the Tupian *lingua geral* of Amazonia, though she never had occasion to learn Portuguese. Unlike her mistress and the other respectable ladies of the town, she was probably free to come and go in the streets during off-hours and on holidays and to maintain her own circle of male and female friends among the teeming population of free and slave Indians and blacks, *mestiços,* and déclassé white people who made up the great bulk of the inhabitants of the town. During her suit for freedom Francisca appeared in person before the judge who was hearing her case, as did all the witnesses on both sides, most of them men. But the widow Anna de Fonte was too ladylike for such public goings-on and had her testimony recorded by a scrivener in the privacy of her home.

Perhaps the most remarkable feature of Francisca's life in Pará was the mere fact that unlike many another slave she managed to survive there for at least two decades and retain some life-affirming spirit and determination about her in the process. Among other things, she survived the terrible epidemic of smallpox that devastated the town in 1724 and 1725, brought the economy to a standstill, and drove the population into the streets in mournful processions of penitence. Many of her friends must have died then, horrible deaths with bodies covered by stinking pustules that made it seem as if they were rotting before the life had quite gone out of them. Francisca may somehow have avoided the plague altogether; she may even have been among the fortunate few who benefited from the pioneering experiment with inoculation (the transfer of pus from the sores of the ill into incisions made in the arms of the healthy), which was carried out by a Carmelite friar of the city during that time. It is more likely that she came down with the pox but somehow managed to survive, probably with her face disfigured, like many of her contemporaries in America and Europe and elsewhere, with the pockmarks that served as the badge of triumph over the principal killer of the age.

Some very dim light is shed on Francisca's life in Pará by the collection of witnesses who were assembled to testify both for and against her in the hearings resulting from her suit for freedom in 1739, when she was nearing forty. Angelico de Barros Gonçalves, her lover, was a master tailor some ten years her junior, who would seem to have been the *mestiço* son or grandson of an Angelico de Barros who had served a term as *comandante* of the Fortress of the Rio Negro some thirty years before. With family ties to the slave trade, like those of nearly everyone else in Pará, he seems to have preferred the less adventurous urban style of life for himself. Angelico recalled having heard from Anacleto da Costa Rayol himself the story of his paramour's being handed over as a free woman to the slave traders by Chief Amu. But the tailor's testimony was given little credit because he was an interested party determined to obtain freedom for his "concubine," one who had in fact petitioned the government in his own right to have Francisca removed from Dona Anna de Fonte's house not long before. Similarly, little attention was paid to Angelico's illiterate brother-in-law and housemate, Manoel Dias, who claimed under oath to have heard the same story from the Indian woman Rosaura herself. Unaccountably Rosaura, who appears to have been alive in Belém at the time of the inquiry, was not called to testify. Also disregarded was the contribution of a Portuguese volunteer witness named Ignacio Caldeira Lisboa, who was identified as Francisca's lawyer interested only in his fees.

Another of Francisca's prime witnesses was a free Indian woman named Apolinaria, of about thirty years of age. Apolinaria testified through an interpreter, an old transfrontiersman and slaving captain named Diego Pinto de Gaya, because like Francisca and most other inhabitants of the colony of Maranhão and Grão Pará—a century after the establishment of Portuguese rule there—she was unable to make herself understood in Portuguese and was comfortable only in the *lingua geral*. Apolinaria asserted that as a girl of ten she had come down to Pará with Francisca, from the same village of Chief Amu and with the same expedition under Anacleto de Costa Rayol. She had been an eyewitness, she testified, to the handing over of Rosaura and Francisca to Rayol. But she was deemed a witness of "little credibility" because not only was she an "Indian woman of the country" and a "poor person of the lowest degree" (*pobre, vil e infame*), but she was also a whore—and as such she was seen as a person whose testimony could readily be bought and who could be "corrupted by the slightest material interest."

The documents contribute nothing toward our understanding of the meaning of *whore* and *concubine* in the early eighteenth-century society of Pará. Many an Indian or African slave woman of Pará was put to work at the prostitute's trade by her mistress, as a source of steady cash income to a "respectable" household. Either term may well have been loosely used by the clergy and officialdom of the day to refer to patterns of sexual behavior other than those prescribed by the canons of matrimony—canons seldom fully observable by men and women of the impoverished class of *viles e infames* in colonial society. Perhaps the most remarkable implication of this collection of testimonies and comments is that there existed within the tiny urban society of early eighteenth-century Pará a network of friendship and mutual support that might unite an Indian slave housemaid, a free Indian whore, a hard-working tailor, and some others in a joint effort to challenge the system and free one of their number from the oppressive burden of chatteldom. No less remarkable is the suggestion that in the real world of Pará the social barriers erected by slavery and official racial discrimination were less influential in ordering social relations than were the natural bonds of friendship.

Dona Anna de Fonte defended her property rights in Francisca by calling together a number of rather more respectable citizens, people in their forties or older, and all but one of them both white and literate, to affirm that they knew the slave woman to have been brought down in return for Dona Anna's investment of trade goods with Anacleto Ferreira, and that for two decades she had generally been known as a slave in the Fonte household. None of these people was an eyewitness to the events on the Isle of Timoní, and several admitted to having derived their information from Dona Anna de Fonte herself. But no questions were raised about the reliability of their testimonies.

The most remarkable of the widow Fonte's witnesses was a male Indian slave belonging to her brother-in-law, one Clemente, who appears somehow to have been induced to perjure himself for her cause. Clemente insisted through an interpreter that he was a Manao himself and that he remembered the time when his uncle, a chief named Mabiary, had captured Francisca as a teenage girl from one of his enemies and then handed her over to another chief named Exa, who in turn had sold her to Estevão Cardoso of Maranhão. According to Clemente, Cardoso had then brought Francisca down directly to sell in Pará. Despite the lack of any certificate of legitimate enslavement, which he explained by the fact that there had been no official slaving troop on the Negro at the time of this transaction, Clemente thought that Francisca ought to be thought of as a slave just like all the rest.

Francisca's case was first heard by the chief justice of the colony, who found that the woman should be declared a free person. This was because Dona Anna had been unable to produce a certificate of legitimate enslavement and because Francisca had been brought from the *sertão* by people licensed not to go slaving but only to go up after cacao. The widow Fonte then appealed the case to the Council of Missions, a body consisting of the heads of all the religious orders established in Pará, which held final jurisdiction in matters involving the administration of the Indians. The council reversed the justice's decision on the grounds that Francisca's witnesses (and in particular Apolinaria) were unreliable, and that since Francisca had been given to Rayol as a kind of dowry to accompany his bride, Rosaura, she had clearly been viewed as a slave by Chief Amu. Expressing its belief that justice was better served by attending to the "truth" than to the confusing details of the evidence assembled in the case, the council ordered that Francisca return obediently to the service of her mistress. When all was said and done, she was no more or less than an ordinary *escrava resgatada*, a slave bought and delivered by the traders of Pará, who was by custom obliged to work for a lifetime to repay the cost of her purchase.

No more than that can now be known of Francisca and of her life and times in the slave society of Pará. The chances are that her days were numbered, since more than half the population of the colony was to die in the terrible epidemic of measles that swept the valley in 1749. But dim though the reflection of the living person has become, it is an image worthy of a moment's thoughtful attention. Francisca was a member of what was perhaps the most despised, dehumanized, and least vigorous human group that existed in colonial America—the caste of Indian slaves. The intelligence, resourcefulness, vitality, determination, and love of life that moved people like her was seldom acknowledged (at least in writing) even by their contemporaries. Francisca's kind were short-lived, shamelessly exploited, and quickly forgotten. But Francisca was a survivor and a woman who made her mark on several other people's lives and managed in some measure to steer her own course. The result is that we may know her name, and wonder about what sort of human being she must really have been.

Notes

1. Samuel Fritz, S. J., *Journal of the Travels and Labours of Father Samuel Fritz in the River of the Amazons between 1686 and 1723*, Hakluyt Society, 2d series, no. 51 (London, 1922), pp. 62–63.

2. Literal translation of Tupi-Guaraní *cunhamena*, the standard term in Brazilian histories for these transfrontiersmen.

Sources

Most of the original documents for the study of Indian slavery and other aspects of the social history of Pará in the seventeenth and early eighteenth centuries have perished since Francisca's day. They have been lost or fallen victim to the humid heat and mold and borer worms. A good many of them were sold by the pound to a firecracker manufacturer not so many years ago, by a director of the State Archive less appreciative of their contents than of the commercial value of the fine rag paper on which they were written. But the file concerning Francisca's suit for freedom has survived because it was collected with other official papers on the Indian slave trade by a governor sent out to abolish that trade and carry out other administrative reforms in the 1750s. The governor took the papers back to Lisbon when he returned, and they may be consulted there today in the Pombal Collection at the National Library. It is from this slender sheaf of notarized depositions and lawyers' resumés, Codex 642, ff. 100–142, that it is possible to reconstruct at least the bare outlines of Francisca's story today.

Background information for the Indian slave trade from the Rio Negro basin was taken from my dissertation, "A Rich Realm of Nature Destroyed: The Central Amazon Valley, 1640–1750" (University of Wisconsin, 1974), chs. 9–11. Ethnographic notes on the

Manao may be found in Alfred Métraux, "Tribes of the Middle and Upper Amazon," *Handbook of South American Indians,* vol. 3 (Washington, D.C., 1947), pp. 687–712.

Suggestions for Further Reading

The best published treatment in English of the Amazon Indian slave trade and labor system, as well as of other aspects of the struggle between Amerindians and Europeans in that part of the colonial world, is John Hemming, *Red Gold: The Conquest of the Brazilian Indians,* 1500–1760 (Cambridge, Mass., 1978), esp. chs. 11, 15, 18 and 19. Legal aspects are discussed in Mathias Kiemen, *The Indian Policy of Portugal in the Amazon Region, 1614–1693* (Washington, D.C., 1954), esp. ch. 5. For a broader view of colonial Amazonian society, see Charles R. Boxer, *The Golden Age of Brazil* (Berkeley, Calif., 1969), ch. 11; Caio Prado, Jr., *The Colonial Background of Modern Brazil* (Berkeley, Calif., 1971), pp. 69–72 and 242–55; and the articles by David M. Davidson and Colin Maclachlan in Dauril Alden, ed., *Colonial Roots of Modern Brazil* (Berkeley, Calif., 1973).

PART FOUR

Survival Through Competition

Introduction

*M*any people in the colonial world found it possible not only to survive but also to inch their way upward or even to advance rapidly in the social order despite the structural inequalities built around class, race, and sex. Breaking the chains of dependency, these individuals strove for a place where it was possible to operate with some degree of autonomy in competition with others. *Dependency* and *autonomy* are both relative terms of course. Not even the most abject slave was totally dependent, nor was the most successful competitor totally autonomous. No one in the colonial world was free of superior authority and the overriding interest of the metropolis; and even modest success in competition often brought with it the envy and hostility of one's neighbors. But rising in the social order nevertheless meant greater freedom to act at least semi-independently, to take one's chances in the commercial economy, or to strive for position within the civil, military, and ecclesiastical bureaucracies. This freedom was no guarantee of material success or of achieving a higher status, but it did enlarge the social space within which the individual strove for advantage.

Given the tripartite structure of inequality, the chances of success in competition within the colonial world were least favorable if one was female, non-European, and of lower-class origin. They were most favorable if one was male, European, and born with some degree of social distinction. Thus it is not surprising that one or two of the people we encounter in Part IV were male Europeans of respectable lineage. What is remarkable about this group is that none of them was born to privilege or embarked on a career with the advantages of wealth.

Competition was not limited to the world of European colonizers, nor even to the world of the free persons of color gathered in their towns. In Indian communities, or at least in those which operated under strong acculturative pressures from the Europeans, there was plenty of it. The slaves of mine and plantation were not above jockeying for positions of comparative advantage. But competition among the isolated and the unfree in colonial America proceeded according to a different dynamic from that of competition in the world of the Europeans. It was more channeled and restricted by considerations of community interest; and it was less a battle for the accumulation of material possessions than a struggle to improve one's status or to obtain relief from demeaning and debilitating manual labor. However, among the acquisitive Europeans and the other free persons who aped them, the object was simply to get rich and by so doing ensure status and power. "Everyone here," wrote an eighteenth-century North American, "is in a Scramble for Wealth and Power, and there are so many jarring and opposite Interests and Systems, that no real comfort can continue long in any mind which is obliged to act in concert with men of such worldly Spirits."[1]

Among ordinary people in America, the competitive mode of behavior was full of risks. To compete successfully was to raise oneself out of the cellar of society in which the bound laborers, black and white, and the chronically poor lived. But the chances of falling backward were always very great on the slippery slopes of competition. Those who extended their credit too far, took an unreasonable risk, offended someone with great power, or merely fell victim to the unpredictable downturns of the Atlantic economy could plunge from prosperity to dependence and despair once again. This is one reason why the transition to the modern world of market relations and the untrammeled pursuit of profit was a slow and jerky one in every American country.

As late as the end of the eighteenth century, sizable portions of the colonial population still resisted the advancing capitalist ethos, preferring to cling to the peasant and *ancien régime* mentality that stressed communality above competition, sidereal work rhythms to industrial clock time, and religion and family more than the aggrandizement of wealth. We cannot speak of a particular decade or even a century in which the transition to the new outlook occurred in any country. The entire colonial period, from the sixteenth to the early nineteenth century, was an epoch in which the spread of commercial capitalism and the beginnings of industrial capitalism, hastened in the New World by what seemed an abundance of opportunity and unlimited resources, began to transform modes of thought and patterns of behavior. The people in the stories that follow may, therefore, be thought of as participants in this fundamental transformation of life.

Note

1. Richard Peters to William Smith, May 28, 1763, in *Pennsylvania Magazine of History and Biography* 10 (1886): 352.

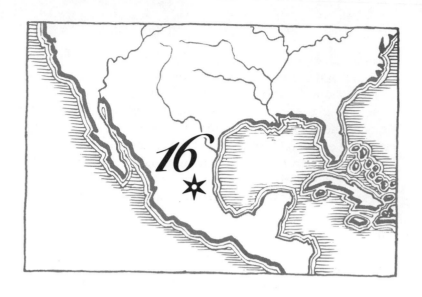

Miguel Hernández:
Master of Mule Trains

JOHN C. SUPER

*M*iguel Hernández was a free mulatto who lived a good, full life in sixteenth-century Mexico. He married, raised a family, and lived to see his children find their own place in the world. He acquired an education and became a community figure in his own way. After years of work and dedication he achieved local economic influence and prominence. Miguel Hernández found success and love during an era of increasing social and racial prejudice. Mexico did not have its social and racial arrangements fully worked out in his day, but increasingly toward the end of the century life was difficult for people of mixed blood.

Miguel Hernández is an important man to know. He is one of those people historians too infrequently encounter who went beyond mere accommodation to create a rich and rewarding life in the face of difficult circumstances. He did so in an orderly and even way, living a relatively prosaic and unassuming life. He was neither a spirited rebel nor an adventurer; he was simply a diligent and persistent man who gradually expanded the horizons of his own world.

Miguel can be recalled today because of his literacy and his knowledge of Spanish legal ways. He was a frequent visitor to the office of several notaries in the town. From the contracts Miguel entered, the will that he wrote, and the contracts and wills written by his friends, it is possible to reconstruct some few aspects of his life. Much of the documentation relating to Miguel would have been impossible to use if he had not been able to sign his name. His signature made it possible to distinguish him from the other Miguel Hernándezes that appeared in the notarial records.

Miguel's signature gives us a more direct, personal understanding of the man. In the absence of a portrait, it is the only likeness of him that endures. With the heavy emphasis on form and style in writing in the sixteenth century, his signature does give something of an intellectual portrait. His signature of 1598 is here reproduced.

His hand was steady and sure, with more attention to the careful formation of each letter than to exaggerated embellishment. Like most men of learning, though, he did have concern for stylistic impression, so there is some flurry and grace to his signature. He obviously held a quill comfortably and confidently. The quality of his hand places him closer to the trained professionals than to the marginally literate men who scratched out crude signatures. Miguel's signature implies that he was literate. Literacy was quite common among sixteenth-century Spaniards in Mexico but was unusual among mulattoes, blacks, and Indians. His literacy therefore immediately placed him in a select group.

Miguel was born in Mexico City in the middle of the sixteenth century, the legitimate son of Pedro Hernández and Ana Hernández, natives of the same city. He was a second generation Mexican, a man of the New World who had few ties with Spain or Africa. He married Ana Hernández (no relation to his mother), who was also born in Mexico City; it is likely that some of their children were born there too. Though details are few on Miguel's background, documentation from later years suggests that he used his legitimacy, literacy, and freedom to good advantage. He did some work as a muleteer, became more familiar with the complexities of trade, and developed personal and financial associations with people of wealth.

Miguel's ties to Mexico City were strong but not strong enough to bind him to a life there. The chances of material gain for men of color at the center of the colonial economy had lessened as life became more settled and orderly after the conquest. Very few blacks and mulattoes, whether slave or free, broke through the legal and social barriers to occupy master positions in the more important crafts or to own valuable property. Thus many of them looked to the provinces for opportunities. Earnest colonists, along with debtors, renegades, and escaped slaves, moved to the provinces to escape the growing rigidity of the social and racial hierarchy of Mexico City.

Miguel Hernández chose the town of Querétaro as his new home. It was a good choice. Querétaro was then a small agricultural and commercial town with a promising future. A man of vision could easily see that the town was on the verge of expansion, though few could have foretold the population jumping from about a thousand in 1590 to over five thousand in 1630. The key to the town's growth was location. Querétaro straddled the highway connecting Mexico City with the silver mines at Zacatecas and the north. The rich agricultural and pastoral lands of the Bajío spread toward the east, producing crops for distribution to the north and south. Commerce, and the transportation system on which it depended, tied the economy together and linked it to larger population centers. Economic growth generated social opportunity. Race, sex, and background influenced a person's place in Querétaro, but they did not determine it. A free man of color with luck and hard work could build a fine life there.

When Miguel arrived in Querétaro, he automatically joined a special group. Since he was free, literate, and skilled as a muleteer, he became one of the leading mulatto citizens. The less fortunate lived for the service of others, bound by the debts that they had accumulated. These men and women labored in fields and factories for two or three pesos each month. With debts that might approach 100 pesos (sometimes incurred to obtain release from jail), such people normally faced years of servitude. Less fortunate still were slaves, the largest group of mulattoes in the town.

Often mulattoes lived on the edge of the law. Contemporaries saw them as dangerous and unstable, as troublemakers who caused more harm than good. They committed (or at least were accused of committing) crimes of assault, rape, drunkenness, and theft more often than Spaniards and Indians. Partly for this reason, local officials from time to time tried to enforce the stringent royal legislation restricting the behavior of mulattoes. In 1597 the town magistrate ordered them to leave the Indian areas because of their corrupting influence. In 1623 the magistrate ordered all free mulattoes and blacks to perform service for Spaniards. Even men with money and good reputation experienced the burden of discrimination. Juan Bautista, a free mulatto, opened a hatter's shop and was thrown in jail for his efforts on the pretext that he was not a professional hatmaker, and that he did not have a license for his shop. The real reason was that the established merchants and manufacturers could more easily intimidate a man of color who did not have powerful friends.

Miguel Hernández carefully sidestepped many of the traps that ensnared other mulattoes and blacks in this society. Like the sure-footed mules that he led, he seldom stumbled as he walked through the Spanish world. His ability to contract large debts without being forced into servitude is strong evidence of the standing he achieved in the community. Miguel managed, at least for some practical purposes, to overcome the stigma of his color. He became a Spaniard in his economic activities, and much of the rest of his life personified the opposite of the nasty stereotypes that Spaniards had of mixed-bloods. Subtleties in the notarial records help to illustrate this. Notaries, who knew Miguel well, at times forgot to add the customary remark that he was a mulatto; at other times they hastily scratched in "free mulatto" above his

16. Mexican muleteers of a later era, from an early nineteenth-century print.

name, adding as an afterthought something that was becoming less important.

After moving to Querétaro, Miguel began building his own freighting business. By the end of the 1590s his success allowed him to expand. In March 1599 he bought six mules for 215 pesos; in August he bought two more for 72 pesos. Business was good enough that he could pay these debts in a year, either in cash or by discounting freight charges. By 1604 he had expanded again, buying eight more mules, not yet entirely paid for. This gave him a train of twenty mules, a substantial investment by local standards. Twenty mules with tack might bring a thousand pesos in the very brisk provincial mule market. The same amount could buy a wheat farm with tools and stock, several thousand acres of grazing land, or a flock of two thousand sheep.

The expansion of Miguel's business can be understood only against the background of a rapidly growing provincial economy. With the catastrophic decline of the Indian population in the sixteenth century, Spaniards were forced to turn from a reliance on Indian surplus to a more direct control over economic production. The rise of the Spanish population and the colonization of the far north hurried this development. Querétaro benefited from the changes. By 1600 Querétaro farmers and ranchers sold maize, wheat, and mutton to hungry urban populations, and just as importantly, local merchants shipped out wool, first in its raw state, then as a manufactured item produced by the town's *obrajes* (woolen factories). With large quantities of bulky goods moving north and south, Querétaro became a transportation center requiring the service of scores of freighters.

Like several other local muleteers at this time, Miguel earned most of his income from hauling wool to the southern markets of Mexico City, Texcoco, and Tlaxcala. For every twenty-five pounds that he hauled, he received about three reales. He supplemented this income with small profits from petty trade. The sale of cloth was a natural consequence of the muleteer's knowledge of prices and markets. Farm workers and artisans owed him a few pesos for rough garments. Here Miguel was similar to other mixed-bloods and Indians who sold bits of cloth, thread, and foodstuffs for a few extra pesos. He differed from them in that once in a while he carried more valuable cloth on consignment from Mexico City people to the province. His wife even bought a dress from one of these Mexico City sellers for thirty-five pesos. Miguel may also have earned a little money from the collection of the tithe, a tax levied by the Church on economic production. One of his debtors was Luis de Vargas, who owed him twenty bushels of wheat—eight for the sale of a saddle and twelve for the tithe. Since merchants almost monopolized the collection of the tithe, it is likely that Miguel was a subcontractor or an agent for a merchant. Finally, Miguel sold mules. Retailing mules that he bought wholesale or selling those no longer needed for his business brought in cash.

To help finance his business, Miguel turned to local landowners and merchants. By 1604 he had open accounts with the merchants Fulano de Oviedo, Hernando de la Vega, and Francisco Vásquez. He had another account with Luis de Tovar, a sharp businessman and one of the fastest rising persons in all of Mexico. Tovar had grown up watching his father wheel and deal in the eastern Bajío wool trade and by the 1590s, when he was in his early twenties, had himself begun to invest directly in the trade. Eventually he invested in large tracts of land and became an important political figure in Mexico. Miguel's association with Tovar was probably a short-run boon to his freighting business, although if the association had continued, Miguel might have ended up simply as an employee of Tovar. Other people contributed to the building of Miguel's business, but only in a small and sporadic way.

The facts that survive from the conduct of the business imply that Miguel was an aggressive and enterprising man, not afraid of taking risks. He seized the opportunity for growth, rushing into debt to increase the size of his mule train. Yet he exercised caution and showed sound judgement by not overexpanding or overextending his credit. Miguel's spirited business temperament paid social and economic dividends. By 1604 he had become a *señor de recuas,* master of mule trains, a smart leap from his status as a simple muleteer (*arriero*) in the 1590s. There were other muleteers in Querétaro, but none of them was addressed as *señor.* Miguel had reached an enviable status in the freighting profession, but he had not reached the top. This position belonged to the owners and masters of the heavy carts and wagons that rumbled between Querétaro and Mexico City. These men were exclusively Spaniards and often figured among the most prominent men in local society. With their large wagons they could easily ship more freight than the muleteers, who were increasingly confined to shorter hauls and harder roads. The lives of some muleteers were like the roads they traveled— rough, continually turning, separated from the mainstream of provincial life.

Miguel Hernández was different. While he never reached the top, he did earn enough to buy valuable property in the town. In 1598 he owned a house and garden worth 500 pesos, a large amount for town property in the 1590s. Apparently he had bought a substantial parcel of urban property just to the west of the center of town after arriving in Querétaro. At this time several Indians, blacks, and mulattoes lived in the area. He sold a section of the land (about 15 × 20 yards) for seventy-two pesos in 1598. He also owned irrigated property just to the north of town, which he sold for thirty pesos. Miguel was profiting from the fast growth of Querétaro in the 1590s.

Miguel also used his new wealth to buy a black slave. By doing so he joined a fairly exclusive group dominated by Europeans. The slave was sick and at 150 pesos may not have been a sensible purchase economically, but the prestige and other social benefits of owning him probably compensated for this.

Miguel had deep ties to Querétaro. His profession made him a man of the road, but his property and his family made him a man of the town. His wife Ana bore four children: Francisco Hernández, Juan Hernández, María Magdalena, and Elvira Martínez de San Miguel. Remarkably, all of them. survived, and were a part of the family in the 1590s. It is to Ana's credit that the family survived as a unit.

What little is known of Miguel's wife is confused by the existence of another Ana Hernández who lived next door. Miguel said that his wife was a Mexican Indian (probably Aztec), but at times she was referred to as a mulatto. The other Ana was definitely a mulatto, who worked as a domestic for two pesos a month in the 1590s. It is probable that

Miguel's wife came from a common Indian family. She made no pretenses about her background, and when she married Miguel she brought no material goods into the marriage. She was illiterate but most certainly Spanish-speaking, even though she at times negotiated contracts with the aid of an interpreter. When Miguel died, Ana turned to her son Juan to help her manage her affairs, giving him power of attorney to represent her and control over her husband's property. Her reliance on Juan was never total. As late as 1622 she appeared in the notary's office to handle family matters.

Miguel's family may have extended beyond his wife and children. Members of a mulatto family headed by another Miguel Hernández appeared in Querétaro. This Miguel had his interests in land, not in transportation and trade. Blacks and mulattoes had the chance to own small rural properties (*ranchos* and *labores*) in the province during this time, but they could not expect to become masters of large agricultural and pastoral enterprises (*haciendas* and *estancias*). Miguel raised crops and a few goats, pigs, and horses on a farm to the south of Querétaro. He also had connections in Mexico City, where he still owned a small house worth 150 pesos in 1600. In that year his family appraised his estate at 1,028 pesos. Miguel's estate shows that small farms could provide more than a subsistence living, but they seldom provided as much opportunity for gain as commerce. Unfortunately, there is no direct proof of the two Miguel Hernández families being related by blood or marriage. Extended mulatto families held together by common social and economic interests may have existed, but they are difficult to document.

There was a woman in Querétaro who has to be considered a member of the family, even though she was not related. She was the widow Ana Enzemoche, an Otomí Indian. Since Ana had no family (as she put it, "not having daughters nor sons, brothers and sisters, nor relatives, nor heirs"), she claimed the Hernández family as hers. She gave María Magdalena a plot of land for her dowry, made both Miguel's daughters heirs to her entire estate, and then appointed Miguel and his wife as executors of her estate. The widow was dear to the Hernández family, as close as any relative could have been.

Miguel's circle of close associations stretched far beyond his family. Many of his friends were his neighbors: Hernando, an Indian singer in the chapel; Cecilia, the Indian wife of a Spaniard; Ana, the mulatto servant; and the many mulattoes and blacks who belonged to Miguel's *cofradía* (confraternity). If this *cofradía* was similar to others in town, its members met often to plan religious festivals, talk about finances and organization, and provide social and economic assistance to widows, orphans, and the sick. Other friends were outsiders, people whom he had met on the road or old acquaintances from Mexico City. When the free mulatto Martín Gracia became ill in Querétaro, he immediately sought out his friend Miguel to help write his will and organize his papers. He gave Miguel control over some houses he owned in Mexico City and charged him with seeing that his daughter received money for a dowry.

He also claimed Spaniards as friends. His closest Spanish friend was Domingo Correa Falcón, a merchant. Their friendship probably began with a business deal, then assumed more permanence when Correa Falcón became Miguel's compadre, the godfather of one of his children. Miguel always referred to Correa Falcón as his compadre and called on him to help settle his estate. Through his membership in the *cofradía* of the Santísimo Sacramento (this was in addition to his membership in the black and mulatto *cofradía*), Miguel associated with the richest landowners, the most active merchants, the most powerful bureaucrats. Miguel knew them all, and in the last years of his life, when he was a *señor*, it is not too difficult to imagine that he looked them in the eye as an equal. He spoke their language, wore their clothes, followed their laws, and succeeded in their businesses.

Many of Miguel's relationships crossed racial and social boundaries. The restrictions that often placed mulattoes and mestizos much closer to the Indian world did not usually apply to him. His life did not fit into any one level of the complex social and racial hierarchy evolving in Mexico; instead it bridged many levels of the hierarchy. His ties with Indians and mixed-bloods were warm and personal. After all, Miguel was still married to an Indian commoner, and his children had been raised among Indians. Yet his occupation and interests threw him headlong into the Spanish world, a world in which he eventually moved with ease. He seemed to walk the cultural bridge without anxiety or doubt. Certainly he curried favor with influential Spaniards. This was natural for anyone chasing the good life in early Mexico. While doing so, he did not suppress his own origins or that of his family. Dodging the past was an established art practiced by many in the sixteenth century, but not by Miguel.

Much more of Miguel's life would be understandable if it were possible to reconstruct more fully the lives of his children after they struck out on their own. This was not possible because of their common surname, and because they were no longer mulattoes. Spanish racial nomenclature was inclusive enough to provide for the offspring of mulattoes and Indian women, but such artificiality did not exist in the province. Children of mulatto and Indian unions with a good social and economic background usually escaped derogatory racial labeling.

It is known for certain that one of Miguel's sons did not follow his father's profession. Juan, who earlier may have been a shepherd, joined the artisan ranks in 1599 when he apprenticed with Bartolomé Vásquez, the best blacksmith in town. Juan agreed to serve for a year and a half in return for bed, board, and clothing. After that time he would be a journeyman, allowed to practice his trade anywhere. Juan probably finished his apprenticeship, since his father guaranteed that he would. Blacksmiths led a decent life in the province. Their position fell somewhere between silversmiths and architects at the top and tailors and carpenters at the bottom. Francisco Hernández also may have been a smith; at least there was another blacksmith in town with that name in 1600. It is reasonable to assume that Miguel's sons had joined the lower ranks of Spanish society.

No definite information is available on Miguel's daughters, but with their substantial inheritance from Ana Enzemoche (which included twenty-nine parcels of land), they should not have lacked suitors. Elvira's name suggests that she was already married or had been married previously. If they did marry, it is likely that they married Indians or mixed-bloods of good standing, since even some Spanish women with dowries had a difficult time finding Spanish husbands around 1600. If they did not marry, they probably had enough money to aspire to a comfortable life in the prestigious local Convent of Santa Clara de Jesús.

Miguel Hernández died suddenly in 1604, leaving his wife and children as survivors. Probably struck by disease or the victim of an accident, he only managed to mark his testament with four heavy strokes, whereas a few days before he still had a fine signature. He quickly called on his compadre to help him with his will. Miguel named his children as heirs, each to share equally in his wealth. He then made his peace with the Church, asking that masses be performed before his special saints. He was anxious to be buried in the Convent of San Francisco, and even before writing his will had made arrangements for this with the guardian of the convent. The guardian readily acknowledged the request because Miguel was a man of substance and virtue. By avoiding the passions that had destroyed many, Miguel had created a life of meaning that was respected by his family and friends.

Sources

The life of Miguel Hernández was reconstructed entirely from Querétaro notarial records, including bills of sale, powers of attorney, letters of apprenticeship, acknowledgements of debts, and service and freighting contracts. The single most important document for understanding Miguel is his testament, a seven-page document written in 1604. His testament is almost a balance sheet of the last years of his life, as it lists his current debtors and creditors in addition to referring to such varied matters as a property line dispute, some clothes that his wife bought, and an old benefactor in Mexico City. These documents are located in the Archivo de Notarias de Querétaro. For easier consultation, most of them can be found on microfilm in the Querétaro microfilm series, Museo Nacional de Antropología e Historia, Mexico City. The following references are to selected documents on microfilm and include the name of the notary, the date, and the roll number. Juan Pérez de Aguilar, 5 September, 1589 (3); Baltasar Martín, 29 October, 1597 (1), 27 July, 1598 (2), 17 August, 1598 (2), 28 January, 1599 (2), 19 April, 1599 (2), 22 February, 1603 (4); Tomás de los Reyes, 21 January, 1601 (1); Hernando de Robles, 21 April, 1604 (5), 1 May, 1604 (5), 24 May, 1604 (2); Gaspar de Porras, 10 November, 1608 (7); Felipe de Santiago, 6 June, 1622 (9).

Suggestions for Further Reading

For a general introduction to the history of Miguel Hernández' town, see my "The Agricultural Near North: Querétaro in the Seventeenth Century," in Ida Altman and James Lockhart, eds., *Provinces of Early Mexico* (Los Angeles, 1977), pp. 231–51. Other studies in the *Provinces of Early Mexico* offer descriptions of individuals who can be compared to Miguel Hernández. For good analyses of significant themes in early Mexican history, consult P. J. Bakewell, *Silver Mining and Society in Colonial Mexico* (Cambridge, Mass., 1971), François Chevalier, *Land and Society in Colonial Mexico* (Berkeley, Calif., 1963), and Charles Gibson, *The Aztecs Under Spanish Rule* (Stanford, Calif., 1964). Very valuable for a personal understanding of the men and women of early Mexico is the work by James Lockhart and Enrique Otte, eds., *Letters and People of the Spanish Indies, Sixteenth Century* (Cambridge, 1975).

For the history of blacks in Mexico, see Gonzalo Aguirre Beltrán, *La población negra de México* (México, 1946), and Colin A. Palmer, *Slaves of the White God: Blacks in Mexico, 1570–1650* (Cambridge, Mass., 1976). To compare Miguel Hernández with other free mulattoes, see Frederick P. Bowser, "The Free Person of Color in Mexico City and Lima: Manumission and Opportunity, 1580–1650," in Stanley L. Engerman and Eugene D. Genovese, eds., *Race and Slavery in the Western Hemisphere: Quantitative Studies* (Princeton, N.J., 1975), pp. 331–368.

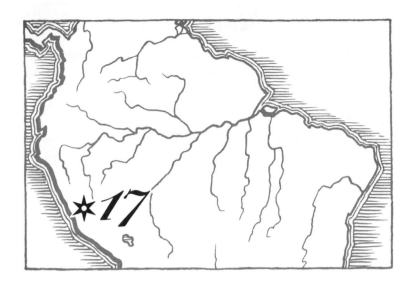

Hernando de Valencia:
Tax Promoter

FRED BRONNER

*T*reasury agent Hernando de Valencia was nearing sixty, an old man by the standard of his day, when he set out from Madrid to Lima at the end of May 1631. His mission was a last chance at success. The Spanish government, dominated by the Count Duke of Olivares, was desperately short of funds for its endless wars to dominate Europe. It had resolved to try to extort revenues from the wealthy Spanish Americans through a package of nineteen hastily conceived expedients known as the *arbitrios*, which were entrusted to Valencia's special care.

For a price, the king's Council of the Indies would fix land grabs, legalize forbidden vineyards, license foodstores, extend *encomiendas* (grants of the right to collect Indian tribute), or sell patents of nobility and lucrative offices. Merchants and officials were to be squeezed for "gracious donations," and Indian leaders coerced into "lending" the funds that had been painfully accumulated by their communities for public enterprises or emergencies. The viceroy of Peru, Count Chinchón, could not be expected to enforce any such measures aimed at extracting revenues from the elite, for he would need their favorable testimony at the official inquest or *residencia* to be conducted at the end of his term. Only an agent on the spot might successfully remind the Peruvian viceroy of his duty.

Having decided this much, Olivares was concerned also to save money. There was no need to send "a great person," a *visitador* or councilor earning up to 6,000 ducats a year, when "a person of papers" such as Valencia might do. His pay was set at 4,000, then trimmed to 3,000 ducats.

To accept such an assignment at such a salary was to undermine one's prestige from the start, a grievous mistake in the status-crazed society of seventeenth-century Peru. Who entered a government office with buckled sword, who sat before whom, covered or bareheaded, on a dais or on a level with the rest, in a leather chair or a velvet chair, at a table parallel to or askew from the tribunal—these were matters of enormous concern among colonial notables and officials. How men greeted one another—*alteza, señoría,* or plain *señor* (but never the intimate *vos*)—was a matter for endless disputes. It was a society in which transatlantic consultations were required to grapple with such weighty problems as the location of signatures: should the financial auditors of the Tribunal de Cuentas endorse the face or the back of viceregal orders? In such a context Valencia's salary-cut was critical. Four thousand ducats a year would have placed him above all the regular crown appointees in Lima except the viceroy. Three thousand placed him below the judges of the highest civil and criminal courts, the Audiencia and Sala del Crímen, and barely above the financial auditors whose equal treatment he was promised. Why did the old man accept such an assignment?

The thumbnail sketch of Valencia that helped the Council of the Indies to pass on his appointment speaks of "twenty years' satisfactory service as royal accountant of grants (*contador de mercedes*), with previous service as a police notary and constable."[1] He was in his teens when apprenticed as a policeman, probably by his father. In 1602 he was making nightly rounds in Valladolid as an underling of two peace officers of the royal court; and soon afterward he advanced from foot to pen work, becoming a police recorder, a *secretario del crímen*, in Madrid. This was still a lowly job, but it gave him access to such men of society as the youthful Chinchón, future viceroy of Peru, whom Valencia "served in his house" and helped recover a rent. The two were great friends, sharing in juvenile capers for a time about 1609; but then Chinchón followed his father in becoming a member of the Council of State and presumably gave up carousing with a lowly scrivener.

For Valencia, the association had involved some unforgettable hobnobbing and even a presentation to the king. Years later, in a memorial to Viceroy Chinchón, he recalled how:

> when the occasion arose to speak about my person, the late Duke of Infantado, swearing by his emblem of knighthood, told Our Lord King Philip III, God rest Him, that I was as good an hidalgo as he.[2]

This hand-to-the-heart had, however, surely been accompanied by a broad wink of the eye. Had the presentee been real gentry, the facts of his origins would have sufficed. But Valencia's claim to noble status must have been modest indeed. He never presented himself as "don" in Lima, where honorific forms of address were cheap among immigrant Spaniards and the crown could sell no patents of nobility because "all [whites] who call themselves hidalgos get away with it."[3] In Spain to be an hidalgo without the "don" meant very little; impoverished hidalgos applied for court jobs as lackeys and coachmen.

The presentation to the king must have occurred at the time of Valencia's promotion from police *secretario* to royal *contador*, in about 1610. During the years that followed, Valencia married and raised a son. With his new position came some leisure for reading and a propensity to parade learning. He quoted antique authors, at times in Latin, and modern essayists on the uses of absolute state power— Comines, Botero, Vera y Zuñiga. He also fancied the lessons of history, searching ancient papers for ways to ensure restitution to the treasury. His professional activities centered on *mercedes* (official favors), which made him less of an accountant and more of a go-between in their dispensation. He surely frequented the Council of the Chamber, which passed out the plums of patronage, and the Council of Finance, which decided on their availability.

Favor, as Valencia well knew, decided an official's standing. Under "the shade and hand" of a superior you could tread on competitors; but the wretches in disfavor were themselves "trod upon" and the butt of gossips. Modest conduct helped ensure favor; but this bore little relation to conventional morality. An official's lapse into sexual irregularities "neither discredited him nor obstructed his promotion, and, if it involved no rape or violence, the courtiers and councilors laughed it off."[4] To be modest was rather to avoid offense to great and small, and, more to the point, to swallow a superior's slights, to bend the knee like a loyal retainer. Modesty was adulation and adulation a conversational formality. "I place myself in the shadow of your greatness and clemency whose herald I shall be while I live," said Valencia after settling a deal.[5] But negotiation through exaggeration made modesty strangely prideful, even ridiculous, as were the requests for crumbs that went with it.

Valencia was well fitted to play this game. He stood tall, gestured impetuously, and let his voice boom. His language shrilled: "Eyes squirting fire—tears of blood—rape, knifing— a corpse with vestiges of manhood." He spoke in the third person, quoting his own witticisms. He boasted of his authority, tossing off the names of his backers at court. He also swore, pulled hair, and drew his sword or dagger when the occasion required.

In the decade following his 1610 appointment, Valencia became sufficiently entrenched to survive the change of reigns in 1621; but he barely survived the administrative reorganization that followed. By 1629 he was trying to wangle a position on a royal council, but the king turned him down. Then, no doubt, he felt obliged to consider the overseas appointment. As reward for his services he obtained the lifetime grant of his salary to his wife, "should he die on his errand," and in 1630 a *cédula* (royal decree) dispatching him to Peru with the promise of a major appointment once he completed his mission: "It is My will to bestow on him, upon his return, a position in My Council of the Indies, commensurate with his endowments and merits."[6] Valencia seems to have understood this as the grant of a councilorship, the most aspired-to pinnacle of a bureaucrat's career; and in Lima he would brag again and again of being "the first lay councilor to have come to this kingdom." But only aristocrats and lawyers had ever served on the council, and Valencia was neither. Also, he should have known the difference between a position in and on the council, a difference that was pointedly noted in a royal reply to one of his requests for money. He had either deluded himself or been duped.

Valencia's mission was a safe bet for Olivares, who stood to win from its success but would not share in its failure. The *contador* was persuaded that he was the best man to play the gadfly to the viceroy. He was encouraged to think "he would return honored and rich"; one of his superiors asked him to help a nephew obtain a viceregal job; even Olivares charged him to be on the lookout for additional means of increasing revenues. Finally, Valencia was offered money by parties interested in the *arbitrios* in Peru.

His old friendship with Chinchón obviously lay behind all these commissions. Valencia might have been enough of a schemer to influence the viceroy much as Olivares was manipulating King Philip. But Valencia, though "modest" enough in dealing with the rich and powerful, was naive enough to put his trust in his royal *cédula* rather than endearing himself to the viceroy. This was a serious mistake. Chinchón, unlike the king, was an activist executive and a compulsive worker who was not easily flattered or outmaneuvered; and he was also a nobleman who hated upstarts.

The journey to America was exhausting and expensive; a voyager's importance was measured by the size of his retinue and baggage train and by the gifts he distributed along the way. Valencia borrowed 6,000 ducats, or two years' pay, "for a passage consonant with his post and station."[7] From Cadiz to Cartagena and Portobelo this still meant the usual fifty-odd days of cramped quarters and spoiled food at sea and unbearable heat during landfalls. We do not know whether the *contador* crossed part of the Panamanian isthmus by boat on the Chagre River or whether he went all the way on the back of a mule or a slave. He tarried in Panama City, sailing down the Pacific in mid-January 1632. After a brisk twelve-day run his ship put in at Paita, whence Valencia took the land route to Lima while his baggage retainers continued the voyage by sea. Half-way down, at Huambacho, he was "lodged and entertained" by a distant relative, don Juan Jacinto de Acevedo, whose wife doña Agustina he was later accused of seducing. Just after he reached the capital and put up at the house of the Inquisitor don Andrés Juan Gaitán at the end of February, news arrived that the ship from Panama had foundered, drowning a third of the 70 Spaniards on board and

17. The judges of Lima's *Audiencia*, early seventeenth century.

nearly all the 125 African slaves. Over a million pesos' worth of merchandise had gone down; and Valencia had lost his only son, a servant, and all his property. His grief may be imagined from the many times he was to mention the event. Nevertheless, he dutifully went to call on the viceroy on his first night in Lima.

Chinchón received him with studied courtesy, refusing to talk business. Some eight days later, Valencia returned to argue his case at length, parading his *cédulas*. Chinchón ordered him to surrender them to the *fiscal* of the Audiencia, Andrés Varona Encinillas. The *fiscal* was the king's solicitor in Lima, and with him present, implied Chinchón, there was no need for Valencia. The *contador* was instructed to return on the following Sunday; and when he did so expecting a private audience, Valencia found Chinchón in the company of a flock of officials. One by one the *arbitrios* were dispatched to different *acuerdos*, joint executive meetings with one or more judges of the Audiencia and high officials, through which the viceroy managed to appear to share his powers while receiving collective backing for his policies. Valencia "forbade this referral as modestly as I could," insisting that the king's orders be carried out directly; but at this Chinchón "became furious," dictated a protest to Olivares, and channeled most of the *arbitrios* to his general fiscal acuerdo. Valencia was invited to these sessions, "the better to enhance his authority," and he was further told not to act without Encinillas, the *fiscal*. "Regarding the *arbitrios*," the viceroy decreed, "your Worships may come and speak to me every Wednesday and Saturday at nine in the morning."[8] Thus the royal *contador* became a twice-weekly solicitor, and a minority of one in Chinchón's *acuerdo*. The viceroy tried to salve his feelings by having his first year's salary paid to him in advance.

The May or June sailing of the Peruvian treasure fleet to Panama was a time of bustle and traffic attended by bickering and bankruptcies. Along with its cargo, the *armadilla* carried passengers bearing hundreds of letters to the court. The viceroy thought of it as a shipment of hostile reports. To neutralize them, he would beef up the remittance of silver as much as he could and doctor his bulletins of achievement. He belittled the *arbitrios* by pointing out that, though quite a few had already been "resolved," the revenue from them came to "less than 10,000 ducats," out of the king's total of over a million. Then, after the fleet's departure, he began to "pour out his venom" against Valencia. Five days before the sailing, the *contador* had described Chinchón as "a fine gentleman, pure, fair, zealous to serve"; three months later he would write that he could no longer "understand or make out this gentleman [whose] retainers were spreading the word that I [Valencia] had brought orders to impose excises, and that the burghers would have to pay for tapers, windows, carriages, and rents."[9]

Besides cottoning up to the rich, Chinchón was contriving to dispose of the *arbitrios*. He had decreed the execution of eight of these and inquired about a ninth before the 1632 fleet, but these were minor measures for the most part; the weightier *arbitrios* were more likely to cause friction. Three days after the fleet left, the *acuerdo* debated the "gracious donations" and decided to postpone them. Valencia himself favored enforcing the other, nonvoluntary *arbitrios* beforehand. This postponement served Chinchón as a welcome precedent for dealing with the *arbitrio* that offered crown legitimation of dubious land titles. The viceroy was violently opposed to this one because he had set up his own title-fixing office in 1630, and the viceregal land titles would be superseded by those of the king. Valencia, however, had already received substantial offers from usurping landlords up and down the coast; and he was adamant in advocating the measure. He cast a lone vote in the *acuerdo* against suspending the lands' *arbitrio*; but his written brief—a harsh plea for absolutism—was kept out of the Book of *Acuerdos*. One *Audiencia* judge went so far as to tell him that the king's right to dispose of lands in Peru had lapsed. That right lasted a hundred years, shot back Valencia, while Peru had only been conquered for ninety-four. (Actually, the centennial of the conquest was only a few weeks away.)

In July, Valencia experienced a triumph when the *acuerdo* adopted the touchy *arbitrio* on vineyards. This compelled vintners to mortgage 2 percent of their produce to the crown so as to legalize their plantings. (The cultivation of the grape in Spain's American colonies had in principle been prohibited for decades, to protect the market for wines produced in Spain.) "All the interested parties are rich and powerful," wrote Valencia, the illegal wine having become "this king-dom's biggest export." Chinchón reacted to this vote with a show of temper and did not dispatch his executive orders implementing it before the end of August.

Meanwhile the viceroy pursued a different delaying tactic to stop the sale of the office of *provincial de la hermandad,* an underpaid suburban police chief "with voice and vote" in the Lima Municipal Council. In this case, the crown was selling instant prestige at the expense of the city fathers and hoping to net 40,000 pesos from it. Thirty thousand were bid at once by Diego de Ayala, the son of an Audiencia judge whose municipal ambitions may have stemmed from a grudge. He had been quarrelling for years with councilman Juan de Lorca over the favors of Juanota, a popular entertainer. But before he had a chance to show up his rival by joining the council, Chinchón suspended the auction. The viceroy acceded to a request of the city councilmen, who were understandably aroused at the suggestion that the dignity of their office might be sold to the highest bidder with the proceeds going to the crown instead of to themselves. Valencia nevertheless pressed the king's *provincialato* suit, though neither em-powered to do so nor trained for legal maneuvering; and in September the Audiencia judges threw his case out of court. Surprisingly, he joined them at about the same time in a unanimous *acuerdo* vote against two *arbitrios* affecting In-dians. Then he returned to the lawsuit; but Chinchón suc-ceeded in entangling the legal procedures and in entrapping Valencia in a court challenge he could not substantiate.

The *contador* meanwhile briefed the viceroy about his plans for Lima's snow monopoly. From Canta, four days' journey away, mule trains brought ice and packed snow to make sherbet for the parched Limeños. On several occasions scarcity combined with summer heat had turned the sale of this delicacy into a riot. While officials squabbled and stole, the populace would go on a rampage of stoning and stabbing. Such mass craving could and had been profitably exploited by the viceroys acting through their retainers. However, in 1615 Viceroy Montesclaros gave the snow franchise to the city of Lima as a going-away gift to ensure the upkeep of the *ala-meda,* the shaded promenade he had laid out on the far shore of the River Rimac. The monopoly had been passed back and forth between the municipal and viceregal authorities; and for a dozen years before Valencia's visit it had been farmed out to a former druggist and naval supplier, Antolín de Reynoso. Valencia won Reynoso over to his project of a crown monopoly, and both men wrote to Madrid to suggest the establishment of this additional *arbitrio*. In the meantime, the *contador* insisted, the arrangements for collecting the snow revenue must not be altered. "Show your orders," retorted Chinchón.

Late in November 1632, Valencia stormed into the viceregal chambers to pour out his bitterness. The *provincialato* case had just taken a turn for the worse, and as for the snow monopoly, "no *cédula* is needed," he insisted, "because I have my orders from the count-duke's mouth." Chinchón would have none of it. "If you don't bring that *cédula*," he said, without finishing the threat. Valencia stormed out again, protesting, "I won't tire you anymore."[10] At Christmas the *contador* was conspicuously absent from the throng of well-wishers at the viceregal palace.

In February 1633, the *acuerdo* approved the "gracious donations," and in March, after a complicated set of court maneuvers, the crown won the right to sell the office of *provincial de la hermandad* after all. The time for the departure of the annual fleet was nearing once more, and Valencia began to work on his report, claiming credit for this latest achievement. He needed the official transcripts of his previous memoranda; but when he applied for them he was sent back and forth between the viceroy's secretary and the secretary of the Audiencia. A petition to Chinchón produced no substantial results. As he renewed the request, he reviewed "the four *arbitrios* of most worth and importance." The *arbitrio* on lands had been suspended; the *provincialato* had been long in doubt; the licensing of food stores was being challenged by Lima's municipality; and the tax on vineyards was not being enforced. Under the circumstances, Valencia insisted on stopping the "gracious donations," since such gifts would only interfere with the other *arbitrios*. Moreover, the drive for voluntary contributions required "a new viceroy from whom *beneficios* and *mercedes* can be expected." Chinchón was thought to be about to leave for Spain, "and in this kingdom they reckon the departing with the dead." At the same time Valencia asked permission to go home "to my post in the Indies Council."[11] The viceroy denied this request, and demanded a full report on all the *arbitrios*.

When the *acuerdo* met in April to discuss Valencia's "gracious gifts" petition, the *contador* brought forth his personal *cédulas* from the king and insisted they be read. The last of them was addressed to Chinchón and instructed him "to admit and hear in gracious audiences what [Valencia] may tell and advise [on the *arbitrios*]." Valencia understood this to mean that "Your Excellency must follow and execute what I tell and advise you punctually and without any leeway." Replied Chinchón, "You would then be my equal or my superior." Valencia's offensive rejoinder ("That is no concern of mine") shocked the other members of the *acuerdo*, who outvoted the *contador* and disregarded his pretension.

Scandal next shook Valencia's position. The news was brought to Chinchón by Damián Bravo, a provincial treasurer who had been a shipmate on the viceroy's passage to Peru. Bravo had it from his brother-in-law, Valencia's longtime retainer, Gaspar Gudiel, whose wife was friendly with a confidante of the lady in question. Chinchón made his own inquiries and found that Valencia was indeed having an affair with doña Agustina de Mendoza, the wife of his onetime host and relative, don Juan Jacinto de Acevedo. The lady was apparently saying that she would rather go to a nunnery than rejoin her husband in Huambacho.

In June, Chinchón wrote to the judge with whom Valencia was lodging that he should advise his house guest "of the risk he was running." Both men were to reply on the back. Valencia answered at length that the charge was a slander and the lady blameless. The idea of an affair being conducted in a household full of male relatives, the lady's mother, and "sixteen or twenty blacks" was absurd. He was indeed in the habit of visiting there but only by coach and in broad daylight. He was friendly with Acevedo, had lent him money, and served as godfather at his daughter's confirmation. Finally, it seemed uncharitable of Chinchón "to make an ant like myself suffer so much," after all his years of services. "I took no vow of chastity when I came to America, though I have acted as if I had."[12]

In July another storm of scandal clouded his horizon at the

feast of Saint Bonaventura, celebrated with solemn mass at the Franciscan monastery. A judge and the presentor of the Sala del Crímen entered the chapel and invited Valencia to join them. They sat on the judges' chairs, set before those of the city council. Presently don Luís de Mendoza, one of Lima's two mayors, came rushing up followed by his colleague and two councilmen, and demanded angrily that Valencia give up his seat. Valencia was just getting off his knees when Mendoza seized the chair but was pushed back. Diego de Ayala, the new *provincial de la hermandad*, dashed to Valencia's side shouting, "Here am I who owe little to the city!" Swords were bared just as the consecrated host was being lifted. Minutes later, when the uproar had subsided, Valencia and Mendoza were put under house arrest and an investigation began.

Shortly thereafter, Valencia appeared to be sowing dissension against Chinchón in a sidewalk talk with some government officials. He brought up the great Mexico City riot of 1624, when Viceroy Gelves had fled for his life from his gutted palace. "By God," said the *contador*, "if all the viceroy's enemies were lined up to one side and all his friends to the other, the friends would be outnumbered."[13] His listeners shut him up indignantly, but for another dozen days none of them reported the conversation to the viceroy. Valencia had already heaped accusations on Chinchón in letters forwarded with the fleet. But on July 30 he sent his Madrid superiors an extraordinary dispatch on the indignities of Saint Bonaventura and the calumny of the married lady. "The bearer," he explained, "is Gaspar Gudiel, who has served me since childhood."

At the inquiry concerning the fracas in church, Valencia testified that Mendoza had drawn his sword first, "defying the king to his face through his agent and future councilor, and showing disrespect to the consecrated host." Mendoza said that Ayala had been the first to draw; and that he had not noticed the elevation of the host because he had forgotten his eyeglasses. Both men were notified the next day that they would have to stand trial in the Sala del Crímen, composed of the very judges who had cooperated with the viceroy in frustrating Valencia's work. He viewed them as "corrupted (*infectos*) against the king's cause," and challenged their right to try him.

Two days later Chinchón was working in his audience hall with two youthful secretaries, when the porter announced Valencia. The viceroy ushered him in, seated him, and bid him put his hat back on. Pale with anger, the *contador* began swinging a chair to show what Mendoza had done to him. His shouts brought in a bevy of staffers, whose testimonies permit a reconstruction of the confrontation that followed. Valencia accused the Sala del Crímen of improper procedure, packed as it was by "my capital enemies"; the viceroy suggested that he consider bringing formal charges against them. Valencia complained that no lawyer would sign his petition and demanded that the viceroy appoint one for him. The viceroy refused and gave him a lecture on legal procedures. Valencia, he said, had been much better treated in Lima than the Madrid *cédulas* required; the *contador* swore that he had not but that honors meant nothing to him with his "councilor's post granted and not just promised," and that he was "better placed in Madrid than any of the officials here, and that in Madrid a criminal judge meant nothing" to him. His only request was that Chinchón ship him off to Spain at the earliest opportunity, or at the very least give him leave to take the next boat to Panama. But the viceroy would not allow even this: "His Majesty has sent you to this kingdom and I am not aware of his royal intent." "Damn it!," cried Valencia, pounding his chest and chair and pushing his hat in, "if you were not the viceroy I wouldn't stand for this!" "Say what you please," replied Chinchón with a smile, "*I* will not lose *my* temper." Valencia attempted to reply but Chinchón had risen. "Calm down," he said. "Go with God and if you have anything further to ask do it in writing."[14]

At a signal, the viceroy's notary served two decrees on Valencia. One forbade him to petition without a lawyer's cosignature; the other enjoined him from dealing with the vines *arbitrio* except through Chinchón's advisors. At this the *contador* left the palace "in utter despair, and, seeing I had no one to turn to, went back to my lodgings whither shortly arrived a second note from the viceroy saying I should take care not to visit the married lady."[15] While Valencia pondered this message, its author met with the judiciary *acuerdo* to consider the *contador*'s "great disrespect" toward the judges in his testimony, which was to be forwarded for further study to Madrid. Two days later Valencia sought asylum in the Franciscan monastery, "fearing some risk," and, with the viceroy's permission, "left the world."

He entered a murky labyrinth. San Francisco was the oldest and bulkiest of Lima's convents, extending over four city blocks and housing some two hundred friars in its multiple cloisters. It also sheltered several bankrupt and homicidal escapees from justice; and a number of the monks had themselves chosen the cloth, "to escape civil law, commit crimes, and devote themselves to wheeling and dealing."[16] In that same month of August the Sala del Crímen declared Valencia a fugitive, ordered his salary stopped, and issued a writ of arrest to hold him in City Hall. On the same day a very disturbed Valencia appeared before the abbot, Fray Martín de Aróztegui, in his slippers, holding on to his sword and nightcap while his collar dangled from his throat, and begged to be hidden from justice. The Franciscan consented and delivered the *contador* to Fray Francisco Casillas, the medic of the convent, who quartered him in an alcove with a tiny courtyard within the infirmary compound. This was walled in except for an opening for his food and feces. (His neighbor, the black cook, complained bitterly about everything passing through *his* window.) In these reduced but secure circumstances the *contador* remained for about a month.

The fugitive next asked Aróztegui to help him escape to Spain. The Franciscan agreed and assigned a friar to accompany him as his guide; but in doing so he seems to have had some understanding with the viceroy. When Valencia learned of this he complained that he had been sold out, "and to think that I had promised to send him a bishop's miter!" By then, however, he had completely won over his guardian Fray Francisco and another monk, and the three laid their plans.

Since guards were said to be posted at the gates, Valencia decided to get out over the adobe wall between the roof of the infirmary and the ravine of the Rimac. His guide was told to help smuggle him to Huaura, just north of Lima, whence he could make his way to Paita, board a vessel to Panama, and catch the wintering Atlantic galleons. Fray Francisco bought him an Indian outfit for disguise, complete with coarse cloak and leggings, cut his beard and hair, and blackened his face. On Saturday, September 17, all was ready. It was a moonless night.

The clock was striking eleven when Valencia gave his

farewell embraces to his friends, who lowered a knotted rope. Below, the guide stood waiting with the *contador*'s mule and a rented black slave. Valencia had barely descended a few feet, however, when he let go of the rope and fell seven yards, landing on top of his companion in flight, dislocating his left arm, and breaking his nose and three teeth. He was bleeding profusely. Strewn about him lay some gold plates, a purse of silver pesos, his sword and machete. The friar and slave lifted him onto the mule and picked up his possessions. They took him to a friend's house in the Indian quarter, the Cercado, and at around midnight called in a surgeon whom Valencia trusted. Six hours, three stitches, and one surgical bleeding later, the disfigured Valencia was swaying in a borrowed sedan chair as he reentered the convent of San Francisco.

The *contador*, whom public opinion had long consigned to Spain, now told visitors, including the surgeon, that he had been thrown and dragged by a mule. Two days later the surgeon pulled his arm into place. A high fever ensued, so he was bled three more times. By the end of October Valencia was arguing that he was no fugitive, and that it was only his sickness that prevented him from appearing before the Sala del Crímen. Before Christmas his lawyers induced the Sala to lift its attachment on his salary, which nevertheless remained unpaid for several months longer. Meanwhile Chinchón insinuated to his superiors that the wounds of the *contador* had been inflicted by doña Agustina's relatives! Valencia, who recovered within two months, decided to counter such slander. He was confident that the grave Franciscan fathers would bear witness that he had lived virtuously while in their care, attending daily mass and keeping his seclusion. But the monks were reluctant, and it was only with great difficulty that he persuaded a few of them to testify while a notary friend transmuted their declarations into official sworn affidavits.

These affidavits of good conduct were endorsed, before being forwarded, with the signature of a high judge of the Sala del Crímen. The judge later denied vigorously having had anything to do with the case; but the notary claimed that the judge had read Valencia's request for depositions carefully, commenting with a toothy smile, "candlewax and molasses!", and that he had visited him in the convent and written there the endorsement of his conduct that the *contador* had forwarded to Spain. The endorsement may or may not have been a forgery; but it was the word of a high criminal judge and knight of Santiago against that of an aged scribe. The notary was indicted and jailed in May 1635. Fifteen months before that, however, he had presided over the taking of depositions in Valencia's cell and elsewhere, had them written out by his asssistants, and himself rounded out the legal points of the document. A fine product it was. Valencia emerged from its folios as a saint in his upright ways, a martyr through his fall from the rope, and a faithful servant of the king who had been threatened and thwarted by the viceroy and his guards. The fact that most of this had been falsely added to the depositions would remain unrecognized in Madrid.

While the monks testifed and the notary contrived, Valencia collected other incriminating evidence, such as a notarized viceregal decree announcing the sale of public offices that made no mention of the royal *cédula* although the offerings were the very ones Valencia had suggested when he first came to Lima, and even the justifying reasons and the price estimates were his. In March, Valencia's lawyer outshouted and outwitted the viceroy's notary to present a petition of the *contador*'s in the Audiencia. But how to get it to Spain? Valencia turned to the *visitador*, an extraordinary crown agent like himself, but one with far more power and prestige. Unfortunately, the *visitador* was too beholden to the viceroy to be of much assistance. Valencia asked him to remit letters to the secretary of the Council of the Indies and to Olivares. Though he may have complied with this request, he refused to reverse a viceregal decree. Valencia then accused the *visitador* (a bishop) of nonfeasance and of sexual irregularities with a wealthy widow.

The *contador*'s own social life, in the meantime, was back to normal. His cell, hung about with silks, "was like a stock-exchange where day and night innumerable well-dressed persons came to conduct business" and fill him in on the latest viceregal misdeeds. The list of visitors reads like a *Who's Who* of Lima's society and bureaucracy. The transactions concerned dispatches to Spain. "They talked business, deals, agreements, and money bags were brought and taken." Valencia readied his own papers with the help of a battery of notaries, while a clerk took down their words. The package was later safely smuggled to Madrid by a member of the viceroy's own household. Valencia, no longer a fugitive, reciprocated these visits, traveling to town by coach and returning late at night. The *contador's* odd hours and arrogant ways with the convent's gatekeepers gave rise to repeated complaints.

A dozen of the monks, old friends as they now were, also frequented his cell. In the evening don Tomá would sing and strum his guitar, accompanied by some professionals who had been hired by Fray Francisco de Jarava, the lecturer in theology. Mornings were the time to banter with veiled women (*tapadas*) in church. (In Lima successive viceroys vainly forbade the female veil.) Similarly, the expensively dressed, promiscuous *mulata* was a pleasurable fixture of church attendance. Valencia favored both *tapadas* and *mulatas.* He would chat endlessly with them, while lingering at the gate with the dark-skinned woman who carried his messages. At one point the abbot ordered the church locked, but Valencia bullied the keeper into reopening it. Besides conversing, he was seen engaging in "dishonest deeds" in the atrium and in the cemetery. There his lascivious speech next to the Chapel of the Miraculous Virgin provoked a warning from one Lima notable, while another threatened him over his behavior in church. One night, in one of its chapels, he was nearly caught in the act of coition.

In August 1634 a batch of dispatches arrived from Madrid. Among them was a *cédula* instructing Valencia to return to Spain "to render account of what has been in your care . . . since Count Chinchón's zeal and care render your reminders unnecessary."[17] Valencia left the convent at once, "accepted with pleasure" the viceroy's notification of the *cédula,* and perhaps paid an old fine that had been imposed by the Sala del Crímen. Yet in November the judges imprisoned him in City Hall. Though we do not know how long he languished among his enemies, the order of arrest was not lifted until the following May. Valencia sailed from Callao with the 1635 fleet at four A.M. on Trinity Sunday, June 3. Darkness prevailed.

And the *arbitrios*? Regarding the legalization of land grabs, Madrid reissued its orders and Lima "obeyed but did not comply"; it was the viceroy who still confirmed such deals. The vineyards measure was temporarily suspended, pending appeal to the Council of the Indies, and was still pending in 1648. The *provincialatos* of all Peruvian cities netted nearly 300,000 pesos, but Diego de Ayala was repeatedly unseated and jailed. The royal snow monopoly was farmed out after Chinchón brutally dispossessed Reynoso. Likewise, the owners of crown-licensed food stores were hounded by city police. In "gracious donations" Chinchón squeezed 80,000 pesos out of Lima; while from the provincial community funds of the Indians he gathered and brought with him to Madrid 100,000 pesos. In the viceroy's final report to his successor, he took full credit for the achievements. One can search this lengthy *relación* in vain for the word *arbitrio*, and only once does it make mention of the Contador Hernando de Valencia.

Notes

1. *Consulta* of April 17, 1630, AGI Indif. 2690.

2. Valencia to Chinchón, August 8, 1633, enclosure 7 of Chinchón to king, May 1, 1634, AGI Indif. 2690, also enclosed with Valencia's dateless letter to king of about the same date, AGI Lima 162.

3. *Libro 23 de los cabildos . . . de los Reyes . . . 1634 hasta 1637* (Lima, 1964), p. 211.

4. Valencia to Chinchón, July 5, 1633, enclosed with Valencia to king, July 30, 1633 and ca. May 1, 1634, both in AGI Lima 162, also enclosure 3 of Chinchón to king, May 1, 1634, AGI Indif. 2690.

5. Valencia to Chinchón, July 28, 1632, enclosure 4 of Chinchón to king, May 17, 1633, AGI Indif. 2690.

6. Enclosure 2 of Chinchón to king, May 17, 1633, AGI Indif. 2690.

7. Valencia to king, Apr. 8, 1634, AGI Lima 6; *Consulta* of May 21, 1631, AGI Indif. 2690.

8. Enclosure 1 of Chinchón to king, May 17, 1633, AGI Indif. 2690.

9. Valencia to king, June 14 and September 18, 1632, AGI, Lima 161; and July 30, 1633, AGI Lima 162.

10. Valencia to Chinchón, March 13, 1633, and testimonies of March 28, 1633 of Fiscal Encinillas and Audiencia Judge Pérez de Salazar; being enclosure 6 of Chinchón to king, May 17, 1633, AGI Indif. 2690.

11. Enclosure 11 of Chinchón to king, May 17, 1633, AGI Indif. 2690; transcript of April 26, 1633, Acuerdo, enclosed with Chinchón to king, "Hacienda 55" of May 9, 1633, AGI Lima 44.

12. See note 4.

13. Enclosure 17 of Chinchón to king, May 1, 1634, AGI Indif. 2690.

14. Enclosure 14 of Chinchón to king, May 1, 1634, AGI Indif. 2690.

15. Valencia to king, ca. May 1, 1634, AGI Lima 162.

16. Fiscal Encinillas to king, May 30, 1629, AGI Lima 160.

17. Enclosures 8 and 9 of Chinchón to king, May 29, 1635, AGI Indif. 2690.

Sources

In writing this story, I have attempted to unravel the contradictory testimonies of two adversaries. The viceroy's may be found in the Archivo General de Indias in Seville, Indiferente *legajo* 2690. Valencia's are in the same archive, Audiencia de Lima 161 and 162. In Lima, the notarial and court records of the Archivo General de la Nación have been of little help for the purpose, but the record of salary payments to Valencia appears in the Archivo Histórico del Ministerio de Hacienda, 71 and 74.

Three contemporary informants have been especially informative. Juan Antonio Suardo, *Diario de Lima*, ed. Ruben Vargas Ugarte, 2 vols. (Lima, 1936) is a naive and detailed diary written in 1629–39 which brings out the city's ceremony, corruption, cruelty and traumatic violence. The author was a minor cleric in the viceroy's service, and he unwittingly reveals the devious ways of his master. Gaspar Escalona Agüero, *Arcae Limensis gazophilatium regium peruvicum* (Madrid, 1647), written by a commonsensical lawyer-official, explains Peru's fiscal administration in dubious Latin and dreary Spanish, including piquant points of status and precedence. Finally, there is the manuscript guide to government finance penned in 1632 by a cantankerous old visionary who hated viceroy Chinchón and had become a "great confidant" of Valencia's, *contador* Francisco López de Caravantes, "Noticia General del Perú, cuarta parte," Biblioteca del Palacio, Madrid, ms. 1634/III.

Other useful information has been extracted from Buenaventura Salinas y Córdova, *Memorial de las Historias del Nuevo Mundo Perú* (Lima, 1957), written in 1630; Antonio Vázquez de Espinosa, *Compendium and Description of the West Indies*, trans. and ed. Charles U. Clark (Washington, D.C., 1942), which describes events in Lima up to 1629; the *Obras del P. Bernabé Cobo*, ed. Francisco Mateos (Madrid, 1956); the *Libro de los Cabildos de los Reyes, 1634 hasta 1637*, ed. Juan Bromley (Lima, 1964); and Diego Pérez Gallego, "Alguna parte del acertado y prudente govierno del Conde de Chinchón," Biblioteca del Palacio, Madrid, ms. 2774, written in 1640.

Since little is known about far more prominent officials, there is no shame in having to admit how little I have uncovered about Valencia's ancestors, living relatives, friends, or resources. I have found no expression of grief over his son's untimely death; and the details of his Atlantic passage have had to be surmised from a lengthy and revealing private letter of the viceroy's describing *his* voyage to Peru, which is to be found in the Biblioteca de la Universidad de Sevilla, ms. vol. 330/122.

Suggestions for Further Reading

The most solid general introduction to the Spanish-speaking world in Europe and America in the seventeenth century is probably the second volume of John Lynch, *Spain under the Habsburgs* (Oxford, 1969). I know of no specific description of the *ambiente* for Spanish officialdom in Lima during this period except for Suardo's lively diary, listed above, which has not been translated into English. For similar material on a later period, see Joseph and Francisco Mugaburu, *Chronicle of Colonial Lima*, trans. and ed. Robert R. Miller (Norman, Okla., 1975). Closer to my story in time as well as theme is John Phelan's exciting *The Kingdom of Quito in the Seventeenth Century* (Madison, Wisc., 1967). Phelan has also pointed out suggestive parallels to present-day Soviet practice in "Authority and Flexibility in Spanish Imperial Bureaucracy," *Administrative Science Quarterly* 5 (1960): 47–65. Intra-government conflict was also common in baroque Mexico. For an exhaustive account, see J. I. Israel, *Race, Class and Politics in Colonial Mexico, 1610–1670* (New York, 1975); and for the flavor of Mexico's squabblings, C. E. P. Simmons, "Palafox and his Criticism: Reappraising a Controversy," *Hispanic American Historical Review* 46 (1966): 394–408.

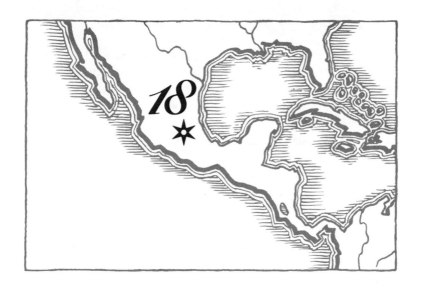

Enrico Martínez:
Printer and Engineer

LOUISA SCHELL HOBERMAN

$\mathscr{A}$s Enrico Martínez, a printer from Seville, stepped off the ship in Veracruz, Mexico, in 1589, his thoughts were those of the classic European immigrant. He wanted to see the New World, of which he had already heard a great deal; he wanted to make his fortune from it; and in doing so he hoped to make it a better place to live for others as well. But Enrico differed from his shipmates in carrying with him more than the immigrant's usual repertory of negotiable talents. His non-Spanish origins, European travels, and scientific knowledge first helped Enrico to establish himself in Mexico City, then over the next forty-three years to attain a high reputation, at least for a while, as a scientist and public official. In the process, however, these differences also forced Enrico into an intense and painful struggle against the obstacles faced by educated people in colonial society.

Most pressing were the external obstacles. Enrico had to find a way to make a living without sacrificing his intellectual interests, yet he was at a disadvantage compared to most thinkers in colonial society, who, as clergymen, enjoyed a steady income from their benefices. He had to pursue his scientific investigations under the cloud of possible censorship or worse by the Inquisition, always suspicious of foreigners. As a person whose special training made him useful to the government, Enrico was thrust into the public limelight without having the family connections or political skills he needed to remain there successfully. Then there were internal obstacles, problems peculiar to Enrico himself. Like anyone else, Enrico had to determine his personal objectives. These also involved him in conflicts. He wanted to find out the truth about the natural phenomena that interested him, but he was frustrated by the still-fumbling astronomy and physics of his day. Enrico felt a sense of public responsibility, once he had put his own affairs in order. He tried to express it by popularizing scientific knowledge through his writing, but this was not easy in a humanistically oriented, Catholic culture. Enrico's major public effort, serving as chief engineer of the drainage works designed to prevent the recurrent flooding of Mexico City, gave him periods of great satisfaction but, as the years went on, increasing anguish as well.

Some of Enrico's difficulties were forced on him by the character of colonial society; others befell him because of the kind of choices he made. His energy and intellectual curiosity led him to challenge several important facets of colonial society. His response to the resistance he met was sometimes courageous, sometimes fearful, but most often resourceful and persevering.

A man in his early thirties when he landed in Veracruz, Enrico had spent most of his life in Spain. Born in Hamburg about 1557, he was taken by his parents to Seville when he was eight and lived there for about ten years. The city Enrico grew up in was the most exciting in Spain at the time. As the only legal port of departure for the Indies, Seville was the required checkpoint for all emigrants to the New World, but it was also a place where people came to settle, to supply the fleets, trade in Indies goods, learn maritime skills, or simply make contact with well-off relatives or townsmen who had already migrated there and might offer a helping hand. Enrico grew up in one of the artisan subgroups of this restless city, the community of printers, who, like other craftsmen, had benefited from the increase in the number of consumers in Seville and the Indies. By the early sixteenth century there were thirty-six presses in Seville to supply the new demand for books. But the printers also thrived because of the vitality of intellectual life in sixteenth-century Spain. The Golden Age saw the achievements of writers, such as Luis Vives, jurists, such as Francisco de Vitoria, and playwrights, such as Lope de Vega; the number of universities grew from eleven to thirty-two over the century, and new secondary schools opened even more quickly. In this dynamic environment foreigners were no novelty in Seville. They were attracted by the same things that attracted Spaniards from elsewhere in Spain. If Catholic, they could live there, and if skilled, they were welcomed. Germans like the Martínez family, originally called Martin, were particularly influential in the printing trade.

In Enrico's late teens, following a familiar pattern, he decided to leave home for a while. Spain could offer little in his main area of interest, the physical sciences, so Enrico went to northern Europe to study. He studied mathematics at the Sorbonne, traveled in Germany and Poland, and spent a year and a half in his native Hamburg, a visit that was later to stand him in good stead. From these journeys Enrico learned to speak German and Flemish and acquired an enthusiasm for astronomy, astrology, physics, and mathematics. Between his return to Spain and his departure for America his activities are something of a mystery. While in Spain during this time, however, he did obtain a valuable piece of royal patronage in the form of the title of *cosmógrafo real,* a title that made him an official consultant in cartography and meteorology. Although this gave Enrico a handy entrée into governmental circles, it was not in itself a source of income. To ensure this Enrico brought with him to New Spain some type and part of a press.

Enrico's decision to settle in Mexico City was well advised. Silver prosperity and a tradition of patronizing learning and the arts had made the city a significant cultural center by the 1590s. Three presses were already in business, however, and competition was stiff. It was difficult to establish oneself without high-placed friends or a lucrative office. Fortunately, Enrico was able to take advantage of an opportunity that came his way late in the 1590s.

After arriving, Enrico had offered his services as a translator to the recently established Inquisition. In 1598 he was able to complement his stock of printing equipment with a press confiscated from a printer convicted of Lutheranism. Although the Inquisition during these years was primarily concerned with prosecuting insincere converts from Judaism, it also found time to try a few hapless Protestants. Enrico was called in to help the judges try one of these, one Adrian Cornelius Cesar, by translating the charges against him into German so that he could be sure of understanding them. Later Enrico was asked to corroborate the accuracy of the accused's account of Lutheran practices. On the basis of his stay in Hamburg, when, he claimed, curiosity alone brought him to Protestant services, Enrico attested that Cesar's description of communion and confession was correct, although he had learned the form of confession only through printed catechisms since the rite took place in wooden compartments "like our own."[1]

The problem of earning a living in a strange city was solved by Enrico's acquisition of the confiscated press. The first book he published from it appeared soon afterward in 1599; in 1674, his son, who bore the name Juan Ruiz, was still printing books. From the government's standpoint, Enrico as translator had acted no differently than Enrico as royal cosmographer. He had served a state agency in carrying out its duties. However, since the Inquisition had access to the property of royal subjects, Enrico's assistance had another aspect. Whether through calculation or accident, he was able to use the Inquisition to improve his own position at the expense of a competitor, for Adrian Cornelius was not only the heir of one printer but the associate of another and he had in fact just hired Enrico to make some type for him. In this instance Enrico found himself on the right side of the arbitrary ethnic-religious lines drawn by Spanish colonial society. He would not always be so lucky.

The power that giveth might also take away, if Enrico did not conform to its edicts. No sooner was he established as a printer than he had to take care what he printed. All books published in the colony had to be licensed by the highest local tribunal. No books on the Inquisition Index, first drawn up in 1551–52, could be published, imported, or read. To contravene this meant prosecution by the Inquisition. This prohibition could not, in fact, be implemented, for illegal books were smuggled into the colonies in significant numbers; but publishing them was a more dangerous activity than merely reading them. For Enrico, this would have meant publishing a nonauthorized version of the Bible or prayer books, Machiavelli's *Discourses,* most of the writings of Erasmus, or an unemended edition of Copernicus' *De Revolutionibus.* One of the three printers in business before Enrico, a Frenchman named Pedro Ocharte, was arrested in 1572 for praising a book containing Lutheran opinions. One of the charges against him was that "as a printer, he should have known better."[2] But Enrico gave suspect literature a wide berth in his subsequent career. He relied on the conventional patrons of printing for his commissions, specializing in announcements of the public presentations of university theses, the acts of the Dominican chapter meetings, and textbooks containing literary selections for use in the Jesuit *colegios.*

Decisions not to do something leave few traces. What did Enrico refrain from publishing so as not to offend the Holy Office? What did he refrain from writing or thinking about himself? The most harmful effect of the Inquisition on intellectual life was that it acted as a deterrent to creative thought, inhibiting the conception of new ideas rather than repressing those already in existence. Enrico was not concerned with controversial religious questions, but he was interested in astronomy and astrology, subjects about which it was also possible to hold mistaken and punishable opinions. His other problem as a thinker in these areas, however, was his own ignorance. Although the Spanish colonies did make advances in botany and metallurgy, they produced no innovations in theoretical science. Without suggesting that all colonial scientists were backward, it is fair to say that as a group in the seventeenth century their awareness and their acceptance of new discoveries lagged behind that of northern Europe. Enrico shared in this backwardness, as can be seen from his own work, a book entitled *Reportorio de los tiempos e historia natural desta Nueva España*, which he published in 1606. The *Reportorio* was the only book of its kind printed in New Spain and one of the few scientific works published in colonial Spanish America. It was a remarkable contrast to the affected and escapist literature of the baroque period in the New World. But the *Reportorio* also bears witness to Enrico's struggle against and compromises with ignorance, isolation, and repression.

The variety of topics in Enrico's book points to the four major objectives that led him to write it. First, he wanted to give a resumé of the current cosmology that would be comprehensible to an untrained reader. Second, he tried to answer theoretical questions raised by certain natural phenomena, particularly those of the New World. Third, Enrico offered an assortment of useful information about crops, weather conditions, and medicine, which he intended to expand in subsequent volumes. Finally, he wanted to make a case for the practice of informed astrology. It was here that he ran the risk of antagonizing the Inquisition, for it was forbidden to make astrological predictions of certain kinds. This objective led Enrico into his most difficult and personally revealing dilemma.

In trying to discover the truth about the natural world, Enrico worked within the Aristotelian-Ptolemean framework approved by the Church. This framework placed the earth at the center of the universe, posited the existence of a prime mover that had set the universe in motion, and held that all things in the natural world behaved according to their qualitative natures or substances. All these propositions were soon to be demolished by Galileo, Kepler, Descartes, and, later, Newton. But these scientists published their innovative writings after 1609, long after Enrico's university days and even after the appearance of the *Reportorio*. Enrico did not have the opportunity, therefore, to challenge the fundamentals of the traditional cosmology. His desire to understand specifics did lead him in some cases to offer explanations that were innovative. At other times, however, the combination of his own ignorance and the ecclesiastical opposition to certain propositions assured that he would simply repeat the errors of the science of his time.

The behavior of the oceans was one subject that interested Enrico. Rejecting several authorities whose theories about the source of ocean tides were contradicted by observation, Enrico gave a reasonable analysis of their origins. When his observations led to theologically unacceptable conclusions, however, Enrico retreated to traditional wisdom even when it conflicted with his own evidence. A good example was his discussion of why, as was believed, the level of the ocean remained constant, despite the continual entry of river water into it. Calculating the volume of water that must enter the ocean daily from the Amazon alone, he found himself concluding that the sea level must indeed rise. Rather than face the contradiction between what he himself calculated (however inaccurately) and what the authorities held, Enrico ended by stating, "although one could give various natural reasons for the accommodation by the sea of all the river water which enters it, this will not be done, since all reasons in the end agree with Holy Writ, that the rivers go forth from the sea and return to it."[3]

When considering American topics, such as the origin of the Amerindians, Enrico was less constrained, since neither the ancients nor the church fathers could have pronounced on topics of which they were unaware. Enrico believed that the Indians arrived on the American continent overland at its northern and southern points. He offered negative and positive evidence for this belief. To have come by sea would have been impossible, given the great distances and the primitive state of navigation in those days. Nor could Plato's Atlantis have been large enough to serve as a bridge, Enrico asserted more arbitrarily. On the positive side, he claimed that a land crossing in the north was verified by the resemblance he had noted between the Indians and the inhabitants of Courland, in present day Latvia. This was rather unlikely proof, unless Enrico were referring to some very southerly Lapps he had seen, but his approach was sound insofar as he was trying to provide new evidence.

However, when Enrico considered the "fact" that the New World was a superior place to live, ignorance combined with local pride led him into some very dubious science. In America, he asserted, "intelligence quickens and bodily strength diminishes." In part, this was due to the "wealth, abundance, and fertility" of the kingdom, which permitted those who in poorer lands were bowed down by the cares of poverty to live better; "relieved from the weight of poverty, they become more vivacious and mentally alert."[4] In part this happy change was due to the warmer climate, which made unnecessary the generation of the body heat that clouded the brain, and in part to the influence of the planet Mars over people of Spanish descent!

REPORTORIO

DE LOS TIEM-
POS, Y HISTORIA NATVRAL
DESTA NVEVA ESPANA.
(✠)
*Compuesto por Henrrico Martinez Cosmographo de su Ma-
gestade Interprete del Sancto Officio deste Reyno.*
✠
Dirigido al Excellentissimo
Señor Don Iuan de Mendoça y Luna Marques de
Montesclaros, Virrey, Gouernador, Presidente y Cappi-
tan General por el Rey nuestro Señor en esta Nueua España &c.

CON LICENCIA Y PRIVILEGIO.
En Mexico.
En la Emprenta del mesmo autor año de 1 6 o 6.

Enrico's American loyalties led him to some bizarre claims, but they also reflect the success of his adaptation to his new environment. He felt at home in Mexico City. In insisting that men improved their minds and their fortunes in the New World, he was generalizing from his own experience as an immigrant. Professionally, Enrico tried to counter the isolation felt by a scientist working in a less creative setting by stressing the importance of America in the world and by devoting part of his *Reportorio* to American topics. But Enrico's Americanism was complemented by a cosmopolitanism that enhanced the value of his work. His approach was to discuss a particular American topic and then make comparisons with Europe. The same occurs in the historical sections of the *Reportorio*, where he recounts part of Aztec history, the discovery of America, and the conquest of Peru, and also offers a panorama of world history, ranging from England to Persia. To some extent this was literary convention, but it also revealed Enrico's orientation.

The *Reportorio*'s bird's eye view of natural science and world history showed Enrico's conception of his task as that of a popularizer of essential knowledge. The fact that the *Reportorio* was later used by scholars of the eminence of Carlos Sigüenza y Góngora should not obscure Enrico's basic objective. Thus many chapters in the work have a practical slant, from the section for budding astrologers on how to tell one's birth sign to that on how to keep corn from rotting. Unfortunately the kind of information Enrico was most eager to share with his readers he had to be most careful about providing.

18.
Title page of Enrico Martínez'
Reportorio (opposite), and the
imprimatur of his Mexico City press.

He was convinced that the most useful information he could give concerned the positions of the moon and other heavenly bodies and his analysis of their influence on weather, health, crops, and human character. Enrico firmly believed astrology, conceptually, to be sound science; he was also fascinated by the practice of it, the sightings of planets, the calculations of their relationship to one another, and the knowledge of their special influences. Yet here he ran the greatest risk of censorship, for the questions of religious dogma raised by astrology occupied the seventeenth-century Inquisition more than the questions of natural science raised by Kepler or Galileo. Astrology was accepted by the Church only if it was limited to the effect of heavenly bodies on inanimate things, and even here the celestial effect was by definition secondary to that of the divine will. To claim that the heavenly bodies determined human affairs was to negate man's free will, a central tenet of Catholic doctrine, for without free will, as Enrico said, "man could not be rewarded for his good works or punished for his bad."[5] Aristotelian physics, unmediated by Church doctrine, had a deterministic component, since Aristotle had asserted that everything on the earthly sphere was subject in the last instance to the prime mover. Statements of this celestial determinism appear in the *Reportorio*. To deal with this problem of determinism, the Church made a distinction between astrology that foretold the behavior of nonhuman things, such as crops, tides, and diseases, and astrology that attempted to foretell human behavior. The former was taught by the professor of astrology at the University of Mexico after 1640; the latter was banned by Pope Sixtus V in 1586.

Enrico thought both kinds of astrology valuable and did not want to confine himself to the former. To avoid punishment, he employed two stratagems. The first was to stress the tentative character of all astrology, because the positions of the planets and stars, and consequently their influence, were constantly changing. This also enabled him to explain away erroneous predictions! The second was to reiterate at the end of any passage in the *Reportorio* that seemed dangerously close to celestial determinism that "man's will was free" or "God was more powerful than all heavenly influences." Enrico's political position here is clear, but his intellectual position is less so, for the need to conform to the

Church's view of astrology forced him to downplay his genuine conviction of its full value.

Among the local problems Enrico discussed in his *Reportorio* was the silting up of Lake Texcoco, the lake in which Mexico City was situated. In 1607 Enrico's interest in this problem brought an abrupt halt to his career as a printer and author. In that year the government began construction of a monumental drainage canal, designed to end the recurrent flooding of Mexico City by draining the excess water out of the Valley of Mexico and conducting it into the Atlantic to the north. As Enrico pointed out in his book, the flooding was getting worse as the capacity of Lake Texcoco to hold the excess during the rainy season diminished, and as the city itself sank into the lake bed under the weight of its heavy buildings. The problem was serious, for periodic floods caused many deaths, destroyed property, demoralized residents, and provoked heavy expenditures to repair the damage. Thus, in 1607, the decision was taken to end the previous reliance on dikes and small runoff canals and to build a large, all-valley drainage canal, known as the *desagüe*. Enrico's plan for this huge project was the one chosen by the authorities, and Enrico was appointed the chief engineer. With this change, the last and most difficult phase of his life began. The press was turned over to his son, the projected sequels to the *Reportorio* were set aside, and Enrico embarked on a new career.

Enrico's involvement in the flood control program brought him face to face with a new series of challenges, which he handled less effectively than earlier ones. He was trained neither as an engineer nor as a politician. Before the establishment of architectural and engineering schools, people were hired for jobs for which they had no special training, but in Enrico's case these gaps in his background had grave consequences.

The conception and initial completion of the *desagüe* was a tremendous achievement. The *desagüe* was 8.2 miles long—the largest public work built in Latin America during the colonial period. Its four-mile tunnel was a unique structure in the West. The tunnel measured from 5.5 to 8.25 feet wide and about 11 feet high throughout; at its deepest point it lay 149 feet below the surface of the earth. As late as 1804, Alexander von Humboldt could write that the building of the *desagüe* tunnel was "a hydraulic operation which in our times, even in Europe, would claim the admiration of engineers."[6] By 1623, however, the *desagüe* had become blocked and useless, regarded by many as a fiasco. In fact it was not put into regular working order until 1900, when the administration of the dictator Porfirio Diaz was able to complete it. Although the present drainage system of the Valley of Mexico is based in principle and partly in fact on the *desagüe* first built by Enrico, it was only fully implemented in the late nineteenth century. Enrico had conceived this solution to the flooding of the city and had built the *desagüe* in 1607–08, but he had not been able to keep it functioning thereafter.

Enrico failed in the short run for four reasons: his own lack of technical expertise, the backwardness of hydraulic engineering at the time, the opposition of interest groups that did not want to pay for the upkeep of the *desagüe,* and the inability of the political system to make them do so. Each of these factors contributed to the major technical problems of the *desagüe:* the blockage of the tunnel by earth and debris and the smallness of both tunnel and canal relative to the water they had to drain.

Lacking the experience of cutting channels through soft earth, Enrico did not reinforce the tunnel walls with masonry; they soon crumbled and clogged the passageway. Due to a mistaken principle of hydraulics, Enrico and his contemporaries believed that this crumbling would be forestalled if the water passing through the tunnel were given a greater current. In fact, the opposite was true and the fastmoving water increased erosion. Faulty and inefficient technology was behind the failure to make the *desagüe* large enough. The tunnel in particular needed to be made deeper in order to maintain the gradient necessary to drain the northern lakes. If it were deepened, however, it hit subsoil springs. Enrico had used the available drainage pumps to good advantage when he opened the tunnel. But they were slow, expensive, and unreliable enough to lead any engineer to avoid counting on them and to make the tunnel as shallow as possible. Thus it was built too small and too high.

Decisions about size, length, vaulting, and machinery to be used on a huge public works project were political as well as scientific, however. The *desagüe* had to be built quickly, economically, without antagonizing important people, and with royal approval. Enrico's ability to act within these constraints enabled him to receive the coveted post of chief engineer, but it was insufficient to help him overcome these obstacles once in office. At fault, too, however, was the political system within which he worked. Contrary to its appearance in law, the colonial political system was highly decentralized. It was elitist but not well-integrated, certainly not authoritarian. Neither its principles nor its procedures were helpful in solving technical problems such as those posed by the *desagüe*.

From the inception of the *desagüe* Enrico was harassed by colleagues who wanted his job. Andrés San Miguel, Alonso Arias, and Adrian Boot were his most prominent enemies. Enrico's foreign origins, his poor record with the *desagüe*, and his background as a printer and scientist rather than an architect made it hard for him to build up a reliable base of political support. But it would be wrong to see his sad loss of credibility merely as an outcome of his personal shortcomings as a politician. At every step these failings interacted with the peculiar character of colonial politics.

In the Spanish colonial system no one official was responsible for a project such as the *desagüe*. Authority over flood control, as over other public issues, was divided among viceroy, high court judges, treasury officials, the local governor, and the city council. Although some of these officials had more power than others, all had to be consulted in each case; then all decisions had to be approved by the crown. It was common for opponents of a particular policy to keep petitioning the crown for its reversal or to refuse to enforce it in their jurisdiction, claiming that it was not practical to implement it at that time. Support freely given during one year might be withdrawn the next. Enrico's numerous reports, countless meetings with high officials, and many trips to City Hall, not to mention the *desagüe* site, were efforts to counter these features of a political system that made decisions too slowly and gave critics too much influence.

Enrico's troubles were also due to the principle that informed the political system. America, as a colony of Spain, was to provide income for the metropolis. Thus, after routine expenses were paid, all revenues were sent back to Spain. If extraordinary expenditures were required, such as the *desagüe*, the money had to be provided by the colonists. The need to obtain this money locally was the chief reason for opposition to the *desagüe*. After an initial contribution the creoles refused to pay more, and they were also reluctant to have their black or Indian workers temporarily appropriated by the state to repair the *desagüe*. The nonwhites, for their part, tried to avoid *desagüe* labor, which paid poorly and was dangerous. If the crown had been willing to finance the *desagüe*, it would have been less damaged by the other features of the political system that had an adverse effect on all public administration. As it was, the *desagüe* was a casualty of New Spain's colonial status.

Following brief imprisonment in 1629 on the ludicrous charge of sabotaging his own work, Enrico entered a period of disillusionment. In that year the run-down condition of the *desagüe* and the unusually heavy rains led to the worst flood disaster in the colony's history. The city was under water until 1634, and the destruction of lives and property was considerable. The city did recover, and Enrico continued to write up new proposals, but his work was carried on under the shadow of failure. When an inspection commission visited the *desagüe* in 1631, its head described Enrico as an unpleasant and somewhat sinister figure, who, "retiring to an obscure apartment with a pretended illness after I came to Huehuetoca [the *desagüe* site], sits hidden in his room surrounded by books on mathematics, spheres, astrolabes, and cross-staffs without attending to his offers and promises."[7] What the commissioner was really describing was an old man trying to hold on to the enjoyment of his studies and whatever self-confidence remained to him. Enrico died at seventy-five in 1632, in a house close to his twenty-five-year albatross, disappointed by the loss of faith in him but still convinced of the superiority of his project.

When Enrico landed in Veracruz in 1589, he brought to his new home a special perspective. As he tried to fit himself into colonial society, his position as a foreigner and a scientist involved him in external and internal conflicts that the less curious and the less ambitious were able to avoid. His fit in the socially stratified, intellectually conservative society of

New Spain was, in other words, imperfect. This was not because Enrico was a revolutionary, but because as he pursued his own particular objectives, he bumped against the sensitive joints of the scaffolding that held this society together. He coped with this friction in different ways. As a printer, he was cautious; as a writer, he edged toward new ideas but fearfully drew back; as an engineer, he was innovative and accurate in his analysis but less skillful in its execution; as a politician, he combined an admirable defense of what he believed right with a less commendable inflexibility and ineptness in attaining it. He persisted but he did not succeed. This was due not only to his mistakes but also to the political and social structure of the colony. Paradoxically, his most socially useful contribution to his environment, the vision of an all-valley flood program and the building of the first *desagüe*, was the one that brought him the most pain.

Notes

1. Archivo General de la Nacion, Inquisición, vol. 165, Expediente 5, F. 44; vol. 306, Exped. 9, Ff. 98–100.

2. Francisco Fernández del Castillo, *Libro y libreros del siglo XVI* (México, 1914), p. 118.

3. Enrico Martinez, *Reportorio de los tiempos e historia natural de Nueva España*, 2d ed. (México, 1948), p. 187.

4. *Ibid.*, p. 178.

5. *Ibid.*, p. 21.

6. Louisa Hoberman, "Bureaucracy and Disaster: Mexico City and the Flood of 1629," *Journal of Latin American Studies* 6 (1974): 212. In "Technological Change in a Traditional Society: The Case of the *Desagüe* in Colonial Mexico," forthcoming, *Technology and Culture*, the author discusses the technical problems in detail.

7. Fernando Cepeda and Fernando Alfonso Carrillo, *Relación universal legítima y verdadera del sitio en que está fundada la muy noble . . . ciudad de México . . . .*, 2 vols. (México, 1637), vol. 1, part 3, p. 14.

Sources

Enrico Martinez' story is chiefly derived from the following primary sources: the *Desagüe* and Inquisition sections of the Archivo General de la Nación in Mexico City, which deal with Enrico's career as an engineer and translator, respectively; Enrico's own *Reportorio*, edited by Francisco Gonzalez de Cossio (note 3); and the history of the *desagüe* published in 1637 by Fernando

Cepeda and Fernando Alfonso Carrillo (note 7). Francisco de la Maza's *Enrico Martinez. Cosmografo e impresor de Nueva España* (México, 1943) was a useful secondary source on Enrico's printing activities in particular, as were Francisco Fernández del Castillo (note 2); Francisco Pérez Salazar, *Dos familias de impresores mexicanos del siglo XVII* (México, 1925); Vicente Andrade, *Ensayo bibliográfico mexicano del siglo XVII* (México, 1889), and José Beristain y Souza, *Biblioteca hispano-americana septentrional,* 4 vols. (México, 1883–97), vol. 4. My discussion of the scientific ideas and general intellectual climate of the colony is based on Elias Trabulse, *Ciencia y religión en el siglo XVII* (México, 1974); Irving Leonard, *Baroque Times in Old Mexico* (Ann Arbor, Mich., 1966); Mariano Picón-Salas, *A Cultural History of Spanish America* (Berkeley, Calif., 1963); and Eli Gortari, *La ciencia en la historia de México* (México, 1963). Antonio Domínguez Ortiz, *The Golden Age of Spain, 1516–1659* (Madrid, 1971) and Jaime Vicens Vives, ed., *Historia social y económica de España y America,* 5 vols. (Barcelona, 1957–59), vol. 3, provided helpful descriptions of social and cultural life in sixteenth-century Spain.

Suggestions for Further Reading

Enrico's life touches on three different aspects of colonial social history: printers and the press, colonial science and religion, and the educational establishment. In addition to the works cited above, two recently republished classics offer a good overview of the colonial press: José Toribio Medina, *La Imprenta en Mexico, 1539–1821,* 8 vols. (Amsterdam, 1965), vol. 1; and José Torre Revello, *El libro, la imprenta y el periodismo en América durante la dominacion española* (New York, 1973). For institutions of higher learning, John Tate Lanning, *Academic Culture in the Spanish Colonies* (New York, 1940) and Julio Jiménez Rueda, *Historia de la cultura en México. El Virreinato* (México, 1960) are very useful. Bernabé Navarro, *Cultura mexicana moderna en el siglo XVIII* (México, 1964) and David Mayagoitia, *Ambiente filosófico de la Nueva España* (México, 1945) also treat the high culture of the colony. Of course the history of scientific ideas can be enjoyably studied through the works of the major writers themselves. For the sixteenth century, José de Acosta's *Historia natural y moral de las Indias,* 2d ed. (México, 1962); for the seventeenth, Carlos Siguenza y Gongora, *Libra astronómica y filosófica* (México, 1959); and for the eighteenth, Jorge Juan and Antonio de Ulloa, *A Voyage to South America,* ed. Irving Leonard (New York, 1964). Finally, a good overview of social types may be found in James Lockhart and Enrique Otte, *Letters and People of the Spanish Indies: The Sixteenth Century* (Cambridge, Engl., 1976).

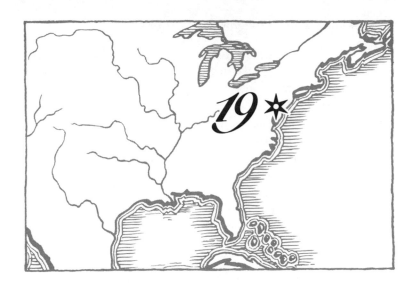

Jacob Young:
Indian Trader and Interpreter

FRANCIS JENNINGS

*O*ur demi-hero first appears in the records as a Dutch mercenary soldier named Jacob Claeson (sometimes spelled Clawson) who came to New Netherland's "South River" colony (Delaware Bay) sometime around the middle of the seventeenth century. He must have had a lot of off-duty time, because he was able to set himself up as a trader with the nearby Indians, and he did so well that several Dutch colonials invested in his business. He had plenty of enterprise. Alone among the Dutch, he learned the language of the most important trading Indians of the region, the Susquehannock tribe. (The Dutch called them Minquas.) Jacob also had the flair essential to salesmen: in business he became "Jacob, My Friend."

In the course of a checkered career he changed his name several times and thus scattered himself in pieces through several archives; but there are enough scraps of surviving evidence to show that Jacob was one of those "little people" who become enmeshed in great events without being very visible in them. In the latter part of the seventeenth century he became the indispensable man in Maryland's diplomacy with the powerful Indian tribes to the north—tribes that Maryland tried to manipulate in peace and war for territorial expansion at the expense of other colonies. The political events are easier to track than Jacob's personal life apart from them, for it is the nature of archives to be more concerned with things than with people. But the man comes through as energetic and resourceful with a capacity for making loyal friends. He needed all his talents, for at one point the quarrels of powerful men suddenly caught him up in such a way that he faced death on the hangman's scaffold. Other quarrels reprieved him, and his friends saved him. Coping with life, in Jacob's day, required more than ability. One had to have a little bit of luck.

The first clue we have to his life is embedded in the correspondence of New Netherland's director-general, Peter Stuyvesant, with their "High Mightynesses," the directors of the Dutch West India Company. In 1660 Stuyvesant was worried about threats against his Delaware Bay colony from the English of Maryland. Stuyvesant's colonists were even more worried. As they compared the difference in size and resources of Maryland's thousands of people and their own hundreds, a number of them decided to join up with the prospective winners in the dispute. Jacob was among those in whom discretion outweighed valor, and he vanished from Stuyvesant's sight. Stuyvesant had two good reasons for singling out Jacob by name in bemoaning the general exodus. The first was that Jacob had forgotten to return "quite a large sum of money"[1] lent to him for his business. The second was Jacob's fluency in the Susquehannock language—a rare skill among Europeans. Stuyvesant feared that the Marylanders would be able to use Jacob's influence among the Indians to the disadvantage of New Netherland.

His fears were well grounded; Jacob did enter the employ of Maryland's Lord Baltimore as an interpreter. But it was a part-time job. Most of Jacob's time was spent at his trading post at the head of Chesapeake Bay or at the home he later reestablished on Delaware Bay. Though primarily a business-man and only sporadically a hired hand, Jacob left no doubt that he had become an Englishman. He ceased being Jacob Claeson and became Jacob Young.

His business was the purchase of furs and animal hides from the Indians, paying for them with European manufac-tured goods such as cloth, kettles, and hatchets, and perhaps some clandestine firearms and rum. It was a lucrative trade in which prices were set unilaterally by the trader for his maxi-mum profit, but it was also full of risks and hazards. Jacob's special trading partners, the Susquehannocks, were an ag-gressive, warlike tribe of the lower Susquehanna valley, whose energetic, wide-ranging activities produced large quantities of marketable peltries. On the debit side of their ledger, however, were frequent interruptions of business by raiding parties from enemy Iroquois tribes of the Finger Lakes region of what is now New York State. Jacob's trading post stood near the mouth of the much-traveled Susquehanna River in a position exposed to attack from either Susque-hannocks or Iroquois, but it enjoyed the immunity that Indians usually granted to traders. Raiding parties passed by Jacob's place without striking it. People would stop in to talk. It was a strategic spot for gathering intelligence of tribal politics and exerting personal influence on the Indians.

Regardless of Peter Stuyvesant's fears, it does not appear from the sometimes cryptic records that Jacob ever swayed the powerful Susquehannock tribe or any other Indians against New Netherland. If he did engage in any clandestine plotting, whatever he might have done was eclipsed by a power much greater than his own when an English fleet suddenly appeared in 1664 to conquer New Netherland. The Dutch colony became New York, but except for a new ruling elite nothing much changed; population, territory, and territorial claims remained the same. We must notice especially that Maryland's lord proprietary continued to claim that both shores of Delaware Bay belonged to Maryland instead of New York.

Lord Baltimore was irritated to see his own intended con-quest anticipated by the Duke of York, and his mood was not improved by contemplation of the power and place of his new adversary, who was not only a duke but brother to the king.

Baltimore's former Dutch opponents had been so weak that they could have been overawed by any well-timed show of force, but the king might make difficulties if an overt move were to be made against a colony belonging to his brother. Baltimore and his henchmen had to change plans. They did not abandon hope of seizing Delaware Bay, but they turned to indirect methods of exerting the necessary force. Because these new methods depended on the manipulation of the Susquehannock Indians, Jacob Claeson/Young—the man who traded with and talked to the Susquehannocks—became essential to the plot.

In brief, the scheme revolved around the seventeenth-century principle of "rights of conquest." What the Marylanders proposed to do was conquer Delaware Bay by indirect action. The native right to the land there belonged to the resident Delaware Indians. If the Delawares were to be conquered in war, their right would pass to their conquerors. If their conquerors were the Susquehannocks, Maryland could acquire an overlord's right to the same territory, because Maryland had made a treaty of alliance with the Susquehannocks that could be presented in an English court as an instrument by which that tribe had subjected itself to Maryland. Thus all the territory formerly acknowledged as belonging to the Delawares would become, via the Susquehannocks, the territory of Maryland. Jacob Young's role in the scheme was to persuade the Susquehannocks to attack the Delawares.

Various complications ensued. The battle-weary Susquehannocks already had a grim war on their hands against the confederated Iroquois tribes, and the Delawares had sent warriors to help defend the Susquehannocks' town against a major Iroquois attack. And the Susquehannocks had been badly hurt by decades of battle and disease. "Wee know," Jacob had written to Maryland's governor, Charles Calvert, that the Susquehannocks "would willingly Imbrace a peace if Obteyned, but are unwilling (through height of Spirit) to sue for itt," and Jacob had added his own plea to negotiate a general peace "which by every one, wee thinke, is much required and most earnestly desired."[2] Calvert ignored the plea. But, regardless of the seduction and pressure from Maryland, the Susquehannocks had no intention of turning suddenly against their Delaware allies. In disgust, Maryland's chiefs abandoned hope of conquering Delaware Bay by means of the Susquehannocks.

The consequences of their scheme were not to be dropped as easily as the scheme itself. When Maryland acquired the Susquehannocks as friends, it also acquired their enemies. The Iroquois began to raid into Maryland's back country, and the aroused gentry immediately declared war on the Iroquois tribes, which were so distant and mysterious that not even their names were known accurately in Maryland. Jacob Young may have been the only European involved in actual fighting in these murky struggles; he apparently led or advised the Susquehannocks effectively enough to make himself heartily disliked in Iroquoia.

In 1675 the situation was transformed. For their own reasons (too complex to include here), Maryland's rulers decided to seek peace with the Iroquois. The source records become very scanty, but they show that the Susquehannocks had once again become Maryland's problem, for the terms on which the Susquehannocks would make peace were not the same as the terms on which Maryland would make peace. Governor Calvert intervened personally—a sure sign that the business at hand was of highest importance. He summoned the Susquehannocks to a meeting, and we cannot doubt that Jacob Young carried the message. At the meeting Calvert "invited" the Indians to move from their home village on the lower Susquehanna River and take up new residence in an abandoned stockaded village on the Potomac River, just below where the city of Washington now stands. It was an imperative invitation, and the Susquehannocks moved.

The result was disaster. Through no fault of their own—without their even knowing how it came about—the Susquehannocks were caught up as victims of the insurrection led by Nathaniel Bacon in Virginia. In July 1675, a party of Virginia militiamen crossed the Potomac into Maryland in hot pursuit of Doeg Indians who had raided a Virginia plantation. In true frontier fashion they killed fourteen unoffending Susquehannocks as well. Elsewhere in Virginia, Nathaniel Bacon excited his back country neighbors with lurid accusations of complicity between Indians and the government. To appease Bacon's followers, the government marched a large troop back into Maryland against the Susquehannocks. Much alarmed, Maryland's government sensed that "rights of conquest" might be used to seize their own lands as they had planned to seize Delaware Bay, and to forestall any such possibility they joined the attack with their own troops. If there was to be a conquest of Indians in Maryland, it would be a conquest by Maryland, never mind the reasons why. The combined force of 1,000 men laid siege to the village on the Potomac that Governor Calvert had designated as the Susquehannocks' residence. Five chiefs were invited out to parley under guarantee of safe conduct. When they came, the guarantee was disregarded and the chiefs were seized and murdered. The deed was obviously intended to demoralize the Indians enough to make them surrender, but it misfired; the furious survivors made their escape in the dead of night and began taking their revenge on the isolated settlers of the backwoods. Then Bacon mobilized his followers and went hunting for them, but instead of fighting Susquehannocks he attacked their enemies, the Occaneechees, who were unfortunate enough to be in possession of a stock of valuable peltry. Bacon was a murderously simple soul whose great goal was to grow rich and powerful by killing Indians and seizing their lands. When Virginia's governor, William Berkeley, tried to stop him he began killing Englishmen too, and such are the ironies of history that Bacon thus acquired fame as a revolutionary democrat!

From the distant Manhattans, New York's governor, Edmund Andros, had informed himself and fretted about these strange events. Andros knew that the botched campaign against the Susquehannocks had been paralleled in New England by another botched effort to conquer Wampanoags and Narragansetts, and he feared the consequences. What would happen if all the tribes united in desperate fury against the English? It was too terrible to contemplate or to leave to the inept management of the men who had started it all. Andros stepped in.

He did not delude himself with the mythologies concocted to justify these wars of colonial aggression. He knew that the Indians would fight to the last man because surrender meant slaughter or, what was worse, sale into West Indian slavery. Andros offered the Indians a better alternative. In return for their cessation from hostilities he offered sanctuary in his colony of New York.

This was not so easily done as said. The Susquehannocks were scattered in the backwoods, and there were other complications, as we shall see. One day, however, Andros received a message from Captain Edmund Cantwell, his deputy on Delaware Bay, that two Susquehannocks had been seen among the Delaware Indians there. Andros immediately instructed Cantwell to bring them to New York for negotiations.

Cantwell made contact, but he and Jacob Young took the Susquehannocks' surviving leaders off to Maryland first to see if a peace could be patched up there. These negotiations failed, and according to simplistic theories of the colonial frontier as an arena of race pitted against race we should expect Andros to line up with Maryland against the Indians. Nothing of the sort happened. Instead, two Susquehannocks journeyed on to New York and parleyed with Andros, who immediately promised them sanctuary within his jurisdiction and demanded nothing in return except good behavior. They sent word to their brethren hiding in the woods, who drifted in to take up residence at Delaware Bay.

There they stayed briefly before most of them moved farther on, all the way north to the Iroquois country. Outmaneuvered, the Marylanders could not trick so they had to treat. They sent a mission headed by Henry Coursey to negotiate with all hostile tribes. Coursey picked Jacob Young to be his interpreter, "without whome I can doe nothing, and what truth is to bee had is from him and none else."[3] They went first to New York City to get Edmund Andros's permission to approach the Iroquois. Coursey's government had thoughtfully provided him with a hundred pounds sterling with which to bribe Andros; the record does not show whether Andros took the money, but he surely did not give the money's worth. The treaties that he finally permitted Coursey to make—through his own interpreter—gave Maryland only peace, with none of the punitive controls that Coursey wanted.

Jacob Young was distraught, but not for Coursey's reasons. Jacob's personal objective had been to bring those Susquehannocks back to their home country, where his trading post was located. Now they were to stay hundreds of miles away from business and profit. Mournfully, he spoke without caution: he "would rather have given 20,000 pounds of tobacco than to come."[4] Jacob had more reason than just a loss of business to be unhappy. At the treaty an Onondaga chief had disclosed that Jacob had been a "great Leader and Captain" in the prolonged Susquehannock-Iroquois wars, and that he had been "a great occasion" of the Iroquois attacks on both Christians and Indians.[5] The remark was ambiguous. It could have meant that Jacob incited attacks or only that his participation in the wars had provoked Iroquois resentment and retaliation. Coursey let the comment pass but remembered it later, to Jacob's great woe.

The treaty was not as comprehensive as Coursey had thought, and its loopholes permitted Susquehannocks to revenge themselves on Maryland's Indian allies. Another treaty being required, back Coursey went to New York (in 1682), and back went Jacob Young as well. A new treaty was signed, but disaster struck Jacob. Rumors had been circulating that he had hired Indians to kill Christians. Jacob sued one rumorer in a Delaware court for defamation and won an apology, but Maryland's gentry paid more heed to the drift of the tales than to the apology. At the 1682 treaty, Henry Coursey bluntly asked the Iroquois whether "some Christian" had stirred them up to make war upon the Piscataway Indians allied to Maryland. An Oneida chief affirmed that Jacob Young had been the man.[6] In ordinary circumstances this dialogue could have been interpreted back and forth by Jacob himself, who would certainly not have permitted such damaging words to pass without modification; but this time the interpreter was one of New York's employees who made no effort to palliate the damaging charge. Henry Coursey recorded it carefully to take back to an irate Lord Baltimore.

His lordship promptly threw Jacob in gaol, and at the next session of the province's general assembly Jacob became the main business on the agenda. Lord Baltimore denounced:

> the Evil Practices of Jacob Young that long Disturber of Our Peace and Quiet: I caused him to be Apprehended and secured in Irons, and do Resolve he shall receive his Tryall this Assembly that so you may all see the Villany of that ungrateful Wretch, who not only hath made a Trade of the Spoils he received of the Indians

that have Yearly Robbed us but by their Means Hath also had the Command of any Man's Life in this Province that he desired to have taken away.[7]

The charge was strong, and what followed made Jacob the unwitting instrument of a battle between the proprietor and the elected branch of his assembly. For Jacob's was a hanging case of treason if Baltimore's accusations were to be accepted, and the uses made by Tudors and Stuarts of treason charges had caused Englishmen to wrap that crime in safeguards of procedure. The "rights of Englishmen" were as precious in the colonies as in England, and the lords Baltimore were as assertively authoritarian as any Stuart. Considering the constant activity of the executioners in their government, one may see unintended sarcasm in the way that scribes frequently abbreviated "His Lordship" to "His Lopp."

Maryland's Upper House was more than willing to do Baltimore's bidding. This was the appointed council of great Catholic landholders, which existed in perpetual tension with the elected Lower House, in which the members were generally Protestant and less wealthy. When the two houses met as the colonial legislature, the Lower House was always on guard against pressures from above to grant more taxes, and its members were highly conscious of the need to preserve legal protection against the anger of their choleric lord. There appear to have been friends of Jacob Young in the Lower House. It is impossible to make out the nature of the relationships in the murky records, but some person or persons put up a fight against Baltimore's efforts to hang Jacob. Stubbornly contesting every nicety of protocol, the Lower House used Jacob Young's case as a means of winning another inch of privilege in its perpetual struggle for real power.

The Upper House began the action, or inaction, against him by sending a delegation to the Lower House to request it to serve as a jury "for the Tryall of a Person that hath so basely betrayed his trust and so ingratefully brought a Charge upon the Province by Instigateing and hireing the Northern Indians to make Warr in this Province."[8]

The charge met an unlooked-for obstacle, and its sequel reminds us that absurdity and farce in history often hide genuine struggles over substantial issues. The gentlemen delegates from the Upper House were proper gentlemen, and they wore swords as proper gentlemen should on state occasions. The Lower House, however, recalled events in England's House of Commons when armed soldiers had invaded it, and the Lower House would have no swords admitted, regardless of the importance of their bearers. The gentlemen were indignant, but the Lower House was adamant—no swords. The gentlemen were also adamant—no swords, no gentlemen—and they stalked off without delivering their message. Jacob Young had won his first reprieve.

Smarting, the Upper House resolved to send the charge against Jacob by their doorkeeper, a hireling who was not entitled to wear a sword, but this was an affront the Lower House would not accept. Once more the message was turned back.

Having established the prerogatives of status, the Lower House sent two of its own members to the Upper House to inquire innocently whether there was anything to communicate regarding Jacob Young. The Upper House seized this seeming opportunity to save face by giving their message to the Lower House's delegates, but the message bounced back once again, still unaccepted, because the Lower House's delegates had "no commission" to carry Upper House messages. Stickling for their due, the Lower House was insisting that the Upper House could not evade the issue of protocol; they must send one of their own members, fully accredited and swordless, if they wanted their message to be recognized and dealt with by the Lower House. For the moment the humiliated Upper House could think of no better response than to refuse thenceforth to receive a Lower House member with his hat on.

What seems to have been the real issue behind this comedy was the reluctance of the Lower House to be pressured into a trial for the extreme crime of treason on the basis of the kind of evidence at hand, and one can sense that more than Jacob Young's fate was in the balance. If such charges could hang Jacob, similar charges might readily be dredged up to hang other persons in Maryland who had incurred Lord Baltimore's displeasure, perhaps even some persons who happened to be obnoxious members of the Lower House. What makes this interpretation the more credible is the apparent recognition by the Upper House that, regardless of protocol and privilege, the charges against Jacob Young would have to be scaled down.

After a day's thought and perhaps some informal consultation, the Upper House resolved that Jacob's crimes would surely be classified as high treason, "could they be proved by two Witnesses Viva Voce upon Oath, *but* such two witnesses are not to be had, they being Indians and far distant from us." This being conceded, the Upper House suggested impeachment for "high Misdemeanors" as an alternative to charges of treason, "so the two Houses may Join in the certain Evidence we have to confine him for Life."[9] This was nicely calculated strategy. It switched roles for the two houses so that the Lower House would prefer charges and the Upper House would become the deciding jury. In such a procedure the verdict was preordained, and life imprisonment in the seventeenth century was scarcely a less severe sentence than hanging. Men did not live long in the gaols of those days.

The Upper House appointed Henry Coursey to deliver this proposal to the Lower House. Coursey was a cunning choice. He impressed the Lower House with his indispensability as a witness, and when he returned with the Lower House's agreement to impeach, he brought also their desire that he be kept available to testify. Whereupon the Upper House laid a snare.

Still smarting from the impertinence of their social inferiors, the Upper House instructed Coursey to testify only if he were permitted to wear his sword into the chamber of the Lower House. Once more he strode up to the doorkeeper of the Lower House, this time in full gentlemanly regalia. But the Lower House was not to be budged. They sent him packing, upon which he quitted the assembly in a huff and went home!

It was a standoff. The Lower House hinted that without Coursey the impeachment of Jacob Young "will be much impeded if not wholly frustrated."[10] The Upper House replied, in effect, that the Lower House had only itself to blame. All were conscious of Lord Baltimore's power and desires. Acrimoniously the proceedings crept along.

There can be no doubt of the ruling gentry's grim intention to make Jacob suffer for something. When the Lower House suggested that the only available evidence against him of any weight consisted of remarks he had made after being imprisoned, the Upper House dismissed the objection as inconsequential, and their remark suggests how much our freedoms today owe to the stubbornness of some of our ancestors: "This house do Say that they conceive it imports little whether the said Words proved by those Affidavits be referred to the fact for which he was Committed or not." Had that rule prevailed to modern times, due process of law would be a grave mockery indeed.

Finally, the Lower House produced a set of articles of impeachment, consisting largely of allegations that Jacob had been too friendly with Indians. The Lower House appointed a lawyer for him, and the lawyer put up a strong defense that was nicely tailored to appeal to the prejudices of the Upper House jurymen. Through this lawyer, Jacob utterly denied every charge and added for good measure several denunciations of the "treachery," "perfidiousness," and "faithlessness" of Indians.

In the end, however, those Indians served him better than the devious ploys of his lawyer. A letter arrived in Maryland with information about Indian attitudes that suddenly slaked the gentry's thirst for Jacob's blood. It reported the message of a group of Susquehannocks living at Delaware Bay. They told a Delaware Swede:

> that whatever could be Alledged against Jacob Young touching any thing concerning the Indian Affairs was all false, that the said Young had always kept off them, the Susquehannocks, from doing more Mishief than they did, or else they would have killed many hundreds more in Maryland than they did, but that they were Stopped through his Means. [And further] that in case the Life of the said Jacob Young be taken away, that they would have 500 lives more for him out of Maryland.[11]

(Maryland's total colonial population at the time was about 16,000.) A sobered Upper House concluded that "it is Absolutly unsafe for the Province to bring the said Jacob to Tryall this Day."

They kept him in gaol a while longer, which was punishment enough for most crimes. Gaols were not heated in those days and winters were cold. The furnishings were stark and the food was garbage. But Susquehannock warnings were not to be lightly flouted, so Jacob was freed after a year of imprisonment. There were conditions attached to his freedom: heavy bond was demanded, and theoretically he was supposed to exile himself from the American continent, but nobody seems to have bothered to follow up on these face-saving devices. Not many of Lord Baltimore's enemies were so lucky.

Once liberated, Jacob headed straight for Delaware Bay, where he had become one of the more substantial citizen-taxpayers. But he was not yet done with Maryland or the Susquehannocks. England's Glorious Revolution of 1688 stimulated a revolution also in Maryland that overthrew the proprietary government, and the revolutionaries resolved to make their own peace with the Susquehannocks, who had by this time returned to their old home on the Susquehanna River. For revolutionaries, who could be better trusted than the man their enemy had tried to kill? They summoned Jacob to make the last treaty between Mayland and the Susquehannocks—a treaty that finally worked. That the tribe's years were numbered anyway is another story; its doom would come finally from a different quarter.

As for Jacob, he became a trusted agent of Maryland's new regime, settled in Cecil County and commissioned as Captain. There were other Indians to be treated with besides Susquehannocks, and Jacob's usefulness became apparent especially when some strange Indians appeared at the head of Chesapeake Bay in 1693. These were Shawnees, newly arrived from the west and seeking to be taken into the Covenant Chain of alliance between the English colonies and their neighboring tribes. But they threw a fright into Marylanders until Jacob established the peacefulness of their errand.

In 1695 he was licensed to keep a public house and ferry on the Susquehanna. We do not know when he had been born, but he was obviously growing older and less inclined to go faring off into the woods on missions to the Indians. The curtain falls there. We can only imagine a moment when Jacob died peacefully in his bed, content that in his time his friends could live at peace.

Unsung in history, Jacob Young was nevertheless one of the men who made history. He never held the sort of power or wealth that attract the attention of chroniclers; his progeny do not seem to have been sufficiently distinguished to excite genealogists; and his easy way of making friends among Indians and lower-class Marylanders has not recommended him to either racists or elitists. Nor can revolutionaries find much inspiration in his cashing in on a revolution made by others. He was not really the stuff of heroic romance: his business methods do not look as though they would stand up under close moral scrutiny, and his escape from the gibbet was none of his own doing.

But he did survive, and the Susquehanna valley would have been even more chaotic without him than it was. He did perform services valuable to Indians and English colonials alike while serving his own interests as well as he could. He stood trial for his life in a contest of political power that edged Maryland one inch farther away from feudal despotism. To be sure, he was there involuntarily and by chance, but he was there, the very center of the struggle.

What morals can be drawn from such an ambiguous life? Many, I suspect, depending on one's taste in these matters. My own preference is for well-worn principles that seem out of fashion for antiheroes nowadays. Storm-tossed and vulnerable as he was, Jacob Young made a moderate success of a far from boring existence by energetic use of what talents he had and by serving his friends so well that they forgot him not when need arose.

Notes

1. Stuyvesant to Directors in Holland, 25 June 1660, in E. B. O'Callaghan and Berthold Fernow, eds., *Documents Relative to the Colonial History of New York*, 15 vols. (Albany, State of New York, 1856–1887), XII, 317. (Cited below as *N.Y.Col.Docs.*)

2. Stockett, Gouldsmith, and Wright to Gov. Calvert, 7 June 1664, in W. H. Browne et al., eds., *Archives of Maryland*, 72 vols. (Baltimore: Maryland Historical Society, 1883–1972), III, 498–499.

3. Coursey to Notley, 22 May 1677, *Arch. of Md.*, V, 247.

4. Trial findings, 19 October 1683, *Arch. of Md.*, VII, 475.

5. Treaty minutes, 21 July 1677, *Arch. of Md.*, V, 255.

6. Treaty minutes, 4 August 1682, *N.Y.Col.Docs.*, III, 326–328.

7. 26 October 1682, *Arch. of Md.*, VII, 333–335.

8. 2 November 1682, *Arch. of Md.*, VII, 348.
9. 4 November 1682, *Arch. of Md.*, VII, 354.
10. 4 November 1682, *Arch. of Md.*, VII, 357.
11. George Oldfield to the General Assembly, 2 November 1682, *Arch. of Md.*, VII, 398.

Sources

Most of the scraps of information used to piece together Jacob Young's story are noted in detail in Francis Jennings, "Glory, Death, and Transfiguration: The Susquehannock Indians in the Seventeenth Century," *Proceedings of the American Philosophical Society* 112, 1 (1968): pp. 26–28, 31–44, 48–50. See also the index references to "Young, Jacob" in that exasperating grab-bag of comprehensiveness, confusion, and ethnocentrism, Charles H. Hanna, *The Wilderness Trail*, 2 vols. (New York, 1911). For Bacon's rebellion, see Wilcomb E. Washburn, *The Governor and the Rebel* (Chapel Hill, N.C., 1957). The details of Jacob's trial are in vol. 7 of the *Archives of Maryland*, ed. William Hand Browne (Baltimore, 1889).

Suggestions for Further Reading

Indian interpreters were individualists by the nature of the breed, but they shared certain circumstances and problems. Two fine biographies have been written about men who practiced the trade in Pennsylvania: Paul A. W. Wallace, *Conrad Weiser, 1696–1760, Friend of Colonist and Mohawk* (Philadelphia, 1945); and Nicholas B. Wainwright, *George Croghan, Wilderness Diplomat* (Chapel Hill, N.C., 1959).

For general background in Indian-white relations on the East Coast in the seventeenth century, see Wilcomb E. Washburn, *The Indian in America* (New York, 1975); Gary B. Nash, *Red, White, and Black: The Peoples of Early America* (Englewood Cliffs, N.J., 1974); and Francis Jennings, *The Invasion of America: Indians, Colonialism, and the Cant of Conquest* (Chapel Hill, N.C., 1975).

For guidance to further reading as far as one may care to go, see Francis Paul Prucha, ed., *A Bibliographical Guide to the History of Indian-White Relations in the United States* (Chicago, 1977).

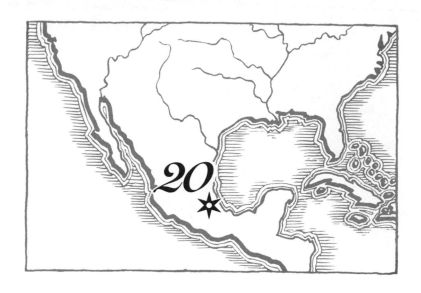

Micaela Angela Carrillo:
Widow and Pulque Dealer

EDITH COUTURIER

*F*or the just motives which I have and with the full consent of my two legitimate sons, my heirs are my five children. . . . To my oldest son, Esteban de Luna, I give the obligation to maintain and care for my three natural daughters . . . so that they do not commit any sins against God."[1] Thus did the self-made Micaela Angela Carrillo secure the consent of her sons to a waiver of the law requiring that parental property be inherited only by children born in wedlock, in order to share her wealth with her illegitimate daughters. But the widow lived for another twenty-three years, and just before her death she executed another will leaving all her remaining property to her youngest daughter, María Antonia Carrillo. Don Esteban, by then her only surviving son, felt cheated and initiated a suit claiming the inheritance. Threatened with the loss of her house, lands, and personal property, the daughter contested the case. It is thanks to the bitterness of this litigation and the survival of the documents recording testimonies about the family's history that we can reconstruct the outline of their mother's life.

This law case reveals the remarkable story of a woman who rose from near destitution on the death of her husband to become an important landowner in the town in which she dwelt. She, as well as her daughter, María Antonia, performed some of the tasks usually reserved for men in the everyday life of the community: they labored in the fields, manufactured pulque, an intoxicating drink which they also retailed, rode horseback, and traded in the city. Micaela exercised authority over her sons as well as her daughters, provided them with property, and arranged for their training in a craft. There is evidence in this tale, moreover, that regardless of the traditional female experiences of this patriarchal society, some women could share in the privileges of men and enjoy some small share of masculine independence.

Micaela Angela Carrillo lived all her life in Nuestra Señora de Asunción Amozoque (present-day Amozoc), a predominantly Indian village about seventeen kilometers east of the large and wealthy Spanish city of Puebla de los Angeles. Puebla, placed strategically on the main commercial route between the colonial capital and its principal port, was a leading center of manufacture and trade. Towns like Amozoque surrounded the city, providing Indian laborers for her pottery factories and some of the markets for her textile mills.

Two features distinguished Amozoque from its neighbors. On top of the church, built by the Franciscans in 1585, there was a star that signaled to *conversos* (Jews who had converted to Christianity but who still secretly practiced the old faith) that a welcome awaited them. We do not know if any members of the Carrillo family were descended from the ancient *converso* community. But members of the family did participate in the famed local industry, which was the production of decorative iron work. Iron spurs from the town were the prized possessions of riders throughout the region. One hundred and fifty years later, Emiliano Zapata, the Mexican populist revolutionary leader, cherished the Amozoc spurs he won in a contest.

Contemporary local records about Amozoque tell us only that the town had a population of around three thousand in the year 1742, of whom 15 percent were classified as Spaniards (largely white), mestizos, and mulattoes, and the remainder as Indians, that is, primarily speakers of the Nahuatl language. Indians occupied the lowest rung of the social ladder of this town, as of the colony as a whole. Both law and custom defined them as a subordinate caste, forbade them to carry arms or ride horseback, and obliged them to wear certain clothing and to pay a head tax known as tribute. The Indian population was divided between a group enjoying some status accepted as nobility, who bore the titles of caciques and *principales*, and a mass of peasants. The elite group enjoyed the right to bear arms, dress in the Spanish manner, ride horses rather than walk, use donkeys, and govern the Indian towns and villages. They were usually exempt from the duty of personal service to Spanish entrepreneurs and householders and paid no tribute. As a result of intermarriage, the hereditary nature of the Indian nobility had become attenuated; nobles were often mestizos, and their status derived more from their wealth than from genealogy.

Amozoque had been a preconquest site of heavy Indian population, but like other indigenous communities of New Spain it had suffered heavily from depopulation due to migrations, the forced labor of colonial society, and a series of devastating epidemics. The government had several times sought to bring additional Indians from the surrounding countryside and smaller towns and villages to live there and to preserve residential segregation. Despite these efforts to concentrate the Indians, the infiltration of whites and others over the long term weakened Indian control of the town. Spanish-owned farms and haciendas proliferated on the outskirts. By the beginning of the eighteenth century, Indian-owned lands were mainly concentrated in the town. Doña Micaela and her family rented and owned lands within Indian Amozoque as well as on the roads leading to the larger farms and haciendas belonging to the wealthier Spaniards.

Doña Micaela's life acquired its separate and special significance apart from her family and was recorded in the archives only because she purchased land and had property worth more than 1,000 pesos. (An agricultural laborer might earn between 35 and 50 pesos a year.) As early as 1744, she had 100 pesos, which she gave to her sister to purchase a house lot. Four years later the lot became the property of Micaela. In 1749, the widow purchased another piece of land and exchanged another lot for property that was contiguous to lands she already owned. By 1756, doña Micaela had five widely scattered pieces of land totalling nearly two acres; and afterward she continued to accumulate land in bits and pieces. As late as 1771, she purchased land next to the property she already owned. The sellers were an Indian family who needed the money to pay their tribute.

Micaela began her life as the daughter of a Spaniard (or perhaps a mestizo who passed for one) named Diego Carrillo, and of the Indian daughter of a *cacique* of Amozoque, María Gutiérrez. Of the father's activities, we know only that he purchased some Indian lands in the vicinity of Amozoque about 1730. From this union at least three children survived to maturity: a son, Francisco, and two daughters, Micaela and María. These three benefited from close ties throughout their lives, borrowing money and renting land from each other and exchanging material aid. As mestizos, they were relieved of tribute payments and enjoyed greater economic opportunities than their Indian neighbors; but the son was prohibited from exercising leadership in the ceremonial life of the town as a result of his impure Indian roots, and neither daughter could have entered a convent, because they were neither white nor Indian.

Micaela Angela Carrillo married a cacique, Juan Tapia y Luna, and thereby strengthened her ties to the hereditary nobility of the town. She later claimed that neither she nor her husband brought any property to the marriage, but it is more likely that one of their parents did provide the couple with enough land on which to build a house and have a small garden.

The new family occupied a half-way position between Indian and Spanish society. Their two sons, Esteban and Pablo, might claim to be either Indian or mestizo and proba-

19. Tapping the *aguamiel* of the maguey plant, from an early nineteenth-century print.

bly knew the Nahuatl language as well as Spanish. Their houses were built in the Indian style, and they participated fully in the economy of the village. They enjoyed the privileges of the Indian nobility, being addressed by local people as don Juan and doña Micaela (in their dealings with Puebla officials, these titles were ignored), riding horses, and being exempt from tribute.

Don Juan Tapia y Luna died during the latter part of the 1730s, leaving his wife and two small sons a piece of land, which doña Micaela later referred to as the *gananciales* or gains from her marriage. The widow was very poor in the early years, unable to maintain her own house and obliged to live with her sister María. Her clothing was made of rough wool and homespun cotton.

Micaela lived by renting maguey plants on other people's land. When the plant was ready to flower, she would go and tap the plant, extracting the *aguamiel,* or sweet tasting sap, which she fermented in a vat of cowhide to make an intoxicating beverage called pulque. It was through the production of this native wine that she supported herself, raised her children, and acquired a few material possessions. Pulque production was one of the most profitable industries in New Spain, including a great number of people from the highest nobility such as the counts of Jala and Regla, to the wealthiest Jesuit institutions, to some of the poorest residents of Indian society. The government derived substantial revenues from taxing those who manufactured and transported it, and from licensing the stores where pulque was sold.

Doña Micaela could rely on a steady income. The maguey plant produced in all kinds of weather, and its product had an assured market in all the towns and cities of highland New Spain. It was a great disadvantage for poor farmers that the plant took between eight and fifteen years to mature, but the owners of large tracts of poor or irregularly watered land could set out hundreds of them and count on a steady return from pulque sales. We may speculate that doña Micaela used a part of her thirty pesos to rent maguey plants that were not yet in production from owners who needed cash, and that eventually from her profits she was able to purchase some of the pieces of land on which they grew. In the meantime, she manufactured the pulque and sold it both in the city and at retail in her home.

During the early years of doña Micaela's widowhood, she gave birth to three illegitimate daughters, the youngest of whom, María Antonia, was born in 1746. She seems never to have revealed their paternity, and all bore her name of Carrillo. They may have been the product of casual liaisons with different men or of a long relationship with a married man. There was no common law union that would have made the father responsible for his daughters; but it is possible that some of the money doña Micaela spent for her land and houses came from this man or men. In failing to remarry, Micaela maintained her independence. Mestizo women often served as heads of their households, and both illegitimate births and consensual unions were commonplace among them. "Natural" children did not suffer grave social prejudice except among upper-class whites in the eighteenth century.

When doña Micaela needed male assistance, she might make use of her brother and brother-in-law, or of an influential compadre. By asking wealthier or more powerful men to act as godfathers to her children, she gained friends who could act as witnesses for her in legal transactions, arrange tax payments, or lend her money. For Micaela, as for many others, the role of the compadre as protector of the child was less important than the benefits derived from his assistance to the parent. The few compadres mentioned in Micaela's wills and in the testimony about her life are probably only a small selection of the symbolic relatives whom she acquired during many years of active participation in the life of her community.

During the 1750s, when she dictated her first will, doña Micaela belonged to four *cofradías*, or Catholic lay sodalities. Each of these organizations, important in the social life of the eighteenth century, was affiliated with a local church or chapel or with a craft guild and was dedicated to the celebration of certain saints' days. In addition, the confraternity contributed to the expenses of burial for its members and acted as a mutual aid society. Of the four to which doña Micaela belonged, three were dedicated to celebrating different feasts of the Virgin (the Virgins of Rosario, Soledad, and Refugio). Indian and mestizo women were quite frequently important members of rural *cofradías* during the colonial period, and it is possible that doña Micaela may have borrowed money from them, marched in their processions, and maintained ties with other members. She bequeathed to them no money in her first will, stating merely that she was "a sister and affirmed as such," and neglected to mention them at all in her second will—a circumstance that suggests some growing isolation from the community around her. Be that as it may, if she was on good terms with any of the *cofradías* at the time of her death, she could reasonably expect that the members would march in her funeral cortège and pray for her soul.

By 1756, both of doña Micaela's sons and one of her daughters had married, but all three of them, along with their spouses and her two younger daughters, aged ten and fourteen, continued to live in their mother's dwellings.

Nonetheless, as early as 1751, she had begun to distribute her property among her children. Each of her sons was to receive a house site, in return for which she extracted from them a promise to permit their half-sisters to receive other properties. Since illegitimate children had no legal right to inherit equally with those born in wedlock, doña Micaela planned to protect them.

The Indian-style house in which her family lived was a group of small unconnected buildings surrounded by a wall of adobe bricks. The entryway was partially paved, and on either side were two *salas* or living rooms. One was roofed with sticks, and the other with boards on a framework of wooden jambs and brick columns; the floors of both were unpaved. There were a number of other smaller buildings, all roofed with the perishable *tejamanil*, a kind of shingle, which had to be replaced every few years. Two kitchens with attached huts completed the residential buildings on the property. The blacksmith's forge, supplied by Micaela to her son Esteban when he began his work as an artisan black-smith, was also on this land.

All these buildings still existed in 1780. Esteban and his family occupied one part of the lot and the widow of Micaela's younger son lived in the other. It was the estab-lishment of quite a well-to-do family by village standards.

At some point after 1756, Micaela and her youngest daughter, María Antonia, moved to another house site, which was located on lands at the edge of town. It had a narrow frontage on the street but was wider toward the back; and 229 maguey plants, far more than the average peasant possessed, were located behind it. At one time the lot had been larger, but María Antonia had sold a piece of land in order to pay to have a special tile roof put on her house. One of the witnesses remembered seeing María Antonia supervis-ing the *albaniles*, or masons. There were two rooms and two smaller huts, which served as a stable and kitchen, and a fifth small hut in bad condition. There was also a *temescal*, or Aztec sweat bath, used for a variety of medicinal purposes, which María Antonia had built. The patio was partly paved, surrounded with walls, and white-washed. She had two fine wooden doors to her house, made with decorative nails and including large locks and keys. She had a table of white wood, about two yards in length, and one box of about a foot and a half, also of white wood, with a lock and key. There were two smaller old chests. One of her most valued possessions was a well, which María Antonia had paid to open and which was valued at twenty-five pesos. It meant that María Antonia did not have to use the common village well as a source for her water. Her property was evaluated twice, once at 300 pesos and another time at 342 pesos.

The inventory of Micaela's moveable goods also tells us a good deal about her. Religious objects were the most prized possessions: two statues of the child Jesus, both on pedestals and made of painted wood; three large oil paintings on cloth in gilded frames, representing the Virgin of the Assumption, Saint Michael, Saint Vincent, and Saint Gaitan, and two small prints of Jesus and Saint Michael complete the list. Saint Michael Archangel, one of the most popular objects of Mexican devotion in the eighteenth century, was Micaela's patron saint; and his feast day on September 29 was certainly celebrated in her household, as well as in the village. Evaluators of the widow's estate appraised all these religious objects at between two reales (a quarter of a peso) each for the prints and seven pesos for the statues. It was common for humble households and modest dowries to include a few of these religious items; and it is likely that doña Micaela treasured them and displayed them in a kind of household shrine.

The other furniture of the household was very simple: various tables, identified only by the kind of plain wood out of which they were fashioned; a long bench, which doña Micaela ordered be cut in two for her daughters, and two smaller benches, which were to be given to her sons. There was a *tarima de tablas,* a kind of low, hard bed; three wooden chests of varying sizes and made of different woods to be divided among her daughters; and a number of mirrors and high-backed benches. Other objects must have existed in the household, such as *petates* or reed mats on which the family slept, a variety of wooden utensils and pottery cooking vessels, and the stone *mano* and *metate* with which they ground their corn—all of them indispensable objects of small monetary value. Micaela's property in small plots of land scattered throughout the community, her house, and the objects mentioned in her will were to be expected in a family of well-to-do Indians, rather than Spaniards or mestizos; and it is interesting that in drawing up both wills she followed Indian rather than Spanish laws of inheritance, in leaving roughly equal amounts to all children regardless of their formal legal status.

More significantly, she certainly responded to the dictates of a loving maternal heart.

During the quarter of a century between the writing of her first will and her second, doña Micaela continued to assist her children and to govern her family. The most needy of her offspring was Esteban, whose poor health (if not his indolence) prevented him from performing the heavy physical labor of a blacksmith. He may have continued to produce pulque and to sell it in his house; but he had numerous children whose support cost him heavily.

The expenses of child rearing began just after birth with elaborate baptismal ceremonies. Doña Micaela contributed heavily to financing these celebrations for her grandchildren. While costly, these ceremonies helped Esteban to accumulate compadres among his friends, clients (called *paniaguados,* in the colorful language of that time, meaning partakers of his food and water), and drinking companions. During these years he held office in various *cofradías* and again relied on his mother's financial aid when called upon to bear the expenses of their fiestas. The *cofradías* may have ceased to be important for Micaela, but they continued to offer prestige and political power to her son. By participating in them, he affirmed his status as a leader in the community.

Despite his mother's assistance and the fact that he received a larger share of her property throughout his life than any of his siblings, Esteban was apparently estranged from Micaela and hardly saw her during her last years. Whether this alienation was based on his resentment of her continued power or on his antagonism to his youngest half-sister, María Antonia, neither Esteban nor any of the principals in the law case explained. Jealousy of his sister certainly continued to influence his behavior for months after Micaela's death.

The most important person for doña Micaela was her youngest daughter, who, following a tradition of the extended family in many societies, never left home but was expected to remain and look after her mother. María Antonia did marry (her mother allegedly borrowed 300 pesos from a compadre to provide her with a splendid wedding), but the marriage did not last long. Her husband proved to be a wastrel and drunkard and after a few years left the household of his wife and mother-in-law. Whether his desertion occurred at their request or at his own initiative is not clear. In any event, María Antonia could not remarry and became totally dependent on her own labor as well as on the prospect of inheriting a part of her mother's property.

Whether or not she would receive the inheritance depended, as it turned out, on María Antonia's ability to prove that she had in fact labored in order to support her mother during the last years of her life. Esteban and his friends gave evidence that María Antonia had been a gay and fun-loving girl, fond of dancing and vain of her appearance, and one who occupied her time in sewing her own clothes and cooking. Cooking and sewing apparently did not count as economically productive activities. The witnesses that María Antonia called in her own defense stated that her sewing was for sale and not for herself; that she had always worked at tapping maguey plants, going out on horseback to her activities as a man might, working to "maintain her mother as though she were the husband."[2] When Micaela died, María Antonia had paid for the funeral with money borrowed from a compadre of her mother's—as Esteban well knew because it was he who had gone to get the money for his sister. Micaela Angela had put aside 80 pesos for the expenses of her last illness and funeral, but as it turned out, clothing and jewelry had to be sold in order to pay these costs.

It was the house and property left by Micaela Angela to her daughter that Esteban was determined to own. Taking advantage of the law that only legitimate children could inherit their parents' property and that natural children along with others could receive no more than 20 percent, he sued for redress. A feeling that he had been defrauded motivated his actions, compounded by his poverty, his need to provide houses for his sons, his jealousy of his half-sister, and perhaps his interest in eliminating her as a competitor in the sale of pulque. Esteban won an initial victory on the point of law, and María Antonia had to leave her house. When she appealed and introduced some of the most respected Spanish merchants, two priests, and other leaders of the town as witnesses on her behalf, the case went in her direction. Moreover, Esteban's witnesses were discredited—as his *paniaguados*, compadres, and debtors. One man was poor and had many children, and hence might have been paid to give testimony; another did not live in Amozoque; another was an habitual drunkard; and still another was an Indian of about sixty years of age, employed as a teacher of catechism to the young boys in the village, apparently an occupation in low repute since it helped to discredit his testimony. María Antonia's nephew and niece, the heirs of Micaela's dead legitimate son, who were entitled to receive his share of the inheritance, resigned their rights in favor of their aunt, stating that their father and their Uncle Esteban had both received fair shares of doña Micaela's property. The judge's final decision gave María Antonia back her house, forced Esteban to pay the court costs, and, as if in retribution for his unfilial behavior, made him liable to tribute payments when it was brought out that he had been claiming both Indian and mestizo rights.

The death of Micaela and the settlement of the family properties provoked a lawsuit and exacerbated a long-standing antagonism between two of her children. This is certainly a common event in the annals of many families. The final quarrel, in fact, highlights Micaela's economic success. She seems to have been inspired by the combination of her mother's and her husband's cacique rank and her father's special position as a Spaniard in this Indian town to struggle hard to rise from the poverty of her early widowhood. The tradition of the control of property by women among the cacique class must have played a part in her enterprising behavior. Another inspiration may have been found in the military qualities of her patron saint, the Archangel Michael, to whom she refers in her last will as "prince of the holy militia, my guardian angel and saint of my name who is to receive prayers in the hour of my death."[3]

Both Micaela and her daughter exemplify the problems and possibilities of women living and working alone, managing to maintain their independence and increase their material comforts through hard work in colonial America. This was no small achievement in an overwhelmingly patriarchal society. But the money doña Micaela made and the property she acquired were soon divided among her children so that they could establish their own households. She did not seek to become an important landowner, so that one member of her family might live in an upper-class manner. The egalitarian nature of the Indian villages would have defeated such aspirations even for a man.

A modern ethnologist studying contemporary communities in the Puebla region observed that this two hundred year old tale had a familiar cast of characters. The circumstance of industrious women producing and selling commodities, buying property with their profits, and providing for the future while the men drank and caroused, may have been as common an occurrence in the eighteenth century as it is in the twentieth.

In the late colonial period women, especially widows, often owned taverns, dispensed pulque from their houses, and travelled to nearby cities to sell this drink in the streets. The two women in the Carrillo family learned to use the new opportunities created by the expansion of the pulque trade to become one of the wealthiest families in their community. But the success of these women in supporting the family in this fashion also had its negative side. While pulque, taken in moderate amounts, seems to have had nutritional value, it was also very commonly consumed in excess. Severe and chronic alcoholism, an element in this story, was a general problem in Mexican peasant society in the 18th century. Micaela's own son Estéban may have been a drunk. The heavy consumption of alcohol provided opportunities for people such as doña Micaela, if they could avoid falling into chronic inebriation themselves, though the trade that sustained her debilitated others. In the 18th century, pulque-making was fast becoming a large-scale industry dominated by the massive production of great haciendas; but in doña Micaela's time and place, it was still possible for an individual villager to seize a corner of the commerical market, use it to support a family and provide for herself in her old age, and in the end leave house and lands so that a daughter might be self-supporting after she was gone.

Notes

1. Archivo de Notarías, Puebla. Papers of notary Josef Benítes de Zárate, 1775–80, fol. 91.
2. *Ibid.*, fol. 135.
3. *Ibid.*, fol. 38.

Sources

The story of this family may be found in the record of judicial proceedings located in the Archivo de Notarías de Puebla, under the name of notary Josef Benítes de Zárate, 1775–80. A microfilm copy exists in the Archive of the Church of the Latter Day Saints, Salt Lake City, Nos. 652058–59. Population figures are taken from Joseph de Villa-Señor y Sánchez, *Teatro Americano* (México, 1746), and from Sherburne F. Cook and Woodrow Borah, *Essays in Population History: Mexico and the Caribbean, Vol. I* (Berkeley, Calif., 1971). Jane Rosenthal, Susan Kellogg, and Asuncion Lavrin read this story from the viewpoints of ethnologist, ethnohistorian, and historian. Anita Aguilar told me of the Amozoc spurs worn by Zapata. All of them provided interesting ideas on this eighteenth-century drama.

Suggestions for Further Reading

The best introduction to village life in central Mexico in the eighteenth century is William B. Taylor, *Drinking, Homicide and Rebellion in Colonial Mexican Villages* (Stanford, Calif., 1979). A succinct view of the problems of race mixture and ethnic categories is Magnus Mörner, *Race Mixture in the History of Latin America* (Boston, 1967); for a more recent interpretation, see John K. Chance, *Race and Class in Colonial Oaxaca* (Stanford, Calif., 1978). On the indigenous nobility, see Delfina López Sarrelangue, *La nobleza indígena de Pátzcuaro en la época virreinal* (México, 1965) and Guillermo Fernández de Recas, *Cacicazgos y nobilarios indígenas de la Nueva España* (México, 1951).

A modern description of the communities surrounding Puebla can be found in Hugo Nutini and Barry L. Isaac, *Los pueblos de habla náhuatl de la región de Tlaxcala y Puebla* (México, 1974); and Alejandra Moreno Toscano has a brief historical introduction to the city and its regions in *Ensayos sobre el desarrollo urbano de México* (México, 1974), pp. 97–110. See also two community studies dealing with the Indian and mestizo family in the twentieth century: William Madsen, *The Virgin's Children: Life in an Aztec Village Today* (Austin, Tex.: 1960), and Hugo Nutini, *San Bernardino Contla: Marriage and Family Structure in a Tlaxcalan Municipio* (Pittsburgh, Pa., 1968).

Some of the flavor of life in colonial Indian towns is contained in *Beyond the Codices: The Nahua View of Colonial Mexico* (Berkeley, Calif., 1976), a sourcebook containing English translations of wills, tax records, land transfers, petitions, and correspondence, and in Ida Altman and James Lockhart, eds., *Provinces of Early Mexico: Variants of Spanish American Regional Evolution* (Los Angeles, 1976). For background on the relationship between Spaniards and Indians, see Charles Gibson, *The Aztecs under Spanish Rule* (Stanford, Calif., 1964).

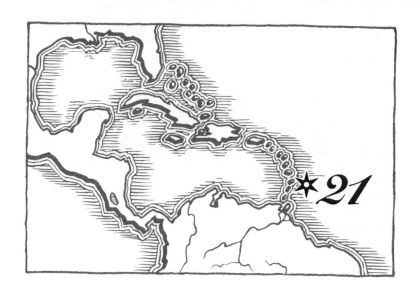

Joseph Rachell
and Rachael Pringle-Polgreen:
Petty Entrepreneurs

JEROME S. HANDLER

*B*y the end of the seventeenth century, the tiny southeastern Caribbean island of Barbados had become
England's richest colony in the New World. Barbados' wealth
derived from the production of sugar, which was primarily
cultivated on large-scale plantations by African slaves. In
addition to slaves, the island contained a minority population of European descent or birth, which included an even
smaller plantocratic group that controlled the island's means
of production, internal legislative apparatus, and other soci-
ety-wide institutions. Gradually, over the years, a third group
emerged comprised of persons whose racial ancestry was
mixed or solely African but who were legally free. Whether
free born or manumitted from slavery, these free blacks and
free "coloreds" were accorded a variety of privileges and

rights not extended to slaves. But because of their racial ancestry they were denied other privileges and rights that white society reserved for itself.

There were very few freedmen during the seventeenth century, but the group increased slowly until there were some two thousand (about half or more being women) at the close of the eighteenth century. At that time freedmen were overshadowed by close to 16,000 whites and over 64,000 slaves.

Despite their small numbers and the fact that they were free subjects of the British crown, by 1721 the Barbadian legislature had legally denied freedmen the right to vote, hold elective office, serve on juries, and testify in court cases or other legal proceedings involving whites. As the years progressed, some other legal constraints were placed on freedmen, but regardless of their legal status at any given time they were always held in a subordinate position and subjected to a variety of discriminatory practices. Some of these practices derived their strength from the legal code, others from social conventions based on the premise of racial supremacy, which permeated all segments of white society. As in other New World slave societies, however, the system allowed some flexibility: although no one in Barbados of known African ancestry could be considered white with respect to social or legal status, some freedmen were able to succeed economically within the occupations to which they were relegated by custom.

Freedmen shunned plantation wage labor. They did not own plantations during the eighteenth century, and few of them were independent small-scale agriculturalists. They were largely an urban group concentrated in Bridgetown, the island's political and commercial center and largest town. There they engaged in a variety of skilled trades and participated actively in the internal marketing system as hawkers or higglers and small shopkeepers. By the end of the eighteenth century, a few women also kept hotels or taverns.

None of these people led dramatic lives in the conventional sense, and most simply coped under very trying circumstances. However, the lives of some of them are worthy of note, because they reveal the possibility of achieving relative economic success by creatively adapting to and strategically exploiting the limited opportunities that Barbados's circumscribed social order provided.

Two of these economically successful freedmen, a black man and a "colored" woman, are the subjects of this essay. Both were born in slavery, and their combined lives spanned the eighteenth century. Although neither was a typical freedman, their very atypicality testifies to remarkable personal characteristics and also reflects various dimensions of the socioeconomic environment in which they lived.

Joseph Rachell: Shopkeeper

The proceeds that freedmen saved from marketing activities, as well as monies they earned in trades, permitted some to acquire the capital to open small shops that sold foodstuffs and hard goods to other freedmen, poor whites, and slaves. As with white-owned shops of comparable scale, the shops owned by freedmen traded in various types of goods that slaves stole from their masters' or others' properties. With low profit margins, a heavy dependence on credit from merchant suppliers and importers, and the burden of the extension of credit to their often impoverished customers, relatively few of these freedmen were able to develop their businesses into mercantile establishments that could compete with the larger enterprises of wealthier whites. For all intents and purposes, freedmen were excluded from larger businesses, not only because whites consciously strove to maintain their dominance in enterprises that traded abroad and supplied the needs of local planters, but also because freedmen largely lacked the capital and credit, and the internal and overseas business and social connections within whose framework such large-scale enterprises operated.

Although some freedmen were able to achieve mercantile establishments by the first few decades of the nineteenth century, during the eighteenth century economically successful freedmen were largely relegated to very small businesses. An outstanding early exception was Joseph Rachell. Born around 1716, Rachell was manumitted before the age of ten, and by the time of his death in October 1766 he had become a Bridgetown merchant with extensive business interests. Nothing is known of his childhood, the circumstances surrounding his manumission, or his early life, and little information is available on his family and social life. At about the age of twenty-five he married Elizabeth Cleaver, a "free mulatto" woman two years his senior, by whom he had at least three children.

The process by which Rachell established and developed his business interests is also unknown, but by his mature years he was a well-known figure in Bridgetown. A contemporary observed that he

> dealt chiefly in the retail way, and was so fair and complaisant in business, that in a town filled with little peddling shops, his doors were thronged with customers . . . his character was so fair, his manners so generous, that the best [white] people showed him a regard, which they often deny men of their own colour.[1]

Rachell was considered "an ingenious, industrious, and upright tradesman." Younger businessmen solicited his advice, and his opinion was often deferred to when the selling price of imported goods was established, and "whenever . . . vessels arrived with a cargo, J. R. was one of the first persons . . . to whom the cargo was offered."[2]

Rachell's trading activities did not extend to England but were largely confined to British colonies in the Caribbean, including Guiana. He also maintained fishing boats and used a group of his slaves as fishermen. In what was an extremely unusual situation for the period, Rachell employed some whites, and they "always spoke of him in a very respectful manner, and particularly revered him for his humanity and tenderness."[3] He was also "extremely kind in lending out money to poor, industrious men" so that they could establish their own businesses or extricate themselves from financial difficulties. Moreover, when a planter or merchant was forced to sell his property for reasons of financial duress or debt, Rachell would often attend the auction, purchase the property at a "fair market price," and then return it to the owner at the same price—frequently having cleared the debt himself before bidding. "By these humane and judicious means," Rachell was able to save "many families from ruin."

Whether the "benevolence of this excellent Negro" was motivated by altruistic sentiments, as the above comments would have us believe, or by a shrewd perception of white society and a practical understanding of the value of building and maintaining a network of allies within it, Rachell certainly could not have afforded to alienate or threaten whites.

In his relationship with an unnamed white man, a wealthy, propertied person who was a colonel in the Barbados militia and who had the reputation of being a "penurious miser," Rachell might have risked such alienation; presumably, however, he would not have undertaken the actions reported in the following episode unless he felt comfortable in his position and had the support of the wider white community. The colonel "used to call frequently at Joseph's shop, on pretence of cheapening cocoa; he was always sure to carry away as much for a taste as his pocket would hold, but never bought any."[4] Rachell was in a quandary, for although he objected to his continued losses he knew that, as a black, he could not bring legal charges against a white man. Finally he struck upon the idea of hiring a white clerk. He ordered the clerk to weigh out a bag of cocoa and to keep that bag under his particular care; whenever the colonel appeared he was only supplied with cocoa from the bag. When the bag was emptied, Rachell claimed payment for the cocoa, notifying the colonel that if payment was not made charges would be brought by the clerk. Although the colonel "stormed, swore, and threatened," he wanted to avoid the expense of a lawsuit "and suggested that being so fairly taken in, there was nothing to be done . . . but to pay the money peaceably. By this innocent stratagem Joseph got rid of the colonel's tasting visits."

Rachell's "charitable" endeavors extended in various directions, and years after his death poor whites talked about the "blessed man, for no poor thing ever went away hungry from his house; and some, who had seen better days, were shewn into a back room, and had victuals set before them."[5] In the early 1750s, the vestry of the parish in which Rachell lived even took the unusual step of providing him an annuity to support the illegitimate daughter of a married or widowed white woman who had died, and Rachell also supported a few impoverished elderly whites who received a modest bequest after his death. When Rachell's fishing boats returned with their daily catch, he would take a portion of the fish to the prisoners in the Bridgetown jail. We are told that he regularly visited the jail, "enquired into the circumstances of the prisoners, and gave them relief, in proportion to their distress and good behavior." Whites often considered freedmen slave-owners as "generally more severe, because [they] are less enlightened owners," but Rachell was viewed as "remarkable [because] he was extremely kind to his Negroes."[6]

Freedmen who were Christians belonged to the Anglican church, the island's official or state church. Rachell was baptized when he was about ten years old and was also married in an Anglican ceremony (a church marriage being an uncommon event among freedmen); as an adult he regularly attended Sunday services at the cathedral in Bridgetown. Although the rector considered him "a very attentive and devout hearer," and although Rachell "was so much esteemed for his honesty that he was commonly admitted to the company and conversation of merchants and planters,"[7] along with other nonwhites he was relegated to a segregated seating area in the cathedral. When he died he was buried in a segregated churchyard in Bridgetown, the social distinctions of Barbadian society being enforced to the last. His funeral was attended by a "prodigious concourse of blacks" and a large number of white people as well.[8] A stone was erected over his grave but without any inscription or memorial. In his will Rachell bequeathed all his real and personal property to his widow "and her heirs forever." Although "possessed of a good deal of property" at his death, the extent and nature of this property is unknown.

The few biographical details that are available on Rachell reveal a man enjoying a certain lifestyle, served by domestic slaves with quality wines at a table lit by spermaceti candles, that was comparable to the lifestyle of whites of similar means. Rachell was clearly a success in Barbadian society and had achieved the maximum status allowed to free black men of his generation. One can only speculate on how he viewed his own behavior and on the extent to which circumstances forced him to demean or compromise himself with whites. Certainly in his outward behavior he had to appear to acquiesce in the norms of compliance and accommodation white society considered appropriate to the behavior of nonwhites. Rachell was not perceived as threatening to the social order and to the maintenance of white supremacy; and he also met certain economic needs of the white community.

Rachael Pringle-Polgreen also met the needs of white society, but in a different way.

Rachael Pringle-Polgreen: Tavern Keeper

Women were much less visible than men in the social and political life of the freedman community, but some women nevertheless accumulated property and achieved a standard of living that rivaled or even exceeded that of many of the males. Shopkeeping was the major vehicle by which freedwomen might become economically successful; and as among men they usually acquired shops by saving monies gained through huckstering activities. Freedwomen also established themselves in shopkeeping by profiting from their sexual relationships with whites.

White males in Barbados—creoles, migrants from Britain, and British naval and military personnel—were regularly involved in interracial sexual relations, which, as elsewhere in New World slave societies, were the major social area exempt from a system that was designed to maintain a distance between whites and nonwhites. The social conventions of the colony neither condemned nor inhibited these relations, and although some freedwomen may not have liked them, they were apparently perceived as devices for social mobility and material security. Just as the slave mistress of a white man could sometimes achieve freedom for herself and her children and acquire material rewards or removal from the more onerous aspects of slavery, such as plantation field labor, so a freedwoman could materially benefit from a sexual alliance with a white man. He could provide her with decent clothes, a house and furnishings, and other goods and property, such as land, a horse and carriage, and even slaves. Also she might inherit from him the goods or money with which she could establish some type of business.

Aside from small shops, by the last quarter of the eighteenth century various hotels or taverns in Bridgetown were owned by women who usually had been the favored mistress of a white man from whom they had gained manumission, or who had worked in the taverns as slaves and were then manumitted by their freedwomen owners.

There were apparently no more than two or three hotel-taverns owned by freedwomen at any one period, but these establishments provided important services in the form of meals, lodging, and washing to island visitors and ship passengers in transit. The taverns were also popular rendezvous for white creoles and British military and naval personnel. Their owners sponsored "dignity balls," formally organized supper dances requiring an admission fee, which were largely attended by "colored" females and which only admitted white men. Another major attraction of the taverns was that they were "houses of debauchery, a number of young women of colour being always procurable in them for the purposes of prostitution."[9]

Understandably, given the services they provided, these hotel-taverns were usually successful businesses; their owners became relatively wealthy and frequently amassed a significant amount of property in the form of houses and slaves. Visitors to Barbados often commented on the resourcefulness of the proprietresses in their business dealings, as well as on their independent spirits, assertiveness, and managerial abilities.

Legendary among these women, and immortalized in a 1796 print by Thomas Rowlandson, was Rachael Pringle-Polgreen; in the late 1770s she became one of the earliest, if not the first, freedwomen to own a hotel-tavern.

Born around 1753, Rachael was the daughter and slave of William Lauder, a Scottish schoolmaster, and an African woman whom he had purchased not long after emigrating to Barbados in about 1750. He first took a position in a Bridgetown "grammer school," a job from which he was dismissed for incompetence in 1762. He then opened a small shop in Bridgetown, which he ran with the assistance of Rachael's mother and presumably Rachael herself—an experience that would serve the daughter well in later years.

By her "juvenile days," Rachael "was a remarkably well-made, good-looking girl, possessing altogether charms that . . . awakened the libidinous desires of her [father] who made many . . . unsuccessful attempts on her chastity."[10] Angered by her failure to respond to these advances, one day the father ordered her whipped. But we are told that just as she was being prepared for the whipping, Thomas Pringle, a British naval officer who was witnessing the scene, "seized the whip . . . and rescuing his panting victim, carried her off in triumph amidst the cheers of a thronging multitude." Lauder was infuriated by Pringle's action; and since his daughter was also his slave, he brought charges against Pringle under a law that prohibited the harboring of a run-away slave. The case was then settled out of court, when Lauder sold Rachael to Pringle "at an extortionate price."

"Not then eighteen," Rachael was established by Pringle in a "small house" in Bridgetown, and soon afterward he manumitted her; she in turn dropped the name of Lauder and adopted that of Pringle. At one point during their relation-ship, the story goes, Rachael became "anxious to strengthen her influence over her benefactor [and] contrived to deceive him." She feigned pregnancy, and when Pringle returned from a tour of duty presented him with a child "as the off-spring of their loves." The child's real mother ruined the deception, however, by demanding that her infant be re-turned; and when Pringle discovered that he had been fooled he not only returned the child but also severed his ties with Rachael. Soon after, his ship sailed for Jamaica and he left Barbados for good. "Rachael, however, was not long without a 'protector'; a gentleman of the name of Polgreen succeeded to the possession of her charms," and she added his name to that of Pringle.

"By her industry" Rachael managed to enlarge the house that Thomas Pringle had obtained for her, and sometime in the late 1770s, when she was in her twenties, she opened her tavern and hotel. Around 1780 her house carried a tax assess-ment of six pounds per annum, which suggests that it was a modest wooden structure such as many others in Bridge-town. Within a year, however, she also owned a "large house" in another section of the city, which was assessed at fifty pounds. Had she been a white male, the ownership of this house alone would have placed her among the small group of people, probably numbering no more than several hundred, whose lands or houses had the ten-pound minimum taxable value that qualified them to vote, hold elective office, and serve on juries. This large house became her major enter-prise—the celebrated Royal Naval Hotel.

The hotel was given its distinctive name after Prince William Henry (later King William IV) visited there in 1786,

20. Rachael Pringle-Polgreen, ca. 1790.

when the naval vessel he commanded docked in Barbados for a week. Half a century later, the editor of a Barbadian newspaper recalled how Rachael walked "with the Prince, actually leaning on the Royal Arm and accompanied by other naval officers and a host of mulatto women as His Highness promenaded the crowded streets."[11]

One legendary episode in the hotel's life took place during the prince's second brief visit to the island. On the night of February 2, 1789, after he and several resident British army officers had dined, they went to the Royal Naval Hotel where, during the course of the evening, the prince "commenced a royal frolic by breaking the furniture, etc." Joined by his fellow officers, they "carried on the sport with such activity, that in a couple of hours every article was completely demolished." While this drunken spree and wanton destruction was going on, Rachael, by now a heavy-set woman of around thirty-six years, was reported to have "sat quite passive in her great arm chair at the entrance door of the hotel" claiming that, as the king's son, the prince had license to do as he pleased. When the prince left, he bid Rachael good night, but "to crown his sport, upset her and chair together, leaving her unwieldly body sprawling in the street, to the ineffable amusement of the laughing crowd." Rachael, we are told, was calm and displayed no anger; but the following morning she sent the prince an itemized bill for seven hundred pounds sterling in damages, which was duly paid and which allowed "Miss Rachael" to refurbish her hotel with more splendor than before.

During the years between the start of her business and July 23, 1791, when she died at around the age of thirty-eight, Rachael Pringle-Polgreen acquired property that was considerable by Barbadian standards for persons of any sex or racial group. In addition to her hotel, she owned at least ten other properties in the same Bridgetown neighborhood. Freedmen and whites of means commonly owned multiple rental properties, but the number of houses that Rachael owned was unusually high. She also possessed a large amount of movable property, and her hotel was elaborately furnished even before its destruction by Prince William Henry. He and his fellow officers destroyed, for example, beds, feather mattresses, "pier glasses," pictures, chandeliers and lamps, decanters, goblets, wine glasses, porcelain, and crockery. The day after the rampage, Rachael placed a newspaper advertisement offering a reward for other missing property, which presumably had been thrown out of the windows: "a small filigree waiter, scolloped around the edge . . . seven silver table spoons, seven teaspoons, two desert spoons marked R. P. in a cypher."[12]

Like Joseph Rachell and many other freedmen, whether free-born or manumitted, Rachael's property included slaves who were employed in various capacities relating to the running of her business. There is no suggestion that she, or most other members of her group, had any compunction against owning slaves; indeed, she probably shared the view of many other freedmen that slaveownership was a fundamental property right that they possessed as free persons. Rachael's last will, made two days before her death, shows that she owned at least nineteen slaves, a substantial number for a person of any racial group living in an urban area. Following a property transmission pattern that was also characteristic of whites, she bequeathed most of her slaves; eleven were inherited by five white legatees, Bridgetown merchants with whom she had close business dealings, and two daughters of one of these merchants; two other slaves were bequeathed to a slave woman who won her freedom under the terms of Rachael's will.

In all, Rachael's will provided for the manumission of six slaves. Although they constituted a minority of the total number of slaves she owned, in terms of islandwide manumission practices for white and nonwhite slaveowners, they represented a disproportionately large percentage of manumissions by one owner at the time of death. Rachael, despite her apparent commitment to and acceptance of slaveownership, seems to have been moved by a sense of loyalty to those who had served her well and with whom she had particularly close ties. Her "charity," however, did not extend to the provision of other property or monies to most of those manumitted; only one manumitted slave received the house and land on which she resided. Rachael ordered her executors, two of the merchant legatees, to use the money raised from the sale of all her other property to pay the required manumission fees as well as her funeral expenses and outstanding debts. All the residual proceeds left from the sale of her property were to be divided equally between two "good friends," the Bridgetown merchants, who between them had also received eight of the slaves Rachael bequeathed, and Thomas Pringle, whose actions had resulted in her freedom many years before.

Aside from the manumitted slaves, all Rachael's legatees were white. She never married and apparently had no children—at least none who were alive at the time of her death; it is not known if she recognized any family connections through her mother. It is one of those anomalies of the slave society that the social relationships to which she attached the greatest importance, as reflected at any rate by the property bequests in her will, were with white people. The greatest homage that white creole society ever bestowed on her, however, was that she was called "Miss Rachael . . . the prefix being then rarely given to black or coloured women."

In their own ways Joseph Rachell and Rachael Pringle-Polgreen were unique individuals in eighteenth-century Barbados. Both had risen from slavery and had succeeded under extremely difficult conditions because of their industry, resourcefulness, and shrewdness. These attributes enabled them to manipulate a circumscribed system to their own advantage. They learned effectively to conduct, and even to enrich, themselves and were able to fill a niche in the socioeconomic order by meeting various needs of white society. They were able to maintain this niche because of their acumen and because their behavior was acceptable by the white-defined standards for the behavior of nonwhites; moreover, they never openly challenged or defied the racial underpinnings of the slave society that confined all freedmen, regardless of education, wealth, and lifestyle, to an inferior and subordinate social status.

We shall never know how Rachell and Pringle-Polgreen really felt about themselves and the society in which they lived. Inwardly they may have rejected many dimensions of the racist ideology that governed white perceptions of nonwhites. There is every indication, however, that their creative adaptation to Barbadian society was facilitated not only because they shared a general lifestyle with white creoles of comparable economic means but also because they identified with white creole values. These values involved a commitment to the concept of private property and slaveownership, and an acceptance of a class system with its concomitant ideology of privilege. By identifying with these values Rachell and Pringle-Polgreen found a measure of security for themselves while abetting the exploitative foundations of Barbadian society.

Notes

I am grateful to Clifford Harper and Shellee Colen for their suggestions on an earlier draft of this chapter, and to Jennifer Griffith for having generously provided miscellaneous information derived from records in the Barbados Department of Archives.
    1. James Ramsay, *An Essay on the Treatment and Conversion of African Slaves in the British Sugar Colonies* (London, 1784), p. 254.

2. William Dickson, *Letters on Slavery* (London, 1789), p. 180.

3. All quotations in this paragraph are from Dickson, *Letters*, pp. 180–181.

4. Quotations in this paragraph are from Ramsay, *Essay*, pp. 258–259.

5. Dickson, *Letters*, p. 181.

6. Dickson, *Letters*, p. 182.

7. Robert B. Nicholls, testimony in *Parliamentary Papers* (London, 1790), vol. 30, p. 333.

8. Dickson, *Letters*, p. 182.

9. John A. Waller, *A Voyage in the West Indies* (London, 1820), p. 6.

10. Unless otherwise noted, all quotations in this section on Pringle-Polgreen are taken from J. W. Orderson, *Creoleana: Or, Social and Domestic Scenes and Incidents in Barbados in Days of Yore* (London, 1842), pp. 94–102.

11. "Extracts from the Barbadian Newspaper," *Journal of the Barbados Museum and Historical Society* 10 (1943): 143.

12. Quoted in Neville Connell, "Prince William Henry's Visits to Barbados in 1786 and 1789," *Journal of the Barbados Museum and Historical Society* 25 (1958): 163.

Sources

The principal source on Joseph Rachell is William Dickson's *Letters on Slavery* (London, 1789). Dickson's account (pp. 180–181) is mainly from a "private journal" whose unnamed author resided in Barbados in 1769 and who derived his information on Rachell from hearsay accounts. James Ramsay's *An Essay on the Treatment and Conversion of African Slaves in the British Sugar Colonies* (London, 1784) has a brief account of Rachell (pp. 254–259) which is based on the oral report of someone who had personally known him. In his testimony before a House of Commons committee investigating the slave trade (*Parliamentary Papers*, London, 1790, vol. 30, pp. 325–360), the Barbadian-born Reverend Robert B. Nicholls provides a few corroborative details which he apparently obtained through hearsay. The dates of Rachell's birth, baptism, marriage, and death, and similar materials on various members of his family, come from the Saint Michael parish registers, located in the Barbados Department of Archives (RL 1/2, p. 270; RL 1/3, pp. 19, 24, 90, 257; RL 1/4, p. 326); the Archives also contain Rachell's will (RB 6/21, pp. 42–43) and that of his wife (RB 6/33, pp. 336–337). The annuity Rachell received from the Saint Michael vestry is reported in "Records of the Vestry of Saint Michael," *Journal of the Barbados Museum and Historical Society*, vol. 24 (1957): 145, 196.

The major source on Pringle-Polgreen's life is J. W. Orderson's novel *Creoleana: Or, Social and Domestic Scenes and Incidents in Barbados in Days of Yore* (London, 1842). Written in the late 1830s, when its author, a prominent white Barbadian creole, was in his seventies, the novel is set in the last quarter of the eighteenth century. The general social conditions and ambience of the period, as depicted by Orderson, are consistent with many other primary sources; moreover, key personages in the sketch of Pringle-Polgreen (pp. 94–102), such as William Lauder (her father), Thomas Pringle, and, of course, Prince William Henry, actually lived. One cannot be certain, however, that various biographical details, such as Lauder's incestuous advances, the circumstances under which Rachael met Thomas Pringle and events in their life together, have not been distorted or even invented.

Information on Pringle-Polgreen's house ownership is contained in the Saint Michael parish levy book, located in the Barbados Department of Archives. This information was published by Warren Alleyne in his "Rachael Pringle Polgreen" (Barbados, 1977), a three-page brochure written to accompany the Barbados Museum and Historical Society's full-scale color reprint of Thomas Rowlandson's 1796 caricature. The Barbados Department of Archives contains Pringle-Polgreen's will (RB 6/19, pp. 435–437) and the Saint Michael parish register (RL 1/5, p. 538), which carries the notice of her burial. Minor sources, all published in the *Journal of the Barbados Museum and Historical Society*, were used to round out various details in Pringle-Polgreen's life: an anonymously authored article, "Rachael of Barbados," *Journal* 9 (1942): 109–111; Neville Connell, "Prince William Henry's Visits to Barbados in 1786 and 1789," *Journal* 25 (1958): 157–164; "Extracts from the Barbadian Newspaper," *Journal* 10 (1943): 139–145; and Neville Connell, "Eighteenth-Century Furniture and Its Background in Barbados," *Journal* 26 (1959): 162–190.

Suggestions for Further Reading

For Barbadian social history during the period of slavery, see Jerome S. Handler, *The Unappropriated People: Freedmen in the Slave Society of Barbados* (Baltimore, Md., 1974); Jerome S. Handler and Frederick W. Lange, *Plantation Slavery in Barbados: An Archaeological and Historical Investigation* (Cambridge, Mass., 1978); and Richard S. Dunn, *Sugar and Slaves: The Rise of the Planter Class in the English West Indies, 1624–1713* (Chapel Hill, N.C., 1972).

There is a small body of literature on freedmen (free "colored" and free black) populations in the British West Indies. Aside from my *Unappropriated People*, other useful works include: Arnold A. Sio, "Race, Colour, and Miscegenation: The Free Coloured of Jamaica and Barbados," *Caribbean Studies* 16 (1976): 5–21; Sheila Duncker, "The Free Coloured and Their Fight for Civil Rights in Jamaica, 1800–1830" (M.A. thesis, University of London, 1960); Mavis C. Campbell, *The Dynamics of Change in a Slave Society: A Sociopolitical History of the Free Colored in Jamaica, 1800–1865* (Rutherford, N.J., 1976); and Edward L. Cox, "Shadow of Freedom: Freedmen in the Slave Societies of Grenada and St. Kitts, 1763–1833" (Ph.D. dissertation, Johns Hopkins University, 1977).

The position of freedmen in other areas of the Caribbean is explored in essays on the French Antilles, Cuba, Haiti, and Curaçao and Surinam in David W. Cohen and Jack P. Greene, eds., *Neither Slave Nor Free: The Freedmen of African Descent in the Slave Societies of the New World* (Baltimore, Md., 1972). In their introduction to this volume, Cohen and Greene offer a useful comparative perspective on various problems relating to freedmen.

✳ NOTE ON CONTRIBUTORS

SOLANGE ALBERRO is a research associate of the Institut Français de l'Amérique Latine in Mexico City and visiting professor at the Instituto Nacional de Antropología e Historia there. She is the author of a number of articles on the role of the Inquisition in colonial Mexican society and is completing doctoral work under the auspices of the Centre des Hautes Etudes de l'Amérique Latine in Paris.

FRED BRONNER is a senior lecturer in Iberian and Latin American History at the Hebrew University of Jerusalem. He has published more than a dozen articles on colonial Peruvian history and edited the works of Simón Bolivar in Hebrew. His *La lucha por el poder en el Perú del siglo xvii* is in press in Lima.

MANOEL DA SILVEIRA CARDOZO has taught at the Catholic University of America since 1940, serving at various times as head of the Department of History. He continues in charge of the Oliveira Lima Library, the most distinguished Luso-Brazilian collection in this country. Works from his pen, largely on the expansion of the Portuguese, have appeared in the United States, Portugal, Brazil, Germany, Spain and Venezuela.

DONALD CHIPMAN is professor of history at North Texas State University. He is the author of *Nuño de Guzmán and the Province of Pánuco in New Spain, 1518–1533* (Glendale, California, 1967), a book on professional football, and several articles. Since 1973 he has served as a contributing editor for the *Handbook of Latin American Studies.* He is currently at work on the descendants of the Aztec emperor Moctezuma II.

EDITH COUTURIER is affiliated with the Department of History at Northwestern University and sometimes teaches at Northern Illinois University. She has been a scholar-in-residence at the Newberry Library as well as a National Endowment for the Humanities Fellow. Her published work includes *La hacienda de Hueyapan, 1560–1936* (México, 1975) and articles in colonial and modern Mexican history. She is co-editor of the Colonial Mexico section of the *Handbook of Latin American Studies.*

J. FREDERICK FAUSZ received his Ph.D. in early American history from the College of William and Mary. In 1976–77 he was a fellow at the Center for the History of the American Indian at the Newberry Library. Currently he teaches colonial history and American Indian ethnohistory at St. Mary's College in Maryland. He has published articles in the *William and Mary Quarterly* and elsewhere.

PAUL B. GANSTER is assistant professor of history at Utah State University. His principal research interests are Andean ethnohistory and colonial social history. Cristóbal Béquer's story is an offshoot of his comparative social history of the secular clergy of Lima and Mexico in the eighteenth century, now nearing completion.

JEROME S. HANDLER is professor of anthropology at Southern Illinois University, Carbondale, and has held research positions at the University of London and the University of the West Indies. He is the author of *The Unappropriated People: Freedmen in the Slave Society of Barbados* (Baltimore, 1974) and *Plantation Slavery in Barbados: An Archeological and Historical Investigation* (Cambridge, Mass., 1978).

LOUISA SCHELL HOBERMAN is assistant professor of history at Wesleyan University and has been a research fellow of the Institute of Latin American Studies at the University of Texas. She is the author of a number of articles in colonial Mexican history.

FRANCIS JENNINGS is director of the Center for the History of the American Indian at the Newberry Library, and of its project for a documentary history of the Iroquois. He is a member of the Executive Board of the Organization of American Historians, and is the author of *The Invasion of America: Indians, Colonialism and the Cant of Conquest* (Chapel Hill, N.C., 1975).

LYMAN L. JOHNSON teaches Latin American history at the University of North Carolina at Charlotte. He has published a number of essays on topics in the social and demographic history of colonial Argentina and is currently at work on a book about the artisan community of colonial Buenos Aires.

MARY KARASCH is associate professor of history at Oakland University. She received her Ph.D. from the University of Wisconsin and is the author of a number of articles on the history of black people and the slave trade in early nineteenth-century Brazil. She is currently engaged in research on frontier society in Goiás.

J. JORGE KLOR DE ALVA is associate professor of philosophy and ethnohistory at San Jose State University, where he is also chairman of the Mexican-American Graduate Studies Department and coordinator of Latin American Studies. He received his J.D. from the University of California, Berkeley and a Ph.D. in History of Consciousness from the University of California, Santa Cruz. He has lectured and published widely in Mexican philosophy and Nahua ethnohistory and is an editor of *Escolios: Revista de Literatura.*

GARY B. NASH is professor of early American history at the University of California, Los Angeles. He is the author of *Quakers and Politics* (Princeton, N.J., 1968), *Class and Society in Early America* (Englewood Cliffs, N.J., 1970), *Red, White and Black: The Peoples of Early America* (Englewood Cliffs, N.J., 1974), and *The Urban Crucible: Social Change, Political Consciousness, and the Origins of the American Revolution* (Cambridge, Mass., 1979).

NEAL SALISBURY, assistant professor of history at Smith College, received his Ph.D. at the University of California,

Los Angeles. His articles have appeared in the *William and Mary Quarterly* and *Proceedings of the Sixth Algonquian Conference.* His book on Indian-European relations in New England from 1500 to 1643 will be published in 1981 by Oxford University Press.

SUSAN A. SOEIRO is a member of the Institute for Research in History in New York. She received her Ph.D. from New York University and has taught at the State University of New York, Stony Brook, and the University of Utah. She is the author of several articles on women in the religious and secular life of colonial Brazil.

JOHN C. SUPER is assistant professor of history at West Virginia University. Since receiving his Ph.D. from the University of California, Los Angeles, he has published several articles on the social and economic history of early Latin America. His book, *Life in Colonial Querétaro: 1531–1810,* will soon be published by the Fondo de Cultura Económica in Mexico City.

DAVID G. SWEET is associate professor of history at the University of California, Santa Cruz. He received his Ph.D. from the Comparative Tropical History Program at the University of Wisconsin, has published articles in colonial Latin American and Southeast Asian history, and is presently completing work on a book about the role of epidemic disease in the colonial history of the Amazon Valley.

RICHARD WHITE is assistant professor of history at Michigan State University, and has been a Fellow at the Center for the History of the American Indian at the Newberry Library. He is currently engaged in research on the ethnohistory of the southeastern United States.

ANN M. WIGHTMAN is completing a dissertation at Yale University on "Demographic Change and the Structure of Indian Society in Seventeenth-Century Cuzco." She is currently a Visiting Instructor in Latin American History at Wesleyan University.

✶ ILLUSTRATION CREDITS

1. *Travels and Works of John Smith* (Edinburgh, 1910).
2. Felipe Huamán Poma de Ayala, *Nueva Corónica y Buen Gobierno* (Paris, 1936).
3. David I. Bushnell, Jr., "Drawings by A. de Batz in Louisiana, 1732–35," *Smithsonian Miscellaneous Collections* 80,5 (1927).
4. Marc de Villiers, "Note sur deux cartes dessinées par les Chikachas en 1737," *Journal de la Societé des Americanistes de Paris,* n.s. 12 (1931).
5. Research Department, Colonial Williamsburg. Used with permission.
6. Drawings by J. J. Codina (1784), published most recently in Alexandre Rodrigues Ferreira, *Viagem Filosófica pelas Capitanias do Grão-Pará, Rio Negro, Mato Grosso e Cuiabá. Iconografia, I* (Rio de Janeiro, 1977).
7. Hercules Florence, *Viagem Fluvial do Tietê ao Amazonas de 1825 a 1829* (São Paulo, 1938).
8 and 9. Muñoz Camargo MS (Historia de Tlaxcala), Hunter Collection, MS 242, University of Glasgow Library. 240v and 241v.
10 and 11. Amedée François Frézier, *Relation du Voyage de la Mer du Sud aux Cotés du Chili et du Pérou* (Paris, 1716).

12. Codex Cocotzin, Bibliothèque Nationale de Paris. Reproduction in Eugène Boban (ed.), *Documents pour servir à l'histoire du Mexique. Atlas* (Paris, 1891). The editors are grateful to Dr. Miguel León-Portilla for his help in locating this rare portrait, and to the Instituto de Investigaciones Estéticas, Universidad Nacional Autónoma de México, for reproducing it.

13. H. P. Biggar, editor, *The Works of Samuel Champlain* (Toronto, 1922–1936), II.

14 and 15. Codina in Ferreira, *Viagem.*

16. Carlos Nebel, *Viaje pintoresco y arqueológica sobre la parte más interesante de la República Mexicana en los años transcurridos desde 1829 hasta 1834* (Paris, 1839).

17. Poma de Ayala, *Nueva Corónica.*

18. Enrico Martínez, *Reportorio de los tiempos y historia natural desta Nueva España* (México, 1606).

19. Nebel, *Viaje.*

20. Print by Thomas Rowlandson in the collection of the Barbados Museum and Historical Society. Made available through the kindness of Mr. Peter Campbell of Bridgetown.

NOTE: The editors are grateful to the photographic services of the University of Texas at Austin, the University of California at Berkeley and Los Angeles, and in particular the University of California at Santa Cruz, for their assistance in the preparation of these illustrations.

Designer:	Eric Jungerman
Compositor:	Dwan Typography
Printer:	Vail-Ballou
Binder:	Vail-Ballou
Text:	VIP Trump Medieval
Display	Phototypositor Snell Roundhand Bold
Cloth:	Holliston Roxite B 53515
Paper:	50 lb. smooth cream